International

D1427621

International Child Law examines and discusses the international legal framework and issues relating to children at both a global and regional level. Analysing both public and private international legal aspects, this cross-disciplinary text promotes an understanding of the ongoing development of child law and the protection of the child.

This second edition has been substantially updated and revised, and three new chapters have been introduced. Together with new material on Sexual exploitation and Children's involvement in armed conflict, a new chapter on Indigenous children's rights responds to the recent United Nations Declaration on the Rights of Indigenous Peoples.

The United Nations Convention on the Rights of the Child remains a central topic, and the mechanisms and policy underlying the Hague Conventions on Intercountry Adoption and Parental International Child Abduction are dealt with in two further chapters. Drawing on a genuine range of legal disciplines, *International Child Law* is a valuable resource for those in the course of study and research in this area.

Trevor Buck is Professor of Socio-Legal Studies at Leicester De Montfort University where his main teaching and research interests include administrative justice, international child law and social security.

International Child Law

Second edition

Trevor Buck,
Alisdair A. Gillespie,
Lynne Ross and
Sarah Sargent

Routledge
Taylor & Francis Group

LONDON AND NEW YORK

Second edition published 2011 by Routledge
2 Park Square, Milton Park, Abingdon, Oxon, OX14 4RN
Second edition published 2011 by Routledge
2 Park Square, Milton Park, Abingdon, Oxon, OX14 4RN

Simultaneously published in the USA and Canada
by Routledge
270 Madison Avenue, New York, NY 10016

Routledge is an imprint of the Taylor & Francis Group, an informa business

© 2005, 2011 Trevor Buck

First published by Cavendish Publishing in 2005

Typeset in Times New Roman by Glyph International Ltd.
Printed and bound in Great Britain by TJ International Ltd,
Padstow, Cornwall

British Library Cataloguing in Publication Data
A catalogue record for this book is available from the British Library

Library of Congress Cataloging-in-Publication Data
International child law / Trevor Buck ... [et al.]. -- 2nd ed.
   p. cm.
Rev. ed. of: International child law / Trevor Buck.
1. Children (International law) 2. Children--Legal status, laws, etc.
I. Buck, Trevor. II. Buck, Trevor. International child law.
K639.B83 2011
346.01'35--dc22   2010006040

ISBN-13: 978-0-415-48716-0 (hbk)
ISBN-10: 0-415-48716-1 (hbk)

ISBN-13: 978-0-415-48717-7 (pbk)
ISBN-10: 0-415-48717-X (pbk)

ISBN10: 0-203-84598-6 (eBook)
ISBN13: 9780-203-84598-1 (eBook)

Contents

Preface

The aim of this book has been to provide the reader with an accessible, informed and scholarly introduction to the international law framework relating to children. This second edition of *International Child Law* follows a similar structure to the first, but has been substantially upgraded with more references to the scholarly literature included in the main text and collated in a general bibliography. This edition contains two introductory chapters, covering Childhood and Children's Rights (Chapter 1) and an Introduction to International Law Sources and Institutions (Chapter 2), which will assist the reader to comprehend the social and legal context of international child law. These chapters are followed by an expanded chapter on the UN Convention on the Rights of the Child (Chapter 3), followed by Child Labour (Chapter 4), International Parental Child Abduction (Chapter 5) and Intercountry Adoption (Chapter 6). This edition focuses on global instruments and initiatives rather than regional ones. Consequently, the 'Child in Europe' chapter from the first edition has been dropped, but there are three additional specialist chapters that appear in this edition on, respectively, Sexual Exploitation (Chapter 7), Children and Armed Conflict (Chapter 8), and Indigenous Children (Chapter 9).

My thanks and acknowledgments to the staff at Routledge for all their help in assisting the task of seeing this project to completion, in particular to Fiona Kinnear and Lloyd Langman; my thanks also to my former colleague, Professor Malcolm Shaw QC, at the University of Leicester, who first suggested to me that I should write this book; thanks also to my present colleagues at Leicester De Montfort Law School, Professor Alisdair Gillespie, Lynne Ross and Dr Sarah Sargent, for their respective writing contributions (see 'List of Contributors'), and to Professor Deborah Lockton for reading and commenting on Chapter 4; and last but never least, many thanks also to my wife Barbara who has, yet again, given me excellent support during the writing process.

Professor Trevor Buck
Leicester De Montfort Law School
United Kingdom
February 2010

List of Contributors

Trevor Buck is Professor of Socio-Legal Studies at Leicester De Montfort Law School, De Montfort University. He has teaching and research interests in international child law, administrative justice and the Social Fund (UK). Trevor was the author of the first edition of *International Child Law* and is the General Editor with overall editorial responsibility for this second edition.

Alisdair A Gillespie is Professor of Criminal Law and Justice at Leicester De Montfort Law School, De Montfort University. He has teaching and research interests in criminal law, especially the sexual exploitation of children, the management of sex offenders and the law relating to covert policing. Alisdair has contributed Chapter 7 (Sexual exploitation) to this edition.

Lynne Ross is Principal Lecturer in Law at Leicester De Montfort Law School, De Montfort University. She has teaching and research interests in Land, international child law and family law. Lynne has contributed to Chapter 1 (Childhood and children's rights) of this edition.

Sarah Sargent is Part-time Lecturer at Leicester De Montfort Law School, De Montfort University. Sarah has practised law in the United States, and has research interests in comparative law, Indigenous children's issues, intercountry adoption and children's rights in international law. She is a PhD candidate at Leicester De Montfort University; her thesis is a comparative legal analysis of the best interests of the child principle in intercountry adoption. Sarah has contributed to Chapter 6 (Intercountry adoption) and Chapter 9 (Indigenous children) of this edition.

Table of Cases

Table of International Legal Instruments

List of Abbreviations

African Charter on the Rights and Welfare of the Child	ACRWC
African Commission on Human and Peoples' Rights	ACHPR
Anti-Social Behaviour Order	ASBO
Asian Human Rights Commission	AHRC
Asian Legal Resource Centre	ALRC
Children and Family Court Advisory and Support Service	CAFCASS
Committee Against Torture	CAT
Committee of Experts on the Application of Conventions and Recommendations	CEACR
Committee on Economic, Social and Cultural Rights	CESCR
Committee on Migrant Workers	CMW
Committee on the Elimination of Discrimination Against Women	CEDAW
Committee on the Right of Persons with Disabilities	CRPD
Committee on the Rights of the Child	CtRC
Department for Children, Schools and Families	DCSF
Economic and Social Council	ECOSOC
Ending Child Prostitution And Trafficking	ECPAT
European Convention for the Protection of Human Rights	ECHR
European Court of Human Rights	ECtHR
European Law Enforcement Agency	EUROPOL
Female Genital Mutilation	FGM
Food and Agriculture Organization	FAO
Foreign & Commonwealth Office	FCO
Human Rights Committee	CCPR
Inter-American Commission on Human Rights	IACHR
Intercountry Adoption Technical Assistance Programme	ICATAP
Intergovernmental Organizations	IGO
Internally Displaced Persons	IDP
International Atomic Energy Agency	IAEA
International Child Abduction and Contact	ICACU
International Civil Aviation Organization	ICAO
International Committee of the Red Cross	ICRC
International Court of Justice	ICJ

International Covenant on Civil and Political Rights	ICCPR
International Covenant on Economic, Social and Cultural Rights	ICESCR
International Criminal Court	ICC
International Criminal Tribunal for Rwanda	ICTR
International Criminal Tribunal for the former Yugoslavia	ICTY
International Fund for Agricultural Development	IFAD
International Labour Organization	ILO
International Maritime Organization	IMO
International Monetary Fund	IMF
International Programme to Eliminate Child Labour	IPEC
International Telecommunication Union	ITU
Millennium Development Goals	MDG
Non-Governmental Organizations	NGO
Office of the United Nations High Commissioner for Human Rights	OHCHR
Optional Protocol to the Convention on the Rights of the Child on the Involvement of Children in Armed Conflict	OPAC
Optional Protocol to the Convention on the Rights of the Child on the Sale of Children, Child Prostitution and Child Pornography	OPSC
Organization for Security and Cooperation in Europe	OSCE
Organization of African Unity	OAU
Organization of American States	OAS
Permanent Court of International Justice	PCIJ
Time-Bound Programme	TBP
United Nations Children's Fund	UNICEF
United Nations Commission on Human Rights (1945–2006)	UNCHR
United Nations Convention on the Rights of the Child	CRC
United Nations Declaration on the Rights of Indigenous People	UNDRIP
United Nations Development Programme	UNDP
United Nations Educational, Scientific and Cultural Organization	UNESCO
United Nations Human Rights Council (2006 – to present)	UNHRC
United Nations Industrial Development Organization	UNIDO
United Nations Permanent Forum of Indigenous Peoples	UNPFII
Universal Declaration of Human Rights	UDHR
Universal Postal Union	UPU
Virtual Global Taskforce	VGT
World Bank	WB
World Food Programme	WFP
World Health Organization	WHO
World Intellectual Property Organization	WIPO
World Meteorological Organization	WMO
World Tourism Organization	UNWTO
World Trade Organization	WTO

Chapter 1

Childhood and children's rights

The international law relating to children is best understood by considering at the outset what we mean when we talk about 'childhood' and 'children's rights'. At first sight, these two concepts seem straightforward, but on closer examination they turn out to be quite contestable notions. 'Childhood' assumes some kind of understanding of what it means to be a child, and, by implication, an adult. 'Children's rights' assumes a background framework of knowledge about 'human rights' of which children's rights can be considered an integral part. To an extent, the project of international law relating to children is one which is predicated on the existence of a universally held definition of 'child',[1] and yet it is self-evident that 'childhood' is experienced very differently by groups of children even within the same nation state. Furthermore, the way in which we perceive childhood and children's rights will have a highly significant bearing on how we view international child law and the international community's approach to legal regulation and standard-setting in this area. This chapter seeks to introduce the reader to these two important concepts.

1.1 Childhood

The following sections include a brief overview of the historical, psychological, sociological and social policy perspectives on childhood. The study of childhood has become a truly multi-disciplinary activity. However, while the focus on childhood tends to be favoured within the academic community, research initiatives that are more highly linked to policy and specific projects have, since the 1990s, tended to concern themselves primarily with child protection (Ennew 2008). Indeed, there are many research centres dedicated to the study of childhood,[2] and the number of 'childhood studies' programmes in higher education has grown.

---

1 See the UN Convention on the Rights of the Child (CRC), article 1, for the legal definition of a 'child'. The text of the CRC is reproduced in Appendix 1. See Chapter 3, section 3.5.2 for commentary on this definition.

2 Centre for the Study of Childhood and Youth, University of Sheffield. Website: http://cscy.group. shef.ac.uk/ (accessed 28 December 2009). Centre for Applied Childhood Studies, University of Huddersfield. Website: http://www2.hud.ac.uk/hhs/acs/index.php (accessed 28 December 2009).

1.1.1 Historical perspective

As one commentator has observed, '[f]or much of history children have not been of particular interest to academics or policy-makers' (Kelly 2005: 375). However, Ariès's (1962) work was the classic historical study of the notion of childhood and his analysis is often referred to in the literature as simply the 'Ariès thesis'. Ariès examined the iconography in art and literature over several centuries to identify an emerging 'discovery of childhood'. He suggested famously that 'in mediaeval society the idea of childhood did not exist' (Ariès 1962). He stated that there had been no distinctive vocabulary of childhood, no distinct dress or games. He argued that infants below 7 years old were recognised as physically vulnerable, but their parents were largely indifferent to them, probably because of the high levels of infant mortality. After 7 years of age, the child was simply regarded as another (smaller) adult. By contrast, from about the fifteenth to the seventeenth century, Ariès suggested a transition had occurred in the prevalent notion of childhood: the child was perceived as a significant family member, to be nurtured and protected. Change started, first, in wealthy households where there were increasing concerns for the moral and educational development of children. Children were becoming creatures to be nurtured and reformed by a combination of rationality and discipline. Ariès reinforced his views by pointing to the historical development of education for the young and the establishment of the 'child' as a central figure in the appearance of the 'family', itself a newly developing institution emerging over the centuries. Ariès argued that these new attitudes to children were then transmitted to the bourgeois class where there was additionally concern for the health and hygiene of children as well as their education. The expansion of the school system brought with it a lengthening in the period of childhood.

Some later studies reinforced these views by examining the history of child-rearing practices. For example, Stone (1990) asserted that in earlier centuries high infant mortality had prompted a low level of affection for children by their parents/carers. In the eighteenth century a new, more affectionate style of child-rearing emerged and traditional practices such as wet-nursing, swaddling and excessive punishment declined. However, by the mid-nineteenth century a reaction, caused by the Methodist revival, had set in whereby the child was perceived as naturally tending towards sinful behaviour and in need of correction by parents and other adults by means of stern discipline designed to break the will (and wilfulness) of a child. This reversion to a more authoritarian family type in turn gave way to a more permissive style in the later Victorian era.

> Only in the closing decades of the Victorian period was there a gradual return to child-centredness and permissiveness caused by a variety of new influences – the decline of religiosity, women's emancipation, family limitation and the new psychological theories of child development. These trends ultimately affected all social classes in the twentieth century, resulting in the

small, modern family characterised by high concentration of affection, a decline in paternal authority, more 'natural' child-rearing practices and more democratic sharing of roles.

(Burnett 1983: 1)

Subsequent commentators have questioned Ariès's thesis and methodology (Pollock 1983), and indeed some of his conclusions do not appear to be sufficiently supported by the evidence. In short, Ariès's (1962) *Centuries of Childhood*

... sparked off a whole series of strictly historical debates: on whether the mediaeval period did in fact have an awareness of childhood, on the key periods in 'the discovery of childhood', on the nature of parent–child relations at various periods, and on the role of the schools to name a few.

(Heywood 2001: 5)

Both Ariès and another historian, Lloyd De Mause, believed in essence that the further one went back in history the worse would be the level of treatment of children. Indeed, De Mause stated that '[t]he history of childhood is a nightmare from which we have only recently begun to awaken' and that '[t]he further back in history one goes, the lower the level of child care, and the more likely children are to be killed, abandoned, beaten, terrorised, and sexually abused' (De Mause 1976: 1–2).

Archard (1993), amongst others, has provided a carefully crafted deconstruction of Ariès's influential thesis. He points not only to the weak evidential basis but also to Ariès's 'predisposition to interpret the past in the light of present-day attitudes, assumptions and concerns'. Furthermore, he argues that Ariès subscribes (wrongly) to a historical understanding of 'modernity' as a linear progression to moral enlightenment. Instead, Archard argues, one can employ a distinction between a 'concept' and a 'conception' to better analyse Ariès's thesis. The argument, in brief, is that to have a 'concept' of childhood is to recognise that there is a distinction between children and adults. To have a 'conception' of childhood is a specification of what the distinguishing attributes are. Archard concludes that all societies at all times have had a concept of childhood, but there have been a number of different conceptions. Historically, we cannot be confident about the reliability of our knowledge in relation to these conceptions. He therefore concludes that Ariès's thesis is flawed by what he refers to as an 'ill judged leap' from 'concept' to 'conception'.

Archard also provides an interesting conceptual framework to accommodate the examination of different 'conceptions' of childhood. He introduces three elements to the notion of childhood: its 'boundaries', 'dimensions' and 'divisions'. The boundary for childhood he defines as the point at which it ends. He argues that any particular society's conception of this boundary may differ according to its culture. Conceptions of childhood frequently locate the relevant boundary in relation to cultural 'rites of passage or initiation ceremonies which celebrate the end of childhood and beginning of adulthood'; according to Archard, '[t]hese are likely to be associated with permission to marry, departure from the parental home or assumption of the responsibility to provide for oneself' (Archard 1993: 23).

Conceptions of childhood may also differ according to their 'dimensions'. Archard suggested that a number of perspectives would render a distinction between children and adults; for example, moral, juridical, philosophical and political. Each society will have its own particular value system which may at any one time favour one or more of these perspectives. Sometimes a society sets the legal age of majority according to a view about one or more of these dimensions. A majority age need not necessarily be consistent with the 'boundary' implied by other dimensions. By way of illustration of this point, Archard points to the origins (in Europe) of the age of majority, which was fixed in the Middle Ages by the capacity of a young boy to bear arms and changed as armour became increasingly heavier and thus demanded greater strength to wear it (Archard 1993: 25). If, however, rationality is the key dimension, then the acquisition of reason is a better test of majority age. Similarly, in societies that focus on the overriding importance of sustaining and reproducing life, 'the ability to work and bear offspring is a strikingly obvious mark of maturity' (Archard 1993: 26).

Archard argues that conceptions of childhood will also depend on how its 'divisions' are ordered and managed. There are in most societies a number of sub-categories between birth and adulthood. Most cultures recognise a period of very early infancy where the child is particularly vulnerable and deserving of adult care; a point that is consistent with the findings of developmental psychology outlined in the following discussion. Some cultures attach importance to weaning; the point where close maternal care finishes. Some societies put particular significance on the point at which a child acquires speech. Roman law specified three age periods of childhood: *infantia* (child incapable of speech); *tutela impuberes* (pre-pubescent child requiring a tutor); and *cura minores* (post-pubescent young person requiring the care of a guardian prior to attaining majority). At any rate, the notion of 'adolescence' or 'youth' in the modern conception of childhood is widely recognised as a period usually involving an apprenticeship for the roles to be required of adulthood. Indeed, the inclusion of the 'middle-aged child', that is, the post-infantile 7-year-old to the pre-adolescent 12-year-old, is arguably a key element of the modern conception of childhood. Archard concluded that:

> ... any conception of childhood will vary according to the ways in which its boundaries are set, its dimensions ordered and its divisions managed. This will determine how a culture thinks about the extent, nature and significance of childhood. The adoption of one conception rather than another will reflect prevailing general beliefs, assumptions and priorities. Is what matters to a

society that a human can speak, be able to distinguish good from evil, exercise reason, learn and acquire knowledge, fend for itself, procreate, participate in running the society or work alongside its other members?

(Archard 1993: 27)

In an influential and controversial work, Pollock (1983) challenged what had become the orthodoxy of Ariès, De Mause and Stone. She argued that the experience of childhood was not as unremittingly gloomy as had been portrayed. Her study was based on her doctoral work which examined over 500 published diaries and autobiographies. She rebutted the notion that there were any fundamental changes in the way parents viewed or reared their children in the period from 1500–1900: '[t]he texts reveal no significant change in the quality of parental care given to, or the amount of affection felt for infants for the period 1500–1900' (Pollock 1983: 3).

The controversies in historical research about childhood are not made easier by the difficulties in locating reliable source materials. One commentator puts it thus:

Ideas about childhood in the past exist in plenitude; it is not so easy to find out about the lives of children. There are sources which can tell us about their numbers in relation to adults, their life expectancy, the ages at which they were likely to start work and leave home and so on, but those seeking to recapture the emotional quality of the lives of children in the past encounter formidable hurdles. The letters and diaries of parents seem to be one way of surmounting the hurdles, but they tend to be written only by the articulate and well-to-do, and in them our view of the child is mediated through the perceptions of the adult. Children themselves have sometimes left behind written materials, but too often what they write in their diaries tells us more about the genre of diary writing and the desires and expectations of adult readers than about the experience of being a child.

(Cunningham 2005: 2)

In essence, what emerges from the historical analyses is that the notion of childhood is a culturally transmitted idea that may have changed significantly over past centuries, though there is little consensus about the detail of how and why these changes in perception have occurred. At the least, this brief survey of the historical perspective of childhood ought to suggest that the aim of universal norm-creation underlying international human rights instruments, such as the UN Convention on the Rights of the Child (CRC), may not necessarily be consistent with the core notion of childhood prevalent in any one society at any one time in history. In recent years there appears to be some renewed academic interest in the history of childhood. Indeed, in 2003, the History Faculty at the

University of Oxford established the first Centre for the History of Childhood in the United Kingdom.[3]

The CRC defines the child as meaning 'every human being below the age of 18 years unless under the law applicable to the child, majority is attained earlier' (article 1). In Archard's terminology, this is the 'boundary' of childhood as defined in international law. Given the high degree of 'cultural relativity' (see section 1.3 below) inherent in the conception of childhood, it is perhaps surprising that the international community was ever able to agree on this important age limit. Equally, the proviso contained in article 1 (see further, section 3.5.2) allows for a majority age of less than 18 years, a result achieved partly by virtue of sensitivity to cultural diversity and in part by the diplomatic awareness that such flexibility would encourage a maximum number of ratifications. International human rights instruments, aimed at achieving a universalist code, are likely to be vulnerable to the criticism that the negotiation and implementation of such agreements will carry the cultural preferences of the most powerful actors responsible for their creation and implementation. If we view the CRC as a paradigm of international norm-creation, then equally we must address carefully the cultural relativist critique (Harris-Short 2001). The issue of cultural relativity is examined in more detail in section 1.3.

1.1.2 Psychological perspectives

As we have seen in the previous section, Ariès pointed to the development of education as historical evidence of a major shift in historical attitudes towards the nature of childhood. Similarly, an understanding of the developmental psychology of children has been enhanced by the adoption of universal education, at least in some countries. It is perhaps unsurprising that such an investment of resources is based upon some pre-existing theory of learning. The particular shape of an education system in any society must be based on a view about the ability of children to receive and process knowledge, in other words, cognitive development.

Piaget (1952, 1960) provided a highly influential analysis of how the processes of thought were structured through his theory of learning. He realised that a child's mind was different from merely being a small version of an adult's mind. In essence, Piagetian theory attempts to explain how humans adapt to their environment via the process of the child's 'assimilation' (taking in new encounters)

---

3 Centre for the History of Childhood. '[I]t is hoped that its creation will help to foster interest in this burgeoning area of historical research within and without the University. The Centre exists both to promote research into the history of childhood and to encourage links between historians and childcare professionals in the belief that close association between the two will be of mutual benefit.' Available at: http://www.history.ox.ac.uk/research/clusters/history_childhood/index.htm (accessed 28 December 2009).

and 'accommodation' (revising cognitive constructs) of experience. Piaget suggested that the developmental process involved the individual in a search to achieve a balance between assimilation and accommodation. This balance is what Piaget describes as *equilibrium*.

On the basis of empirical studies, Piaget identified a model of the child's intellectual growth through separate chronological stages. First, the sensory-motor stage (infancy) immediately after birth. In this period, which he asserted lasted until around 2 years old, the infant's adaptation to his/her environment is shown by motor activity without the use of abstract reasoning. At first, infants use motor reflexes to interact with their environment. The infant relies on seeing, feeling, sucking and touching to learn about his/her environment. Infants eventually learn that their environment is not simply an extension of themselves. The infant develops a sense of causation in learning to move an object by hand. Children acquire the concept of 'object permanence' at about 7 months old, that is, an understanding that an object (or person) still exists when not in view. For example, a young infant will lose interest in a toy when it is covered up, but an older infant will actively seek it out. Following an understanding of object permanence, the infant performs motor experiments ('directed groping') and learns how to manipulate objects. An increase in the child's physical mobility allows the child to develop new intellectual abilities. Some symbolic abilities – for example, language – are developed at the end of this stage.

Piaget's second 'pre-operational stage' (toddler and early childhood) lasts until the child is around 2–7 years old. In this period a child will acquire language skills, and memory and imagination are developed, but thinking is done in a non-logical, non-reversible manner. This stage is characterised by what Piaget terms egocentric thinking; that is, they will only view the outside world from their own perspective. For example, a 3-year-old may well hide behind a chair in the belief that as s/he cannot see anyone else and no-one else can see him/her. Pre-operational children will develop an internal representation of the outside environment that allows them to provide a description of people, events and feelings. Children can be observed using memory and imagination during this stage.

Piaget's third stage, 'concrete operations' (elementary and early adolescence), was said to last for children from around 7–12 years old. Such children are capable of taking into account another person's point of view and can appreciate more than one perspective at the same time. The beginning of this period is marked by the acquisition of the principle of 'conservation'. This is an understanding that the number, volume, mass, liquid, weight, area and length of objects does not change when the particular configuration of the object(s) is changed. For example, a child will appreciate that two identical lengths of ribbon, one rolled up into a ball and the other laid flat, retain the same length. Children also acquire the idea of reversibility; that is, some changes can be undone by reversing an earlier action. For example, one can regain the flat ribbon by rolling out the ball. Children become capable of mentally visualizing this type of action without the need to see it actually performed. Egocentric thought decreases. A child develops the ability to coordinate two dimensions of an object simultaneously, arrange structures in sequence, and transpose differences between items in a series, and will have a better idea of time and space. During this stage, a child begins to reason logically, but can only think about actual, concrete, physical objects; they cannot yet manage abstract reasoning.

The final stage of Piaget's theory is 'formal operations' (adolescence and adulthood), acquired by children from around 11 or 12 years old into adulthood. Children at this stage will be capable of thinking logically and in the abstract and can reason theoretically, though some people may never reach this stage. Early on at this stage there is a return to egocentric thought processes. However, thinking is not tied exclusively to events that can be observed. Some research studies have suggested that only around 40–60 per cent of college students reach this stage! The stage is characterised by the ability to construct hypotheses and systematically test these to resolve a problem. In particular, an ability arises to reason hypothetically, or contrary to the known facts. For example, an argument based on the premise that the world is flat could be processed.

The impact of Piaget's theory on, for example, education curricula has been immense. The lasting influence of Piaget can be seen in the 'Early Childhood Studies' courses available in university education and other departments.[4] One key point to his theory should be noted. This is that a child could only pass from one stage to another when the appropriate levels of maturity and external stimuli were present. The theory thus acknowledges both the importance of the child's biological maturation *and* the differential influence of the external environment; in other words, 'nature and nurture'. In the absence of good conditions to sustain both, a child is unlikely to progress to his or her fullest potential. However, subsequent researchers in developmental psychology do not accept Piaget's theory uncritically. For example, the theory does not clearly explain why development from one stage to another happens. The theory largely ignores individual differences in cognitive development and provides little explanation for why some individuals may proceed faster than others from one stage to another. Also, the actual functioning of a person at a particular time may vary considerably in relation to understanding of spatial, mathematical and other concepts, to the point where placing that individual in one of Piaget's stages becomes meaningless. In order to remove some of these weaknesses scholars, known as 'neo-Piagetian' theorists – for example, Demetriou *et al.* (2000) – have adapted Piaget's theory to develop new understanding of cognitive and developmental psychology.

Indeed, there is an increasing body of evidence in the last 30 years that young babies, for example, do far more representational 'thinking' than merely the

---

4 A UCAS search produced 269 such courses available in 2010. See http://www.ucas.ac.uk/students/coursesearch/coursesearch2010/ (accessed 28 December 2009).

motor reflexes which Piaget underlined at this (first) stage (Sutherland 1992). Nevertheless, Piaget's contribution has been enduring and indeed the very concept of the cognitive development of the child makes much sense when applied, as in the *Gillick* case[5] in the United Kingdom, to determine the point at which teenagers can be regarded as sufficiently mature to understand the meaning and consequences of important decision-making which may have significant effects upon their lives. As we shall see, one of the key dilemmas in discussions of 'children's rights' (see section 1.2.1) is the nature and extent of the child's autonomy across a range of decision-making areas. The insights of developmental psychology have much to contribute towards a more rounded understanding of children's ability to conduct and understand fully the consequences of their own independent action.

1.1.3 Sociological perspective

In the 1980s and 1990s, academic societies started to pay specific attention to the sociology of childhood. For example, in 1998 a research committee of the International Sociological Association was dedicated to the study of childhood.[6] One explanation for the marginalisation of interest in children is their general marginalisation in society. Adult perspectives on children often focus on what children are to become rather than appreciate what they are. Since all children are expected to grow up, there is a tendency to focus on the end product, that is, the adult, rather than to concentrate on the child and the 'here and now' aspects of childhood. Children are often viewed as passive consumers of a culture already established by adults. Society can be seen, within traditional social theory, as maintaining its integrity through a process of 'socialisation'. Individuals are in effect guided into suitable roles via a wide range of institutional and other processes. The notion of socialisation itself involves society's values being lodged into individuals' personalities. Social theory has often recognised the child as particularly in need of such socialisation in order to provide the appropriate induction into the adult world.

However, it is the family that has the expected primary role to ensure that this process of socialising the child is carried out effectively. It is useful in this context to distinguish two different models of the socialisation process: the deterministic and constructivist models (Corsaro 2005).

The deterministic model is based on the idea that the child is essentially appropriated by society, that is, trained into becoming a useful member of society. On the one hand, the child's potential future contribution to society is recognised. On the other hand, the underlying assumption is that without the appropriate

5 [1986] A.C. 112.
6 International Sociological Association: Research Committee 53 (Sociology of Children). Available at: http://www.isa-sociology.org/rc53.htm (accessed 29 December 2009).

application of socialisation the child will remain a threat to the good order of society. The child's role in this conceptualisation is essentially a passive one. Furthermore, there are 'functionalist' and 'reproductive' models contained within this deterministic approach.

The functionalist approach in the 1950s and 1960s emphasised the need to maintain order and balance in society and therefore looked at children in terms of how they can be best prepared to take up useful places in the adult world. Theorists such as Talcott Parsons advocated such an approach and viewed the child as a threat to the intricate balance required to maintain society. Parsons saw the child as a 'pebble "thrown" by the fact of birth into the social pond' (Parsons and Bales 1956). The child's point of origin, the family, will be the first element to feel the effects of this potential disruption, followed by schools and then other social institutions and processes. Eventually, the child internalises the values, norms and standards of the wider society. A key criticism of the functionalist approach, however, was that the internalisation of the requirements for society's good order could simply be viewed as a sophisticated method of social control. It assumed that the status quo would be maintained. In other words, these social-isation processes were viewed as a means to reproduce social inequalities.

The reproductive model of society therefore tended to analyse more deeply the nature of such inequality in a more critical manner and not just assume that the function of society was merely to reproduce itself without improvement or any fundamental change. As regards the impact on children, such an approach takes greater note of the existence and nature of social conflict and inequality. The deterministic approach as a whole can be criticised in that it will tend to overem-phasise the outcomes of socialisation and underestimate the active roles played by the individual. Some advocates of the deterministic approach have advanced a behaviourist understanding of childhood, emphasising the value of training in skills needed for functional living and the need for a clear system of rewards and punishment which would determine appropriate socialisation.

In contrast to the notion of society appropriating the child, the 'constructivist' model focuses on how the child appropriates society. The contribution of developmental psychology, in particular Piagetian theory, is particularly important here. The child is conceptualised as extracting information from his or her environment in order to construct his or her own interpretation of society. Piaget's 'stage' analysis of intellectual development (see section 1.1.2 above) confirms children's differing qualitative understandings of their environment and their interactions with it as compared to adults. Piaget's concept of 'equilibrium' also provides a view of the child as being more active and self-determining than a picture of the child determined by irresistible societal forces. Though Piaget believed there was an inherent tendency for children to compensate for environmental intrusions (he termed this 'equilibrium'), nevertheless, 'the nature of the compensations is dependent on the *activities of children in their social-ecological worlds*' (Corsaro 2005: 11–12).

Lev Vygotsky is another significant constructivist theorist who underlined children's active rather than passive roles. He believed that their social development, however, was based on *collective* rather than individual (Piaget) action. He argued that language and other cultural tools are developed collectively by societies over the course of history and are acquired by children in order to actively participate and contribute to that culture. Vygotsky had a notion of 'internalisation' whereby every function in the child's development appeared not only on the social level at first, that is *between* people (interpsychological), but also on the individual level, that is *inside* the child (intrapsychological) (Vygotsky 1962). The following commentary provides a useful illustration of how such a conception can be seen to operate.

Consider Vygotsky's conceptions of self-directed and inner speech. By self-directed speech, Vygotsky is referring to the tendency of young children to speak out loud to themselves, especially in problematic situations. Piaget saw such speech as egocentric or emotional and serving no social function. Vygotsky, on the other hand, saw self-directed speech as a form of interpersonal communication, except that in this case the child is addressing himself as another. In a sense, the child is directing and advising himself on how to deal with a problem. In experimental work, Vygotsky found that such speech increased when children were given a task like building a car with construction toys or were told to draw a picture. Vygotsky believed that, over time, self-directed speech was transformed or internalized from the interpersonal to the intrapersonal, becoming inner speech or a form of thought. We can grasp his ideas when we think about how we first learn to read. Most of our early reading as young children is done out loud as we read to ourselves and others. Over time we begin to mumble and then to mouth the words as we read, and eventually we read entirely at a mental level. In short, the intrapsychological function or skill of reading has its origins in social or collective activity – reading out loud for others and oneself. For Vygotsky internalization occurs gradually over an extended period of time.

(Corsaro 2005: 14–15)

In addition, Vygotsky posed a model of development in which children were constantly in between their actual and potential developmental levels (the 'zone of proximal development'), interacting with others in order to acquire more skills and information. Children gradually appropriated the norms and values of society through this collective process of sharing and creating culture.

Although constructivist models are capable of providing a picture of the child as a more active participant in society, there are two essential weaknesses with this general approach. First, most constructivist theory focuses on *individual* child development. Even Vygotsky's notion of collective action at the interpersonal level becomes obscured with an overemphasis on the intrapersonal level, the process of an individual child's internalisation of culture. Second, the focus is usually on the endpoint of the developmental cycle, the transition from immaturity to adult maturity. Corsaro offers the notion of 'interpretive reproduction' as a theoretical perspective which refocuses attention on collective interactions and children's own creative generation of culture:

> The term *interpretive* captures the *innovative* and *creative* aspects of children's participation in society. In fact, … children create and participate in their own unique peer cultures by creatively taking or appropriating information from the adult world to address their own peer concerns. The term *reproduction* captures the idea that children are not simply internalizing society and culture, but are actively *contributing to cultural production and change*. The term also implies that children are, by their very participation in society, *constrained by the existing social structure and by societal reproduction*. That is, children and their childhoods are affected by the societies and cultures of which they are members. These societies and cultures have, in turn, been shaped and affected by processes of historical change.
>
> (Corsaro 2005: 18–19)

Corsaro has produced a graphic representation of his model (Figure 1.1). The spokes represent a range of fields that comprise various social institutions. Cultural information flows to all parts of the web along these spokes. The child

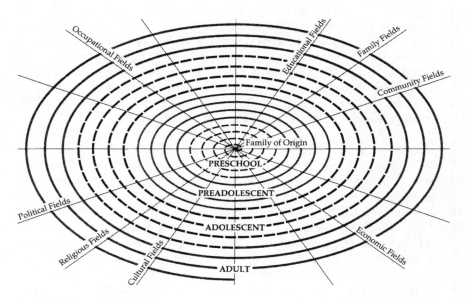

Figure 1.1 The orb web model.

Source: Corsaro (2005: 26).

enters his or her culture at the point of origin, the family. Children begin however to participate in relations outside the family from an early age, as is represented in the figure by the spiral lines. They 'begin to produce and participate in a series of peer cultures' (Corsaro 2005: 25). There are four distinct peer cultures represented: preschool, pre-adolescent, adolescent and adult. Corsaro argues that these peer cultures are not stages through which children progress. They are not, for the most part, pre-existing structures, but are produced and participated in by the children themselves.

It can be seen that one key element of the recent sociological theorizing about childhood has been the focus on the child as an active social agent:

> In sociology this has been codified … as a call for children to be understood as social actors, shaping as well as shaped by their social circumstances. This represents a definitive move away from the more or less inescapable implication of the concept of socialization: that children are to be seen as a defective form of adult, social only in their future potential but not in their present being. And yet this rallying point of children's agency is embedded in and related to a much wider process through which the individual voices and presence of children is now being recognised and accounted for.
>
> (James *et al.* 1998: 6)

Consequently, this approach avoids viewing children as somehow outside of the mainstream of society and also avoids any marginalisation of children by viewing them only as emerging members of the wider community.

Another key theme in the sociological perspective on childhood, sometimes referred to as 'generational order', has been the way in which children are categorised by age for different purposes which does not necessarily reflect children's own needs but instead may be seen as structural requirements in society to maintain social order (Mayall 2003). Consequently, social inequalities are also intimately related to the sociological understanding of childhood. Some sociological work focuses on the accounts that children themselves have of their lives and relations with parents and other adults. Children themselves make important points on questions relating to autonomy and interdependence. Some commentators have called for more attention to be paid to children's own perspectives:

> Whilst Western liberal thinkers have regarded the autonomous, independent moral agent as the highest form of life, children regard relationships as the cornerstone of their lives. It is of crucial importance to them to work with and through family relationships, to care about those who live elsewhere as well as those they live with. … Thus any account of how the social order works, in terms of values ascribed by varying social groups to dependence, independence, and inter-dependence, needs to take account of children's views.
>
> (Mayall 2000: 256)

One commentator has observed that the 'new sociology of childhood'[7] has become 'the dominant theoretical framework, for anyone seeking a sociological understanding of childhood and children' (King 2007: 194). He observes that the new sociology of childhood is distinct from the 'socialization' and development psychology research of previous decades. It can also be seen that this renewed sociological emphasis on the child's competence, autonomy and active agency and voice fits comfortably around the legal-oriented perspective of 'children's rights' which is examined in further detail in section 1.2.1 below. Indeed, as King observes,

> One of the difficulties faced by the new sociology of childhood has been that of establishing a clear demarcation line between what claims to be a new theoretical understanding of children and the discourse of children's rights.
>
> (King 2007: 194)

1.1.4 Social policy perspectives

The way in which the concept of childhood has been viewed historically, the theories of child development, and the constructivist account of childhood from the sociological perspective, discussed earlier, cannot provide a complete picture without an understanding of a society's approach to formulating and developing social policy in child-related matters. To an extent, the approach to building social policy relating to children will reflect a society's distilled understanding (derived from many disciplines) of how children fit into the overall order of that society. An understanding of international child law is enhanced by an ability to locate it within the context of the wider social policy framework at the international, regional or national level. At the international level, this can be identified in the programmes pursued by the United Nations, for example, via UNICEF (see section 2.4.1.2). At the regional level, for example in Europe, we shall need to look at the key institutions – the Council of Europe and the European Union (EU) (see section 2.5.2.1) – to determine how policy is determined and delivered. Indeed, there are indications that both these institutions are becoming active participants in progressing child policy. The Council of Europe has issued a number of conventions related to family and child matters.[8] The EU has in the

---

7 For example, Corsaro (2005), James and Prout (1997), James *et al.* (1998), Jenks (1996) and Qvortrup *et al.* (1994).
8 For example: ETS 005 Convention for the Protection of Human Rights and Fundamental Freedoms (opened for signature 4/11/1950 – entry into force 03/09/1953); ETS 035 European Social Charter (18/10/1961 – 26/2/1965); ETS 058 European Convention on the Adoption of Children (24/04/1967 – 26/04/1968); ETS 085 European Convention on the Legal Status of Children born out of Wedlock (15/10/1975 – 11/08/1978); ETS 105 European Convention on Recognition and Enforcement of Decisions concerning Custody of Children and on Restoration of Custody of Children (20/05/1980 – 01/09/1983); ETS 160 European Convention on the Exercise of Children's Rights

past sidelined child-related issues on the basis that they are not directly related to the overall EU project of the single market. However, this appears to be changing.

> In recent years, the pendulum has swung from a steadfast resistance on the part of the EU and nation States to EU intervention in children's rights, towards a growing eagerness to engage the institutions in a range of issues affecting children. Indeed, the broadening scope of EU activity has made it increasingly difficult to justify maintaining a hands off approach; all aspects of EU law and policy have a direct or indirect impact on children's lives such that it is no longer a question of *why* the EU should be enacting child-focused provision, but rather, *what* it should be doing to minimise the adverse effects of EU law and policy for children.
>
> (Stalford and Drywood 2009: 170–71)

Finally, at the national level, government activity in the relevant ministries, in addition to local government organs and voluntary agencies, will implement policy and feed back both strategic and operational lessons learned from such implementation.

It would appear that a key driver of social policy formulation in relation to children is a society's dominant perception of the state–family relationship. Fox Harding (1996) has described seven potential models describing this relationship. At one end of this typology there is an authoritarian model, where the state sets out to compel and prohibit certain family behaviour, thereby severely limiting personal freedom. At the other end there is a *laissez-faire* model where state intervention is minimal and where family life is seen as a private matter unsuitable for legal intervention. It is arguable that at present the British government, for example, best reflects one of Fox Harding's models located between these two extremes, in which the state will substitute for and support families when they fail. In this model the state recognises that, in the normal course of affairs, the family should be left alone and is the best place for children to be raised. However, when the family breaks down a state duty arises to mitigate the resulting damage, protect family members and support the formation of a substitute family, for example, by arranging an adoption. Indeed, this approach is probably comparable to the position in several other European states. The way in which article 8 of the European Convention on Human Rights (ECHR) (right to respect for private and family life, home and correspondence) is drafted, and its practical operation, are based on the assumption that the individual is in need of protection from arbitrary interference by the state and therefore any state interference must

(25/01/1996 – 01/07/2000); ETS 163 European Social Charter (revised) (3/5/1996 – 1/7/1999); ETS 185 Convention on Cybercrime (23/11/2001 – 1/7/2004); ETS 192 Convention on Contact concerning Children 15/5/2003 – not yet in force); ETS 201 Convention on the Protection of Children against Sexual Exploitation and Sexual Abuse (25 October 2007 – not yet in force).

be credibly justified on specified grounds. It can be seen that those grounds in effect may describe circumstances where private and family life have become dysfunctional and therefore justify a higher degree of state involvement, subject always to the proportionality principle that requires the particularities of state interference to be in proportion to the overall aims of that interference.

In countries where this type of state–family relationship prevails, the social policies in relation to children have tended to focus on interventions deemed necessary to address situations where families fail. The classic example is where parents, for a variety of reasons, are no longer perceived as capable or available to look after their children properly. Consequently, in many countries including the United Kingdom, child policy has often tended to gravitate towards a concentration on the state's *social services* for children. A comparable child welfare approach is also found in the education and health sectors. In these sectors, the state only intervenes, at least with coercive techniques, when clear dysfunctions are evident.

Furthermore, social policy relating to children is often viewed as *either* 'welfarist' *or* 'rights-based', though these two approaches are not necessarily mutually exclusive. The former usually refers to an underlying policy aimed at protecting children who are seen as vulnerable members of society in need of guidance and control. The role of parents, schools, social services and the state is to protect, nurture and provide fulfilling opportunities for children's development. Rights-based policy is designed to support children's own participation in decision-making and is based on a conception of children having distinct rights that can be asserted, morally and legally. As we have seen, this approach also very much resonates with the dominant sociological image of the child as a competent, autonomous and active social agent. The dichotomy in current debates between welfarist and rights-based policy should not hide other complexities of child welfare policy and the subtle changes in perceptions about the acceptability of state intervention in the family. For example, Hendrick (1997), in an examination of British child welfare, shows that there was a shift in around the 1870s 'from a simple concern with child reformation and rescue, usually by placing children in either philanthropic or Poor Law institutional care, to a far more complex notion and practice of welfare'.

The precise boundaries of state intervention also depend on the way in which the major social problems involving children are perceived. If the physical, emotional or sexual abuse of children is regarded as a manifestation of the individual pathology of the abuser, then detection, treatment and/or punishment of the offender are likely to be of central concern in social policy initiatives. On the other hand, if child abuse can be explained to an extent by a social structure that harbours poverty and inequality, then other initiatives are required. The UK government committed itself in 1999 to a policy that would halve child poverty by 2010 and eradicate it by 2020. Despite the difficulties in formulating an adequate measure of child poverty, this initiative does represent a real attempt to apply more holistic thinking to the structural inequalities affecting children. Indeed, one of the last pieces of legislation of Gordon Brown's administration prior to the May 2010 election was the Child Poverty Act 2010 (c.9) that provided a statutory basis to the commitment made by the British Government to eradicate child poverty by 2020. Its stated purpose was to give new impetus to the government's commitment, and to drive action across departments. It also aimed to define success in eradicating child poverty and create a framework to monitor progress at a national and local level. Indeed, the successive New Labour administrations since 1997 have generally a rather good record in driving forward child welfare programmes and children's rights. The 'Sure Start' initiative[9] is another example of such 'joined-up' government thinking. Indeed, the creation in June 2007 of a discrete Department of State devoted to 'Children, Schools and Families' (DCSF) along with a Secretary of State with lead responsibility for all policies affecting children in England, and the creation of a co-ordinated and CRC-compliant 'Children's Plan for England' (Secretary of State for Children, Schools and Families 2007), are further indications of how child policy has become increasingly mainstreamed in the United Kingdom. However, there are areas where child policy is failing, as evidenced by the Committee on the Rights of the Child's (CtRC) 'concluding observations' on the UK's performance – see sections 3.4.2 to 3.4.4 – in particular, matters in relation to the administration of juvenile justice. It also seems likely that the global recession, commencing in July 2007, will prompt re-examination of existing policy frameworks and a search for new policy paradigms.

It may often be difficult to identify clearly what the social policy is of a particular community towards its children. Sometimes this is precisely because the policy, if it exists at all, is relatively incoherent and uncoordinated. The 'concluding observations' emanating from the CtRC (see Chapter 3) in response to national reports are full of such criticisms. The country reports submitted by state parties to the CtRC and the latter's 'concluding observations' are a useful source of information about a state's policy on child-related matters. Another informative source is the official documentation, along with critical commentary from non-governmental organisations (NGOs) and academic commentary. For example, a government Green Paper issued in the United Kingdom in 2003, 'Every Child Matters' (Chief Secretary to the Treasury 2003), provided a useful snapshot of a number of child-related policies. Ostensibly, the paper was a response to the public inquiry into the death of 8-year-old Victoria Climbié that was set up after

---

9 'Sure Start' is the Government's programme to deliver the best start in life for every child by bringing together early education, childcare, health and family support. The Early Years, Extended Schools and Special Needs Group, within the DCSF, is responsible for delivering Sure Start. Sure Start covers a wide range of programmes, both universal and those targeted on particular local areas or disadvantaged groups within England. Responsibility for early education and childcare issues lies with the devolved administrations in Scotland, Wales and Northern Ireland. Available at: http://www.dcsf.gov.uk/everychildmatters/earlyyears/surestart/whatsurestartdoes/ (accessed 29 December 2009).

an English jury found her carers guilty of murder and child abuse in January 2001.[10] More broadly, however, 'Every Child Matters' provided some analysis and framework of policy that could address the problems identified in such child abuse inquiries and in relation to other children's issues. For example, it identified the consistent failings in child protection services first brought to public attention in the United Kingdom in the Maria Colwell inquiry (DHSS 1974):

> The common threads which led in each case to a failure to intervene early enough were poor co-ordination; a failure to share information; the absence of anyone with a strong sense of accountability; and frontline workers trying to cope with staff vacancies, poor management and a lack of effective training.
>
> (Chief Secretary to the Treasury 2003: 5)

Child protection policy that is based on intervention only in circumstances where the family unit has broken down obviously raises issues about the extent of family dysfunction that might justify such intervention, via care and supervision orders, for example. The threshold legal test[11] for such orders – 'significant harm' or its likelihood – marks the point at which local authority social services can take compulsory action. In addition, our understanding of the background state–family configuration will also impact upon the decision-making involved in placing children once they are ingested into the public care system. Consistently with the standards set out in the CRC (see section 3.5.5), planning the child's future will take place initially on the understanding that the ultimate aim is to rehabilitate the family unit. Where this is not possible 'permanency planning' will follow, that is, placing the child with a new adoptive family. However, such decision-making is of course fraught with difficulties; in what circumstances does the underlying aim of rehabilitation become a hopeless cause and the alternative of adoption a realistic one? Although the 'paramountcy principle' is now relevant to adoption-order decision-making[12] as it is to other decisions relating to the upbringing of children,[13] the policy impulse underlying the history of adoption legislation in the United Kingdom has not always focused exclusively on the welfare of children, but has at different times since the first Adoption Act in 1926 focused on the needs of the adoptive family, the needs of the birth family and the needs of the state/local authority in managing adoptions. For example, the Adoption

---

10 See the report of the inquiry (Health Committee 2003).
11 See Children Act 1989, s.31(2).
12 'The paramount consideration of the court or adoption agency must be the child's welfare, throughout his life'. (Adoption and Children Act 2002, section 1(2)).
13 'When a court determines any question with respect to—
     (a) the upbringing of a child; or
     (b) the administration of a child's property or the application of any income arising from it,
     the child's welfare shall be the court's paramount consideration'. (Children Act 1989, section 1(1)).

and Children Act 2002 can be seen as a legislative vehicle intended to address specifically the local authorities' needs to reduce the overall numbers of children languishing for too long in local authority care. In recent years, there has been an increase in the number of children returned to local authority care by their adoptive parents. It would appear that such children are so damaged by their early life experiences that adoption placements also become an unrealistic option. Institutional care in a children's home may be the last resort available.

Conversely, the Webster case in 2009[14] illustrated the problems that can arise when the agencies involved with child protection misread or misunderstand the signs of dysfunction or breakdown, and adoption takes place, only for later events to show that the original family was blameless. Mr and Mrs Webster were exonerated of the claim that they had abused one of their children, but since three children had been adopted by the time due process had acknowledged the error, the adoptions could not be reversed – the child's welfare was paramount. In this instance the paramountcy principle prevented the children from being returned to their natural parents. Although there is a need to protect children, especially the most vulnerable, nevertheless the action taken must be proportionate. Adoption can provide a child with a loving family and, hopefully, prevent the tragedies referred in preceding discussion. Conversely, if the decision to free up for adoption is taken without recourse to all relevant agencies and careful examination of the evidence, then unfortunate situations like that of the Webster family could be repeated.

The 'Baby P' case in 2008–09 has revealed a range of difficulties bearing upon child protection policy in the United Kingdom. P was a 17-month-old boy who died after suffering over 50 injuries in an 8-month period during which he was repeatedly seen by social services in Haringey, London. The London Borough of Haringey had also been the subject of inquiry in the Victoria Climbié inquiry several years earlier. P's mother, her boyfriend and the boyfriend's brother were all eventually convicted of causing or allowing the death of P, the mother having pleaded guilty to the charge. Haringey and other agencies were widely criticised. Following the conviction, three inquiries and a nationwide review of social service care were launched, and the Head of Children's Services at Haringey was removed by direction of the government minister. A further nationwide review was conducted by Lord Laming into his own recommendations concerning Victoria Climbié's killing in 2000 (Laming 2009).

Lord Laming's report concluded, inter alia, that many local authorities had not implemented his previous recommendations from the Victoria Climbié inquiry in 2001 (Laming 2009). The government's response to Lord Laming's report confirmed the need for a 'comprehensive approach to children through national strategies' (DCSF 2009: 31). It also confirmed the government's own commitment

---

14 *Webster (The Parents) v. Norfolk County Council & Ors (Rev 1)* [2009] EWCA Civ 59 (11 February 2009).

to placing the child as the active agent within the safeguarding structure of child protection:

> Crucially, Lord Laming has stressed the importance of placing the child at the centre of all that we do. That means understanding the perspective of the child, listening to the child and never losing sight of the child. Just as the centrality of the child drives our policies so too should it drive day-to-day practice at the front line.
>
> (DCSF 2009: 4)

1.2 Human rights

Children's rights can be properly understood only in the context of the wider human rights framework. The devastating impact of the Second World War and the founding of the United Nations in its aftermath have been the most recent modern inspiration behind the human rights movement in the twentieth century. Early legal codes in mediaeval times, which appear to include 'rights', on closer inspection turn out merely to reflect how powerful groups in that society at that time were realigning themselves. Thus the *Magna Carta* (1215)[15] in England, for example, is concerned more with the privileges of the barons and Church–State relationships than with matters of common humanity. Similarly, the English *Bill of Rights* in the seventeenth century[16] set out the ground rules for a new settlement between King and Parliament. Philosophers in the eighteenth and nineteenth centuries generated thinking about 'natural rights' and 'natural law', that is, the rights attached to a human by virtue of nature, rather than by status or any other classification. The American (1776) and French (1789) Revolutions drew on such ideas for their inspiration. The US Declaration of Independence (4 July 1776) famously stated that 'we hold these truths to be self-evident; ... that all men are created equal, that they are endowed by their Creator with certain unalienable Rights, that among these are Life, Liberty and the pursuit of Happiness.' John Locke (1632–1704), the English philosopher, believed there was a natural-law right to life, liberty and property. The French Republic produced its Declaration of the Rights of Man and of Citizens (26 August 1789). In the nineteenth century a number of recognisable human rights issues were becoming increasingly controversial, for example, slavery, serfdom, bad working conditions and child labour. Social movements sprang up in response; for example, labour unions, racial and religious minority groups, women's rights and national liberation

---

15 Confirmed and reissued in the reign of King Edward I, Magna Carta (1297) (c. 9). Clauses 1 (freedom of Church of England), 9 (liberties and customs of City of London etc.) and 29 (no imprisonment except by lawful judgment of his peers) are still in force today. Other important rights, for example, habeas corpus, have been incorporated into more modern statutes.
16 1688 (c.2) 1 Will and Mar Sess 2.

movements. The idea that every human being was equally deserving of respect and dignity and could be regarded as a right holder – capable of asserting rights against other individuals and the state and that governments had a duty to respect, promote and protect such rights – was beginning to appear.

The political consensus achieved by the Allies in the immediate post-war period allowed the conditions necessary for a synthesis of these ideas to emerge. There are several references in the United Nations Charter of 1945[17] to human rights, in particular in the preamble, where it is stated that the peoples of the United Nations are determined 'to reaffirm faith in fundamental human rights, in the dignity and worth of the human person, in the equal rights of men and women and of nations large and small'. Article 68 of the Charter required the UN's Economic and Social Council to set up a UN Commission on Human Rights (UNCHR)[18] (see Chapter 2). Its first task, through the chairmanship of Eleanor Roosevelt, was to produce an international bill of human rights. It was decided that this should be in the form of a declaration (not binding in international law) rather than a binding treaty. It was envisaged that the document should be short, inspirational and accessible, and would be followed at a later date with more detailed (and binding) treaty provisions. The result was the Universal Declaration of Human Rights of 1948 (UDHR).[19] Article 1 stated that '[a]ll human beings are born free and equal in dignity and rights. They are endowed with reason and conscience and should act towards one another in a spirit of brotherhood.' Eighteen years later the (binding) treaty provisions appeared in the form of the International Covenant on Civil and Political Rights of 1966 (ICCPR) and the International Covenant on Economic, Social and Cultural Rights of 1966 (ICESCR). These two covenants reflect respectively the so-called 'first generation' (civil and political) and 'second generation' (economic, social and cultural) rights.

Despite its formal non-binding status, the UDHR has become the accepted gold standard of international human rights. It has almost certainly become part of what is termed 'international customary law' (see section 2.2.2). It has inspired similar human rights instruments to be produced at the regional level. For example, the European Convention on Human Rights (Rome, 1950), the American Convention on Human Rights (the 'Pact of San Jose', Costa Rica, 1969) and the African [Banjul] Charter on Human and Peoples' Rights (Nairobi, 1981). The 50th anniversary of the UDHR was celebrated by the adoption of the Asian Human Rights Charter: A Peoples Charter (Kwangju, South Korea, 1998).

---

17 The Charter of the United Nations was signed on 26 June 1945, in San Francisco, at the conclusion of the United Nations Conference on International Organization, and came into force on 24 October 1945. The Statute of the International Court of Justice is an integral part of the Charter: see generally, section 2.4.1.

18 The UNCHR was replaced by a United Nations Human Rights Council (UNHRC) in 2006: see section 2.5.1.1.

19 The Declaration was passed by the UN's General Assembly on 10 December 1948.

Individual countries too are increasingly incorporating these now well-known human rights standards into their own domestic law. Britain passed her Human Rights Act in 1998 and the Australian Capital Territory has produced Australia's first Bill of Rights in its Human Rights Act of 2004.

Some of the provisions of the UDHR relate to the family and children. Article 12, for example, states that '[n]o one shall be subjected to arbitrary interference with his privacy, family, home or correspondence, nor to attacks upon his honour and reputation. Everyone has the right to the protection of the law against such interference or attacks.' Article 16(3) states that '[t]he family is the natural and fundamental group unit of society and is entitled to protection by society and the State.' Article 25(2) interestingly provides that '[m]otherhood and childhood are entitled to special care and assistance. All children, whether born in or out of wedlock, shall enjoy the same social protection.' Article 26 contains a right to education which should be free and compulsory at the elementary stage and 'directed to the full development of the human personality and to the strengthening of respect for human rights and fundamental freedoms'.

The historical development of human rights outlined in the preceding discussion and the emergence of the UN 'Treaty bodies' (see section 2.5.1.2 and Table 2.1) that now deal with particular categories of human rights issues, including the CtRC's supervision and monitoring of the CRC, have raised the issue of how far children's rights should be differentiated from the general international human rights instruments. The problem with the latter is that they have tended to focus on the rights of parents. There may also be obligations on parents and institutions towards children but these are likely to be unenforceable by children. One commentator points out that making the case for the recognition of children's rights has led to an assumption that children have different rights from adults, with different justifications, rather than accommodating children as an integral part of the same human rights protection regime (Sawyer 2006). However, she argues that:

> ... children should be regarded as essentially human beings who are equally entitled to rights. If children are to have special rights or accommodations on the basis of their particular vulnerability or inexperience, those should be additional to, rather than instead of, ordinary protective and constitutional rights. The starting-point should be recognition of children's legal personality as a construction as important as that of parents' rights'.
>
> (Sawyer 2006: 13)

Clearly, this reinforces the point that in order to be effective, any instrument that purports to provide for children must be child-centred and independent of adult bias. Hence the view that a more appropriate way forward in providing for children would be to grant them defined 'rights' – a trend that became increasingly popular following the end of the First World War and which eventually led to a fully-fledged code of children's rights in the form of the CRC in 1989.

1.2.1 Children's rights

Even before the modern development of international human rights law, as outlined in the preceding section, the League of Nations (1919–1946) had shown an interest in protecting and providing welfare services for children, in particular those orphaned and displaced in the wake of the First World War. In 1919 a Committee for the Protection of Children was set up by the League of Nations. Eglantyne Jebb (1876–1928), the founder of the British Save the Children Fund and the Save the Children International Union in Geneva, was an early campaigner for children and succeeded in getting the League of Nations to adopt a Declaration on the Rights of the Child in 1924 . This was in fact the first declaration of human rights adopted by any inter-governmental organisation and preceded the UDHR by 24 years. The 1924 Declaration was reaffirmed by the League of Nations in 1934. As can be seen from an examination of the text, the 1924 Declaration contains five principles directed to creating the conditions necessary for children to be protected and to enable them to develop into citizens who will contribute to their communities. However, the text of this document portrays the child as a *passive* object of concern rather than as an *active* subject capable of asserting rights against others. The intention behind the Declaration of 1924 was not to create a binding treaty but merely to create guiding principles for those working in international child welfare. The Declaration reflects a paternalistic view of child welfare where adults are clearly in total control of children's destinies. There is no suggestion here about welcoming or encouraging children's participation in decision-making or other aspects of children's self-determination.

The Declaration of the Rights of the Child of 1924 was revisited and revised by the United Nations in the form of the Declaration of the Rights of the Child of 1959. A much more robust language of rights is deployed in the Declaration of 1959 which sets out ten principles in a more expanded form than the Declaration of 1924. Indeed, some commentators have regarded the Declaration of 1959 as the 'conceptual parent' to the UN Convention on the Rights of the Child of 1989 (Van Bueren 1998: 14). Although the UDHR of 1948 contains some material specifically addressed to children, there are more specific formulations of rights directly affecting family and child issues contained in the two UN International Covenants issued in 1966 (i.e. ICCPR and ICESCR).

The ICCPR of 1966 contains a robust right of the child to be protected from discrimination, a right to a name and nationality:

1. Every child shall have, without any discrimination as to race, colour, sex, language, religion, national or social origin, property or birth, the right to such measures of protection as are required by his status as a minor, on the part of his family, society and the State.
2. Every child shall be registered immediately after birth and shall have a name.
3. Every child has the right to acquire a nationality.

(ICCPR, article 24)

The status of the family as 'the natural and fundamental group unit of society' referred to in the UDHR is reaffirmed in article 23, which also sets out a principle of equality of spouses during marriage and at dissolution and that '[i]n the case of dissolution, provision shall be made for the necessary protection of any children.'[20] The ICESCR of 1966 contains a strongly worded provision giving protection to children against economic and social exploitation, in particular setting out standards to regulate child labour. State parties to the Covenant recognise that, inter alia:

> Special measures of protection and assistance should be taken on behalf of all children and young persons without any discrimination for reasons of parentage or other conditions. Children and young persons should be pro- tected from economic and social exploitation. Their employment in work harmful to their morals or health or dangerous to life or likely to hamper their normal development should be punishable by law. States should also set age limits below which the paid employment of child labour should be prohibited and punishable by law.
>
> (ICESCR, article 10(3))

Rights to health (article 12) and education (article 13) are also included in detailed formulations in the ICESCR.

In short, the modern human rights movement in the post-war era has produced increasing concern about the rights of children. This has been reflected both in the development of the more robust textual formulations found in the two International Covenants of 1966 and in the further development of UNICEF and other inter-governmental organisations and NGOs working for improvements in children's lives: see section 2.4.1.2. The account of how the UN's International Year of the Child in 1979 eventually led to the production of the UN Convention on the Rights of the Child in 1989, which has become, in effect, the template for the international legal rights of the child, is taken up in more detail in Chapter 3: see section 3.2. For the purposes of this chapter, however, it is useful to consider further what 'children's rights' actually means.

There is now a considerable academic literature relating to the subject of children's rights. As Fortin (2009: 3) notes, the literature gravitates around three themes:

- how to identify children's rights;
- how to balance one set of rights against another in the event of a conflict between them; and
- how to mediate between children's rights and those of adults.

---

20 ICCPR, article 23(4).

1.2.1.1 Theories of children's rights[21]

There are two fundamental, moral philosophical debates that have exercised theorists who have grappled with the notion of children's rights. First, there is a 'choice' or ' will' theory of rights.[22] A theory of rights, it is said, assumes that the person asserting those rights will have a choice as to when and whether to exercise them. As children at various levels of maturation will not be likely to have the competence to exercise such choices in all circumstances, it has been questioned whether they can properly be described as having 'rights' at all. If rights are basically premised on the notion that the right holder must be competent to make such choices, then it might follow that, at least in circumstances where it is clear that a child would lack competence to choose, that child could not be properly described as a right holder. There are a number of difficulties with this approach. As Fortin (2009: 12) remarks, '[t]he assertion that children, who are too young and incompetent to claim rights, therefore have no rights, has an unattractive logic.' Indeed, if one applied the same approach to, for example, the position of a severely mentally ill or disabled adult, the 'unattractiveness' of the logic would increase still further. In order to circumnavigate such a stark conclusion, it could be conceded that there may be correlative duties on parents and other adults or institutions to provide a remedy for children (or severely mentally ill or disabled adults) who are not competent to make their own choices. Thus a child's right might obtain some, albeit indirect, recognition from the existence of such correlative duties placed on adults in respect of (incompetent) children. However, this theory can be criticised on the basis that it over-emphasises the existence of remedies. MacCormick (1982), for example, argues that it is only *because* a child has a right to care and nurture that the legal imposition on adults/ institutions to provide such protection is justified; the existence of the right presupposes the remedy. In addition, the choice theory fails to provide children with a secure standpoint in the face of parents or institutions who are failing in their correlative duties to protect. As we know from the considerable literature on child abuse, it is frequently the case that the greatest threat to a child's emotional, physical and sexual integrity comes from parents and other close family members and friends.

Second, this approach can be contrasted with the so-called 'interest' theory of rights intended to address some of the problems of the 'choice' theory.[23] According to the interest theory, rights are based upon whether a child has an interest that is in need of protection rather than merely based upon whether

---

21 See Freeman (1983: ch. 2), which provides an extended discussion of the concept of children's rights; and the extremely useful summary of the theoretical discussions of this concept in Fortin (2009: 3–30).

22 Advocates of the 'choice' theory include: Hart (1984) and Feinberg (1980).

23 Advocates of the 'interest' theory include: MacCormick (1982: 154–56), Raz (1996: 165–92) and Campbell (1992).

the right holder is actually capable of asserting or waiving his or her claim. If society generally recognises that children have a need for care and protection, then it ought to be possible to construct rights upon such foundations. In other words, from the identification of 'interests' there should emerge a collection of 'moral rights' and some of these will be transformed into 'legal rights'. One formulation of a moral right, favoured by Fortin (2009: 14), is 'a good of such importance that it would be wrong to deny it or withhold it from any member of C (a given class)' (MacCormick 1982: 160). However, this does not assist greatly in the task of identifying which interests can be transformed into moral rights; it appears merely to beg the same question using different terminology. What constitutes a 'good' of 'such importance' that it would be 'wrong' to deny or withhold it? As regards the transformation of moral into legal rights:

> Most commentators accept that moral rights are translated into legal rights if there is some recognition of their importance by the rest of society and consequently the imposition of correlative legal duties on others regarding the fulfilment of those rights.
>
> (Fortin 2009: 15)

The core point of the interest theory is that children ought not to be denied access to concrete legal rights merely because some children will not be sufficiently mature to make informed choices in their exercise and operation. However, the proponents of the interest theory would not claim that all children's interests are suitable to be transformed into moral rights and subsequently legal rights. A weakness of the interest theory is the uncertainty involved in identifying the relevant interests and the mechanisms that might operate to transform such interests into moral rights and then into legal rights. Which 'interests' should be rights-protected and why? By what criteria are we to assess the various interests of children for inclusion in a list of potential moral and legal rights?

Although there is no definitive resolution to this problem, Eekelaar at least provides a practical classification of children's interests which might be capable of transformation into moral/legal rights. In order to meet the problem that children might not be competent to properly formulate their interests, he suggested that the adult should 'make some kind of imaginative leap and guess what a child might retrospectively have wanted once it reaches a position of maturity' (Eekelaar 1986: 170). He ordered children's interests into three groups: 'basic', 'developmental' and 'autonomy' interests. Children's basic interests refer to the child's need for immediate physical, emotional and intellectual care. Children's developmental interests are concerned with children's needs to optimise their full developmental potential by having equal access to appropriate resources. A child's autonomy interests relate to the need for children to be free to make independent decisions about their lives. Importantly, Eekelaar advocated that where autonomy interests conflicted with basic and/or developmental interests the latter interests should prevail.

The problem is that a child's autonomy interest may conflict with the developmental interest and even the basic interest. While it is possible that some adults retrospectively approve that they were, when children, allowed the exercise of their autonomy at the price of putting them at a disadvantage as against other children in realizing their life-chances in adulthood, it seems improbable that this would be a common view. We may therefore rank the autonomy interests subordinate to the basic and the developmental interests. However, where they may be exercised without threatening these two interests, the claim for their satisfaction must be high.

(Eekelaar 1986: 171)

So, for example, the autonomy demonstrated by a child's decision to smoke cigarettes would be overridden by the recognition of basic (and development) health interests. Using the 'imaginative leap' notion referred to earlier, Eekelaar justifies this view on the basis that adults would be unlikely to retrospectively approve behaviour that would clearly prejudice their life-chances in adulthood.

As regards the underlying debate between the application of 'choice/will' or 'interest' theory, Fortin has argued that the emerging case law under the Human Rights Act 1998 has suggested that a young person's claim to exercise autonomy based on Convention rights has been dependent on that person's ability to comprehend what is involved in the decision itself. This is an approach that conforms to the 'choice/will' theory, but in practice, it is neither a logical nor a safe approach. On the other hand, an interest theory of rights 'allows conceptions of the child's welfare to be accommodated within conceptions of his interests or rights', and the interest theory does not compel any rejection of the idea of children making choices.

Children may indeed have some rights to self-determination based on their interest in choice, without having a right to complete autonomy. An analysis based on an interest theory of rights withholds the right to complete autonomy, including the right to make all fundamental decisions regarding his future, until the teenager reaches a required level of maturity, measured not only by reference to his powers of comprehension. At this level, he is deemed to be on a par with adult rights holders, with no paternalistic interventions available to protect him from the hazards of dangerous decision-making. Before then the courts are entitled to deny him the right to reach decisions which will materially threaten his adult wellbeing. Such a stance is a morally coherent one, reflecting the view that the status of minority carries a legal significance. It is designed to protect children from the dangers of adulthood, more particularly from making life-threatening decisions.

(Fortin 2006: 325)

In addition to the underlying moral philosophical debates around choice and interest theories, there are a number of other typologies of children's rights.

Freeman proposes four categories: welfare rights, protective rights, those grounded in social justice and those based on children's claims to more freedom from control and more autonomy over their lives [Freeman 1983]. This is similar to another fourfold classification of rights proposed by Wald, described as 'Rights Against the World', 'Protection from Inadequate Care', 'Rights to an Adult Legal Status' and 'Rights Versus Parents' [Wald 1979]. Campbell suggests a fourfold classification according to the minor's status as person, child, juvenile and future adult [Campbell 1992]. Arguably, Bevan's scheme which simply divides children's rights into two broad categories: protective and self-assertive, has a more pragmatic relevance [Bevan 1989]. It reflects the fundamental conflict currently underlying the whole of child law as it is developing in practice – that is the conflict between the need to fulfil children's rights to protection and to promote their capacity for self-determination.

(Fortin 2009: 17)

1.2.1.2 Autonomy, paternalism and participation

A key controversy in child law and policy is the extent to which the child can be properly regarded as having a right to autonomy or self-determination. This very much reflects the focus on the active agency of the child identified in our discussion of the sociological perspective on childhood (section 1.1.3). It also reflects the way in which childhood is a 'social construction', a point brought out by our discussion of the historical perspective on childhood (section 1.1.2). The notion of active agency has been increasingly recognised and supported by the strengthening of a human rights culture, enhanced in the United Kingdom by the passage of the Human Rights Act in 1998. However, the process of legal recognition of children's autonomy had started over a decade before the Human Rights Act, in the landmark case of *Gillick*.[24]

In this case, the Department of Health and Social Security had issued guidance to area health authorities on family planning which contained a section dealing with contraceptive advice and treatment for young people. It stated that attempts would always be made to persuade children under the age of 16 who attended clinics to involve their parent or guardian at the earliest stage of consultation, and that it would be most unusual to provide contraceptive advice to such children without parental consent. However, the guidance underlined the need not to abandon the principle of confidentiality between doctor and patient, and stated that in exceptional cases it was for a doctor exercising his or her clinical judgment to decide whether to prescribe contraception. The plaintiff, who was the mother of five girls under the age of 16 years, wrote to her local area health authority

---

24 *Gillick v. West Norfolk and Wisbech Area Health Authority* [1986] AC 112, [1985] 3 All ER 402.

seeking an assurance from them that no contraceptive advice or treatment would be given to any of her daughters without her knowledge and consent. The area health authority refused to give such an assurance and stated that in accordance with the guidance the final decision must be for the doctor's clinical judgment. The plaintiff challenged the legality of the guidance. The House of Lords held[25] that the National Health Service legislation indicated that Parliament regarded contraceptive advice and treatment as essentially medical matters and that there was no statutory limit on the age of the persons to whom contraceptive facilities might be supplied; and that a girl under the age of 16 years had the legal capacity to consent to medical examination and treatment, including contraceptive treatment, if she had sufficient maturity and intelligence to understand the nature and implications of the proposed treatment; that the parental right to control a minor child deriving from parental duty was a dwindling right which existed only in so far as it was required for the child's benefit and protection; that the extent and duration of that right could not be ascertained by reference to a fixed age, but depended on the degree of intelligence and understanding of that particular child and a judgment of what was best for the welfare of the child; that the parents' right to determine whether a child under 16 should have medical treatment terminated when the child achieved sufficient intelligence and understanding to make that decision itself; that although in the majority of cases parents were the best judges of matters concerning the child's welfare, there might be exceptional cases in which a doctor was a better judge of the medical advice and treatment that would conduce to a child's welfare and where it might be desirable for a doctor to give a girl, in her own best interests, contraceptive advice and treatment, if necessary without the consent or even the knowledge of the parents; and that, accordingly, the department's guidance did not contain advice that was an infringement of parents' rights.

The support which this case appeared to give to a child's autonomy of decision-making, subject to being recognised as of sufficient understanding and maturity in relation to the decision, was much heralded at the time, and the appearance of the iconic 'Gillick-mature child' in public debate in the United Kingdom has persisted. However, it was followed in the early 1990s by two decisions which tended to dilute the child's right to make autonomous decisions (Douglas 1992). In both *Re R (a minor) (wardship: consent to treatment)*[26] and *Re W (a minor) (medical treatment: court's jurisdiction)*[27], the Court of Appeal ruled that the court could override a young person's decision to withhold consent from life-saving treatment (anti-psychotic drug treatment and treatment for *anorexia nervosa* respectively). While *Gillick* continued to support children's autonomous decision to consent to treatment, a distinction was drawn in these two cases from

---

25 Lord Brandon of Oakbrook and Lord Templeman dissenting.
26 [1992] Fam. 11, [1991] 4 All ER 177.
27 [1993] Fam. 64, [1992] 4 All ER 627.

s to *refuse* consent to treatment. As pointed out in a case from the
: Court of Canada:

> To date, no court in the United Kingdom has allowed a child under 16 to
> refuse medical treatment that was likely to preserve the child's prospects of
> a normal and healthy future, either on the ground that the competence thresh-
> old had not been met ..., or because the court concluded that it had the power
> to override the wishes of even a '*Gillick*-competent' child ...
>
> (A.C. v. Manitoba (Director of Child
and Family Services)[28], para. 57)

In *R (on the application of Axon) v. Secretary of State for Health (Family
Planning Association intervening)*,[29] a mother of two girls aged 12 and 15 years
had had an abortion 20 years previously and experienced grief, guilt and depres-
sion for many years afterwards, and wanted to ensure that she should be informed
and consulted in the event that her daughters sought medical advice on sexual
matters. She sought judicial review in respect of guidance, issued by the
Department of Health in 2004, on the advice and treatment by health professionals
of young people under the age of 16 in relation to sexual matters including
contraception, sexually transmitted infections and abortion, on the basis that the
guidance misrepresented the law as laid down in *Gillick* and infringed the
claimant's right to respect for family life under article 8 of the ECHR. The
Administrative Court held that *Gillick* remained authoritative on the lawfulness
of the provision by health care professionals of confidential advice and treatment
on contraception to young people under the age of 16 without parental knowledge
or consent, and provided appropriate guidelines. The guidance issued by the
Department of Health did not misrepresent or misapply the *Gillick* decision.
Since the Department's guidance provided that confidential treatment and advice
could only be given where the child understood the advice and its implications,
there was nothing in the guidance which interfered with parents' rights to respect
for family life under article 8[30] of the ECHR, and that, accordingly, the guidance
was lawful.

Shortly after the House of Lords' decision in *Gillick*, the 'mature minor'
doctrine was applied in Canada.[31] More recently, the Supreme Court of Canada,

---

28 2009 SCC 30 (2009), 26 June 2009.

29 [2006] EWHC 37 (Admin), [2006] QB 539.

30 It was additionally held, *per curiam*, that *any* interference with a parent's rights under article 8(1)
would be justified under article 8(2) as being in 'accordance with the law' and 'necessary in a
democratic society' for the 'protection of health' or for the 'protection of the rights of others' and
was proportionate.

31 In *J.S.C. v. Wren* (1986), 76 A.R. 115 (C.A.), a 16-year-old girl had received medical approval for
a therapeutic abortion, but her parents sought an injunction to prevent it because the age of majority was 18. Based on *Gillick*, Kerans J.A. concluded that the girl was capable of consenting to the
abortion on her own behalf.

in *A.C. v. Manitoba (Director of Child and Family Services)*,[32] has had to grapple with the question of a child's autonomous decision-making in the context of a life-threatening scenario. C, a devout Jehovah's Witness, was admitted to hospital when she was 14 years and 10 months old, suffering from lower gastrointestinal bleeding caused by Crohn's disease. She refused to consent to the receipt of blood. The Director of Child and Family Services apprehended her as a child in need of protection, and sought a treatment order from the court under section 25(8) of the Manitoba Child and Family Services Act, by which the court may authorise treatment that it considers to be in the child's 'best interests'. There is a presumption in section 25(9) of the Act that the best interests of a child 16 or over will be most effectively promoted by allowing the child's views to be determinative, unless it can be shown that the child does not understand the decision or appreciate its consequences. Where the child is under 16, however, no such presumption exists. The applications judge ordered that C receive blood transfusions, concluding that when a child is under 16 there are no legislated restrictions of authority on the court's ability to order medical treatment in the child's 'best interests'. C and her parents appealed the order, arguing that the legislative scheme was unconstitutional because it unjustifiably infringed C's rights under sections 2(*a*), 7 and 15 of the Canadian Charter of Rights and Freedoms. The Court of Appeal upheld the constitutional validity of the impugned provisions and the treatment order.

The Supreme Court of Canada held (Binnie J. dissenting) that the appeal should be dismissed and that sections 25(8) and 25(9) of the Child and Family Services Act were constitutional. The majority (LeBel, Deschamps, Charron and Abella JJ) found that when a young person's best interests are interpreted in a way that sufficiently respects his or her capacity for mature, independent judgment in a particular medical decision-making context, the constitutionality of the legislation was preserved. The statutory scheme struck a constitutional balance between what the law has consistently seen as an individual's fundamental right to autonomous decision-making in connection with his or her body, and the law's equally persistent attempts to protect vulnerable children from harm. The 'best interests' standard in section 25(8) operated as a sliding scale of scrutiny, with the child's views becoming increasingly determinative depending on his or her maturity. The more serious the nature of the decision and the more severe its potential impact on life or health, the greater the degree of scrutiny required. Interpreting the 'best interests' standard in this way navigates the tension between an adolescent's increasing entitlement to autonomy as he or she matures and society's interest in ensuring that young people who are vulnerable are protected from harm. The Supreme Court took the view that this approach brought the 'best interests' standard in line with the evolution of the common law (including *Gillick*) and with international principles.

---

32 2009 SCC 30 (2009), 26 June 2009.

; latter point was a reference to the CRC in which article 3 describes 'the
terests of the child' as a primary consideration in all actions concerning
children: see section 3.5.3.2. Articles 5 and 14 of the CRC require state parties to
respect the responsibilities, rights and duties of parents to provide direction to the
child in exercising his or her rights 'in a manner consistent with the evolving
capacities of the child'.

Similarly, article 12 requires state parties to 'assure to the child who is capable
of forming his or her own views the right to express those views freely in all
matters affecting the child, the views of the child being given due weight in
accordance with the age and maturity of the child': see section 3.5.3.4.

There are, of course, a number of legal duties to take into account children's
views in child law.[33] Although these may fall short of full participation rights in
decision-making, they do often signal at least the beginnings of a fuller acknowledgment of children's capacities and autonomy. Thus, although it may be inappropriate, even positively damaging, to give a younger child the final decision
about which parent s\he may want to live with in the context of a parental dispute,
it may be suitable to ensure some consultation with the child to ascertain their
wishes and feelings in order to improve the overall decision-making process.
After all, the airing of a child's views is good practice for more central
participation in decision-making to be undertaken later on in adulthood.

If a child cannot be regarded as fully autonomous, then it follows that there is
a need for some adult and/or state constraint on a child's autonomy, commensu-
rate with the maturity and competence of the developing child and the prevalent
view within that society of the respective responsibilities of parents, the wider
family and the state. Most commentators now accept the justification for at least
some paternalistic intervention. Raz (1996) justifies paternalistic coercion on the
basis that it may be grounded on the general trust reposed by the child in the
person or body exercising such coercion. Thus a child may sufficiently trust and
respect his or her parents to understand at least the legitimacy of their coercive
action in relation to specific behaviours. Paternalism is often criticised as an agent
of oppression and the concept resonates with feminist notions of paternalistic
structures of society to explain sex discrimination and gender-based inequalities.
In the context of the child and parent relationship, however, paternalism is arguably a key component once it has been accepted that the best interests of children
lie in both welfarist protection and the encouragement of participatory decision-
making. Indeed, the theories of rights discussed earlier 'provide a substantial
body of wisdom supporting the view that paternalism can be justified as a means

---

33 For example, under the 'welfare principle' contained in section 1 of the Children Act 1989, when
a court is considering making, varying or discharging an order under Part IV of the Act, or making
etc. a section 8 order, where that order is opposed, it must have regard in particular to a welfare
checklist which includes 'the ascertainable wishes and feelings of the child concerned (considered
in the light of his age and understanding)' (s.1(3)(a)).

of protecting children's long term interests. The minor status has a moral and legal justification which the courts may decide requires asserting' (Fortin 2006: 325). Other advocates of children's rights, while affirming that '[t]he language of rights can make visible what has for too long been suppressed' (Freeman 2007: 6), have had little difficulty in retaining a suitable place for liberal paternalistic intervention, particularly in relation to life-threatening decision-making by adolescents (Freeman 1983: 54–60; Freeman 2007: 15).

If the principle of the need for at least some paternalistic intervention is accepted, then the argument will often turn to how the occasions on which such intervention is appropriate can be properly identified. This has remained an almost irresolvable issue in the literature. On the one hand, there is a need to respect children's interests in making choices, in practising their autonomy. On the other hand, there is a need to override some of their decisions which would otherwise damage their lives. The problem is particularly acute at the threshold of adult responsibility seen in older teenagers. Most parents of adolescents will have experienced the dilemma of when to exert authority over their child on the basis that this is in their best interests, or to allow the child to follow his or her own choices which, though disapproved, will provide the child with a sense of being taken seriously and an opportunity to learn better the practice of autonomous decision-making. As Fortin wisely puts it:

> The ideal formula would authorise paternalistic interventions to protect adolescents from making life-threatening mistakes, but restrain autocratic and arbitrary adult restrictions on their potential for autonomy. Finding it may prove problematic.
>
> (Fortin 2009: 29)

Perhaps a more pragmatic way to examine children's rights is to focus on their 'participation rights'. This phrase refers to the way in which a child may participate in a range of decision-making. The advantage of using this type of language is that it allows a finer calibration of the extent to which a child may participate in any one particular decision according to the child's own maturity and the nature of the decision in question. Article 12 of the CRC obliges state parties to assure to the child who is capable of forming his or her own views a right to express views about matters affecting him or her; it also confers on the child a right to be heard in any judicial or administrative proceedings affecting the child. This is a key provision of the CRC, and its importance has been underlined by the CtRC's production of recommendations following a day of general discussion (Day of Discussion 2006) and a detailed and analytical General Comment No. 12 (2009): see section 3.5.3.4.

> A widespread practice has emerged in recent years, which has been broadly conceptualised as 'participation', although this term itself does not appear in the text of article 12. This term has evolved and is now widely used

to describe ongoing processes, which include information-sharing and dialogue between children and adults based on mutual respect, and in which children can learn how their views and those of adults are taken into account and shape the outcome of such processes.

(General Comment No. 12, 2009: para. 3)[34]

This idea of a continuum of children's participation has an immediate practical appeal and indeed has been taken up enthusiastically by child advocates and practitioners. Roger Hart produced a useful model of a 'ladder of participation'[35]: see Figure 1.2. The first three rungs of the ladder are not categorised as true child participation. 'Manipulation' refers to situations where children may be used as a means to an (adult) end. Hart gives the example of pre-school children being deployed by adults in demonstrations without having any understanding of the issues. 'Decoration' refers, 'for example, to those frequent occasions when children are given T-shirts related to some cause' and this rung is distinguishable from 'manipulation' in that 'adults do not pretend that the cause is inspired by children. They simply use the children to bolster their cause in a relatively indirect way' (Hart 1992: 9). 'Tokenism' refers to situations where children are apparently given a voice but have little or no choice about the subject or style of communicating it and little or no opportunity to formulate their own opinions. The remaining five rungs of the ladder are categorised as constituting children's participation. 'Assigned, but informed' refers to, for example, situations such as sending a scout troop that is informed about the problem of spectators' rubbish at a sports event and is volunteering to assist with clearing up. Hart also uses the example of the children assigned to the 71 world leaders attending the World Summit for Children in New York in 1990.[36] 'Consulted and informed' refers to situations where children are not only consulted for their views but also informed of the outcome of the decision-making process in hand. Hart provides the example of the corporate world where, at Nickelodean, a TV company based in New York, new ideas for programmes are designed in consultation with children and they are informed of the result. 'Adult-initiated, shared decisions with children' refers to projects that may be initiated by adults, but the decision-making is shared with young people. Hart provides the example of children's news publishing which

---

34 The General Comment recommends that all processes, in which children are heard and participate, must conform to a number of benchmarks: see General Comment No. 12 (2009: para. 134(a) to (i).

35 This model was based on Arnstein's (1969) model relating to adult participation in the political process.

36 'On 29–30 September 1990 the largest gathering of world leaders in history assembled at the United Nations to attend the World Summit for Children. Led by 71 heads of State and Government and 88 other senior officials, mostly at the ministerial level, the World Summit adopted a Declaration on the Survival, Protection and Development of Children and a Plan of Action for implementing the Declaration in the 1990s'. Available at: http://www.unicef.org/wsc/ (accessed 1 January 2010).

The Ladder of Participation

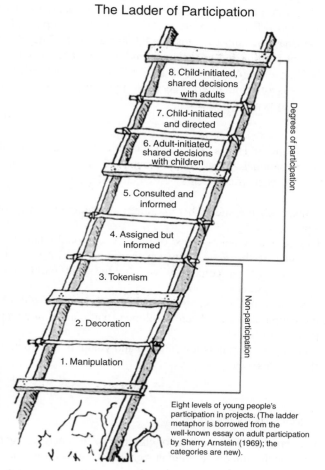

8. Child-initiated, shared decisions with adults

7. Child-initiated and directed

6. Adult-initiated, shared decisions with children

5. Consulted and informed

4. Assigned but informed

3. Tokenism

2. Decoration

1. Manipulation

Degrees of participation

Non-participation

Eight levels of young people's participation in projects. (The ladder metaphor is borrowed from the well-known essay on adult participation by Sherry Arnstein (1969); the categories are new).

Figure 1.2 The 'ladder of participation'.

Source: Hart (1992: 8).

often involves a high degree of responsibility. 'Child-initiated and directed' refers to situations where children, in their play, conceive and carry out complex projects. Hart provides the illustrative example of a large dam system which children under 8 years of age, as many as 50 at a time, built on a sandbank behind a school in Vermont, USA (Hart 1992: 14). The final rung of the ladder – 'Child-initiated, shared decisions with adults' – is illustrated by Hart with the following example:

A group of New York City high school students formed a coalition to petition the Board of Education for a relevant programme of sex education;

they had seen too many of their peers leave school pregnant. They worked with the Planned Parenthood organization to write a proposal, but unfortunately the Board of Education lost the 8,000 signatures. They persisted, and a subsequent petition led to meetings and a favourable response from the school's Chancellor. As a result of these efforts, peer counsellors were hired in the schools offering referral services and information on problems of pregnancy and venereal disease.

(Hart 1992: 14)

A useful critique of Hart's 'ladder of participation' and related theories of children's participation is provided by Thomas (2007). He concludes that the components of a theory of children's participation should:

a) encompass all the sites where children's participation may or may not take place;
b) be located in a broader context of inter-generational relations;
c) understand the distinction between 'participation' meaning activity that children engage in conjointly with adults, and children and young people's autonomous activity;
d) accommodate the new kinds of participatory practice with children and young people that have been developed (particularly in countries of the majority world);
e) account for the demands for children and young people to have the same political rights as adults.

(Thomas 2007: 215)

1.2.1.3 Children's rights movement

The growing international recognition of children's rights can be regarded as one element of the general interest in human rights that followed the Second World War. In Europe this was characterised by the European Convention on Human Rights in 1950, prompted by the previous experience of arbitrary state interference with individual liberties. There has been an increased awareness of sex and race discrimination issues. Indeed, the civil rights movement in the United States demonstrated a broad concern about the 'rights' of minority groups. The US Supreme Court had ruled in 1967 that 'neither the Fourteenth Amendment nor the Bill of Rights is for adults alone'[37] and that children could likewise benefit from the US Constitution's procedural safeguards. The minority legal status of children came to be regarded in some quarters as oppressive and as a means to conceal the abuse of power over children, both by parents and the state. The American so-called 'child liberationists' took this to extremes. They suggested that it was essentially a form of oppression to exclude children from the adult world and

---

37 *Re Gault* 387 US 1 at 13.

adult freedoms. Holt (1974), for example, argued that children of any age should have the vote, they should be able to work for money, direct their own education and be paid a guaranteed minimum state income. Thus the movement for children's rights was unfortunately closely associated with simply giving adult freedoms to children. This was a gross distortion of the true position, as any cursory examination of the structure and content of the UN Convention on the Rights of the Child would reveal.

Some commentators now believe that the liberationists did little to serve the cause of children's rights precisely because of this lasting association (Fortin 2009: 4). However, other social movements have equally gone through stages of militant ideology in their development. Such militant interludes have arguably performed the valuable function of challenging conventional orthodoxies, and have acted as precursors to more measured responses.

In retrospect, the liberationists' views do appear to have been formulated without due regard to the obvious facts of varying physical and mental competence found in children. Their views ignore, for example, all the carefully worked and tested body of knowledge concerning children's cognitive development (see section 1.1.2). The liberationists' views can also be regarded as potentially dangerous to the extent that they may encourage children to taken on adult responsibilities before proper preparation for such roles. Campbell (1992), for example, stressed the need for children not to have their experience of childhood stolen from them under the guise of offering them adult responsibilities. On one view, the focus on the need for children to make their own decisions and exercise autonomy, if taken too far, will inevitably lead to the boundary of adulthood and childhood being redefined. However, the radical approach of the liberationists has at least established that children are not inherently incapable of informed and rational decision-making, at even quite young ages, contrary to what many people might have otherwise thought.

Some commentators, in particular Goldstein et al. (1973, 1980), have argued strongly for family autonomy from the state, that is, a model of minimum state interference in the privacy of family life [a similar position to the *laissez-faire* model of Fox Harding (1996) outlined in section 1.1.4 above]. There have been recent public debates influenced by this orientation. One commentator has noted the significant differences between the experience of childhood now and in past centuries:

> Children in the past have been assumed to have capabilities that we now rarely think they have. ... So fixated are we on giving our children a long and happy childhood that we downplay their abilities and their resilience.
>
> (Cunningham 2006)

Another commentator further develops this picture of children and argues that childhood is becoming undermined by 'risk aversion':

> Activities and experiences that previous generations of children enjoyed without a second thought have been relabelled as troubling or dangerous,

while the adults who still permit them are branded as irresponsible. At the extreme, as in the examples above, society appears to have become unable to cope with any adverse outcomes whatsoever, no matter how trivial or improbable. While such episodes may be rare, they fit a pattern of growing adult intervention to minimise risk at the expense of childhood experience. Adult anxieties typically focus on children's vulnerability, but they can also portray children as villains, again recasting normal childhood experiences as something more sinister.

(Gill 2007: 10–11)

The assumption of those advocating a minimalist state intervention role is that parents should be entitled to raise their children as they think best. While this perspective is reflective of the general human rights drive to prevent arbitrary state interference, it also poses a threat to the integrity of children's rights. If legal systems are premised on minimum state intervention in family life, as many are, there equally may be little opportunity for supporting children's choices where these conflict with parental views. The assumption underlying the minimalist state intervention model of the centrality of the parental role may be in danger of being translated into a parental immunity from any type of appropriate account-ability. But these positions need not be mutually exclusive. It is no doubt possible to constrain both state and parental authority within reasonable limits, thus reflecting a desired balance of authority in relation to children.

1.2.2 International children's rights

Although it is reassuring to find theoretical justifications for children's rights, the approach of legal positivism has simply been to point to the existence of such rights in contemporary legal instruments. At the international level this is now easy; one can identify, in addition to the references in the UDHR of 1948 and the two international covenants of 1966, the forty substantive rights as set out in the CRC of 1989. The speed at which the CRC was ratified and the number of nations involved strengthen the argument, at least on a pragmatic basis, that this convention has established itself as the key international instrument that sets out the fundamental principles of international children's rights: see generally, Chapter 3. Indeed, that argument is further advanced by the view that the CRC may constitute a special form of international law which can be regarded as having a 'fundamental' status, that is, *jus cogens* (see section 2.2.5). On the other hand, it has been said that the CRC, and indeed other international treaties, are vehicles for 'manifesto' rights, that is, rights that reflect mere aspirations. Some commentators note that the proliferation of international human rights instruments may have led to a 'devaluation' in the currency of rights talk (Wellman 1999). Fortin identifies article 27 (the child's right to an adequate standard of living) of the CRC as a provision that it is difficult to imagine could ever be legally enforced due to its 'exteme vagueness' (Fortin 2009: 18). However, once we move away from expectations of concrete legal enforceability, even such provisions as article 27 may be seen as offering more than mere rhetoric. Upon closer examination, article 27 does at least provide a useful normative legal standard, namely that parents have the 'primary responsibility' for securing favourable living conditions, and the state by implication has a secondary responsibility to assist parents and other carers in these tasks and 'in case of need provide material assistance and support programmes, particularly with regard to nutrition, clothing and housing'. It thus provides a useful structure, defining the relationship between parents and state, in which the 'right' to an adequate standard of living can be operationalised. It also contains a more detailed obligation on states to secure the recovery of maintenance for children.[38]

Lawyers and policy makers are often concerned more with the way in which legal rights, that is, those contained in valid international and domestic instruments, are formulated and structured, rather than their philosophical pedigree. How do individual rights relate to other associated rights in the same or related instrument? For example, article 27 of the UN Convention on the Rights of the Child is especially linked to article 6(2) ('child's right to survival and development') and article 24 ('the right to enjoyment of the highest attainable standard of health'). Inevitably most rights, especially the social, economic and cultural rights, can only be successfully implemented by balancing them against other rights and interests. One of the reasons for the wide recognition of the important status of the CRC is precisely its form and structure and the origins of its drafting. Chapter 3 deals with this in greater detail, but suffice it to say here that the CRC combines civil and political rights ('first generation rights') – for example, articles 13, 14 and 15 – with social, economic and cultural rights ('second generation rights') – for example, articles 24, 26 and 27. Indeed, consistently with the structure of general human rights instruments, securing second generation rights often proved to be a necessary precondition for meeting first generation rights. Freedom of expression, for example, can be conducted more effectively only when a society has created reasonable conditions of economic security and social order. The way in which the international community continues to perceive children's rights through its legal instruments and programmes provides a unique opportunity to examine how that community is constantly revising and setting its priorities in relation to children.

As will be seen (section 3.5), the 'Concluding Observations' of the CtRC on country periodic reports submitted to it under the reporting process give specific direction to state parties about the shortcomings that need to be addressed in order to further the cause of children's rights as formulated in the CRC. However, one of the key weaknesses in the system is the lack of 'teeth' if the state party is somewhat dilatory in addressing these issues.

---

38 CRC, article 27(4).

1.3 Childhood, children's rights and cultural relativism

Our discussion of both the concepts of childhood and children's rights in this chapter also raises a range of issues about 'cultural relativism' – a term first used in anthropological research, implying that human beliefs and activities can only be understood in terms of their own culture. It should be noted that this concept should not be confused with 'moral relativism', that is, a belief that all cultures are both separate and equal and that any value system, however different from another, is equally valid. The problem of cultural relativism in international human rights law was highlighted at the time the United Nations was in the process of preparing the UDHR in 1947–48. The Executive Board of the American Anthropological Association produced a statement on human rights and put the question thus:

> The problem is thus to formulate a statement of human rights that will do more than just phrase respect for the individual as an individual. It must also take into full account the individual as a member of the social group of which he is a part, whose sanctioned modes of life shape his behavior, and with whose fate his own is thus inextricably bound.
>
> Because of the great numbers of societies that are in intimate contact in the modern world, and because of the diversity of their ways of life, the primary task confronting those who would draw up a Declaration on the Rights of Man is thus, in essence, to resolve the following problem: How can the proposed Declaration be applicable to all human beings, and not be a statement of rights conceived only in terms of the values prevalent in the countries of Western Europe and America?
>
> (American Anthropological Association 1947: 539)

Consequently, one can see how any international human rights instrument, such as the CRC which seeks to achieve a universal standard, may be significantly weakened in terms of its legitimacy and ultimately its implementation if it is seen to be an exclusive product of the cultural values held principally by the powerful nations who were in a position to manage and direct its drafting. It would appear, for example, that at least in the early years of the drafting process of the CRC '[t]he industrialised countries were significantly over-represented at all stages' and fears that the outcome would be 'a heavily Northern-oriented text were widespread and justified' and only mitigated by the participation of a few developing countries in combination with a last-minute surge of delegates from the South, many from states with Islamic law (Cantwell 1992: 23).

Equally, although cultural differences must be respected, conversely this must not become an excuse for practices that are widely perceived as unacceptable (Harris-Short 2001: 306). International human rights law has frequently been criticised in two respects. First, that it lacks universality and in fact has been construed according to an ethnocentric view of the world usually associated with the influence of the more powerful nations of the North. Alternatively, it is conceded that the normative standards may be culturally 'neutral', but consequently they will lack any substantial meaning in terms of their practical implementation. It is certainly true that any perusal of the CRC's *travaux préparatoires* (Detrick 1992) shows quickly the negotiated and mediated nature of some of the legal standards that eventually emerged in the final text. Some would argue, however, that a high number of active state participants in the drafting process should ensure that there is reasonable attention to cultural diversity in framing such standards in the first place.

Cultural relativism is also a significant aspect of how international legal standards are viewed by individual nations and put into practice. For example, a state that has become politically and economically weak, which may have suffered years of warfare, civil strife, poverty and hunger, is likely to have very different priorities from some of the well-established and relatively secure industrialised nations. There will not only be a difference in the resources available to act on appropriate programmes, but there will also be differences in how such nations may construe the key underlying assumptions, relationships and concepts behind the standards. For example, it can be seen that the African nations, in their production of the *African Charter on the Rights and Welfare of the Child* (see section 2.5.2.2), have proceeded on the basis of a different view about the nature of the family unit and the relationship of individuals to the family and to the wider community.

The way in which the CRC was drafted, the nature of the standards finally agreed, and the way in which the CtRC has interacted with state parties in their examination of reports, are all alive with cultural implications. As will be seen in the detailed discussion of the CRC in Chapter 3, it contains an ideological commitment to minimal state interference in family affairs, shown both by the way in which certain articles of the CRC have been framed and the CtRC's comments in respect of countries that appear to have a quite different view of the relationship between the state and the family (see section 3.5.5). 'Traditional and customary practices' are also frequently criticised by the CtRC as obstacles in achieving the standards set out in the CRC – for example, such practices impinging on the 'basic health and welfare' provisions of the CRC: see section 3.5.6.4. Yet anthropologists may well point out that such practices can have a positive influence, underwriting the community's social solidarity and shared belief systems.

In theory, the ability to make declarations and reservations on ratifying the CRC allows room to accommodate such differences, but within a unified international framework. It can be argued that a generous provision for reservations and declarations in international treaties should be a mandatory element of the required consensus-building in the international community. Equally, the way in which the CtRC probes individual state parties for their reasons and justifications for such departures from the CRC's standards reflects a mechanism of dialogue that is actively exploring cultural sensitivities but remains within the overall international framework. The balance to be achieved in advancing concrete international rights in this area and allowing sufficient flexibility to encompass cultural sensitivity is not an easy one to strike.

Chapter 2

Introduction to international law sources and institutions

2.1 Introduction

This chapter provides an outline of some of the key sources, concepts and institutions that are necessary for an understanding of the international law relating to children. Those already familiar with international law sources and institutions might wish to omit this chapter, though it contains references to child law related examples that illustrate some of the general international law points discussed. A number of topics, discussed in some detail in general international law textbooks (e.g. Brownlie 2008; Kaczorowska 2008; Shaw 2008), are omitted here as they have little connection specifically with the realm of international child law. Thus the reader will find little about the law of the sea, territorial sovereignty, state succession and other concepts and institutions which do not relate directly to the subject of this book. However, an understanding of international child law will require some basic knowledge of the international legal system, how disputes are resolved and the nature of some of the key international institutions that have an important role to play in this field.

The study of international law is characteristically divided into private international law (known as 'conflict of laws') and public international law. Private international law refers to the body of laws that regulate private relationships across national borders. It deals largely with cases within legal systems where there is a foreign element to consider. Public international law, on the other hand, deals mainly with relations between states and the operation of international bodies. International child law in fact encompasses both subdivisions of international law. For example, there are a number of conventions emanating from the Hague Conference on Private International Law (see section 2.4.2) that seek to enhance judicial and administrative co-operation on intercountry adoption and child abduction. There are also a number of human rights standards from the United Nations (see section 2.5.1) and from regional institutions (see section 2.5.2) that are directly relevant to children.

2.2 Sources of international law

Unlike most domestic legal orders that are based on the existence, in some form or another, of a distinct legislature, an executive and a judicial power, the international legal order is not constructed in this way. As yet there is no unified world government with law-making and executive authority to issue international laws that will be applied and interpreted by a global court system. The arrangement of international institutions does have some similar features to state governance, but there are important points of distinction. However, there is an authoritative statement of the sources of international law to be found in the Statute of the International Court of Justice 1945,[1] which most commentators would agree has been universally accepted, even though it technically applies only to the sources that the International Court of Justice (ICJ) (see section 2.4.1.1) must apply.

(1) The Court, whose function is to decide in accordance with international law such disputes as are submitted to it, shall apply:

   (a) international conventions, whether general or particular, establishing rules expressly recognised by the contesting states;
   (b) international custom, as evidence of a general practice accepted as law;
   (c) the general principles of law recognised by civilized nations;
   (d) subject to the provisions of article 59,[2] judicial decisions and the teachings of the most highly qualified publicists of the various nations, as subsidiary means for the determination of rules of law.

(2) This provision shall not prejudice the power of the Court to decide a case *ex aequo et bono*,[3] if the parties agree thereto.

(Statute of the International Court of Justice 1945, article 38)

The sources of international law set out in this Statute are discussed in the following sections.

2.2.1 International treaties and conventions

Treaties are known by a number of different names: Agreements, Statutes, Declarations, Pacts, Conventions, Charters, Covenants and Protocols, etc. In essence, they involve the creation of a written agreement with which the states participating in them will be bound in international law. The procedural and other matters relating to the making of treaties have developed over time into rules of customary international law (see following discussion) which have themselves

---

1 The Statute of the International Court of Justice is an integral part of the Charter of the United Nations, which was signed on 26 June 1945 and came into force on 24 October 1945.
2 Article 59 states: 'The decision of the Court has no binding force except between the parties and in respect of that particular case.'
3 According to what is right and good; in equity and good conscience.

been consolidated and extended by the Vienna Convention on the Law of Treaties 1969. Treaties are traditionally divided into two types: there are 'law-making treaties' that are intended to have a general relevance; and 'treaty-contracts' intended only as binding between two or a few states. A good example of a law-making treaty in this context is the United Nations Convention on the Rights of the Child 1989 (hereafter the 'CRC'). The CRC is, as we shall see in Chapter 3, a comprehensive statement of an agreed international vision of children's rights. An example of a treaty-contract is any one of the many bilateral extradition treaties that regulate the surrender by one government to another of an accused or convicted person. The United Kingdom, for example, has extradition relations with more than 100 territories by way of both multilateral extradition conventions and agreements, or under bilateral extradition treaties. Extradition relations are regulated in the United Kingdom by the Extradition Act 2003.

It is in the nature of a law-making treaty that its success in establishing anything approaching a global or general effect will often depend on the political support that it receives from the nations of the world. Thus, for example, although the Hague Convention on Jurisdiction, Applicable Law and Recognition of Decrees Relating to Adoptions 1965 represented an attempt to manage certain adoption issues at the international level, the lack of state ratifications[4] deprived this instrument of ever having any significant impact. This convention has now been 'denounced' by each of the ratifying countries and has ceased to have effect in international law. A new international instrument, the Hague Convention on Protection of Children and Co-operation in respect of Intercountry Adoption 1993 (hereafter the 'Hague Convention on Intercountry Adoption') (see Chapter 6), has superseded it. A treaty will normally specify two commencement dates: first, when it comes into force in international law; and second, the date when any particular ratifying state is bound by it in international law. For example, the Hague Convention on Intercountry Adoption specifies, first, that this convention will enter into force in international law 'on the first day of the month following the expiration of 3 months after the deposit of the third instrument of ratification, acceptance or approval'.[5] Second, it will 'thereafter' enter into force 'for each State ratifying, accepting or approving it subsequently, or acceding to it, on the first day of the month following the expiration of 3 months after the deposit of its instrument of ratification, acceptance, approval or accession'.[6] The Hague Convention on Intercountry Adoption 1993, as will be seen in Chapter 6, has so far been agreed by 81 states, including some very influential nations.[7]

---

4 Austria, Switzerland and the United Kingdom ratified this Convention.
5 Hague Convention on Intercountry Adoption, article 46(1).
6 Hague Convention on Intercountry Adoption, article 46(2)(a).
7 As at 12 February 2010. The ratifications and other details relating to the convention can be examined in the convention's 'status table' or 'status chart'. These are now invariably available online: see http://www.hcch.net/index_en.php?act=text.display&tid=25 for the status tables relating to all the Hague conventions.

All other things being equal, the greater the international support for such international instruments, the more likely it will be that the potential for achieving the underlying aims of the instrument can be realised.

However, states that have not ratified a treaty will not be bound by its terms in international law. Thus, the United States and Somalia are not bound by the CRC. Remarkably, all the other (193) countries of the world have ratified this convention. However, as we shall see later, there may be aspects of an international instrument that can be regarded as part of international customary law and therefore will bind states that have not ratified. States will normally 'sign' treaties as a preliminary step to indicate their forthcoming agreement in the later 'ratification'.[8] It should be noted, for example, that although the United States and Somalia have not ratified the CRC, they are both 'signatories' to it. The act of signature is not without any legal effect.[9]

The use of treaties as a primary means of international law-making has been so widespread that there was a need for an authoritative statement of the principles and formalities of treaty-making. This was achieved in the Vienna Convention on the Law of Treaties 1969 (hereafter the 'Vienna Convention'). There is also a Vienna Convention on Treaties between States and International Organizations 1986. The Vienna conventions reflected and codified existing international customary law, in particular, the basic international law principle that treaties bind the parties to them and must be performed in good faith (*pacta sunt servanda*).

International law and international relations are closely entwined and the process of a state agreeing to any particular treaty is often influenced by political considerations at the domestic, regional and international level. Multilateral treaties between a larger number of countries will often involve both compromise in the drafting process and some flexibility as to the ability of countries to opt out of particular clauses. Treaties therefore often contain provisions that allow countries to state 'reservations' and/or 'declarations' upon signature or ratification. The legal effect is that a country that states a reservation will not be bound by the relevant provision from which it has reserved its agreement. Article 19 of the

---

8 'Where signature is subject to ratification, acceptance, or approval ..., signature does not establish consent to be bound. However, signature qualifies the signatory state to proceed to ratification, acceptance, or approval and creates an obligation of good faith to refrain from acts calculated to frustrate the objects of the treaty.' (Brownlie 2008: 610). See also article 19 of the Vienna Convention.
9 Article 18 of the Vienna Convention provides that: 'A State is obliged to refrain from acts which would defeat the object and purpose of a treaty when:

    (a) it has signed the treaty or has exchanged instruments constituting the treaty subject to ratification, acceptance or approval, until it shall have made its intention clear not to become a party to the treaty; or
    (b) it has expressed its consent to be bound by the treaty, pending the entry into force of the treaty and provided that such entry into force is not unduly delayed.'

Vienna Convention provides some ground rules about such reservations.[10] This provision, in effect, acts as a background template of rules where the individual treaty is silent. Consequently, whenever we wish to know what the precise scope may be for making reservations it is important to read any relevant provisions of the particular treaty in issue alongside the Vienna Convention. Some treaties specify what types of reservation may be made and then go on to exclude expressly the making of any other type of reservation, in which case the default 'template' provided by article 19 of the Vienna Convention cannot apply. For example, the Hague Convention on the Civil Aspects of International Child Abduction 1980, an instrument we shall take a closer look at in Chapter 5, specifies that only certain types of reservation may be made and expressly states that '[n]o other reservation shall be permitted'.[11]

The Vienna Convention also provides some important provisions about treaty interpretation:

1. A treaty shall be interpreted in good faith in accordance with the ordinary meaning to be given to the terms of the treaty in their context and in the light of its object and purpose.

2. The context for the purpose of the interpretation of a treaty shall comprise, in addition to the text, including its preamble and annexes:

   (a) any agreement relating to the treaty which was made between all the parties in connection with the conclusion of the treaty;

   (b) any instrument which was made by one or more parties in connection with the conclusion of the treaty and accepted by the other parties as an instrument related to the treaty.

3. There shall be taken into account, together with the context:

   (a) any subsequent agreement between the parties regarding the interpretation of the treaty or the application of its provisions;

   (b) any subsequent practice in the application of the treaty which establishes the agreement of the parties regarding its interpretation;

   (c) any relevant rules of international law applicable in the relations between the parties.

---

10 For example, article 19 of the Vienna Convention provides that:
 'A State may, when signing, ratifying, accepting, approving or acceding to a treaty, formulate a reservation unless:

(a) the reservation is prohibited by the treaty;

(b) the treaty provides that only specified reservations, which do not include the reservation in question, may be made; or

(c) in cases not falling under subparagraphs (a) and (b), the reservation is incompatible with the object and purpose of the treaty.'

11 Article 42.

4. A special meaning shall be given to a term if it is established that the parties so intended.

(Vienna Convention, article 31)

A careful reading of this provision shows a structured approach to interpretation: it commences with a focus on 'ordinary meaning' but never loses sight of the 'context' to guide the meaning of terms in the treaty and its underlying 'object and purpose'. The extended description of the 'context' and other factors to be taken into account in article 31(3) and (4) allows any interpretative exercise to comply with some of the practical outcomes of the norms and behaviour of the international community in respect of the treaty in question. The important status of preparatory works (*travaux préparatoires*) as supplementary means of interpretation should also be noted:

Recourse may be had to supplementary means of interpretation, including the preparatory work of the treaty and the circumstances of its conclusion, in order to confirm the meaning resulting from the application of article 31, or to determine the meaning when the interpretation according to article 31:

(*a*) leaves the meaning ambiguous or obscure; or
(*b*) leads to a result which is manifestly absurd or unreasonable.

(Vienna Convention, article 32)

Preparatory works can, in any event, provide a wealth of background and contextual information about the origins of the treaty in question. For example, there are explanatory reports available in respect of the Hague Conventions: the reports by Pérez-Vera (1980) on the child abduction convention (see Chapter 5) and by Parra-Aranguren (1994) on the intercountry adoption convention (see Chapter 6). Similarly, explanatory reports in relation to the conventions emanating from the Council of Europe have been published. For example, there is an explanatory report[12] relating to the Council of Europe Convention on the Protection of Children against Sexual Exploitation and Sexual Abuse 2007, referred to in Chapter 7. The Council of Europe explanatory reports are prepared by a committee of experts and published with the authorization of the Committee of Ministers, though they often contain a cautionary note that such reports cannot constitute a complete, authoritative interpretation.[13]

---

12 This can be accessed at: < http://conventions.coe.int/Treaty/EN/Reports/Html/201.htm> (accessed 3 November 2009).

13 'The text of this explanatory report does not constitute an instrument providing an authoritative interpretation of the Convention, although it might be of such a nature as to facilitate the application of the provisions contained therein.' Ibid., para. II.

2.2.2 International customary law

As discussed in the previous section, the law on international treaties was first developed by the emergence of rules of 'international customary law'. Indeed, international customary law rules appeared in relation to a range of subject matter. It is tempting to think in modern times that the role of custom as a source of law is merely a residual one. This is generally the case within the municipal (domestic) legal systems of developed nations. However, at the international level, the role of custom as a source of law has remained creative rather than merely residual, precisely because the international legal order lacks the better defined and authoritative institutional framework generally found in domestic legal orders. The appearance of international customary law can be a flexible and responsive mode of law-making in a changing world; and one that may be necessary to preserve international legal order. Shaw refers to the analogy of a gradual formation of a path, and then road, across vacant land (Shaw 2008: 79) to explain the concept. In essence, two requirements are needed for a rule of international customary law to be recognised:

- the material facts of the alleged customary rule must be found in state practice; and
- states must subjectively believe that such practice is binding.

The first element then is to establish that the material facts of the alleged custom can be found in a 'state practice'. The second element, whether states subjectively believe the practice is binding, is termed the *opinio juris*. General customary rules ought normally to be uniform and consistent in relation to both the above requirements, though one should not be prescriptive about this; the context and nature of the customary rule may give a different emphasis as to how these requirements are viewed. In domestic legal systems, the duration of an alleged custom is often of importance.[14] In international law, customs can appear instantly. For example, the customary rule about state sovereignty over air space appeared around the time of the First World War and the rule of non-sovereignty of space appeared at the time the first satellites were being launched in the 1950s and 1960s: see generally Haanappel (2003: 1–10).

In theory, all states can participate in the formation of international customary law. However, the influence and power of particular nations on specific issues may mean that an individual state's contribution to international discussion on certain issues will lead the direction of international law-making on those issues.

---

14 In English law, the question whether any custom ranks as a source of law depends on judicial recognition following the application of several tests; see Ward and Akhtar (2008: 7–8). One of these tests is famously whether it has been so regarded since 'time immemorial', a notion itself defined by Statute in the thirteenth century as a reference to 3 September 1189, the date of the coronation of King Richard I.

For example, the United Kingdom, a powerful maritime nation in the nineteenth century, had a key influence on the formation of the international law of the sea and prize law. Russia and the United States had a crucial influence on the formation of space law. However, matters affecting human rights generally, and children's rights in particular, are unlikely to be viewed explicitly in this way. The core ethic of human rights law is the recognition of the dignity of an individual person irrespective of nationality. In principle, it would seem ironic if it were only the economically powerful nations that had significant influence in designing the structure of international human rights law. On the other hand, the postwar emergence of the United Nations system itself and the United Nations Universal Declaration of Human Rights 1948 can be seen as international architecture, heavily influenced by the victor nations of the Second World War. As one commentator puts it, 'scholars should not jump too quickly to the conclusion ... that altruism must motivate the establishment of morally attractive international norms' (Moravcsik 2000: 48). It would be difficult and probably ethnocentric to assert that there might be some principled basis for certain nations to claim some special distinctive role or superior moral authority in relation to forming legal standards that are relevant specifically to children's rights. On the other hand, to ignore the influence of power relations embedded in the international community in this field would be naïve. The drafting process of a multilateral treaty is ultimately a diplomatic process not immune from the influence of power politics. The way in which such instruments are perceived and acted upon (or not acted upon) after they subsequently emerge into the body of international law is also a process often more driven by the shape of international relations than a result of applying principles from the legal text of an international instrument.

As we have seen, the first requirement for a rule to have the status of customary law is to show a 'state practice'. The state practice must be uniform and consistent with the alleged rule of customary law, and a range of materials may evidence this. For example, the state's official publications, diplomatic exchanges, resolutions made by the General Assembly of the United Nations, drafts produced by the International Law Commission and the cumulative practice of international organizations may be good evidence of customary law. Some states have produced extensive digests and yearbooks containing their own state practices relevant to the international community which have particular authority, for example, the *British Yearbook of International Law*; Lowe and Crawford (2009) for the latest volume at the time of writing, and the *Digest of US Practice in International Law* (Cummins 2008 for the latest version). The municipal law of a state may in certain circumstances be evidence of a state practice. Ultimately, the identification of state practice which may form the basis of customary law is a somewhat circular exercise, as reflected in the following formulation: 'state practice covers any act or statements by a state from which views about customary law may be inferred' (Akehurst 1974).

The second requirement for establishing a rule of international customary law – establishing the *opinio juris* – involves a subjective belief by a state that its practice is binding. As might be expected, a high threshold is required to prove this requirement. It also follows that protests by states may occur, with the result that the legitimising process of custom formation is broken. However, it is again difficult to be prescriptive about this process. Sometimes state protests may themselves contain the seeds of a new customary rule. On occasion two customary rules may co-exist for a while side-by-side. For example, in the 1960s some countries used the customary three-mile rule, that is, national rights were limited to waters extending from the coast to three nautical miles (the 'cannon shot' rule). Others used the customary twelve-mile rule that had developed in the post-war period onwards as nations laid claim to mineral resources, to protect fishing and to enforce pollution control in their territorial waters.[15] An important feature of rules of international customary law is that these will be binding on all states unless that state has objected to it from the start. In some states, including the United Kingdom, international customary law may be regarded as being automatically incorporated into municipal law according to the 'incorporation doctrine' (see section 2.3). It can therefore be very important from both a national and an international perspective to determine whether an international rule has become part of customary law.

The relationship and status of treaties and customary law has been a difficult issue in international law discourse. Historically, custom preceded the more modern liking for formal treaty-making. On the other hand, treaties, though often desired because they were more certain, tended to have an element of codification of the existing (relevant) customary law. However, where a treaty has effectively codified a part of customary law, it is not the case that the treaty provision has necessarily entirely substituted the customary source of law. The ICJ (see section 2.4.1.1) held in the *Nicaragua Case*[16] that a customary rule about a state's right of self-defence had not been superseded by a provision of the United Nations Charter;[17] the two sources of law co-existed. In the context of international child law, for example, it is arguable that international customary law protects the child against sexual, economic and other forms of exploitation analogous to slavery, similar to the protection offered in some of the articles relating to such exploitation contained in the CRC; see also the concept of *jus cogens* in this context at section 2.2.5.

---

15 Maritime international customary rules have been codified in the United Nations Convention on The Law of The Sea, signed at Montego Bay, Jamaica, 10 December 1982; entry into force: 16 November 1994 (one year after the sixtieth state signed the treaty).

16 ICJ Reports, 1986, p 14; 76 ILR, p 349.

17 'Nothing in the present Charter shall impair the inherent right of individual or collective self-defence if an armed attack occurs against a Member of the United Nations, until the Security Council has taken measures necessary to maintain international peace and security. Measures taken by Members in the exercise of this right of self-defence shall be immediately reported to the Security Council and shall not in any way affect the authority and responsibility of the Security Council under the present Charter to take at any time such action as it deems necessary in order to maintain or restore international peace and security.' (UN Charter, article 51).

2.2.3 General principles of law recognised by civilised nations

Every legal system, including the international legal order, will have gaps where it may appear there is no law, or where the law is silent on a particular matter. Where there is no treaty or customary law rule, case law may well fill some of these gaps; but in the international legal system there is often a lack of case law in particular areas, either because the subject has not been litigated or because there is no court-like forum that forms part of the international arrangements at issue. This is so in relation to the operation of the CRC, which establishes no international court forum comparable to, say, the ICJ or, at the regional level, the European Court of Human Rights located in Strasbourg. However, an accepted standard of international law is that every international situation is, as a matter of law, capable of being determined (Shaw 2008: 99). One of the functions therefore of the 'general principles of law' in the context of article 38 is to fill such gaps where necessary. The provenance and content of these general principles are somewhat contested by scholars, but it is thought that they may include legal principles that are common to a large number of systems of municipal law. However, it is much more difficult to precisely identify these principles, and indeed some commentators regard them as a sub-category of either treaties or custom rather than a discrete but limited source of law. On one view, general principles tend to be preconditions for the operation and efficiency of the international legal system as a whole. For example, the key general principle that international agreements are binding and must be carried out in good faith (*pacta sunt servanda*) is a presupposition without which the whole of treaty law would lack the key quality of legal obligation. Similarly, 'equity' and 'equitable principles' are often regarded as part of the general principles of international law. There is also the principle of 'good faith', reflected in the United Nations Charter, which provides that 'all Members, in order to ensure to all of them the rights and benefits resulting from membership, shall fulfil in good faith the obligations assumed by them in accordance with the present Charter.'[18] Again, principles of equity and good faith can be viewed as preconditions for a well-ordered international legal order. A leading British authority on international law concludes:

> Although generalised principles or concepts that may be termed community value-judgments inform and pervade the political and therefore the legal orders in the broadest sense, they do not themselves constitute as such binding legal norms. This can only happen if they have been accepted as legal norms by the international community through the mechanisms and techniques of international law creation. Nevertheless, 'elementary principles of humanity' may lie at the base of such norms and help justify their existence

---

18 United Nations Charter 1945, article 2(2).

in the broadest sense, and may indeed perform a valuable role in endowing such norms with an additional force within the system.

(Shaw 2008: 109)

In practice, the appeal to the so-called 'general principles of law' may derive either from municipal law analogies or from international law. However, the extraction of principles from municipal law will need to be at a sufficient level of generality to come within the formulation in article 38(1)(c) of the Statute of the International Court of Justice. The ICJ and its predecessor, the Permanent Court of International Justice (PCIJ), have managed on occasion to extract general principles from municipal legal systems.[19] Brownlie (2008: 19) cautions against an over-rigid categorization of this residual source of law. He points to the following examples of general principles: principles of consent, reciprocity, equality of states, finality of awards and settlements, the legal validity of agreements, good faith, domestic jurisdiction, and the freedom of the seas.

2.2.4 Judicial decisions and publicists' writings

Article 38 of the Statute of the International Court of Justice appears to establish a hierarchy of sources as judicial decisions, and the writings of publicists are said to be a 'subsidiary' means for the determination of rules of law. There is no equivalent in international law to the doctrine of precedent. Even the decisions of the ICJ are expressly stated[20] to have no binding force except as between the parties and in relation to the case in hand. Nevertheless, some of these cases do have considerable influence and authority and decisions of the ICJ and PCIJ have sometimes found their way subsequently into treaty provisions. In any event, court decisions may provide useful interpretations of existing treaty provisions. An example is the *Guardianship Case*,[21] a rare child law case heard by the ICJ, which had to consider various provisions of the Hague Convention on Guardianship 1902 (see further, section 2.4.1.1).

The phrase 'judicial decisions' in article 38 also includes international arbitration awards and the rulings of national courts. Supreme Court decisions in federal states, for example, may be considered when examining the issue of border disputes. In some areas, certainly in the past, writers have had a key influence on the formation of the law. 'Writers such as Gentili, Grotius, Pufendorf, Bynkershoek and Vattel were the supreme authorities in the sixteenth to eighteenth centuries and determined the scope, form and content of international law' (Shaw 2008: 112).

---

19 For example, *Chorzów Factory case*, PCIJ, Series A, No. 17 (1928), p. 29. It is thought one of the most significant general principles is that of good faith: see *Nuclear Tests (New Zealand v. France)*, I.C.J. Reports 1974, p 457 at 473.

20 Statute of the International Court of Justice, article 59.

21 *Application of the Convention of 1902 Governing the Guardianship of Infants (Netherlands v. Sweden) (1957–1958)*: judgment 28 November 1958. ICJ Reports, 1958, p 55.

Their influence, however, has waned, due in part to the greater production of treaty law. Though the historical importance to international law of the writings of jurists as a source in its own right has declined, the leading textbooks are routinely consulted by states, courts and international organizations, perhaps more so than in the past given the increased growth in international law instruments and their increasing significance in international affairs.

2.2.5 Hierarchy of sources and jus cogens

If there is a hierarchy of sources in international law, then one can say that judicial decisions and juristic writings are given a 'subsidiary' role under the terms of article 38 of the Statute of the International Court of Justice. The 'general principles of law' appear to function as a limited supplement to custom and treaty. The priority order between custom and treaty is generally that the later in time will have priority. However, there are some rules of international law that are regarded as so fundamental that the usual relationship between custom and treaty will be disrupted. The theoretical basis is that there are some obligations that each state has towards the international community as a whole, for example, outlawing aggression, genocide, prohibition of torture, protection from slavery and racial discrimination. The Vienna Convention provides that a treaty will be void if 'it conflicts with a peremptory norm of general international law'.[22] The rule, known as *jus cogens*, also applies to customary rules. Such a peremptory norm cannot be derogated from by local custom. In short, such norms are binding on all nations; they cannot be derogated from, nor can they be usurped by treaty provision. In the context of child law, this is an important issue. As discussed in further detail in Chapter 3, there are significant arguments that can be made that part of the CRC can be regarded as containing norms of the character fulfilling the requirements of *jus cogens*. Van Bueren (1994a: 55–6), for example, argues by analogy that the sexual and economic exploitation of children is comparable to slavery and should therefore be recognised as a 'peremptory norm of general international law' capable of overriding conflicting treaty provision and binding nations that have not ratified the treaties that provide protection against such exploitation of children.

2.3 The relationship between municipal (domestic) and international law

The details of the relationship between municipal and international legal orders are complex: see further, Shaw (2008: 129–194) and Brownlie (2008: 31–54). There are essentially two key debates about this relationship that are outlined in this section. The first debate concerns 'monist' and 'dualist' doctrines of international law. The older, monist doctrine asserts that municipal and international law

---

22 Article 53.

are part of a single, integral legal order and, if there is a conflict between the two, international law ('the law of nations') should prevail. The dualist doctrine, by contrast, asserts that the two systems exist separately; they do not affect each other, and it therefore follows that neither system prevails over the other. The two systems have different fundamental concerns. International law, it is argued, is primarily about the legal relationships between *states*, whereas municipal law is mainly concerned with the horizontal legal relationships between citizens and the vertical relationships between the sovereign state and its *citizens*. A third strand of thought, a modification of the dualist doctrine, has emerged which acknowledges the separate realms of municipal and international law and concludes that there is therefore little conflict of obligation possible between the two systems. A state's practice on a particular issue may well be in breach of its obligations under international law. This will be a matter for remedial action, if there is any available, in the international community. However, any 'conflicting' municipal legislation of a sovereign state will remain supreme unless specifically repealed in response to international 'naming and shaming' and other pressures. In fact, the practice of legislatures and the courts is sometimes thought to be a more reliable way to understand the relationship between municipal and international law.

An examination of such practice leads us to the second key debate about the doctrines of *transformation* and *incorporation* that focus on the practical problem of how municipal courts should deal with international legal standards. The doctrine of transformation (which is based on a 'dualist' understanding) asserts that municipal law will not be able to fully digest rules of international law unless there has been an explicit act of adoption. This will be achieved according to the constitutional machinery appropriate for the nation concerned. In the United Kingdom, for example, it will be by the passage of an Act of Parliament. By contrast, the doctrine of incorporation (based on a 'monist' understanding) holds that international law is automatically part of municipal law without the need for a constitutional ratification procedure. However, it should be noted immediately that the doctrine of incorporation is only to be applied to international customary law. The position with international treaties is treated differently. A lengthy case law development, dating back to the eighteenth century, has produced an acceptance of the doctrine of incorporation (of international customary law) in English common law. The landmark case was *Trendtex Trading Corp v. Central Bank of Nigeria*.[23] The Court of Appeal affirmed that the incorporation doctrine was the correct one and that international law did not know a rule of *stare decisis* (binding precedent). The municipal courts could implement changes in international customary law without waiting for any binding case precedents to be overturned in the House of Lords. Later cases have reaffirmed that '[c]ustomary international

23 [1977] 2 WLR 356 (CA).

law is part of the common law',[24] a position also accepted in the Scottish courts.[25] However, the certainty in choice of doctrine does nothing to resolve the problem that municipal courts may still have in identifying clearly what the relevant international customary rule is.

Treaties, however, are not incorporated automatically within the United Kingdom. The constitutional position is that, although the executive authority (the Crown) signs and ratifies international treaties, which then will have effect within international law, there is an additional need for the legislature (Parliament) to produce an Act, before that treaty will have binding legal effect recognised by the municipal courts. Depending on the government's political will on the matter, and the terms stated in the treaty to be met for it to enter into force, a long period of time might expire between ratification and domestic enactment. For example, the UK Government was one of the first countries to sign (4 November 1950) and ratify (8 March 1951) the European Convention on Human Rights, which came into force in international law on 3 September 1953. However, the British courts only started to apply the Convention directly, by virtue of the Human Rights Act 1998, 50 years later: the latter Act being commenced on 2 October 2000. As will be seen in Chapter 3, the CRC was signed and ratified by the UK Government in 1989, but it has not yet been enacted through Parliament and therefore does not have binding legal effect in UK courts.[26] This issue was raised in the discussions conducted by the parliamentary Joint Committee on Human Rights in scrutinising the operation of the CRC. Their report noted the following:

> We do not accept that the goal of incorporation of the Convention into UK law is unrealisable. We believe the government should be careful not to dismiss all the provisions of the Convention on the Rights of the Child as purely 'aspirational' and, despite the ways we have listed above in which the CRC is currently able to exert influence, we firmly believe that children will be better protected by incorporation of at least some of the rights, principles and provisions of the Convention into UK law. ... We believe that the assent of Parliament to these rights and principles, which could be secured by incorporation, would be a positive step towards enlarging and reinforcing the 'culture of respect for human rights' which we wish to see in the United Kingdom, as well as enhancing their democratic legitimacy.
>
> (Joint Committee on Human Rights 2003: 14, para. 22)

---

24 *R v. Bow Street Metropolitan Stipendiary Magistrate ex p Pinochete Ugarte (No. 3)* [2000] 1 AC 147, 276 (HL).

25 2001 SLT 507, 512.

26 It is interesting to note, however, the gathering political pressures to incorporate the CRC in the United Kingdom. For example, a Children's Rights Bill [HL Bill 8] contained provisions that would incorporate the CRC on much the same basis as the Human Rights Act 1998 incorporated the ECHR. The Bill was a Private Member's Bill moved by Baroness Joan Walmsley and received a first reading in the House of Lords on 19 November 2009, to coincide with the 20th anniversary of the adoption of the CRC.

However, an unincorporated international treaty does have some, albeit limited, significance in municipal law. Under English law, a rule of statutory interpretation has developed to assist with possible conflicts between unincorporated international treaty provisions and domestic legislation. The rule presumes that Parliament could not, at least without express words, have legislated contrary to the state's international obligations.[27] However, this presumption can be relied upon only in cases of ambiguity, not in cases where the statute offers a discretion. On the other hand, some cases have been more proactive in pointing to an unincorporated treaty provision to resolve a gap in municipal law.[28] However, this approach to utilising unincorporated treaties as an 'aid to construction' in statutory interpretation in the United Kingdom falls a long way short of allowing international law to properly enter the body of municipal law.

2.4 International organisations and institutions

The following sections contain some basic information about the main international organizations and institutions, in particular those that are connected to international children's rights. The references in this section should provide the reader with signposts to more specialist reading if required. Section 2.4.1 deals broadly with the UN system. The human rights bodies within the United Nations are dealt with in more detail in section 2.5.

2.4.1 The United Nations

The United Nations (UN) was established on 24 October 1945 by 51 nations in response to the Second World War, to preserve peace through international co-operation and collective security. UN membership is now global. Membership of the UN involves accepting the obligations of the UN Charter 1945, a treaty that sets out some principles of international relations. The UN Charter provides that:

1. There are established as principal organs of the United Nations: a General Assembly, a Security Council, an Economic and Social Council, a Trusteeship Council, an International Court of Justice and a Secretariat.
2. Such subsidiary organs as may be found necessary may be established in accordance with the present Charter.

(Charter of the United Nations, article 7)

---

27 *Garland v. British Rail Engineering Ltd* [1983] 2 AC 751; *R v. Secretary of State for the Home Department ex p Brind* [1991] 1 AC 696.
28 *Derbyshire County Council v. Times Newspapers Ltd* [1992] QB 770, at 830.

The six 'principal organs' are set out in The United Nations System chart.[29] In fact, there are now only five active organs. The Trusteeship Council[30] was originally established to provide international supervision of eleven Trust Territories. All of these territories have now achieved independence or self-government. The Council suspended operations on 1 November 1994 with the independence of Palau, the last remaining trust territory. All of the principal organs are based at the UN headquarters in New York, other than the ICJ which is located at The Hague in the Netherlands.

The General Assembly, established under the UN Charter,[31] is the main deliberative and policy-making organ of the UN and is made up from representatives of all (192) Member States. Shaw comments that '[t]he Assembly is essentially a debating chamber, a forum for the exchange of ideas and the discussion of a wide-ranging category of problems' (Shaw 2008: 1212). It provides a unique forum for multilateral discussion of all the international issues covered by the Charter. It meets in regular session from September to December each year, and thereafter as required. Each Member State in the Assembly, however powerful, has one vote. Votes taken on certain key issues, such as recommendations on peace and security and the election of Security Council members, require a two-thirds majority of Member States. Other questions are decided by simple majority. In recent years there has been an effort to achieve consensus without the need to make decisions by way of a formal vote in order to strengthen the legitimacy of the Assembly's decisions.

At the time of writing there were plans under way to enhance the General Assembly's role, authority, effectiveness and efficiency. The landmark Millennium Declaration was adopted by the Assembly in 2000[32] and reflected the Member States' commitment to create a new global partnership and to attain specific goals to attain peace, security and disarmament in addition to development and eradicating poverty, safeguarding human rights and promoting the rule of law, protecting our common environment, meeting the special needs of Africa and strengthening the United Nations. Some of these have time-bound targets, with a deadline of 2015, and have become known as the 'Millennium Development Goals' (MDGs). With the close of the general debate, the Assembly allocates items among its six main committees. The committees then prepare and present draft proposals and decisions for consideration at a plenary meeting of the Assembly. The Assembly also has two further supplementary committees: a credentials committee tasked with examining the credentials of representatives of Member States; and a general committee that reviews the progress of the

---

29 See <http://www.un.org/aboutun/chart_en.pdf> (accessed 11 February 2010).
30 UN Charter, Chapters XII and XIII, articles 75–91.
31 Chapter IV, articles 9–22.
32 A/Res/55/2, 8 September 2000. Available at: http://www.un.org/millennium/ (accessed 12 May 2010).

General Assembly and its main committees. The six main committees[33] and the Secretariat carry the General Assembly's work forward when it is not in session. The Third Committee (the Social, Humanitarian and Cultural Committee) is frequently allocated agenda items concerned with a range of social, humanitarian and human rights issues. It also examines the special procedures of the UN Human Rights Council (UNHRC) established in 2006.[34] The UNHRC is elected by and reports to the Assembly. The Third Committee interacts with various special rapporteurs, independent experts and chairpersons of working groups of the UNHRC. It discusses the advancement of women, the protection of children, indigenous issues, the treatment of refugees, the promotion of fundamental freedoms through the elimination of racism and racial discrimination, and the promotion of the right to self-determination. The committee also addresses important social development questions such as issues related to youth, family, ageing, persons with disabilities, crime prevention, criminal justice and drug control. At the time of writing the Third Committee had formulated two draft proposals relating to the protection of children: one on the girl child, and another on the rights of the child (UNGA 2009, 2009a). The Assembly's resolutions and recommendations are not strictly binding in international law, but obviously they may have great moral authority, particularly where there is a unanimous resolution. Brownlie (2008: 15) comments that although General Assembly resolutions are not in general binding, such resolutions 'provide a basis for the progressive development of the law and the speedy consolidation of customary rules'. A number of programmes, funds and other bodies, for example, the United Nations Children's Fund (UNICEF) and the Office of the High Commissioner for Human Rights (OHCHR), report directly to the General Assembly.

The Security Council[35] has the onerous task of maintaining international peace and security and convenes when necessary. It is organised so as to be able to function continuously; a representative of each of its members must be present at all times at UN Headquarters. Five Council members are permanent – China, the Russian Federation, the United Kingdom, France and the United States, 'chosen on the basis of power politics in 1945' (Shaw 2008: 1206). There are also an additional ten members elected by the General Assembly for periods of 2 years. Decisions of the Council, other than procedural matters, require nine votes and the absence of a veto by one of the five permanent members. It has been declared that the issue of whether a matter was procedural or not was itself subject to a

---

33 First Committee (Disarmament and International Security); Second Committee (Economic and Financial); Third Committee (Social, Humanitarian and Cultural); Fourth Committee (Special Political and Decolonization); Fifth Committee (Administrative and Budgetary); and Sixth Committee (Legal).

34 The United Nations Human Rights *Council* (UNHRC) is the successor body to the United Nations *Commission* on Human Rights (UNCHR) and a subsidiary body of the UN's General Assembly. See further, section 2.5.1.1.

35 UN Charter, Chapter V, articles 23–32.

veto.[36] The Council attempts to resolve disputes peacefully and in some cases will undertake investigation and mediation itself. The Council has frequently issued cease-fire directives and it also sends United Nations peacekeeping forces to troubled areas, often to keep opposing forces apart and to facilitate peaceful settlements. The Council can impose economic sanctions and trade and arms embargoes, and has authorised the use of collective military action to ensure its decisions are carried out. A recalcitrant Member State may be suspended from exercising the rights of UN membership by the General Assembly on the recommendation of the Council, and a persistent violator of the principles of the Charter may be expelled from the United Nations by the Assembly on the Council's recommendation. The Presidency of the Council rotates monthly, according to the listing of its Member States. The Council has a number of subsidiary bodies, including the Counter-Terrorism Committee, established by Council resolutions[37] following the attack on the twin towers of the World Trade Center in New York City on 11 September 2001.

The Economic and Social Council[38] (ECOSOC) coordinates the economic and social work of the United Nations. It has 54 member governments elected by the General Assembly for overlapping periods of 3 years. Seats on ECOSOC are allotted according to geographical representation with fourteen to the African states, eleven to Asian states, six to Eastern European states, ten to Latin American and Caribbean states, and thirteen to West European and other states. ECOSOC holds several short sessions and preparatory meetings with members of civil society throughout the year. It holds a four-week substantive session in July, alternating between New York and Geneva. This is organised in five segments (High-level, Coordination, Operational Activities, Humanitarian Affairs and General). A ministerial declaration is generally adopted on the theme of the High-level Segment, which provides policy guidance and recommendations for action. ECOSOC has a number of functional and regional commissions and standing committees and expert bodies that report to it, for example,[39] the Economic Commission for Africa. At the 2005 World Summit, heads of state and government mandated ECOSOC to hold annual Ministerial Reviews and a biennial Development Cooperation Forum. The objective of the former is to assess progress in achieving internationally agreed development goals. The objective of

---

36 'This "double-veto" constitutes a formidable barrier. Subsequent practice has interpreted the phrase "concurring votes of the permanent members" in article 27 in such a way as to permit abstentions. Accordingly, permanent members may abstain with regard to a resolution of the Security Council without being deemed to have exercised their veto against it' (Shaw 2008: 1207).
37 Security Council resolution 1373 (2001), adopted unanimously on 28 September 2001. See http://www.un.org/sc/ctc/index.html. (accessed 12 May 2010).
38 UN Charter, Chapter X, articles 61–72.
39 Also, the Commission on Human Rights which came to an end in 2006.

the latter is to enhance the coherence and effectiveness of activities of different development partners.

The ICJ,[40] sometimes referred to as the 'World Court', consists of 15 judges elected by the General Assembly and the Security Council. The ICJ decides claims between nations, but the nations' participation in this process is voluntary. The ICJ also provides advisory opinions to the General Assembly and the Security Council: see further, section 2.4.1.1.

The Secretariat[41] is headed by the Secretary-General of the UN, currently Ban Ki-moon of the Republic of Korea, the eighth Secretary-General, who was appointed by the General Assembly on 13 October 2006 on the recommendation of the Security Council for a 5-year, renewable term which commenced on 1 January 2007. The Secretariat conducts the administrative work of the UN, as directed by the other organs of the United Nations. As of 30 June 2009 the Secretariat had some 40,000 staff members around the world (UN Secretary-General 2009). There are UN offices at the headquarters in New York, and also in a number of other locations, for example, Geneva, Vienna, Nairobi, Addis Ababa, Bangkok, Beirut and Santiago. The UN Charter specifically provides that the Secretary-General and the staff of the Secretariat 'shall not seek or receive instructions from any government or from any other authority external to the Organization' and that each Member State must respect the 'exclusively international character of the responsibilities of the Secretary-General and the staff and not to seek to influence them in the discharge of their responsibilities'.[42]

The principal organs of the United Nations are linked to the 'specialised agencies' through cooperative agreements. The specialised agencies are autonomous organizations working with the United Nations and each other through the coordinating machinery of ECOSOC. There are currently 17 such agencies.[43] The oldest of these agencies, the International Labour Organization (ILO), is explained in further detail in section 2.4.1.4 and is referred to extensively in Chapter 4. The specialised agencies, together with the UN and its principal organs, are sometimes known collectively as the 'UN family' or the 'UN system'.

---

40 UN Charter, Chapter XIV, articles 92–96.
41 UN Charter, Chapter XV, articles 97–101.
42 UN Charter, article 100.
43 Food and Agriculture Organization (FAO); International Atomic Energy Agency (IAEA); International Civil Aviation Organization (ICAO); International Fund for Agricultural Development (IFAD); International Labour Organization (ILO); International Maritime Organization (IMO); International Telecommunications Union (ITU); United Nations Educational, Scientific and Cultural Organization (UNESCO); United Nations Industrial Development Organization (UNIDO); Universal Postal Union (UPU); World Bank (WB); World Food Programme (WFP); World Health Organization (WHO); World Intellectual Property Organization (WIPO); World Meteorological Organization (WMO); World Tourism Organization (UNWTO); International Monetary Fund (IMF).

The work of the United Nations in establishing the Universal Declaration of Human Rights in 1948 and the two UN Covenants in 1966 has been outlined already in Chapter 1. In recent years, the United Nations has changed its focus from providing international legal 'standard setting' to ensuring that human rights standards are implemented. The Office of the United Nations High Commissioner for Human Rights (OHCHR) was created in 1993[44] as part of a package of wider reforms to the United Nations. The OHCHR is part of the UN's Secretariat. The High Commissioner has the rank of Under-Secretary and reports to the General-Secretary of the United Nations and to the General Assembly. The OHCHR seeks to prevent violations of human rights and works with governments to further the observance of human rights standards. The system of the UN's human rights protection is explored in further detail in section 2.5.

The importance of the United Nations for the development of children's rights was underlined in a 'Special Session on Children' of the General Assembly held in May 2002.[45] It was the first session devoted exclusively to children and the first to include children as official delegates. The aim of the session was to review progress since the 'World Summit for Children' in 1990[46] and to revitalise commitment to children's rights. The document produced from this special session, 'A World Fit for Children', that was adopted by a resolution of the General Assembly (UN 2002), included a (non-binding) declaration that reaffirmed a commitment to promoting and protecting the rights of children and to a number of principles and objectives aimed at eradicating child poverty, discrimination, poor education, protection from harm, exploitation, disease and war. 'A World Fit for Children' also contained a detailed plan of action that recognised, *inter alia*, that:

> Chronic poverty remains the single biggest obstacle to meeting the needs, protecting and promoting the rights of children. It must be tackled on all fronts, from the provision of basic social services to the creation of employment opportunities, from the availability of microcredit to investment in infrastructure, and from debt relief to fair trade practices. Children are hardest hit by poverty because it strikes at the very roots of their potential for development – their growing bodies and minds. Eradication of poverty and the reduction of disparities must therefore be a key objective of development efforts.
>
> (UN 2002: para. 18)

The plan of action concluded that the promotion of healthy lives for children, providing quality education, protecting children from abuse, exploitation, violence

---

44 The OHRC's website: <http://www.ohchr.org> (accessed 2 November 2009).
45 See the archived materials at: <http://www.un.org/ga/children> and: <http://www.unicef.org/specialsession/> (accessed 2 November 2009).
46 See the archived materials at: <http://www.unicef.org/wsc/> (accessed 2 November 2009).

and armed conflict and combating HIV/AIDS 'are achievable goals and are clearly affordable for the global community'.

2.4.1.1 The International Court of Justice (ICJ)

The ICI, the successor body to the Permanent Court of International Justice (PCIJ) (1922–1940), is the principal judicial organ of the United Nations. It is located at The Hague in the Netherlands. The Statute of the International Court of Justice (annexed to, and an integral part of the UN Charter[47]) is the main constitutional document constituting and regulating the Court. The General Assembly and Security Council elect the 15 judges of the ICJ to a 9-year term of office. The Court cannot have more than one judge of each nationality and these judges must have the relevant qualifications for high judicial office in their respective countries. The Court has two main roles: to hear and decide 'contentious cases' between states, and to give 'advisory opinions' on legal questions referred to it by authorised international bodies. As regards contentious cases, it is only state parties that may appear before the Court, which is only competent to hear a case if the states concerned have accepted its jurisdiction. The procedure is defined in its Statute and in essence includes a written and an oral stage, after which the Court deliberates in private and then delivers its judgment in public. There is no appeal from the judgment of the ICJ. Failure to comply with a judgment may result in the other party having recourse to the Security Council.

The first case entered in the General List of the Court was submitted on 22 May 1947.[48] There have been 146 cases entered in the General List between that date and 12 May 2010. These have concerned a number of issues, for example, territorial sovereignty, land and marine boundary disputes, diplomatic relations, hostage taking and the right of asylum. There is, however, only one judgment to date directly relevant to children, and that concerned the issue of guardianship.

In the *Guardianship Case*,[49] a Dutch infant, living in Sweden, had been placed under the protective upbringing regime (*skyddsuppfostran*) of the Swedish authorities after the death of her mother. The Netherlands claimed that the Swedish measure of protective upbringing was incompatible with the obligations under the Hague Convention of 1902.[50] Under this Convention the application of the national law of the infant was expressly extended to both the person and the property of the infant. On the facts, this would have led to the child being handed over to a Dutch guardian. However, the ICJ reasoned that the Convention of 1902 had been designed to deal with conflicts of private law rules and would give

---

47 See UN Charter, Chapter XIV, articles 92–96.
48 *Corfu Channel* (*United Kingdom v. Albania*) (1948), ICJ Reps 15.
49 ICJ Reports, 1958, p 55.
50 The 1902 Convention was replaced by the Hague Convention Concerning the Powers of Authorities and the Law Applicable in Respect of the Protection of Infants 1961.

preference to the national law of the infant in only those cases. Here, however, it held that the Convention of 1902 did not cover the social purpose of the Swedish protective upbringing regime; therefore there was no failure by Sweden to observe its obligations under the Convention of 1902 and the Netherlands' claim was rejected (by twelve votes to four).

The ICJ's function to provide advisory opinions is available only to international organizations. The UN Charter provides that it is only the General Assembly or the Security Council that may request advisory opinions of the Court. Other organs of the United Nations and the 'specialised agencies' authorised by the General Assembly may also request advisory opinions on legal questions within the scope of their activities.[51] There have been suggestions that the power to request advisory opinions could be given to the Secretary-General and to states and national courts (Schwebel 1984, 1988). In principle, the Court's advisory opinions are not binding in character, but there is provision to agree in advance that the advisory opinion will be binding. The Court has given 25 advisory opinions since 1946, concerning, for example: the conditions of admission of a State to membership in the United Nations; reparation for injuries suffered in the service of the United Nations; the international status of South West Africa (Namibia); certain expenses of the United Nations; certain judgments rendered by the United Nations administrative tribunal; Western Sahara; questions relating to the privileges and immunities of human rights rapporteurs; the legality of the threat or use of nuclear weapons; and the legal consequences of the construction of a wall in the Israeli-occupied Palestinian territory. A recent request for an advisory opinion has been made to test whether the unilateral declaration of independence of Kosovo is in accordance with international law.[52] This request was made in 2008 and was still ongoing at the time of writing. In general, it would seem that the ICJ 'is now playing a more central role within the international legal system than thought possible two decades ago' (Shaw 2008: 1114). The President of the ICJ, Judge Hisashi Owada, in a recent address to the United Nations General Assembly, stated that:

> ... the increased recourse to the International Court of Justice by States for the judicial settlement of their disputes points to the consciousness among political leaders of the importance of the rule of law in the international community. ... The importance of the rule of law is crucial against the backdrop of the deepening process of globalization. Law does not replace politics or economics, but without it we cannot construct anything that will last in the international community.
>
> (ICJ, Press Release No. 2009/31, 2 November 2009)

51 UN Charter, article 96.
52 See 'Accordance with International Law of the Unilateral Declaration of Independence by the Provisional Institutions of Self-Government of Kosovo', ICJ Press Release No. 2008/34, 10 October 2008.

2.4.1.2 The United Nations Children's Fund (UNICEF)

The United Nations Children's Fund was created by the General Assembly on 11 December 1946 to provide emergency food and healthcare for children in countries that had been devastated by the Second World War. In 1953, UNICEF became a permanent part of the UN system and its name was shortened (from the original 'United Nations International Children's Emergency Fund'), but it has continued to be known by the popular acronym based on the old name. UNICEF's 36-strong executive board is elected by ECOSOC to guide its work. Members are elected for 3-year terms and the board regularly makes reports to ECOSOC. UNICEF has a strong presence in most countries. Its priorities are to support children to obtain the best start in life, to reach every child with life-saving vaccines, to support girls' education, and to work with young people to prevent the spread of HIV/AIDS. There are a number of national committees that raise funds for UNICEF. Each country office initiates a 5-year programme in collaboration with the host government, and focuses on practical ways in which to achieve the rights of children and women in accordance with the principles laid down in the CRC and the UN's Convention on the Elimination of All Forms of Discrimination against Women 1979. A situation report is produced at the beginning of each programme cycle. The overall policy on children is made at the UN headquarters. UNICEF helps to provide humanitarian aid in times of civil commotion and war, supplying food, safe water, medicine and shelter. It has also advanced the idea of 'children as zones of peace' and 'corridors of peace' to help protect children where there is armed conflict. A former United States Secretary of Agriculture, Ann Veneman, became executive director of the organization in May 2005 with an agenda to increase the organization's focus on the Millennium Development Goals.

2.4.1.3 The International Law Commission (ILC)

When the United Nations was established, there was little support by those framing the UN Charter to give the United Nations direct law-making powers. However, there was support for a power to undertake studies and make recommendations for 'encouraging the progressive development of international law and its codification'.[53] The General Assembly established the ILC for this purpose in 1947,[54] along with a Statute of the International Law Commission. The ILC meets annually and is composed of 34 members elected by the General Assembly for 5-year terms. The members serve in an individual capacity, reflecting their expertise, rather than as mandated government representatives. The topics for their work are sometimes referred to them by the General Assembly or

---

53 See UN Charter, article 3(1).
54 United Nations General Assembly Resolution A-RES-174(II), 21 November 1947.

ECOSOC, and they are also initiated by the ILC itself. It is provided that the ILC 'shall concern itself primarily with public international law, but is not precluded from entering the field of private international law'.[55] In fact, it has predominantly dealt with public international law matters. The Statute of the International Law Commission also makes a distinction between its two main tasks. 'Progressive development' means 'the preparation of draft conventions on subjects which have not yet been regulated by international law or in regard to which the law has not yet been sufficiently developed in the practice of States'. 'Codification' means 'the more precise formulation and systematization of rules of international law in fields where there already has been extensive State practice precedent and doctrine'.[56]

The ILC's work has resulted in a number of treaties that have made a significant contribution to the international legal order, for example, the Vienna Convention on the Law of Treaties 1969, the Vienna Convention on Succession of States in respect of Treaties 1978, the Vienna Convention on Diplomatic Relations 1961, the Vienna Convention on the Law of Treaties between States and International Organizations or between International Organizations 1986 and the Draft Articles on the Responsibility of States for Internationally Wrongful Acts 2001.

2.4.1.4 The international labour organization (ILO)

As we have seen, the (currently 17) 'specialised agencies' of the UN[57] are a privileged and integral part of the UN system. The ILO is of particular interest to international child lawyers as its activities cover child labour related matters (see further, Chapter 4). ILO became the first 'specialised agency' of the UN system in 1946. It was originally founded in 1919 and is the only surviving creation of the Treaty of Versailles of 1919 that established the League of Nations. Its principal task is to establish international labour standards in the field of labour rights. It also provides technical assistance, for example, in the fields of employment policy, labour law and industrial relations, working conditions and labour statistics. Its general aims and purpose were set out in the Declaration of Philadelphia in 1944 and this document is now annexed to ILO's constitution. ILO has a unique tripartite structure: workers' and employers' organizations participate as equal partners, along with governments, in its principal organs. The tripartite structure is reflected in all three of its main bodies – the International Labour Conference, the Governing Body and the International Labour Office.

The Member States of ILO (currently 183) meet in Geneva at the International Labour Conference in June of each year. Two government representatives and

---

55 Statute of the International Law Commission, article 1(2).
56 Statute of the International Law Commission, article 15.
57 See note 43 above for a list of all 17 specialised agencies.

one worker delegate and one employer delegate represent each Member State. Delegations are usually headed by Cabinet-rank ministers, but individual delegates can vote freely, even against their own delegation. The conference plays a key role in discussing and adopting international labour standards. It elects the Governing Body and adopts the budget.

The Governing Body is the executive council, consisting of 28 government, 14 worker and 14 employer member representatives. It meets three times a year in Geneva. Ten of the government seats are held permanently by states of chief industrial importance,[58] and representatives of the remaining government seats are elected at the conference every 3 years. It sets the agenda for ILO's policy and presents the programme and budget for approval by the conference. It will also elect a Director-General for a 5-year term to lead the International Labour Office. This latter body is ILO's permanent secretariat and carries out the work of the organization under the scrutiny of the Governing Body. The Office employs some 1,900 officials of over 110 nationalities at its Geneva headquarters and in 40 field offices. In addition, some 600 experts undertake missions in all regions of the world under the programme of technical cooperation.

2.4.2 The Hague Conference on Private International Law

The Hague Conference on Private International Law (hereafter the 'Hague Conference') is not part of the UN system; its origins predate the formation of the League of Nations in 1919. The Hague Conference is an intergovernmental organization whose main purpose is 'to work for the progressive unification of the rules of private international law'.[59] Relationships of a personal, family or commercial nature between individuals and companies in more than one country have become increasingly common in the modern world. One main function of the Hague Conference is to resolve the differences that may occur between the various legal systems involved through the formulation and adoption of 'private international law' rules. The Hague Conference has also developed its role as a centre for international judicial and administrative cooperation in the area of private law, especially in the fields of protection of the family and children, civil procedure and commercial law.

The first session of the Hague Conference was convened in 1893 by the Netherlands government. Six sessions were held prior to the Second World War and the seventh session, held in 1951, saw the introduction of a Statute of the Hague Conference on Private International Law, which made the Hague Conference a permanent intergovernmental organization. The twentieth session was held in 2005. There were at the time of writing 69 Member States of the Hague Conference: the European Community as a discrete entity is also a member of the Hague

---

58 Brazil, China, France, Germany, India, Italy, Japan, the Russian Federation, the United Kingdom and the United States.
59 Statute of the Hague Convention on Private International Law 1955, article 1.

Conference. There has been an increasing tendency for non-Member States both to participate in proceedings and to ratify Hague Conference conventions.

The work of the Hague Conference has been to draw up multilateral conventions over a number of private international law fields including conflict of laws issues, the recognition of companies, jurisdiction and foreign judgments, and international judicial and administrative cooperation. Hague Conference activities are organised by a secretariat, the 'Permanent Bureau', headed by a Secretary General. The Permanent Bureau's main role is to make the necessary preparations for the plenary sessions and for the Special Commissions. The Permanent Bureau will undertake some of the preliminary research on a convention or treaty and then refer it to a Special Commission made up of government experts. The drafts are then discussed and adopted at the plenary session. These sessions meet roughly every 4 years and additional 'Extraordinary Sessions' are convened on an *ad hoc* basis. The Standing Government Committee of Private International Law formally sets the agenda for the plenary session under the Statute. However, more direct influence by Member States has evolved so that recommendations are made by the Special Commissions and then to the plenary sessions. At the plenary session each Member State has one vote, and non-Member States, invited to participate on an equal footing, also have a vote. By tradition, the President of the plenary session has always been the person leading the Netherlands delegation, reflecting its historical origins. The Conference has adopted 39 conventions since 1951.

Special Commissions are also used frequently to monitor the operation of particular conventions. This has occurred, for example, in relation to both the child abduction convention and the intercountry adoption convention.[60] A Special Commission on the implementation of the 2007 Child Support Convention and Protocol (see following discussion) took place in November 2009. The Secretary General submits the budgets of the Permanent Bureau and the Special Commissions annually for approval by the Council of Diplomatic Representatives of Member States.

The Hague Conference has also been active in its outreach activities. It has organised international judicial seminars, for example, on child custody and the international protection of children. There are three modern Hague conventions that have been particularly influential in the development of international child law and have been very successful Hague conventions in their own right. These are the Hague Conventions on: the Civil Aspects of International Child Abduction 1980 (see Chapter 5); the Protection of Children and Cooperation in respect of Intercountry Adoption 1993 (see Chapter 6); and Jurisdiction, Applicable Law, Recognition, Enforcement and Cooperation in Respect of Parental Responsibility and Measures for the Protection of Children 1996. More recently, the Hague Conference has produced two further family-law-related agreements: the Hague Convention on the International Recovery of Child Support and Other Forms of Family Maintenance

---

60 At the time of writing there were plans to hold a further Special Commission on the practical operation of the Hague Intercountry Adoption Convention in June 2010: see http://www.hcch.net/index_en.php?act=progress.listing&cat=8 (accessed 12 May 2010).

2007 and the Hague Convention Protocol on the Law Applicable to Maintenance Obligations 2007 (which supplements the convention of 2007).

2.4.3 The International Criminal Court

The International Criminal Court (ICC), comparable in some ways to the UN's ICJ (see 2.4.1.1), began operating on 1 July 2002 following international discussions initiated by the General Assembly and established by the Rome Statute of the International Criminal Court 1998.[61] Its official seat is in The Hague but its proceedings may take place anywhere. It is the first permanent international court charged with trying those who commit the most serious crimes under international law, that is, crimes against humanity, war crimes and genocide. However, the ICC is not part of the UN system. It is functionally independent of the UN in terms of personnel and financing, but some meetings of the ICC governing body, the Assembly of States Parties to the Rome Statute, are held at the UN. There is an agreement between the ICC and the United Nations that governs how the two institutions work with each other.[62] Although at the time of writing 110 states were members of the Court, its authority is weakened by the absence of China, India, Russia and the United States from membership. It can exercise jurisdiction only where the accused is a national of a state party, the alleged crime took place on a state party's territory, or a situation is referred to it by the UN's Security Council. The Court is intended to supplement existing national courts and can exercise jurisdiction only where national courts cannot or will not investigate or prosecute such crimes. The ICC is a court of last resort. The ICC Prosecutor can initiate an investigation on the basis of a referral from any state party or from the UN's Security Council. In addition, the prosecutor can initiate investigations on the basis of information received from individuals or organizations. To date, Uganda, the Democratic Republic of the Congo and the Central African Republic have referred situations occurring on their territories to the Court. In addition, the Security Council has referred the situation in Darfur, Sudan (a non-state party). At the time of writing, the Court has indicted around a dozen individuals.

The ICC's first trial, of Congolese militia leader Thomas Lubanga, began on 26 January 2009, following an application for arrest made on 12 January 2006.[63] The outcome of this trial is of particular interest to international child lawyers as M. Lubanga is allegedly responsible for war crimes consisting of:

Enlisting and conscripting of children under the age of 15 years into the *Forces patriotiques pour la libération du Congo* [Patriotic Forces for the

---

61 The Rome Statute was adopted at a diplomatic conference on 17 July 1998, and entered into force on 1 July 2002.
62 *Negotiated Relationship Agreement between the International Criminal Court and the United Nations,* ICC-ASP/3/Res.1, entry into force 22 July 2004.
63 ICC-01/04-01/06, *The Prosecutor v. Thomas Lubanga Dyilo.*

Liberation of Congo] (FPLC) and using them to participate actively in hostilities in the context of an international armed conflict from early September 2002 to 2 June 2003 (punishable under article 8(2)(b)(xxvi) of the Rome Statute);

Enlisting and conscripting children under the age of 15 years into the FPLC and using them to participate actively in hostilities in the context of an armed conflict not of an international character from 2 June 2003 to 13 August 2003 (punishable under article 8(2)(e)(vii) of the Rome Statute).

(ICC website <http://www.icc-cpi.int/Menus/ICC>, accessed 24 October 2009)

The context and progress of this case is given further examination in Chapter 8 (Children and Armed Conflict).

2.5 Human rights protection

The overview of the development of human rights protection in Chapter 1 provides some detail about the introduction of the Universal Declaration of Human Rights (UDHR) of 1948 and the two UN Covenants (see section 1.2.1), dealing respectively with first generation (civil and political) and second generation (economic, social and cultural) rights, introduced in 1966. The UDHR, made by resolution of the General Assembly, is not strictly binding in international law. However, it is generally treated as having entered into international customary law. The declaration and the two (binding) covenants have laid the foundation of international human rights law, and their provisions have found their way into the written constitutions of a number of states and subsequent human rights treaties. There have also been further UN treaties dealing with particular subject areas of human rights concerns, for example, the Convention on the Prevention and Punishment of the Crime of Genocide in 1948, the Convention on the Elimination of All Forms of Racial Discrimination in 1965, the Convention on the Elimination of All Forms of Discrimination against Women of 1979, the Convention against Torture and Other Cruel, Inhuman and Degrading Treatment or Punishment of 1984, the International Convention on the Protection of the Rights of All Migrant Workers and Members of their Families in 1990 and the UN Convention on the Rights of the Child of 1989, along with its two Optional Protocols in 2000: see further, Chapters 3, 7 and 8.

2.5.1 Global protection – UN machinery

There are two types of body within the UN system that promote and protect human rights. First, those created under the UN Charter, and second, those established by international human rights treaties.

2.5.1.1 UN Charter bodies protecting human rights: OHCHR and UNHRC

Most of these entities receive administrative support from the Office of the High Commissioner for Human Rights (OHCHR), which is, as we have seen, a subsidiary body of the UN's Secretariat. The interrelationship between the various human rights themselves and the need for the United Nations to treat human rights pervasively within all its activities was recognised in the Vienna Declaration and Programme of Action adopted in 1993.[64] This declaration emphasised that all human rights were universal, indivisible and interrelated; and it called for, *inter alia*, the creation of OHCHR to spotlight and coordinate human rights activities. The OHCHR (see also section 2.4.1) was established some months later, and the first incumbent took office in 1994. The OHCHR is based at the *Palais Wilson* in Geneva and the UN headquarters in New York City. The idea behind the OHCHR is to have a centre with strong moral authority to lead the human rights movement and to enhance the UN's ability to implement human rights standards. The OHCHR has forged links with non-government organizations (NGOs), academic institutions and others to promote human rights education, in addition to its involvement in preventative work. One of the aims of the OHCHR is to assist in mainstreaming human rights thinking throughout the UN system. The OHCHR is broadly tasked with a liaison role between all the human rights bodies within the UN and beyond.

The United Nations Human Rights *Council* (UNHRC) is a part of the UN system and is the successor body to the United Nations *Commission* on Human Rights (UNCHR) and a subsidiary body of the UN's General Assembly. The General Assembly established the UNHRC[65] in 2006 in order to replace the previous body, which had been discredited for having countries with poor human rights records as members; for example, Sudan, China, Cuba and Zimbabwe. The resolution to establish the new body was approved by 170 members of the (then) 191-nation General Assembly. The United States voted against the resolution. It had wanted a smaller body to be created, with members chosen primarily for their commitment to human rights. The new Council comprises members who are elected by secret ballot by an absolute majority of the General Assembly, and there is provision for periodic reviews of membership with the possibility of suspension for any state accused of systematic human rights violations. The UNHRC adopted an 'Institution-building package' on 18 June 2007 to guide its future work. This provides that it will undertake a 'Universal Periodic Review' to assess human rights situations in all the 192 UN Member States. In September 2007

---

64 The importance of the rights of the child is given specific attention in article 21 of the Vienna Declaration and Programme of Action 1993.
65 General Assembly resolution, A/RES/60/251 (15 March 2006).

an Advisory Committee was established which provides expert advice and serves as the UNHRC's think tank. The Advisory Committee has eighteen members: five from African states; five from Asian states; three from Latin American and Caribbean states; three from Western European and other states; and two members from Eastern European states. There is also a complaints procedure, established in 2007, which allows individuals and organizations to bring complaints about human rights violations to the attention of the UNHRC. The 'Working Group on Communications', consisting of five independent experts (serving for 3-year terms) and representative of the five regions, make determinations whether a complaint deserves investigation. If it does, the complaint is passed to the 'Working Group on Situations' which again consists of five members (for a term of 1 year), geographically representative of the five regions. This group then reports to the UNHRC and makes recommendations about the course of action to be taken.

The UNHRC consists of 47 seats, occupied by members elected by the General Assembly for a term of 3 years, which can be occupied for no more than two consecutive terms. The seats are distributed among the UN's regions: 13 for Africa, 13 for Asia, six for Eastern Europe, eight for Latin America and the Caribbean, and seven for Western Europe and others. The first election of members was held on 9 May 2006.

'Special procedures' is the general name given to the mechanisms established by the UNHRC's predecessor body, the Commission on Human Rights, to address either specific country situations or thematic issues. At the time of writing there were 30 thematic and eight country mandates, which are provided with personnel, logistical and research assistance by the OHCHR. Special procedures are either an individual (called 'Special Rapporteur', 'Special Representative of the Secretary-General', 'Representative of the Secretary-General' or 'Independent Expert') or a working group usually composed of five members (one from each region). The mandates of the special procedures are established and defined by the resolution creating them. Mandate holders of the special procedures serve in their personal capacity and do not receive salaries or any other financial compensation for their work. The independent status of the mandate holders is crucial in order for them to be able to fulfil their functions impartially. Various activities can be undertaken by special procedures, including responding to individual complaints, conducting studies, providing advice on technical cooperation at the country level, and engaging in general promotional activities.

Most special procedures receive information on specific allegations of human rights violations and send urgent appeals or letters of allegation to governments asking for clarification. In 2009, a total of 689 communications were sent to governments in 119 countries: 66 per cent of these were joint communications of two or more mandate holders.[66] Mandate holders also carry out country visits.

---

66 See <http://www2.ohchr.org/english/bodies/chr/special/index.htm> (accessed 25 October 2009) and OHCHR (2010, 7).

Some countries have issued 'standing invitations'. As of September 2009, 65 countries had extended standing invitations to the special procedures.[67] The UNHRC has reviewed special procedures, and all thematic mandates that have been reviewed have been extended.[68] Some new thematic mandates have also been established: on contemporary forms of slavery and access to safe drinking water and sanitation. A new mandate on cultural rights was established in March 2009. Most country mandates have also been extended, with the exception of Belarus, Cuba, the Democratic Republic of the Congo and Liberia. At its 11th session, the UNHRC created the mandate of independent expert on the situation of human rights in the Sudan for a period of 1 year. A mandate holder's tenure in a given function, whether a thematic or a country mandate, will be no longer than 6 years (two terms of 3 years for thematic mandate holders).

2.5.1.2 UN human rights treaty bodies

In addition to the 'Charter' bodies, there are also a number of human rights 'treaty bodies': see generally, OHCHR (2005). At present there are eight such bodies that monitor the implementation of the principal human rights treaties. These are set out in Table 2.1.

The treaty bodies carry out various functions in accordance with the provisions in the treaties that established them. These include consideration of state parties' reports and consideration of individual complaints or communications, if prescribed under the relevant treaty. In addition, they issue, from time to time, 'General Comments' and organise 'Days of Discussion' on treaty-related themes. In principle, once a state ratifies one of the relevant treaties it will have acquired a legal obligation to implement the rights contained in the treaty. In order to provide some further assurance over and above the act of ratification/accession that a state will in fact implement its legal obligations under the treaty, there is a further obligation under the treaty for the government of a state party to submit regular reports to the monitoring committee established under that treaty.

The reporting system is common to most of the UN human rights treaties, though there are some differences in detail. For example, an initial report is usually required 1 year after joining and then every 4 or 5 years. An initial report to the Committee on the Rights of the Child (CtRC), however, is only required after 2 years and then periodically after 5 years.[69] In addition to the report from the government of a state party, the treaty bodies may also receive reports on treaty-related matters from non-governmental organizations (NGOs), UN agencies, other intergovernmental organizations, academic institutions and the press.

---

67 Ibid.
68 In June 2007, at its Fifth Session, UNHRC adopted Resolution 5/2, containing a Code of Conduct for special procedures mandate holders.
69 UN Convention on the Rights of the Child (CRC), article 44(1).

Table 2.1 Human rights treaty bodies and treaties

Human rights treaty body	Treaty/protocols monitored
The Human Rights Committee (CCPR)	International Covenant on Civil and Political Rights (1966) and its optional protocols
The Committee on Economic, Social and Cultural Rights (CESCR)	International Covenant on Economic, Social and Cultural Rights (1966)
The Committee on the Elimination of Racial Discrimination (CERD)	International Convention on the Elimination of All Forms of Racial Discrimination (1965)
The Committee on the Elimination of Discrimination Against Women (CEDAW)	Convention on the Elimination of All Forms of Discrimination against Women (1979) and its optional protocol (1999)
The Committee Against Torture (CAT)	Convention against Torture and Other Cruel, Inhuman or Degrading Treatment (1984)
The Committee on the Rights of the Child (CtRC)	Convention on the Rights of the Child (1989) and its optional protocols (2000)
The Committee on Migrant Workers (CMW)	International Convention on the Protection of the Rights of All Migrant Workers and Members of their Families (1990)
The Committee on the Right of Persons with Disabilities (CRPD)	International Convention on the Rights of Persons with Disabilities (2006)

As we shall see in Chapter 3, there is a strong role for NGOs in the reporting process to the CtRC. Having received all relevant reports, the treaty bodies and government representatives will examine the reports and then publish their concerns and recommendations in the form of 'concluding observations'. Some of the treaty bodies (but not the CtRC) also conduct further monitoring in the form of an inquiry procedure, the examination of inter-state complaints and the examination of individual complaints. Furthermore, some of the treaty bodies (CCPR, CERD, CAT and CEDAW) can receive petitions from individuals in certain circumstances. There are attempts to coordinate the activities of the treaty bodies' committees through an annual meeting of chairpersons and inter-committee meetings.

As we shall see in some greater detail in Chapter 3, the CtRC, established under the UN Convention on the Rights of the Child 1989, is composed of 18 independent experts who act, like the members of the other treaty body committees, in their 'personal capacity' rather than as government representatives.[70] The CtRC examines country reports – both the official government report and reports from any relevant NGOs – and then responds at the end of this process with its 'concluding observations'. The CtRC also reviews additional reports from states which have ratified either or both of the two Optional Protocols to the

---

70 CRC, article 43(2), as amended.

CRC: the Optional Protocol on the involvement of children in armed conflict 2000 (OPAC) and the Optional Protocol on the sale of children, child prostitution and child pornography 2000 (OPSC).[71]

2.5.2 Regional protection

The global protection of human rights, reflected in particular by the UN's Universal Declaration of Human Rights 1948 and the two International Covenants of 1966, has inspired the spread of international human rights law in the regions of the world. This section provides, by way of example, a brief (and by no means exhaustive) overview of the regional human rights protection systems available in Europe, Africa, Asia and the Americas.

2.5.2.1 Human rights protection in Europe

The regional organization most associated with human rights protection in Europe is the Council of Europe. The European Union (EU) has also contributed to the support of the human rights agenda. Although hopes for human rights development were focused on the UN institutions after the trauma of the Second World War, '[t]hese hopes met with early frustration as the Cold War immobilised human rights at the United Nations for a long time' (Tardu 2003: 35). In addition to the Council of Europe and the EU, one can also add a third system of institutional support for human rights protection, in the form of the Organization for Security and Cooperation in Europe (OSCE) which had 56 participating states at the time of writing. Since this organization emerged from the Helsinki Conference in 1975 it has developed three dimensions: political-military; environmental-economic; and the 'human dimension'. As regards the latter, it has adopted various policies and programmes including the creation of an Office of the Special Representative and Coordinator for Combating Trafficking in Human Beings. The OSCE's commitments are not legally binding but do exert moral and political influence and are usually consistent with global initiatives emanating from the United Nations.

The Council of Europe, which has its headquarters in Strasbourg in north-eastern France, is Europe's oldest political organization, founded in 1949.[72] It now comprises 47 member countries, including 21 countries from Central and Eastern Europe. Observer status has been granted to five states: the Holy See, the United States, Canada, Japan and Mexico. The Council of Europe is distinct from the 27-nation EU, but no country has ever joined the European Union without

---

71 In May 2010, there were 117 signatories and 137 parties to OPSC, and 125 signatories and 132 parties to OPAC.
72 The ten founding member states were: United Kingdom, Sweden, Norway, the Netherlands, Luxembourg, Italy, Ireland, France, Denmark and Belgium.

first belonging to the Council of Europe. The Council of Europe, it can be claimed, represents the 'greater Europe', in particular since the accession of over 20 countries of Central and Eastern Europe since November 1990.

The Council of Europe was established to advance parliamentary democracy and the rule of law and to develop regional agreements in Europe to standardise member countries' legal and social practices. It was also intended to promote a European identity that would cut across the different European cultures. Since the late 1980s, it has acted as a political anchor and human rights watchdog for Europe's post-communist democracies. It has, in particular, been active in helping Central and Eastern European countries, via a variety of technical assistance and other programmes, to carry out and consolidate a range of social, political and constitutional reforms to resonate with economic reform.

The Council of Europe's political aims were revised at the Vienna Summit in October 1993. The Heads of State and Government viewed the Council of Europe as the guardian of democratic security, an essential complement to military security. An action plan was adopted during the second Summit in Strasbourg in October 1997. The action plan was intended to strengthen the Council of Europe's work in four areas: democracy and human rights, social cohesion, the security of citizens and democratic values, and cultural diversity.

The principal bodies of the Council of Europe are the Committee of Ministers, the Parliamentary Assembly and the Congress of Local and Regional Authorities. There is also a 1,800-strong Secretariat to the Council of Europe led by a Secretary-General. The Committee of Ministers is the Council of Europe's key decision-making body. The Council of Europe has been responsible for the introduction of over 200 treaties or conventions.[73] Some of these international legal instruments are open to non-member states. The content of these treaties and conventions ranges from human rights to the fight against organised crime, data protection and cultural co-operation.

The Council of Europe is most renowned for the establishment of the European Convention for the Protection of Human Rights and Fundamental Freedoms 1950 (ECHR).[74] The ECHR was produced in response to the concerns in the immediate post-war period about arbitrary state interference with individual human rights. In particular, it followed and was partly modelled on the United Nations' extremely influential Universal Declaration of Human Rights of 1948 (see sections 1.2 and 2.5). The United Kingdom had been closely involved in drafting the ECHR and was the first country to ratify it.[75] The ECHR initially established two bodies: first, the European Commission on Human Rights, which made decisions

---

73 At the time of writing the Council of Europe had produced its 207th treaty: see the full list of Council of Europe Conventions at: http://conventions.coe.int/Treaty/Commun/ListeTraites. asp?CM=8&CL=ENG (accessed 12 May 2010).

74 Opened for signature on 4 November 1950; entry into force on 3 September 1953.

75 The United Kingdom signed the ECHR on 4 November 1950 and ratified it on 8 March 1951.

on questions of admissibility and produced reports on the merits of such petitions. If there was no friendly settlement of the issue at this stage, an application would proceed to the European Court of Human Rights (ECtHR) at Strasbourg. A single unified ECtHR replaced the Court and the Commission on 1 September 1998.

In 1966, the UK Government made a declaration under the ECHR that gave British citizens the right of individual petition to the ECtHR. For over 30 years since, an increasing number of cases from the United Kingdom arrived at the Strasbourg court, including a number of family law cases. However, the position was unsatisfactory as it took an average of 5 years to get a hearing in Strasbourg, at an average cost of about £30,000. The 'rights' under the ECHR could not be enforced directly in British courts, as Parliament had not yet incorporated the convention into domestic law. The first New Labour administration achieved legislative reform – the Human Rights Act 1998 – to incorporate the ECHR into UK law. The Human Rights Act 1998 came into force on 2 October 2000. This Act has, in essence, produced a new principle of statutory construction whereby the courts and tribunals must interpret domestic legislation compatibly with convention rights where at all possible. If a compatible interpretation is not possible, then the higher courts – the House of Lords, the Judicial Committee of the Privy Council, the Court of Appeal, the High Court and the High Court of Justiciary (Scotland) – are empowered to make a 'declaration of incompatibility'. In order to preserve the British constitutional principle of 'parliamentary sovereignty', a declaration will merely prompt the relevant government minister to steer appropriate amending legislation through Parliament. However, a minister will not be compelled to do so, though it is envisaged that remedial parliamentary action will be taken in practically all cases in response to a declaration of incompatibility (Home Secretary 1997: para. 2.10).

In addition to the courts' pervasive duty to construe legislation compatibly with convention rights, the ECHR also permeates the British legal system by imposing a general duty on 'public authorities' (defined to include courts and tribunals) to act compatibly with the relevant rights. A human rights issue can now arise in any of the domestic courts or tribunals, either as a free-standing issue or (in a much greater number of cases) as a corollary point in any other legal proceedings. When considering such points, the courts and tribunals are under a mandatory duty to 'take into account' the case law from the ECtHR at Strasbourg. A creative feature of the Strasbourg court's jurisprudence has, over the years, been its willingness to read in positive obligations on states to Convention rights rather than merely constraining the reach of the ECHR to negatively prevent arbitrary state interference with citizens.[76]

The ECHR and the European Social Charter 1961 (the latter revised in 1996) are both generic human rights treaties, addressing 'first' and 'second generation' rights respectively, and they both contain some specific provisions relevant to the

---

76 This is sometimes referred to as the 'horizontal effect' of Convention rights.

rights of children.[77] There are also a number of other conventions that deal more specifically with particular issues relating to children: for example, the Convention on the Legal Status of Children Born out of Wedlock 1975; the Convention on Contact Concerning Children 2003; Convention on Action against Trafficking in Human Beings 2005; Convention on the Protection of Children against Sexual Exploitation and Sexual Abuse 2007; Convention on the Adoption of Children (revised) 2008.

The European Union, currently with 27 member states and three candidate countries[78] has a number of programmes aimed at human rights issues and has established a Fundamental Rights Agency. Efforts to tackle trafficking, especially in women and children, have become a political priority for the Union and it has run a number of cross-border programmes to address trafficking in human beings. The Union also ensures that a clause stipulating the maintenance of human rights standards is inserted into all agreements on trade or cooperation with third countries. For example, the Cotonou Agreement,[79] a trade and aid pact which links the Union with 78 developing countries in Africa, the Caribbean and the Pacific, provides that EU trade concessions can be suspended and aid programmes reduced or curtailed if any country falls below such human rights standards. It has imposed sanctions for human rights breaches on Burma (Myanmar) and Zimbabwe. The main decision-making body of the Union, the Council of the EU, has produced over the past decade comprehensive annual reports[80] on human rights activities. These contain accounts of EU initiatives and instruments in third countries, European Parliament actions on human rights, thematic issues, EU action in other international fora (e.g. the UNHRC, the General Assembly, the Council of Europe and the OSCE), country-focused issues and some analysis of the effectiveness of EU actions and instruments. 'Thematic issues' include regular contributions of sections on the rights of the child and children in armed conflict. The EU Annual Report on Human Rights for 2008, for example, reported that at the 62nd session of the United Nations General Assembly:

> ... the resolution on the rights of the child initiated by the European Union in cooperation with the Latin American and Caribbean Group of countries (GRULAC) established the mandate of the Special Representative of the UN Secretary-General (UNSRSG) on violence against children, charged with

---

77　For example, ECHR, article 8 (right to respect for private and family life, home and correspondence) and European Social Charter (1996 revised), article 7 (right of children and young persons to protection), article 17 (right of children and young persons to social, legal and economic protection).

78　Candidate countries applying for membership at the time of writing were: Croatia, the former Yugoslav Republic of Macedonia, and Turkey.

79　The agreement was signed on 23 June 2000 in Cotonou, Bénin. It was concluded for a 20-year period from March 2000 to February 2020, and entered into force in April 2003.

80　*EU Annual Reports on Human Rights, 1998–2009.* Available at: http://www.consilium.europa.eu/cms3_fo/showPage.aspx?id=970&lang=en&mode=g (accessed 2 November 2009).

promoting the prevention and elimination of all forms of violence against children.

(Council of the European Union 2008: 63)

The same annual report also refers to the adoption by the Council, in December 2007, of new EU guidelines on the rights of the child (Council of the European Union 2007). The guidelines promote the rights of the child worldwide, in particular by advancing the implementation of the CRC and its two Optional Protocols. The combination of several robust conventions emanating from the Council of Europe and the increasing strength of the children's rights agenda in the European Union provides a powerful system of human rights protection in Europe which has also influenced the development of international human rights protection in other regions of the world.

2.5.2.2 Human rights protection in Africa

The African Union, known prior to 9 July 2002 as the Organization of African Unity (OAU), is the principal intergovernmental organization in the African continent and consists of all 53 nations of the African continent. It was constituted in the early 1960s and the OAU Charter was adopted by the African Heads of State on 25 May 1963 in Addis Ababa, Ethiopia, where the Organization has remained since. The OAU Charter was abrogated and replaced by the Constitutive Act of the African Union on 11 July 2000 in Lome, Togo.

The main human rights document is the African Charter on Human and Peoples' Rights, often referred to as the 'Banjul Charter' because it was endorsed in Banjul, the capital of the Gambia, shortly before it was finally approved in Nairobi, Kenya, by the 18th Assembly of the Organization for African Unity (OAU) on 16 June 1981. The Banjul Charter became effective after the 26th instrument of ratification on 21 October 1986. All 53 African states have now ratified it. Since the signing of the Banjul Charter critics have disparaged the African human rights system for its failure to establish a court that would safeguard and enforce the rights guaranteed in the Charter (Adjami 2002). An African Commission on Human and Peoples' Rights (ACHPR), provided for in articles 30–61 of the Banjul Charter, was established by the OAU in 1987. Its mandate is fourfold: to promote human and peoples' rights, to protect those rights, to interpret Charter provisions, and to perform other tasks allocated to it by member states.[81] The ACHPR is located in Banjul and meets twice a year in sessions lasting for around 10 days, usually in March/April and in October/November. However, commentators point out that, despite some positive developments

---

81 Banjul Charter, article 45.

in the ACHPR's individual complaint mechanism, 'its decisions are non-binding, and attract little, if any, attention from governments of member states'.[82]

The text of the Banjul Charter was influenced by the UN Declaration of Human Rights 1948 and the UN's two International Covenants of 1966, but there are some distinctly African concepts and approaches that depart from Western concepts of human rights. There are a number of provisions that reflect African communal traditions, stressing every individual's responsibility to the family and to the wider local and national communities. The Banjul Charter also contains a concept of 'duties' that is subsumed under the notion of human rights. 'Human rights', in the Banjul Charter, refers to rights and their correlative duties. There is also a different category of rights in the Charter – 'peoples' rights'. There is not a hard and fast definition of peoples' rights, but the term does denote a more collective notion of rights and contrasts sharply with the Western liberal notion of 'individual' rights which permeates the global UN human rights treaties. The definition of 'people' or 'peoples' in the Charter is given according to the African philosophical concept of 'peoples'. According to African socialism, a person belongs to a community or society and is governed by societal rules of existence and behaviour, better known as the extended African family codes. A person is an integral member of a group animated by a spirit of African solidarity (Don Nanjira 2003: 22).

The Banjul Charter also marks a departure from other human rights documents in that it effectively authorises African states to intervene in the domestic affairs of another African state if human rights are violated. The rights contained in the Charter can be divided into four categories: civil and political rights (articles 3–14); economic, social and cultural rights (articles 15–18); peoples' rights (articles 19–24); and duties to respect, promote and protect human rights (articles 25–29). The Banjul Charter did not originally have a court mechanism to implement it. The ACHPR operates a reporting procedure[83] in which it considers, every 2 years, state reports on state activity to give effect to the Charter rights. There is also a 'communication procedure', a complaint system through which an individual, NGO or group can petition the Commission about violations.[84] The Commission can then make recommendations to the state concerned and to the OAU Assembly.

The changeover from the OAU to the African Union is also being accompanied by the introduction of an African Court of Justice. This was authorised under the Constitutive Act of the African Union 2000 and its powers and procedures are spelled out in the Protocol to the African Charter on Human and Peoples' Rights on the Establishment of an African Court on Human and Peoples' Rights 1998

---

82 See the 'Coalition for an effective African Court on Human and People's Rights' website at: <http://www.africancourtcoalition.org/editorial.asp?page_id=16> (accessed 2 November 2009).

83 Banjul Charter, article 62.

84 See Banjul Charter, article 56, for the criteria.

adopted in Ouagadougou, Burkina Faso, 10 June 1998. Resonating with the UN Charter's provision in respect of the International Court of Justice, the African Court is expressed as the 'principal judicial organ of the Union'. It consists of 11 judges, and no two judges will be nationals of the same state. Article 14(2) of the Protocol states that: 'The Assembly shall ensure that in the Court as a whole there is representation of the main regions of Africa and of their principal legal traditions.'

The judges are elected by the Assembly and serve for a 6-year term, renewable on one occasion only. State parties, various organs of the African Union, the Commission and African intergovernmental organizations are all eligible to submit cases.[85] States that are not members of the African Union are not allowed to submit cases, nor will the Court have jurisdiction to deal with a dispute involving a state that has not ratified the Protocol. It is intended that the Court's activities are 'complementary' to the protective mandate of the Commission.[86] For example, it is provided that the Court may give an 'advisory opinion' on any legal matter relating to the Charter or other relevant human rights instrument 'provided that the subject matter of the opinion is not related to a matter being examined by the Commission'.[87] The Protocol entered into force on 25 January 2004 and eleven judges have been elected.[88] However, interpretation of African Union law will not be automatically controlled by the African Court of Justice. It is therefore less likely to become a vehicle for legal integration than the European Court of Justice (ECJ) has within the EU framework. The Court is further limited in that only those member states of the African Union which have ratified the Protocol will be subject to its jurisdiction. Delay has occurred in establishing this Court, not least the decision of the African Union in July 2004 to merge the court with the African Court on Human and Peoples' Rights (ACHPR), as also envisaged under the provisions of the Protocol. The underlying intention to merge the ACJ and the ACHPR is based on a desire to save funding and avoid problems of overlapping jurisdictions. Once formally merged with the ACHPR, the Court will be located in an Eastern region member state of the African Union. Mauritius has offered to host the Court.[89]

A Protocol on the Statute of the African Court of Justice and Human Rights (ACJHR) was issued on 1 July 2008.[90] This Protocol merges the African Court on Human and Peoples' Rights and the Court of Justice of the African Union into

---

85 Protocol to the African Charter on Human and Peoples' Rights on the Establishment of an African Court on Human and Peoples' Rights 1998, article 5.

86 Ibid., article 2.

87 Ibid., article 4(1).

88 See <http://www.africa-union.org/root/au/organs/Court_of_Justice_en.htm> (accessed 2 November 2009).

89 See <http://www.aict-ctia.org/courts_conti/acj/acj_home.html> (accessed 2 November 2009).

90 At the time of writing this Protocol had 18 signatories and 1 ratification (Libya).

one single court.[91] The Protocol thus replaces the Protocol to the African Charter on Human and Peoples' Rights on the Establishment of an African Court on Human and Peoples' Rights (adopted in 1998) and the Protocol of the Court of Justice of the African Union (adopted in 2003).[92] The Statute of the African Court of Justice and Human Rights is contained in the annex to the Protocol.

The African Charter on the Rights and Welfare of the Child 1990 (ACRWC) appeared shortly after the appearance of the CRC in 1989 and was the first comprehensive regional treaty on the rights of the child (Lloyd 2002). Arguably, African states had been under-represented in the drafting process of the CRC. There have been a number of aspects that were omitted from the CRC and were in need of a specific African response: for example, the situation of children living under the apartheid regime in South Africa, practices in Africa such as female genital mutilation, and the severe socio-economic conditions of the African continent. There are a number of cultural features, for example, the strong role of the extended family in matters of adoption and fostering, which were not suitably reflected in the CRC. However, the African version is undoubtedly modelled on the CRC and shares its key underlying principles: for example, the principle of non-discrimination,[93] the best interests principle,[94] the right to life, survival and development[95] and the participation and evolving capacities principles.[96]

The ACRWC has established an African Committee of Experts on the Rights and Welfare of the Child ('the Committee'), composed of 11 members sitting in their personal capacity. They are elected by the Assembly of Heads of State and Government of the African Union. The Committee is convened twice each year and had its first session in July 2001. The members serve a non-renewable 5-year term. Initial reports from states ratifying the ACRWC are to be received after 2 years and thereafter every 3 years.

The Committee is authorised under the ACRWC[97] to receive 'communications' from states concerning any relevant issue. These can be submitted by any individual, group or NGO recognised by the OAU or the African Union, a member state or the United Nations. This is a much more robust model of grievance procedure than merely the reporting procedure available under the CRC. Finally, there is a potentially rigorous investigation procedure[98] available to the Committee that can use any appropriate investigative method in relation to any issue covered

---

91 Protocol on the Statute of the African Court of Justice and Human Rights, issued on 1 July 2008, article 2.
92 Ibid., article 1.
93 African Charter on the Rights and Welfare of the Child, articles 3 and 26.
94 Ibid., article 4.
95 Ibid., article 5.
96 Ibid., articles 4, 7, 9(2), 11(4) and 12.
97 Ibid., article 44.
98 Ibid., article 45.

by the ACRWC. However, despite the promising formal framework of the ACRWC, there are weaknesses. The slow pace of ratifications has meant that it was not until 29 November 1999 that the treaty received the 15th instrument of ratification and entered into force.[99] There were, at the time of writing, 45 of the 53 African states that had ratified it.

2.5.2.3 Human rights protection in Asia

While the Americas, Europe and Africa have all established regional human rights treaties and institutions to protect human rights through multilateral action, Asia has been the last major region remaining without an international human rights enforcement mechanism. In part this has been because of the view that international human rights principles have been derived largely from a 'Western' perspective that is in conflict with certain core Asian values. Some commentators have argued that international human rights do not sit easily with some Asian countries that feel these threaten their sovereignty, though developments may change this.

> Utilizing their sovereignty as a shield from international interference, Asian states have refused to recognise the universality of human rights, preferring instead to enforce higher priority policies, such as economic development, social stability, and financial success. Human rights in Asia are difficult concepts to define because of the changing nature of international law and the wariness of Asian states of encroachments on their sovereignty. Despite this difficulty, the increasing pressure of international custom through documents such as the recent NGO-proposed Charter is moving Asian states toward creating an organization to define and protect human rights. NGOs and states must therefore accommodate each other to some extent, if such an organization is to come into existence.
>
> (Harris 2000: 21)

The Asian emphasis on harmony within the family and within the state, along with more pronounced support for communitarian values, has been a frequent debate amongst scholars (Bauer and Bell 1999). Some argue that such characteristically Asian values tend to conflict with the Western-style support for 'individual' rights. There are others who contest any easy contrast between Western and Asian approaches:

> I have disputed the usefulness of a grand contrast between Asian and European values. There is a lot we can learn from studies of values in Asia and Europe, but they do not support or sustain the thesis of a grand dichotomy.

---

99 As required by the African Charter on the Rights and Welfare of the Child, article 47(3).

Contemporary ideas of political and personal liberty and rights have taken their present form relatively recently, and it is hard to see them as "traditional" commitments of Western cultures. There are important antecedents of those commitments in the form of the advocacy of tolerance and individual freedom, but those antecedents can be found plentifully in Asian as well as Western cultures.

The recognition of diversity within different cultures is extremely important in the contemporary world, since we are constantly bombarded by oversimple generalizations about "Western civilization," "Asian values," "African cultures," and so on. These unfounded readings of history and civilization are not only intellectually shallow, they also add to the divisiveness of the world in which we live.

(Sen 1997: 30)

There are a growing number of NGOs in Asia devoted to the promotion and protection of human rights, for example, the Asian Centre for Human Rights based in New Delhi, India. This centre maintains a particular focus on India, Sri Lanka, Bangladesh, Nepal and the Philippines. There are also two organizations based in Hong Kong. One is the Asian Human Rights Commission (AHRC), founded in 1986 by a group of jurists and human rights activists. This is an independent, non-governmental body, which seeks to promote greater awareness and realization of human rights in the Asian region and to mobilise Asian and international public opinion to obtain relief and redress for the victims of human rights violations. A related organization, the Asian Legal Resource Centre, holds general consultative status with the UN's ECOSOC. The aims of such bodies have been further strengthened by a declaration of an Asian Human Rights Charter on 17 May 1998 in the city of Kwangju in South Korea, at a meeting jointly organised by the Asian Human Rights Commission in Hong Kong and the Kwangju Citizens' Solidarity group. The occasion also marked the 50th anniversary of the UN's Universal Declaration of Human Rights 1948 and the commemoration of the Kwangju Massacre (18 May 1980).[100] This Charter is a significant step along the way to bringing Asia into line with the rest of the world's approach to international human rights protection. It is interesting to note that the Asian Human Rights Charter suggests that although the protection of human rights should be pursued at the international, regional, national and local levels, '[t]he primary responsibility for the protection of rights is that of states, therefore priority should be given to the enhancement of state capacity to fulfil this obligation.'[101] It also

---

100 A pro-democracy uprising that ended when South Korean soldiers opened fire. Official estimates of resulting deaths are around 500, though NGOs and human rights groups have estimated there may have been as many as 2,000 killed.

101 Asian Human Rights Charter 1998, para. 16.1.

suggested there should be an inter-state Convention on Human Rights formulated in regional forums with the collaboration of national and regional NGOs, to be enforced by an international Commission or Court.[102] As regards children's rights, the Asian Human Rights Charter states the following:

CHILDREN

10.1 As with women, their oppression takes many forms, the most pervasive of which are child labour; sexual slavery; child pornography; the sale and trafficking of children; prostitution; sale of organs; conscription into drug trafficking; the physical, sexual and psychological abuse of children within families; discrimination against children with HIV/AIDS; forced religious conversion of children; the displacement of children with and without their families by armed conflicts; discrimination; and environmental degradation. An increasing number of children are forced to live on the streets of Asian cities and are deprived of the social and economic support of families and communities.

10.2 Widespread poverty, lack of access to education and social disloca-tion in rural areas are among the causes of the trends which increase the vulnerability of children. Long-established forms of exploitation and abuse, such as bonded labour or the use of children for begging or sexual gratification are rampant. Female infanticide due to patriarchal gender preference and female genital mutilation are widely practised in some Asian countries.

10.3 Asian states have failed dismally to look after children and provide them with even the bare means of subsistence or shelter. We call on Asian states to ratify and implement the Convention on the Rights of the Child. We also call on communities to take the responsibility for monitoring violations of children.s rights and to press for the implementation of the UN Convention in appropriate ways in their own social contexts.

(Asian Human Rights Charter 1998, paras 10.1 to 10.3)

2.5.2.4 Human rights protection in the Americas

The inter-American human rights system is derived from the American Declaration of the Rights and Duties of Man in Bogotá, Colombia, in April 1948. This was followed by the creation of the Inter-American Commission on Human Rights (IACHR) in 1959, which has its headquarters in Washington, DC. The IACHR is an autonomous organ of the Organization of American States (OAS). It represents all of the member states of the OAS. It has seven members who act independently without representing any particular country. The members of the

---

102 Ibid., para. 16.2.

IACHR are elected by the General Assembly of the OAS. Its mandate is prescribed in the OAS Charter, the American Convention on Human Rights 1969 and the Commission's Statute. There is also an American Court of Human Rights, which is also an organ of the OAS. In the 1960s the IACHR started to conduct 'country visits' to monitor human rights protection, and examined complaints or petitions regarding specific cases of human rights violations. The case reports of the IACHR can be found in the Annual Reports of the Commission, or independently by country.[103] The American Convention on Human Rights ('The Pact of San José, Costa Rica') appeared in 1969 and entered into force on 18 July 1978. It has been ratified by 25 countries.[104] The Convention has not been ratified by Canada, nor by some of the English-speaking Caribbean nations. The United States signed the Convention but has never ratified it. Trinidad and Tobago deposited a denunciation of the Convention in 1998.[105] The IACHR's publication of reports occurs where states have not responded satisfactorily to an initial report made confidentially to the state challenged in the petition. As an alternative to the publication of a second report, the IACHR can opt instead to refer the matter to the American Court of Human Rights. This decision is made on the basis of the best interests of human rights in the Commission's judgment.

The 'Pact of San José' provides protection of civil and political rights, including the right to life:

1. Every person has the right to have his life respected. This right shall be protected by law and, in general, from the moment of conception. No one shall be arbitrarily deprived of his life.

(American Convention on Human Rights, article 4(1))

This provision reflects beliefs concerning abortion, perhaps not an unsurprising result given that the Convention was drafted by predominantly Roman Catholic countries. There is also one provision specifically addressed to the rights of the child:

---

103 For the *Annual Reports of the Inter-American Commission on Human Rights*, see http://www.cidh.oas.org/annual.eng.htm (accessed 31 October 2009).

104 Argentina, Barbados, Brazil, Bolivia, Chile, Colombia, Costa Rica, Dominica, Dominican Republic, Ecuador, El Salvador, Grenada, Guatemala, Haiti, Honduras, Jamaica, Mexico, Nicaragua, Panama, Paraguay, Peru, Suriname, Trinidad and Tobago, Uruguay and Venezuela.

105 Following a decision of the Judicial Committee of the Privy Council – *Pratt and Morgan v. Attorney General for Jamaica* [1994] 2 AC 1 – Trinidad and Tobago denounced the Convention on the basis that the delay in the time taken for appeal processes to the Inter-American Court of Human Rights in capital punishment cases was outside of the time frame required by the Privy Council's decision to dispose of such cases without such delay, constituting cruel and unusual punishment.

Every minor child has the right to the measures of protection required by his condition as a minor on the part of his family, society, and the state.

(American Convention on Human Rights, article 19)

In contrast to the comprehensive list of civil and political rights protected there is only one cursory article addressed to economic, social and cultural rights.[106] This latter weakness in the exposition of second generation rights was addressed by an Additional Protocol to the American Convention on Human Rights in the area of Economic, Social and Cultural Rights (the 'Protocol of San Salvador'), opened for signature in San Salvador, El Salvador, on 17 November 1988. There has also been a second Protocol to the American Convention on Human Rights to Abolish the Death Penalty, adopted at Asunción, Paraguay, on 8 June 1990. The American Convention had already constrained the circumstances in which the death penalty could be imposed: for the most serious crimes; no reinstatement once abolished; not to be used for political offences or common crimes; not to be used against those aged under 18 or over 70, or against pregnant women.[107] The Protocol formalises state parties' commitment not to impose capital punishment in any peacetime circumstance.

---

106 Article 26 (Progressive Development). 'The States Parties undertake to adopt measures, both internally and through international co-operation, especially those of an economic and technical nature, with a view to achieving progressively, by legislation or other appropriate means, the full realization of the rights implicit in the economic, social, educational, scientific, and cultural standards set forth in the Charter of the Organization of American States as amended by the Protocol of Buenos Aires.'

107 Article 4(2)–(5).

Chapter 3

The United Nations Convention on the Rights of the Child

3.1 Introduction

The United Nations Convention on the Rights of the Child 1989 (CRC) is in many ways distinctive amongst international treaties and unique in terms of international law generally. It was produced after a lengthy drafting process that started in 1978. The participation of non-governmental organizations (NGOs) in both the drafting process and the reporting mechanism is also significant. Another remarkable feature has been the way in which states have been eager to sign and ratify the CRC. On the first day the CRC was opened for signature (26 January 1990), no less than 61 states parties signed, somewhat of a record for an international treaty. The CRC entered into force in international law on 2 September 1990. A remarkable feature of the CRC is quite simply the near-global ratification it has received. There are 193 parties to the CRC; only Somalia and the United States remain to ratify it (see section 3.6). Detrick, who has provided a detailed and authoritative annotation of each of the substantive articles of the CRC, concluded:

> While the Convention on the Rights of the Child may not be the last – or complete – word on children's rights, it is the first universal instrument of a legally binding nature to comprehensively address those rights. As such, it forms a universal benchmark on the rights of the child – a benchmark against which all future claims for evolution will and must be answered.
>
> (Detrick 1999: 721)

The CRC contains not only civil and political rights ('first generation rights') but also social, economic and cultural rights ('second generation rights'). It is the first, comprehensive, *rights-based* international treaty specifically constructed to protect and enhance the position of children. It marks a step change in the international law of children's rights. Prior to the CRC, the international community had begun to recognise the child at least as a legitimate 'object' of international law. However, the CRC goes further and recognises the child as a more active 'subject' of international law who can be a holder of rights and participate in important decision making.

The CRC is a good example of the 'globalization' process as applied in the international legal realm, the worldwide convergence of normative legal standards. In its relatively short existence, it has established itself as the central international instrument on children's rights and has influenced the operation of international, regional and domestic law and policy. It can be reasonably claimed that the appearance of the CRC justifies the study of 'international child law' as a discrete subject in its own right. The CRC does more than establish an authoritative text of children's rights; it has also provided the international community with a powerful vehicle to institute programmes of action and shape policy initiatives to further advance their practical implementation. However, as will be seen, the CRC, along with the machinery it has established and the way in which it has been received by the international community, has not been immune from defects and weaknesses.

3.2 Background and history

The Declaration of the Rights of the Child of 1924, emanating from the old League of Nations, was in fact the first human rights document approved by an inter-governmental institution and preceded the Universal Declaration of Human Rights itself by 24 years. The Declaration of 1924 was merely a non-binding resolution of the League of Nations, though it carried significant moral force. It was reaffirmed by the League of Nations in 1934. In 1959, the General Assembly of the United Nations unanimously adopted a new text of the Declaration of the Rights of the Child, containing 10 major principles. This document did not have international legal binding force either, but its *unanimous* adoption by the General Assembly legitimated its persuasive authority. The language used in the text of the Declaration of 1959 reflects the conception of a child as more than merely a passive recipient of international humanitarian aid, but rather as an active participant in the enjoyment of human rights and freedoms.

However, the states that accepted the Declaration of 1959 also opposed the creation of a legally binding treaty on the subject of children's rights. Interest in such a treaty was not to arise until 20 years later when the UN General Assembly proclaimed 1979 as the 'International Year of the Child'. In 1978, Poland submitted a draft text for a Convention on the Rights of the Child. Various states, parties took the view that the Polish text merely replicated the Declaration of 1959 and did not provide an adequate update given the changes in social, economic and cultural development that had occurred in the previous 20 years. Furthermore, it was thought that the revision of the 1959 principles was worded too vaguely for a convention that was now intended to be legally binding. In 1979, the United Nations Commission on Human Rights (UNCHR)[1] organised an open-ended

---

1 The United Nations *Commission* on Human Rights (UNCHR) was abolished and replaced by the United Nations Human Rights *Council* (UNHRC) in 2006, in part because the former body had been discredited for including countries with poor human rights records: see further, section 2.5.1.1.

working group to review and expand the original Polish text. Any of the 43 states that were then represented in the UNCHR (there are now 53 states) could participate; other UN members could send observers and contribute from the floor, and intergovernmental organizations could also contribute. NGOs could also send observers but with no absolute right to speak, but their requests to take the floor were rarely refused (Detrick 1999). The working group adopted a principle of consensus working, so that no votes were taken during the course of the CRC's drafting. This was to encourage as many states to ratify as possible. A report was issued on each of the working group's sessions and discussed by UNCHR, and in turn through the Economic and Social Council (ECOSOC) and by the General Assembly. The working group held 11 sessions between 1979 and 1988. The industrialised countries were over-represented in the drafting process, giving rise to criticisms that the CRC was a 'Northern' oriented document. However, there were active contributions from some of the developing countries, in particular Algeria, Argentina, Senegal and Venezuela, and in 1988 there was a 'sudden last minute surge of delegates from the South, many from States with Islamic law' (Cantwell 1992: 23). The general thaw in East–West relations in the mid-1980s made a significant difference to the atmosphere of debate in these working group sessions. In the early 1980s, the delegations working on the drafts of the CRC and the Convention against Torture were working, literally, along the corridor from each other, and on occasion the delegations traded concessions in their respective groups.

> The NGOs' contributions were in many respects remarkable. It is generally acknowledged in the international community that the NGOs had a direct and indirect impact on [the CRC] that is without parallel in the history of drafting international instruments.
>
> (Cantwell 1992: 24)

The *ad hoc* group of NGOs was able to identify no less than 13 substantive articles for which they claimed primary responsibility, and a further similar number of articles to which they had a less direct but nevertheless important input. Although every clause of the CRC was fully debated, Cantwell (1992: 26) has identified four key areas of principal controversy that occurred during the drafting process: (i) the definition of the minimum age of the child (article 1); (ii) freedom of religion (article 14); (iii) adoption (article 21); and (iv) the age at which children should be permitted to participate in armed conflict (article 38). The working group finally adopted a text in December 1988 and it was then transmitted to the General Assembly for approval and adoption through the UNCHR and ECOSOC. After 10 years of negotiation the CRC emerged, its wording clearly influenced by the Universal Declaration of Human Rights of 1948 and the two (legally binding) International Covenants issued in 1966. The UN General Assembly unanimously adopted the CRC on 20 November 1989.

It was opened for signature on 26 January 1990. The CRC entered into force on 2 September 1990.[2]

There are two elements that go towards the explanation of how children's issues emerged at the top of the international agenda in the 1990s (Black 1996): first, the movement for children's rights, culminating in the CRC in 1989 (see section 1.2.1.1); and second, the child survival campaign resulting in the World Summit for Children in 1990. The latter was concerned mainly with health and other issues relating to children. In September 1990, a large gathering of world leaders – 71 heads of state and 88 other senior officials, mostly at ministerial level – assembled at the United Nations in New York. The summit adopted a Declaration on the Survival, Protection and Development of Children and a Plan of Action for Implementing the Declaration in the 1990s.[3] The Declaration and Plan of Action contained a number of targets for improving both the survival of children and their opportunities for positive growth and development. These included the reduction of infant and under-five child mortality, the reduction of maternal mortality, the reduction of severe and moderate malnutrition among under-five children, universal access to safe drinking water, greater food supply and sanitary means of sewage disposal, universal access to basic education, the completion of primary education, the reduction of the adult illiteracy rate and the improved protection of children in difficult circumstances.

3.3 The UN Convention on the rights of the child

The following sections focus in some detail on the institutional framework and the processes and principles of the CRC. The Committee on the Rights of the Child (CtRC) is the key body created by the CRC to monitor the progress made by states parties. The CRC does not contain provisions to create a court-like forum following the model of the European Court of Human Rights established under the European Convention on Human Rights. The sole sanction lies in the reporting procedures set out in the Convention. Four of the eight human rights treaty bodies (see generally, section 2.5.1.2) – the Human Rights Committee (CCPR), the Committee on the Elimination of Racial Discrimination (CERD), the Committee Against Torture (CAT) and the Committee on the Elimination of Discrimination Against Women (CEDAW) – do have petitioning procedures,

---

2 Thirty days after the deposit of the 20th instrument of ratification or accession: see CRC, article 49(1). The difference between ratification and accession (as regards the CRC) is that those initially 'signing' must ratify whereas states that have not signed 'accede'. The act of signature does not bind the party to ratify, though in practice this does usually follow. However, the act of signature on its own is not without legal effect. Such a state is bound not to do anything that would defeat the object and purpose of the relevant treaty until the state has made its intention not to ratify clear: see article 18 of the Vienna Convention on the Law of Treaties 1969.

3 Available: <http://www.unicef.org/wsc/declare.htm> (accessed 3 November 2009).

and it is likely that children's advocates in the future will want to advance the case for the development of more robust complaints procedures under the CRC and its two Optional Protocols. Indeed, in an oral statement made by the current chair of the CtRC – Ms Yanghee Lee of the Republic of Korea[4] – to the Third Committee (Social, Humanitarian and Cultural) (see section 2.4.1) of the General Assembly, she reported:

> [T]he Committee has furthermore given consideration to the NGO initiative of creating an individual complaints mechanism through the adoption of an Optional Protocol to the Convention. The Committee has given close attention to this issue and considers that such a procedure would significantly contribute to the overall protection of children's rights. The Committee looks forward to any discussions that may be initiated in this regard and notes that the establishment of an individual complaints mechanism would be in line with the mechanisms that exist or are envisaged for all other human rights treaties.
>
> (Lee 2008: 4)

However, it should be noted that at present there is no individual complaint or petition remedy available under the CRC, though the CtRC does recommend from time to time that children or their representatives refer to other treaty bodies to pursue such remedies in appropriate cases.[5]

3.3.1 The Committee on the Rights of the Child (CtRC)[6]

The CRC provides for the establishment of a specialist CtRC, the purpose of which is to examine the progress made by states in achieving the realization of the obligations established under the CRC.[7] There was originally a Committee of 10 child law and policy experts elected by the states parties. Members of the CtRC serve in their 'personal capacity'; they do not hold a mandate from their respective countries. An equitable geographical distribution and representation of the principal legal systems is taken into consideration in their selection.[8] The membership of the Committee was increased to 18 by an amendment to

---

4 Professor Yanghee Lee has been a member of the CtRC since 2003 and has served as its Chair since May of 2007. She was re-elected as Chair of the Committee in May 2009. Her membership term will expire on 28 February 2013.

5 See 'Overview of working methods of the Committee on the Rights of the Child', CtRC website. Available: <http://www2.ohchr.org/english/bodies/crc/workingmethods.htm> (accessed 4 November 2009).

6 The CtRC's website: <http://www2.ohchr.org/english/bodies/crc/index.htm> (accessed 3 November 2009).

7 See CRC, article 43.

8 CRC, article 43(2).

the CRC[9] that came into force in 2003. The Committee has a small permanent secretariat at the Office of the High Commissioner for Human Rights (OHCHR) in Geneva. Each member of the CtRC, like the Committees of the other seven human rights treaty bodies (see Chapter 2, Table 2.1), is an independent expert of 'high moral standing and recognised competence in the field' and not a delegate acting under a national mandate. CtRC's primary function is to receive and comment upon the states parties' periodic reports. It meets in Geneva for three sessions each year, normally in January, May and September. The CtRC held its first session in October 1991.[10]

The CtRC also publishes its interpretation of the content of human rights provisions in the form of 'General Comments'. It also holds, in accordance with its rules of procedure,[11] a 'Day of General Discussion' on a thematic issue each year on the first Friday of its September session. These days of discussion are public meetings open to representatives of states parties, UN agencies and bodies, NGOs, national human rights institutions, professional groups, academics, youth groups and other interested parties. The CtRC sometimes chooses to develop a General Comment from an article, provision or theme that has been discussed earlier in one of its General Days of Discussion. It has in the past also published 'Recommendations/Decisions' (Recommendations Nos 1–8, 1998–2005), but none of the latter have appeared since 2005. In its early years the members of the CtRC undertook some informal visits to states parties. These were discontinued in 1997 but were reinstated in 2003.

3.3.2 The reporting process under the CRC

Each of the Committee's three annual sessions comprises a 1-week pre-sessional meeting and a 3-week plenary meeting. The legal framework for the reporting process is contained in articles 43–45 of the CRC and in the CtRC's Rules of Procedure (Committee on the Rights of the Child 2005) that have been established under article 43(8) of the CRC. The Secretary-General provides the necessary staff and administrative facilities to service the work of the CtRC. There is a primary legal duty for states parties to submit reports to the CtRC both

---

9 CRC, article 50. In the 4 months following the communication of the proposal of amendment, less than one third of the States Parties indicated that they favoured a conference of States Parties for the purpose of considering and voting upon the proposals in accordance with article 50(1) of the Convention. Consequently the 'conference' referred to in article 50(1) of the Convention was not convened.

10 At the time of writing the 2010 sessions planned were: the 53rd session, 11–29 January 2010; the 54th session, 24 May–11 June 2010; and the 55th session, 13 September–1 October 2010.

11 Rules of Procedure, r.75 states that: 'In order to enhance a deeper understanding of the content and implications of the Convention, the Committee may devote one or more meetings of its regular sessions to a general discussion on one specific article of the Convention or related subject.'

on the *measures* they have adopted to give effect to the CRC and on the *progress* made on the enjoyment of those rights.[12] The 'initial report' must be submitted within 2 years of the date the CRC entered into force for that state and thereafter every 5 years. The text of article 44 emphasises that these reports should contain 'sufficient' information to provide the CtRC with a 'comprehensive' understanding of its implementation of the CRC, but need not repeat basic data in subsequent periodic reporting cycles. Since 2002, the guidance advises that reports should not exceed 120 standard pages.[13] The CtRC devotes 1 day (two meetings of 3 hours each) to its public examination of states party reports. If a state submits a report that falls below that standard, the CtRC may request additional information, indicating the time limit within which this should be supplied.[14] The CtRC has a wide discretion to request 'further information relevant to the implementation of the Convention' and may also request 'additional reports or information in the intervening period [between the regular reporting periods]'.[15] The CtRC, through the Secretary-General, must also indicate 'the form and contents of reports or information' to be supplied to it.[16] This has been done in the form of a document setting out 'General Guidelines' regarding the form and content of initial and subsequent periodic reports to be submitted by states parties and for the participation of partners (e.g. NGOs) in the pre-sessional working groups (Committee on the Rights of the Child 1991, 1995, 1995a).

There is nothing in the CRC itself to indicate any consequence or sanction for the non-submission of reports. However, the rules of procedure state that non-submission will result in the CtRC sending a 'reminder' warning letter to the states party concerned, and if the party remains recalcitrant the Committee can report this to the General Assembly.[17] A states party submitting a report will be notified of the date, duration and place of the session at which its report will be examined, and representatives of the state will be invited to attend in order to answer questions put by the Committee.[18] The CtRC welcomes state delegations that have significant involvement in the strategic decisions relating to the rights of the child on the basis that this is likely to have greater impact on policy-making and implementation activities. The CtRC usually appoints two of its members as 'country rapporteurs' to lead discussions with individual states party delegations. Under article 45(a) of CRC, the 'specialised agencies' (see section 2.4.1), the United Nations Children's Fund (UNICEF) and 'other UN organs' are entitled to be represented where the Committee are considering the implementation of any

---

12 CRC, article 44.
13 Decided by CtRC at its 30th session in 2002, CtRC/C/118.
14 Provisional Rules of Procedure, r.69.
15 Ibid., r.66(2).
16 Ibid., r.66(3).
17 Ibid., r.67.
18 Ibid., r.68.

provisions of the CRC falling within their mandates. The Committee may also invite the UN bodies and 'other competent bodies as it may consider appropriate' to provide expert advice and to submit reports in areas falling within their activities. It is made clear in the CRC's *travaux préparatoires* that 'other competent bodies' includes NGOs in this context (Detrick 1992: 25), a point also made clear in the CtRC's 'Guidelines for the participation of partners' (Committee on the Rights of the Child 1995a). Article 45(a) is a key provision as it provides the international legal authority for NGOs to be consulted and contribute to the Committee's examination of the 'official' state report. The Committee has acknowledged the key role of the coalition of NGOs in supporting the reporting process: see General Comment No. 5 (2003: para. 59).

The Committee must itself submit reports about its activities every 2 years to the General Assembly through ECOSOC,[19] and the procedural rules add that the Committee may also 'submit such other reports as it considers appropriate'.[20] The Committee may also recommend to the General Assembly that the Secretary-General undertake on its behalf a study on a specific issue relating to children's rights. The Committee is empowered under article 45(d) of CRC to make 'suggestions and general recommendations' based on the information received via the reporting process.

There is also a comparable reporting regime in relation to the obligations imposed by the Optional Protocol to the Convention on the Rights of the Child on the sale of children, child prostitution and child pornography (OPSC), and the Optional Protocol to the Convention on the Rights of the Child on the involvement of children in armed conflict (OPAC) (see section 3.7).[21] It is required that each states party must submit an initial report within 2 years following the entry into force for that states party, providing information on the measures it has taken to implement the provisions of the Protocol(s). Following the submission of this 'comprehensive' initial report, states parties are then obliged to submit any further information with respect to the implementation of the Protocol(s), in accordance with article 44 of CRC. States parties to the Optional Protocol(s) who are not parties to the main CRC[22] must submit subsequent reports every 5 years. In 2008 and 2009, the CtRC had considered a total of 59 state reports under the main Convention and under the two Optional Protocols. Table 3.1 shows the numerical throughput in each of the sessions from January 2008 to September 2009.

It can be seen from Table 3.1 that the CtRC was dealing with around ten state reports in each of its three sessions held in January, May and September every year. While it is still dealing separately with a number of 'initial reports' in relation

---

19 CRC, article 44(5).
20 Rules of Procedure, r.64.
21 See OPAC, article 8 and OPSC, article 12.
22 The United States is not a party to CRC, but it has ratified both OPSC and OPAC.

Table 3.1 Numbers of state reports considered by the Committee on the Rights of the Child, 2008, 2009, under CRC and the two Optional Protocols

Session No.	Month	CRC	OPSC	OPAC	Totals
2008					
47th session	January	2	3	5	(10)
48th session	May	5	2	3	(10)
49th session	September	3	4	3	(10)
(2008 total)		(10)	(9)	(11)	(30)
2009					
50th session	January	5	2	3	(10)
51st session	May	6	2	2	(10)
52nd session	September	5	2	2	(9)
(2009 total)		(16)	(6)	(7)	(29)
Totals (2008 + 2009)		26	15	18	59

to the two Optional Protocols (see section 3.7), this is likely to remain the pattern. However, as explained earlier, once a state has submitted its initial report under the Optional Protocol(s) further periodic reports will be submitted along with that state's reporting obligation under the main convention, a situation that is likely to assist a more efficient report-processing system.

In practice, a state's report will first be sent to the Secretariat of the Committee at the OHCHR in Geneva (see Figure 3.1). The Committee will examine it at the next available session and has attempted to examine reports within 1 year of receipt. The Committee will then seek written information from other sources, such as NGOs and inter-governmental organizations. The Committee holds a pre-sessional working group, which is a private session composed of Committee members, where an initial review of the states party's report is carried out. NGOs and inter-governmental organization representatives may be invited to the pre-sessional working group.

> The Committee has systematically and strongly encouraged NGOs and NHRIs (National Human Rights Institutions) to submit reports, documentation or other information in order to provide it with a comprehensive picture and expertise as to how the Convention is being implemented in a particular country. The Committee welcomes written information from international, regional, national and local organizations. Information may be submitted by individual NGOs or national coalitions or committees of NGOs.
>
> (NGO Group 1998: 3)

The working group will then prepare a 'list of issues' that is submitted to the states party. Governments are requested to respond to these questions in writing

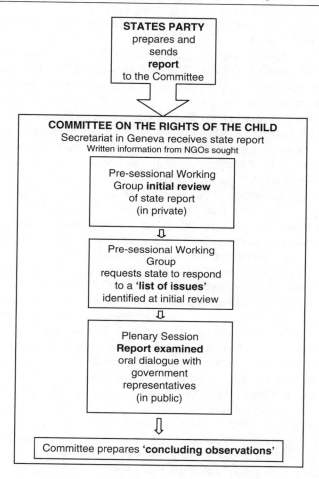

Figure 3.1 The reporting process of the Committee on the Rights of the Child.

before the plenary session. During its plenary session, which is held in public, the Committee examines the report in the presence of the government representatives, who are invited to respond to the questions and comments made by Committee members. After this dialogue, the Committee prepares, in a closed meeting, its 'concluding observations', which summarise the main points of discussion and pinpoint the key issues requiring further action by the states party. Concluding observations usually contain the following elements: an introduction; positive aspects including the progress achieved; factors impeding implementation; main subjects for concern; suggestions and recommendations addressed to the states party. The concluding observations are made public on the last day of a CtRC session during the adoption of the session report. It is assumed that the concerns indicated in the CtRC's concluding observations will be addressed in the country's next periodic report (Committee on the Rights of the Child, 2009).

A significant weakness of the CtRC, as with some of the other human rights treaty bodies, has been the delays in managing the states party reporting process. This is all the more serious in the context of the CtRC because, as explained earlier, the reporting process remains the core sanctioning mechanism available under the CRC. The problem of delay is twofold. First, there has been delay by the CtRC itself in managing the reporting process. Second, there have been delays by some states parties in producing their initial and periodic reports. As regards the former problem, the CtRC has made some efforts to manage the reporting process more efficiently. In January 2000, the CtRC increased its workload to examine 27 reports per year, rather than 18 as previously. Several of the Committee's 'Recommendations' (Recommendation No. 3, 2002; Recommendation No. 4, 2002; Recommendation No. 5, 2003) to date have been concerned with trying to address the delays experienced in the reporting cycle.

In January 2002, the Committee recommended a system of combined reports for states where the reporting cycle had been delayed. In May 2002, the Committee recommended that reports should not be over lengthy and should focus more on key developments and progress in actual implementation. In January 2003, the Committee added an additional rule requiring a combined second and third report where the second periodic report was due between 1 and 2 years following the dialogue with the Committee about its initial report. In September 2003, another recommendation acknowledged that there was a 2-year delay between the submission of reports and consideration by the Committee, and noted there were 13 initial reports and around 100 second periodic reports overdue (Recommendation No. 5, 2003). It also acknowledged the extra workload caused by the reporting procedures under the two Optional Protocols that would be expected from January 2004. The CtRC proposed to work in two chambers in order to clear a target of 48 reports a year rather than 27 as previously (Recommendation No. 6, 2003). However, it can be seen from Table 3.1 that, 5 years on, this target had not been achieved; the throughput of report consideration by CtRC, despite these organizational reforms, is still running at around 30 each year. As regards the second problem, to ensure that states parties submit their reports on time, there has been some effort to rectify the situation.

At its twenty-ninth session (see CRC/C/114, paragraph 561), the Committee decided to send a letter to all States parties whose initial reports were due in 1992 and 1993, requesting them to submit that report within one year. In June 2003, similar letters were sent to three States parties whose initial reports were due in 1994 and never submitted. The Committee further decided to inform those States parties in the same letter that should they not report within one year, the Committee would consider the situation of child rights in the State in the absence of the initial report, as foreseen in the Committee's 'Overview of the reporting procedures' (CRC/C/33, paras. 29–32) and in light of rule 67 of the Committee's provisional rules of procedure (CRC/C/4).

(Committee on the Rights of the Child 2009)

The twofold problem of delay – prevarication in the submission of country reports, and the CtRC's own inability to process work expeditiously – is not unknown in relation to some of the other human rights treaty bodies. If the problem is not successfully managed, the impact is likely to be corrosive of the underlying aims of the CRC and the resulting demoralization within the international community may threaten the legitimacy of this type of international human rights instrument.

3.4 CRC and the United Kingdom

This section examines the United Kingdom's relationship with the CRC and its record in the CtRC's reporting process. The United Kingdom signed the CRC on 19 April 1990 and ratified it on 16 December 1991. As explained in Chapter 2, the CRC came into force generally in international law on 2 September 1990, in accordance with article 49(1), following the deposit of the twentieth instrument of ratification or accession. It came into force in respect of the United Kingdom on 15 January 1992 in accordance with article 49(2).[23]

3.4.1 The United Kingdom's reservations and declarations

Upon signature, the United Kingdom made the following reservation:

> The United Kingdom reserves the right to formulate, upon ratifying the Convention, any reservations or interpretative declarations which it might consider necessary.
>
> (UN Treaty Collection: http://treaties.un.org/)

Upon ratification, the United Kingdom made two declarations in order to clarify the definition of a 'child' and 'parents' respectively:

> The United Kingdom interprets the Convention as applicable only following a live birth.
> The United Kingdom interprets the references in the Convention to 'parents' to mean only those persons who, as a matter of national law, are treated as parents. This includes cases where the law regards a child as having only one parent, for example where a child has been adopted by one person only

---

23 'For each State ratifying or acceding to the Convention after the deposit of the twentieth instrument of ratification or accession, the Convention shall enter into force on the thirtieth day after the deposit by such State of its instrument of ratification or accession'. (CRC, article 49(2)).

and in certain cases where a child is conceived other than as a result of sexual intercourse by the woman who gives birth to it and she is treated as the only parent.

(UN Treaty Collection: http://treaties.un.org/)

The former interpretative declaration ensured that the United Kingdom's implementation of the CRC would not vest any rights in the foetus. Article 1 of the CRC defines a 'child' to mean 'every human being below the age of eighteen years unless under the law applicable to the child, majority is attained earlier'. This definition, however, although setting the upper age limit of 18 years to define a 'child', fails to specify when childhood begins. In fact, this was a deliberate diplomatic omission as this precise point had been a highly contentious issue during the drafting of the CRC where some countries with anti-abortion agendas wished to ensure that the 'right to life' was extended to the human foetus (Detrick 1992). The omission of any definitive reference to the point at which childhood commences allowed countries like the United Kingdom to ratify the CRC and, if they chose to do so, to make a suitable declaration of their position to clarify this matter and ensure that their ratification would not have the legal effect of undermining their abortion laws. On the other hand, a clause in the preamble[24] of the CRC provided some encouragement to nations that were more driven by an anti-abortion agenda. The latter declaration concerning the definition of 'parents' ensures that the United Kingdom's adoption legislation, that allows single persons to adopt a child, and the conferment of legal 'parent' status (i.e. 'parental responsibility') on single mothers who choose to conceive a child by way of artificial insemination by donor (AID), does not conflict with the CRC.

Along with these two declarations, the United Kingdom also made four reservations upon ratification. One of these concerned 'children's hearings' (a Scottish tribunal system that had dealt for some years in juvenile justice matters). Article 37(d) of the CRC provides children with rights of access to legal and other appropriate assistance and the right to challenge the legality of any deprivation of liberty before a court or other competent, independent and impartial authority, and to a prompt decision on any such action. The United Kingdom reserved its right, with respect to article 37(d), to continue its operation of children's hearings, an operation that in some cases involved a child being detained for up to 7 days prior to attending the hearing where legal representation at the hearing was not allowed, though the tribunal's decisions were subject to appeal. The text of the declaration pointed out that '[c]hildren's hearings have proved over the years to be a very effective way of dealing with the problems of children in a less formal, non-adversarial manner.' The United Kingdom withdrew this reservation on 18 April 1997. The reservation was rendered unnecessary by the implementation

---

24 'Bearing in mind that, as indicated in the Declaration of the Rights of the Child [1959], "the child, by reason of his physical and mental immaturity, needs special safeguards and care, including appropriate legal protection, before as well as after birth"'. (Ninth preambular paragraph, CRC).

of the Children (Scotland) Act 1995, which now provides[25] that where a child is deprived of his or her liberty by being kept in a place of safety under a warrant by the Children's Hearing, an appeal to the Sheriff in respect of the issue of the warrant by the Children's Hearing must be disposed of within 3 days of the lodging of the appeal. In addition, there is an appeal from the Sheriff's decision to that of the Sheriff Principal. There is therefore prompt access to a local court and a local appellate court with access to legal representation and legal aid. The more comprehensive and direct system of appeals to a court allows access to legal aid and representation.

A second reservation made upon ratification concerned young workers. UK employment legislation used to treat persons under the age of 18 but over school-leaving age (i.e. 16- and 17-year-olds) not as 'children', but as 'young people'. Article 32 of the CRC provides that states parties recognise the right of the 'child' to be protected from economic exploitation and in particular exploitation in the employment context. In consequence, the United Kingdom reserved the right to continue to apply article 32 subject to its existing employment legislation.

The United Kingdom withdrew this reservation on 3 August 1999. This reservation had become unnecessary as the United Kingdom had implemented two European Community directives.[26] The withdrawal has also been helped by the United Kingdom's ratification of both the Minimum Age Convention, 1973 (ILO Convention No. 138) and the Elimination of the Worst Forms of Child Labour Convention, 1999 (ILO Convention No. 182).[27]

A third reservation concerned immigration and nationality issues. The United Kingdom reserved the right 'as it may deem necessary from time to time' to apply domestic legislation concerning the entry into, stay in and departure from the United Kingdom of those who do not have the right to enter or remain in the United Kingdom and were not UK citizens. However, following a public consultation in 2008 and legislation that places a duty on the UK Border Agency to keep children safe from harm, the government announced its withdrawal of this reservation, which came into effect on 18 November 2008.

A fourth reservation upon ratification was focused upon article 37(c) concerning the rights of the child deprived of liberty to be treated with humanity and dignity, and in particular that children in places of detention or prisons should not have to share accommodation with adults, unless it was considered in the child's best interests. The United Kingdom reserved a right not to apply article 37(c) of the CRC 'in so far as those provisions require children who are detained to be accommodated separately from adults'. Following a review in 2008 of the arrangements for accommodating children and young persons remanded or sentenced to custody,

---

25 Children (Scotland) Act 1995, section 51.
26 Council Directive 94/33/EC of 22 June 1994 on the protection of young people at work; Council Directive 93/104/EC of 23 November 1993 concerning certain aspects of the organization of working time.
27 This latter ILO Convention is discussed in detail in Chapter 4, section 4.2.3.

the government concluded that all custodial establishments for under-18s in England and Wales were able to comply with the terms of article 37(c), and Scotland and Northern Ireland confirmed that they too no longer needed the reservation. The United Kingdom also withdrew this reservation on 18 November 2008.

A further declaration was deposited on 7 September 1994 by the United Kingdom stating that it reserved its right 'to extend the Convention at a later date to any territory for whose international relations the Government of the United Kingdom is responsible'. In a communication received on this date the United Kingdom indicated that the CRC would apply to:

> Isle of Man, Anguilla, Bermuda, British Virgin Islands, Cayman Islands, Falkland Islands (Malvinas), Hong Kong, Montserrat, Pitcairn, Henderson, Ducie and Oeno Islands, St. Helena, St. Helena Dependencies, South Georgia and the South Sandwich Islands, Turks and Caicos Islands.

In this regard, the Secretary-General received an objection, on 3 April 1995, from the government of Argentina, rejecting the extension of the application of the CRC to the Malvinas Islands, South Georgia and the South Sandwich Islands, and reaffirming its sovereignty over those islands. Finally, in anticipation of the transfer of sovereignty over Hong Kong from the United Kingdom to China scheduled for 1 July 1997, both governments sent communications to the Secretary-General on 10 June 1997 informing him of the transfer. China also notified the Secretary-General that the CRC, with the reservation made by China and the United Kingdom combined, would also apply to the Hong Kong special administrative region.

3.4.2 The United Kingdom's initial report and the CtRC's response (1994–95)

The United Kingdom's obligation to submit its initial report within two years of the date of entry into force for the United Kingdom[28] required a submission before 15 January 1994; it was submitted shortly after that date (United Kingdom 1994).[29] The Committee's concluding observation (CO United Kingdom 1995) appeared on 15 February 1995. The UK government's approach to the presentation of its initial report to the CtRC had been heavily influenced by the perceived achievement of the passage into UK law of the Children Act in 1989 (Kilkelly 1996). The UK's delegation had advanced the view that this Act had not only consolidated several child law related statutes, but was also perceived as a

---

28 CRC, article 44(1)(a).
29 The UK's initial report (CRC/C/11/Add.1) is dated 28 March 1994.

significant restructuring of the United Kingdom's child law regime, in effect providing the United Kingdom with a child law system in advance of the standards set out in the CRC. For example, it was claimed that the welfare 'paramountcy' principle, a key element of the Children Act 1989,[30] was preferable to the 'best interests' principle contained in article 3 of the CRC. The CtRC did not share that view (CO United Kingdom 1995). Indeed, the CtRC had a number of concerns about the United Kingdom's approach. It was concerned about the broad nature of the reservations made upon ratification and questioned whether these were compatible with the object and purpose of the Convention, in particular the reservation concerning nationality and immigration. The CtRC also doubted whether the United Kingdom had an effective and independent coordinating mechanism to implement and monitor the CRC, and suggested the establishment of permanent mechanisms for monitoring the Children Act 1989 and the CRC. It noted the paucity of information on the plight of children in Northern Ireland and the absence of safeguards to prevent the ill-treatment of children under the emergency legislation.

The CtRC was further concerned about implementation of the general principles of the CRC. In particular, the CtRC noted that the 'best interests' principle did not appear in health, education and social security legislation. One further item of concern, revisited in the CtRC's subsequent reports on the United Kingdom, was the persistence of corporal punishment. It was concerned about the imprecise nature of the common law concept of 'reasonable chastisement' (which serves as a defence to the crime of assault) on the basis that it could be interpreted in a subjective and arbitrary manner. The CtRC was equally concerned that private schools were still permitted to administer corporal punishment to children in attendance, a position that seemed to be incompatible with article 28(2) (school discipline administered consistently with human dignity). In general, the administration of juvenile justice in the United Kingdom received a number of criticisms from the CtRC. It noted, for example, the low age of criminal responsibility (8 years[31] in Scotland, 10 years in England and Wales and Northern Ireland) and observed that the national legislation relating to the administration of juvenile justice appeared to be incompatible with articles 37 and 40. The CtRC also suggested

---

30 '(1) When a court determines any question with respect to—
    (a) the upbringing of a child; or (b) the administration of a child's property or the application of any income arising from it, the child's welfare shall be the court's paramount consideration.' (Children Act 1989, section 1).

31 At the time of writing the Scottish Parliament was considering plans to raise the age of criminal responsibility in Scotland to 12 years. See Criminal Justice and Licensing (Scotland) Bill 2009, clause 38. Children between the ages of 8 and 16 can currently be prosecuted at the discretion of the Lord Advocate in Scotland. The policy memorandum on the Bill (above) stated that 'This is considered by many to be contrary to international standards and the United Nations Convention on the Rights of the Child (article 40(3)(a)) which suggests that 12 is the minimum acceptable age at which children should be held accountable for their actions before full (adult) criminal justice proceedings.' (para. 190).

the United Kingdom could do much more to make the provisions and principles of the CRC more widely known to adults and children alike, in accordance with article 42, and suggested that teaching about children's rights should be incorporated into the training curricula of relevant professionals such as teachers, the police, judges, social workers, health workers and personnel in care and detention institutions. Furthermore, greater priority should be given to incorporating the general principles of the CRC, particularly the child's right to make their views known and to have those views given due weight (article 12), into the legislative and administrative measures and in policies undertaken to implement the rights of the child. The CtRC noted the need for the United Kingdom to address, on an urgent basis, the issues of sexual exploitation and drug abuse as they affect children. It also recommended proactive measures for the rights of children belonging to Gypsy and Traveller communities, including their right to education, and that a sufficient number of adequately appointed caravan sites for these communities be secured.

3.4.3 The United Kingdom's second periodic report and the CtRC's response (1999–2002)

The CtRC was equally robust in its criticisms of the United Kingdom's record as outlined in the second periodic report. The due date for the United Kingdom's initial report was 15 January 1994 and consequently, in accordance with article 44, the due date for its second periodic report ought to have been in January 1999. However, the CtRC's concluding observations on that report appeared much later, in October 2002 (CO United Kingdom 2002). The CtRC did note several positive aspects. It welcomed the United Kingdom's withdrawal of two of its reservations (see section 3.4.1 above) made upon ratification: (i) concerning access to legal assistance in children's hearings in Scotland (article 37(d)), withdrawn on 18 April 1997; and (ii) concerning young workers and employment legislation (article 32), withdrawn on 3 August 1999. The CtRC also signalled its approval of the enactment of the Human Rights Act 1998, and the peace process in Northern Ireland which had led to the establishment of a Northern Ireland Human Rights Commission and the appointment of a police ombudsman for Northern Ireland. Furthermore, it approved of the establishment of a Children and Young People's Unit and the development of new child-focused government structures and the completion of the abolition of corporal punishment in schools throughout England, Wales and Scotland.

However, the CtRC had a number of concerns. It expressed concern that there was no formal process to monitor whether new domestic legislation was compatible with the principles and provisions of the CRC. Also, although the CtRC noted the United Kingdom's national objective to halve child poverty by 2010 through locally targeted services for children, it remained concerned that the CRC was not implemented according to the 'maximum extent of ... available resources' of the states party as stipulated by article 4.

The progress of devolution in the United Kingdom had emphasised the greater need for appropriate coordination. The CtRC was concerned that there was as yet no overarching strategy plan based on the CRC to be applied throughout the United Kingdom, though the CRC had been used as a framework in the strategy for children and young people developed by the Welsh Assembly (National Assembly for Wales 2000) and the CtRC welcomed the establishment of an independent Children's Commissioner in Wales.[32] As regards progress on the CRC's 'general principles', the CtRC was concerned that the principle of non-discrimination (article 2) had not been fully implemented for all children in all parts of the United Kingdom and that there was unequal enjoyment of rights, in particular for children with disabilities, children from poor families, Irish and Roma travellers' children, asylum-seeker and refugee children, children belonging to minority groups, children in care, detained children and children aged between 16 and 18 years old. The CtRC had further criticisms to make of the United Kingdom's juvenile justice system, in particular, the frequent use of physical restraint in residential institutions and in custody, as well as the placement of children in juvenile detention and in solitary confinement in prisons. The CtRC welcomed the abolition of corporal punishment in all schools in England and Wales and Scotland following its recommendations in 1995, but remained concerned that the abolition had not yet reached private schools in Northern Ireland. While the Welsh Assembly had adopted regulations prohibiting corporal punishment in all forms of day care, including childminding, this legislation had not yet been extended to other parts of the United Kingdom.

The CtRC expressed concern about the prevalence of child deaths arising from violence and growing levels of neglect within families, in schools, in institutions, in the care system and in detention. It also noted the absence of adequate, systematic follow-up of child deaths and that crimes committed against children below the age of 16 were not recorded. The CtRC recommended the introduction of a system of statutory child death inquiries and the development of a coordinated strategy for the reduction of all forms of violence against children. The CtRC remained concerned about the high rate of teenage pregnancies, the incidence of mental health problems, the rate of suicide and the rising incidence of sexually transmitted diseases among young persons. As regards 'special protection measures', the CtRC expressed concern that the ongoing reform of the asylum and immigration system failed to address the particular needs and rights of asylum-seeking children, despite the establishment in 1994 of the Children's Panel of Advisers.[33] The CtRC was concerned that detention of these children was incompatible with the principles and provisions of the CRC, and that the dispersal system might impede better integration, and that placement in temporary accommodation of children seeking asylum might infringe their basic rights such

32 See Children's Commissioner for Wales Act 2001.
33 The Refugee Council accommodates the panel, a 23-strong team, under Home Office funding.

as access to health or education. The CtRC was 'deeply concerned' that about one third of the annual intake of recruits into the armed forces was below the age of 18 years, that the armed services targeted young people and that those recruited were required to serve for a minimum period of 4 years, increasing to 6 years in the case of very young recruits: see Chapter 8, section 8.1.2.3. The CtRC welcomed the 2001 national plan for safeguarding children from commercial sexual exploitation and other measures to combat the sexual exploitation of children, but remained concerned that trafficking for sexual exploitation was still a problem and that sexually exploited children were still criminalised by law. It recommended the United Kingdom carry out a study on the scope, causes and background of child prostitution, and review its legislation and continue to implement policies and programmes in accordance with the Declaration and Agenda for Action and with the Global Commitment adopted at the 1996 and 2001 World Congresses against Commercial Sexual Exploitation of Children (see Chapter 7). The CtRC was particularly concerned that the age of criminal responsibility was still set at 8 years in Scotland and at 10 years in the rest of the United Kingdom. The CtRC was 'deeply concerned' at the increasing number of children who were being detained in custody as a result of recently increased court powers to issue detention and restraining orders. The CtRC concluded that deprivation of liberty was not being used only as a measure of last resort and for the shortest appropriate period of time, in violation of article 37(b) of the CRC. The CtRC recommended that the United Kingdom establish a system of juvenile justice that fully integrated into its legislation, policies and practice the provisions and principles of the CRC, in particular articles 3 (best interests principle), 37 (no torture or other cruel etc. treatment or punishment), 40 (right of accused to be treated with dignity), and in accordance with the United Nations Standard Minimum Rules for the Administration of Juvenile Justice of 1985 (the 'Beijing Rules'), the United Nations Guidelines for the Prevention of Juvenile Delinquency of 1990 (the 'Riyadh Guidelines'), the United Nations Rules for the Protection of Juveniles Deprived of their Liberty of 1990 (the 'Havana' Rules), and the Vienna Guidelines for Action on Children in the Criminal Justice System of 1997. The CtRC recommended that no child should be tried as an adult, irrespective of the circumstances or the gravity of the offence, and that the privacy of all children in conflict with the law was fully protected consistently with article 40(2)(b)(vii) (accused child to have privacy fully respected) of the CRC.

Finally, the CtRC invited the United Kingdom to submit its next periodic report before the due date established under the Convention for the fourth periodic report (15 January 2009) in the form of a combined third and fourth periodic report. It invited the United Kingdom to submit its combined report 18 months before the due date of the periodic report, on 15 July 2007. It also requested that its next report contain information from all the Overseas Dependent Territories and Crown Dependencies of the United Kingdom of Great Britain and Northern Ireland.

Following this reporting round, the CRC was reviewed by the Westminster Parliament's Joint Committee on Human Rights. The Joint Committee noted that: '[u]nless and until any of its provisions are incorporated ... the role of the

Convention within the United Kingdom will be principally as the source or a set of child centred considerations to be used when evaluating legislation, policy making and administrative action.' However, the Joint Committee clearly shared many of the concerns of the CtRC, for example, about the juvenile justice system and the number of children in custody and those committing suicide.

The Joint Committee also recommended the case for a Children's Commissioner for England.[34] On the reporting process generally, the Joint Committee stated:

> We conclude that the reporting process under the Convention has the potential to provide impetus to develop a culture of respect for children's rights within government, and focus attention on the impact of policy, practice and legislation upon children. The quality of the dialogue between the government and the UN Committee could certainly be improved. Both sides need to give attention to how this might be achieved, but the government is the partner with the resources, and therefore the prime responsibility, to make the principles of the Convention a reality in the lives of children in the UK.
>
> (Joint Committee on Human Rights 2003: para. 115)

3.4.4 The United Kingdom's third and fourth (combined) periodic report and the CtRC's response (2008)

The United Kingdom's combined third and fourth periodic report (United Kingdom 2008) was submitted in February 2008 and the CtRC's concluding observations appeared on 20 October the same year (CO United Kingdom 2008). On the positive side, the CtRC welcomed the United Kingdom's decision to withdraw its two remaining reservations made upon ratification (relating to nationality/immigration and young offenders – see section 3.4.1). It also approved of a number of measures relating to children's rights, for example: the Children's Plan for England of 2007 (Secretary of State for Children, Schools and Families 2007), which directly refers to the provisions and principles of the CRC;[35] and the creation of the Department for Children, Schools and Families (DCSF) along with a Secretary of State with lead responsibility for all policies affecting children in England. It also welcomed the references that the domestic courts had been making to the CRC.[36] The CtRC also noted with appreciation that, since consideration of

---

34 See Children Act 2004, ss. 1–9. The first Children's Commissioner for England, Professor Aynsley-Green, was appointed in March 2005. Maggie Atkinson took over as Children's Commissioner in February 2010.

35 See Secretary of State for Children, Schools and Families, 2007: 159–161.

36 For example, in *Re E (A Child)* [2008] UKHL 66, para. 60, Lord Carswell opined that although the CRC had not been incorporated into domestic law, '[t]he requirement [of the 'best interests' principle in the CRC] is nevertheless a consideration which should properly be taken into account by the state and its emanations in determining upon their actions. It is accordingly a matter which may be relevant in determining whether the actions of the police satisfied the obligations placed upon them by art.3 of the Convention.' See further, section 3.4.5.

its second report in 2002, the United Kingdom had ratified or acceded to a number of human rights instruments.[37]

3.4.4.1 General measures of implementation (articles 4, 42 and 44(6))

The CtRC noted with regret that some of their previous recommendations had not been fully implemented: in particular, recommendations relating to: the incorporation of the CRC in UK law; budgetary allocations to deploy the maximum use of resources; dissemination and awareness of the CRC; non-discrimination; corporal punishment; education; asylum-seekers; and juvenile justice. While welcoming the announced withdrawal of the remaining two reservations (i.e. relating to young offenders and immigration/nationality), the CtRC regretted that the United Kingdom had maintained its reservation with regard to the applicability of article 32 (relating to young workers) to its Overseas Territories and Crown Dependencies. The CtRC welcomed the United Kingdom's efforts to harmonise its legislation with the CRC, particularly its adoption of the Children Act 2004 for England and Wales which, inter alia, created the Children's Commissioner for England, and the enactment of the Childcare Act 2006. However, the CtRC remained concerned that the principles of the Convention were not duly taken into account in all pieces of legislation throughout the country. The CtRC also reiterated its previous calls for a single, high-profile, coordinating mechanism. Despite some welcome initiatives, such as the 'Every Child Matters' initiative in England, the CtRC remained concerned that the CRC was not regularly used as a framework for the development of strategies throughout the United Kingdom. The CtRC welcomed the establishment of independent Children Commissioners in all four devolved regions of the United Kingdom but expressed disappointment that their independence and powers were limited and that these offices had not been established in full compliance with the 'Paris Principles'.[38]

The CtRC recommended that all four Children Commissioners should be independent under the criteria set out in the Paris Principles and that these office-holders should be mandated to receive and investigate complaints from or on behalf of children concerning violation of their rights. In this regard, the CtRC drew attention to its General Comment No. 2 (2002) on the role of independent national human rights institutions in the promotion and protection of the rights of

---

37 OPAC, on 24 June 2003; the Optional Protocol to the Convention against Torture and Other Cruel, Inhuman or Degrading Treatment of Punishment, on 10 December 2003; the Optional Protocol to the Convention on the Elimination of All Forms of Discrimination against Women, on 17 Dec 2004; the 1993 Hague Convention No. 33 on Protection of Children and Cooperation in Respect of Intercountry Adoption, on 27 February 2003; and the Protocol to Prevent, Suppress and Punish Trafficking in Persons, Especially Women and Children, supplementing the United Nations Convention against Transnational Organized Crime, on 9 February 2006.

38 Principles relating to the Status of National Institutions (the 'Paris Principles'). Adopted by General Assembly resolution 48/134 of 20 December 1993.

the child. The CtRC also regretted the lack of any consistent budgetary analysis and 'child rights impact assessment', which made it difficult to identify the extent of expenditure allocated to children across the United Kingdom, and reminded the United Kingdom of its recommendations about deploying maximum resources under article 4, as laid out in its general Day of Discussion (2007). The CtRC recommended that child rights impact assessments should be regularly conducted to evaluate how the allocation of budget is proportionate to the realization of policy developments and the implementation of legislation. The CtRC also reiterated its concern that there was no systematic raising of awareness about the CRC and that levels of knowledge about the CRC were low amongst children, parents and professionals working with children. It repeated its calls for the CRC to be included in the statutory national curriculum to ensure that its principles and values were fully integrated into the structure and practice of all schools. The CtRC also encouraged the United Kingdom to involve civil society in promoting and implementing the CRC, including people's participation in the planning stage of policies as well as in the follow-up to the CtRC's concluding observations and the preparation of the next periodic report.

3.4.4.2 General principles (articles 2, 3, 6 and 12)

The CtRC welcomed the United Kingdom's efforts to mainstream a child's right to non-discrimination (article 2) into its anti-discrimination law (the forthcoming Equality Bill[39]). However, it remained concerned about particular groups of children, whom the CtRC thought might benefit by taking affirmative actions: Roma and Irish travellers' children; migrant, asylum-seeking and refugee children; lesbian, bisexual, gay and transgender children, and children belonging to other minority groups. Worryingly, the CtRC also pointed out the general climate of intolerance and negative public attitudes towards children, especially adolescents, which appears to exist in the United Kingdom, including in the media. The CtRC remained concerned about the lack of integration of the best interests principle (article 3) in legislative and policy matters relating to children, particularly in the areas of juvenile justice, immigration and freedom of movement and peaceful assembly. The CtRC welcomed the introduction of statutory child death reviews in England and Wales, but expressed concern that six more children had died in custody and at the high prevalence of self-harm in custody since its last examination of the United Kingdom. While welcoming the United Kingdom's abolition of the use of plastic baton rounds for riot control in Northern Ireland, the CtRC was concerned that they had been replaced by 'attenuating energy projectiles', whose less harmful nature had not been proven. In addition, the CtRC was concerned at the authorization of taser guns for police officers in England and Wales, and also in Northern Ireland as a pilot project, and that in both cases

---

39 Now the Equality Act 2009 (c.15).

they could be used on children. The CtRC welcomed the arrival of the Childcare Act 2006 which required local authorities to have regard to the views of young children when planning services for children, as well as the requirement on inspectors to consult children when visiting schools and other institutional settings, but remained concerned that there had been little progress in enshrining article 12 in general education law and policy. It approved of the support forums for children's participation, such as the United Kingdom Youth Parliament, Funky Dragon in Wales and the Youth Parliament in Scotland.

3.4.4.3 Civil rights and freedoms (articles 7, 8, 13–17 and 37(a))

The CtRC expressed concern over the use of Anti-Social Behaviour Orders (ASBOs) in addition to 'mosquito devices'[40] and the introduction of 'dispersed zones', in so far as these had the potential to violate children's rights to freedom of movement and peaceful assembly which were subject to limited restrictions.[41] The CtRC was also concerned about the fact that DNA data relating to children were retained in the national DNA database irrespective of whether a child was ultimately charged or found guilty of an offence. It was also concerned that children were insufficiently protected from media representation and public 'naming and shaming' on TV reality shows following the imposition of ASBOs. Although the CtRC noted that efforts had been made by the United Kingdom to review its use of physical restraint and solitary confinement to ensure that these measures were not used unless absolutely necessary and as a measure of last resort, it remained concerned that physical restraint on children was still used in places of deprivation of liberty. As regards corporal punishment, the CtRC further noted that although amendments had been made to legislation in England, Wales, Scotland and Northern Ireland which restricted the application of the defence of 'reasonable chastisement', this defence had not been removed. It approved of the commitment of the National Assembly in Wales to prohibit all corporal punishment in the home, but noted that under the terms of devolution it was not possible for the Assembly to enact the necessary legislation. It noted concern that the United Kingdom had failed to explicitly prohibit all corporal punishment in the home, and emphasised its view that the existence of any defence in cases of corporal punishment of children did not comply with the principles and provisions of the CRC, as this would imply that some forms of corporal punishment were acceptable. It also noted concern that corporal punishment was lawful in the home, schools and alternative care settings in virtually all overseas territories and crown dependencies, and adverted to its general comment on this subject (General

---

40 These are high-frequency ultrasound devices, often capable of being heard only by persons under the age of around 25, and therefore particularly painful when heard by children.
41 See CRC, article 15(2).

Comment No. 8, 2006).[42] The CtRC recommended the prohibition of all corporal punishment in the family and the repeal of all legal defences throughout the United Kingdom and its overseas territories and dependencies. The CtRC also recommended that the United Kingdom implement the recommendations of the UN Secretary-General's study of violence against children (Pinheiro 2006), taking into account the recommendations of the Regional Consultation for Europe and Central Asia.[43]

3.4.4.4 Family environment and alternative care (articles 5, 18(1) and (2), 9–11, 19–21, 25, 27(4) and 39)

The CtRC was concerned that many families lacked appropriate assistance in the performance of their child-rearing responsibilities, notably those families in a crisis situation due to poverty. The CtRC was concerned about the insufficient resources invested in staff and facilities to support children deprived of parental care. It was concerned that some children could land up in the care system because of parental low income and that there was an increasing number of such children, including a high percentage of children of African descent, children with disabilities and children from ethnic minorities. Children in alternative care were moved between places too frequently and there was insufficient contact with parents and siblings. There was inadequate monitoring of alternative care and children had limited access to complaint mechanisms. In making its recommendations to address these matters, the CtRC urged the United Kingdom to take into account its recommendations, issued at the day of general discussion, on children without parental care (Day of Discussion 2005). The CtRC was also concerned about the delays in waiting for adoption of children of African descent and children of ethnic minorities by families of the same ethnic origin. It was concerned about the problem of violence, abuse and neglect of children and the lack of any comprehensive nationwide strategy. In particular, there was no sufficient system of recording and analysing abuses, and measures of physical and psychological recovery and social reintegration for victims were insufficiently available.

3.4.4.5 Basic health and welfare (articles 6, 18(3), 23, 24, 26 and 27(1)–(3))

The CtRC recommended, with regard to children with disabilities, that the United Kingdom should take necessary measures,[44] taking into account the CtRC's general

---

42 Similar recommendations concerning corporal punishment have been made by some of the other human rights treaty bodies, e.g. CCPR, CEDAW and CESCR.
43 Held in Ljubljana from 5–7 July 2005. See: http://www.unicef.org.uk/press/news_detail_full_story.asp?news_id=570 (accessed 13 May 2010).
44 In the light of the Standard Rules on the Equalization of Opportunities for Persons with Disabilities of 1993, A/RES/48/96, General Assembly, 20 December 1993.

comment on the rights of children with disabilities (General Comment No. 9, 2006), to develop protective legislation, programmes and services for children with disabilities and to include children with disabilities in the development of a comprehensive national strategy. It also urged the United Kingdom to consider ratifying the UN Convention on the Rights of Persons with Disabilities of 2006 and its Optional Protocol. The CtRC was concerned about the persistence of inequalities in access to health services, as evidenced by the widening gap in infant mortality between the most and the least well-off groups. The CtRC was further concerned that, while one in ten children in the United Kingdom had a diagnosable mental health problem, only around 25 per cent had access to the required treatment and care and children could still be treated in adult psychiatric wards. It was also concerned that the implementation of the International Code of Marketing of Breastmilk Substitutes continued to be inadequate and that an aggressive promotion of breastmilk substitutes remained common. The CtRC remained concerned at the high rate of teenage pregnancies, especially among girls from a lower socio-economic background and in the Overseas Territories, in particular Turks and Caicos Islands, and recommended renewed efforts to provide adolescents with appropriate reproductive health services and education. It also expressed its concern at the incidence of use of alcohol, drugs and other toxic substances by adolescents. The CtRC recommended that the United Kingdom needed to study the root causes of these problems to provide targeted preventive measures and to strengthen mental health and counselling services. The CtRC, though welcoming the United Kingdom's commitment to ending child poverty by 2020 and the Childcare Act 2006 requirement on local authorities to reduce inequalities among young children, also noted its concern about the persistence of child poverty, particularly in Northern Ireland where 25 per cent of children reportedly lived in poverty, and in relation to Traveller children. The CtRC encouraged the United Kingdom to establish measurable indicators of poverty to achieve their policy target of eradicating child poverty.

3.4.4.6 Education, leisure and cultural activities (articles 28, 29 and 31)

As regards children's rights to education, the CtRC noted the persistence of significant inequalities with regard to school achievement of children living with their parents in economic hardship and the persistence of disadvantage amongst the following groups: children with disabilities, children of travellers, Roma children, asylum-seeking children, dropouts and non-attendees for different reasons (sickness, family obligations etc.), and teenage mothers. The CtRC was also concerned about the participation of children in schooling in an environment where they had few consultation rights, in particular no right to appeal their exclusion (which the CtRC urged should only be used as a last resort) or the decisions of a special educational needs tribunal. Bullying in schools remained a widespread problem and the number of school exclusions remained high, particularly from disadvantaged groups of children. The problem of segregation of education was

of 11 continued in Northern
the 11+ transfer test in Northern
's rights to play, that despite the
children's play[45] such rights were
l Kingdom because of poor play
ilities. The CtRC was further con-
e in recent years was pushing chil-
to ASBO-related policing.

ticles 22, 30, 38,

a new asylum procedure in March 2007
sidered by specially trained interviewing
Border Agency had engaged in the reform
d asylum-seeking children. However, it
of asylum-seeking children who continued
ded that the United Kingdom should inten-
sily
on of asylum-seeking and migrant children is
always used as a last resort and for the shortest appropriate period of
time, in compliance with a 37(b) of the CRC. It also recommended that
consideration be given to amending the 2004 Asylum and Immigration (Treatment
of Claimants etc.) Act[46] to allow for a guaranteed defence for unaccompanied
children who enter the United Kingdom without valid immigration documents.
As regards the Optional Protocol to the Convention on the sale of children, child
prostitution and child pornography (OPSC), the CtRC welcomed the announced
forthcoming ratification.[47] The CtRC expressed concern at the lack of data on
child victims of sexual exploitation, including in the Overseas Territories. The
CtRC reminded the United Kingdom that it should always consider, both in legislation and in practice, child victims of these criminal practices, including child
prostitution, exclusively as victims in need of recovery and reintegration and not
as offenders. It also recommended that the United Kingdom ratify the Council of
Europe Convention on the Protection of Children against Sexual Exploitation and
Sexual Abuse 2007,[48] and welcomed the United Kingdom's stated intention to

45 See Secretary of State for Children, Schools and Families (2007: 28–30).
46 Section 2 provides that it is an offence 'if at a leave or asylum interview he does not have with him,
    in respect of any dependent child with whom he claims to be traveling or living, an immigration
    document which—
    (a) is in force, and
    (b) satisfactorily establishes the child's identity and nationality or citizenship.'
47 The United Kingdom's became a signatory to OPSC on 7 September 2000, and ratified it on 20
    February 2009.
48 The United Kingdom's signed this Convention on 5 May 2008, but has not yet ratified it.

ratify the Council of Europe Convention on Action against Trafficking in Human Beings 2005.[49] As regards the administration of juvenile justice, the CtRC remained concerned that the age of criminal responsibility was still set at 8 years in Scotland and 10 years in England, Wales and Northern Ireland. There were still cases where children could be tried in an adult court, and the number of children deprived of their liberty indicated that detention was not always being applied as a measure of last resort. The CtRC recommended that the United Kingdom fully implement international standards of juvenile justice, in particular articles 37, 39 and 40 of the CRC, in addition to the relevant general comment (General Comment No. 10, 2007) along with the 'Beijing Rules', the 'Riyadh Guidelines' and the 'Havana Rules'.

The CtRC also expressed concern that ASBOs, which were civil orders, could be converted into criminal offences in cases where such an order was breached. It was concerned at the apparent ease of issuing such an order and its application to a broad range of prohibited behaviour, despite the serious (criminal) consequence of a breach. The CtRC recommended an independent review of ASBOs, with a view to abolishing their application to children.

Finally, the CtRC invited the United Kingdom to submit its fifth periodic report by 15 January 2014. It also invited the United Kingdom to submit an updated core document, in accordance with the requirements of the 'common core document' in the harmonised guidelines on reporting under the international human rights treaties, including guidelines on a common core document and treaty-specific documents, approved at the fifth Inter-Committee Meeting of the human rights treaty bodies in June 2006.[50]

3.4.5 The United Kingdom courts and the convention on the rights of the child

The CtRC has approved of an increasing tendency for the British courts to make reference to the CRC in their judgments. The synopses of five illustrative cases below provide some indication as to how the CRC is starting to be received into the UK's legal system.

In *Dosoo v. Dosoo (Sheriff Court of Lothian and Borders at Edinburgh)* (11 March 1999),[51] in an action for divorce, the residence/contact with boys aged 14, 12 and four and a half was contested by the children's mother and father. A welfare report was prepared that recorded the older boys' views. The two older

---

49 The United Kingdom's signed this Convention on 23 March 2007 and ratified on 17 December 2008. It came into force in international law in respect of the United Kingdom's on 1 April 2009.
50 'Harmonized guidelines on reporting under the international human rights treaties, including guidelines on a common core document and treaty-specific documents: Report of the Inter-Committee Technical Working Group', HRI/MC/2006/3, 10 May 2006. Available at: http:// daccess-dds-ny.un.org/doc/UNDOC/GEN/G06/419/42/PDF/G0641942.pdf?OpenElement (accessed 13 May 2010).
51 1999 Fam. L.R. 80.

boys had specifically requested that their views would be kept confidential as they feared repercussions from their father. The father applied to have the report disclosed to him arguing, inter alia, that a refusal would constitute a breach of natural justice and would be contrary to articles 6 and 8 of the European Convention on Human Rights (ECHR). The solicitor acting for the boys argued that, according to the terms of the Children (Scotland) Act 1995, the overriding concern had to be the welfare of the children and section 6 of the Act had adopted the terms of article 12 of the CRC which required that children should be able to express their views freely. Sheriff Robertson refused the father's motion and concluded, inter alia:

> [T]he Children (Scotland) Act 1995 must be applied in issues relating to children and s6 thereof and OCR [The Ordinary Cause Rules 1993)] 33.20(1) have given effect to Art 12 of the UN Convention on the Rights of the Child. I agree that for a child to be able to express his views "freely" he must be able to feel confident in privacy if he so wishes and the court should respect that privacy except in very compelling circumstances. For the reasons indicated above I have not been satisfied that such circumstances exist at the present stage in this case and I have concluded that the motion should be refused.[52]

K v. HM Advocate (Privy Council) (29 January 2002)[53] was a decision concerning two cases relating to the requirement that, in criminal proceedings, the defendant should be brought to trial 'within a reasonable time' within the meaning of article 6 of the ECHR. In the first case two police officers were accused of committing perjury at a trial in April 1998, but their case did not arrive for trial until late 2000. The High Court had ruled that this delay was unreasonable in what was apparently an extremely simple case. In the second case, K, born December 1984, was cautioned and charged in October 1998 with rape, sodomy and other indecent practices committed over the previous 20 months against three younger cousins. After various delays, an indictment was served in January 2001. The High Court had held that the 27 months between October 1998 and January 2001 was substantially too long, having regard in particular to K's age and the failure to treat the case with increasing urgency as time went on. It is also observed in this case that the European Court of Human Rights (ECtHR) had taken account[54] of both the CRC and the 'Beijing Rules' when considering proceedings involving children.

---

52 1999 Fam. L.R. 80, para. 80–18.
53 2002 S.L.T. 229.
54 *V v. United Kingdom*, 16 December 1999, (2000) 30 E.H.R.R. 121. This case, aka the 'Bulger Case', concerned two 11-year-old boys who were convicted of the abduction and murder of a 2-year-old boy. One of the boys convicted complained that his trial in public in an adult Crown Court and the punitive nature of his sentence violated his right not to be subjected to inhuman or degrading treatment or punishment as guaranteed under article 3 of the ECHR. He further complained

The Privy Council held that the reasonable time requirement had, when dealing with children, to be read in the light of CRC[55] and the 'Beijing Rules',[56] under both of which criminal proceedings, if brought at all, had to be prosecuted with all due expedition. Furthermore, delay was particularly undesirable where children were concerned and the 27-month period in K's case was one which on its face gave ground for real concern and no satisfactory explanation had been given for the lapse of time. Finally, the considerations that pointed towards a breach of the reasonable time requirement also pointed towards discontinuance of the proceedings as the only appropriate remedy.

In *Re E (A Child)* (House of Lords (Northern Ireland)) (29 January 2002),[57] an outbreak of disorder had occurred in Northern Ireland on 19 June 2001. The disorder developed into abuse towards and attacks by Protestant families on (Roman Catholic) girls going to and from the Holy Cross Girls Primary School. The appellant claimed that her young daughter was frightened and upset by witnessing a violent incident that took place. The police closed the road until the end of the school term. When the new school term commenced in September, the situation escalated and became increasingly violent and dangerous. In early November the police adopted a revised strategy of lower-key policing and eventually the protest by loyalists was suspended on November 23. The appellant argued that the police force had failed in its positive obligations under article 3 of the ECHR to protect the appellant and her daughter from inhumane and degrading treatment and it was alleged that the police had discriminated against them.

The House of Lords held that the police had fulfilled their positive obligation imposed by article 3 of the ECHR and there was no breach of the rights of the appellant or her child. It also held that, with respect to the claim under article 14 of the ECHR, there was no evidence that the police would have handled matters differently if they had been dealing with Protestant parents and children facing a similar Catholic protest. They took all reasonable steps to protect the children.

that he was denied a fair trial in breach of article 6, that he had suffered discrimination in breach of article 14 in that a child aged younger than 10 at the time of the offence would not have been held criminally responsible, that the sentence of detention during Her Majesty's pleasure violated his right to liberty under Article 5, and that the fact that the Home Secretary, rather than a judge, was responsible for setting the tariff violated his rights under Article 6. Finally, he complained under Article 5(4) that he had not had the opportunity to have the continuing lawfulness of his detention examined by a judicial body, such as the Parole Board. He also claimed just satisfaction under article 41 of the ECHR.

55 '(2) ... (b) Every child alleged as or accused of having infringed the penal law has at least the following guarantees: ... (iii) to have the matter determined without delay'. (CRC, article 40 (2)(b)(iii)).

56 'Each case shall from the outset be handled expeditiously, without any unnecessary delay.' United Nations Standard Minimum Rules for the Administration of Juvenile Justice ('the Beijing Rules') 1985, para. 20.

57 [2009] H.R.L.R. 8, [2008] UKHL 66.

It was additionally held[58] that the requirement in article 3(1) of the CRC – that in all actions concerning children the 'best interests' of the child shall be a primary consideration – was a consideration which should properly be taken into account by the state and its emanations. It was also a matter which may be relevant in determining whether the actions of the police satisfied the obligations placed upon them by article 3 of the ECHR.

AK v. Secretary of State for the Home Department (Court of Session (Outer House)) (4 September 2009)[59] was a decision concerning a contested asylum case where a foreign national (K) had petitioned for judicial review of a decision of the Home Secretary refusing to treat new submissions on his behalf as a fresh claim for asylum. He argued, inter alia, that the Home Secretary had failed to take account of the 'best interests' principle as a primary consideration (article 3 of the CRC). He contended that it was not enough for the Home Secretary to concede that the best interests of the child fell within the proportionality assessment under article 8 of the ECHR, as the mere balancing exercise envisaged therein did not satisfy the principle under the CRC. The petition was refused. Lady Clark of Calton observed the following:

> It appears also to be implicit in the submission on behalf of the petitioner that Article 3 of the UN Convention lays down some higher standard protecting the interests of the child so that even a mandatory consideration of the best interests of the child as part of the consideration of Article 8 [ECHR] could not meet that standard and therefore give effect to the principle. I do not accept that. Article 3 of the UN Convention does not elevate the principle to a higher status which would be implied by the words 'the paramount consideration' or 'the primary consideration'. It is also in my opinion not intended to be a reference to the best interests of the child in the very general sense which might be appropriate in care proceedings. What is in issue, in the immigration context, is whether or not the decision affects the Article 8 rights of the child. A failure to give consideration to the best interests of the child would not in my opinion satisfy 'the principle' [i.e. the best interests principle in article 3 of the CRC]. The mere fact that a balancing exercise of circumstances and factors is necessarily involved in Article 8 consideration, does not mean that 'the principle' is not given effect. In my opinion a recognition that the best interests of the child must be considered in the balancing exercise is sufficient to give effect to the principle that it is a primary consideration. Other factors or circumstances may be omitted or discounted because they have not been given that status. But a failure to address the best interests of the child in a case where a child is involved, and the decision

---

58 [2009] H.R.L.R. 8, para. 60.
59 [2009] CSOH 123.

maker is required to consider Article 8 ECHR would in my opinion amount to a failure to give effect to 'the principle'.

When I consider the case law prayed in aid on behalf of the respondent and summarised in paragraph 38, I accept that the case law does indicate that when a tribunal or court comes to consider Article 8 ECHR, that consideration properly encompasses consideration of the best interests of any child affected.[60]

In a case concerning a British couple, *Northumberland CC v. Z, aka 'Re X (A Child)* (Family Division) (16 March 2009),[61] (Y and Z) had brought X (a child) from Kenya to the United Kingdom using means that were illegal in the United Kingdom and in Kenya. They made an application to adopt X but were ruled out as carers and instead the court approved care plans advanced by the local authority and the Kenyan government. The judge, however, stated that Y and Z had acted with the best of motives and no criminal charges were brought against them. The local authority sought disclosure of the transcript of the care proceedings to the police and the UK Border and Immigration Agency, subject to conditions ensuring the confidentiality of the document. The Kenyan government sought the disclosure of a larger body of documentation and undertook not to use the material as direct evidence against Y or Z in any criminal proceedings or in any request for their extradition.

The applications were granted. It was held that, even though Y and Z had acted with the best of motives, in reality, intercountry adoptions could involve dishonesty, subterfuge, criminality and exploitation of the vulnerable. However, Mr Justice Munby also observed that:

The Conventions to which I have referred [the CRC and the African Charter of the Rights and Welfare of the Child 1990[62]] enshrine important principles of public policy, in both the domestic and more importantly the international sphere, to which the court must have close regard. And there are important principles of comity here in play. This is a context in which, to generalise from the point made by Balcombe LJ in *Re F (A Minor) (Abduction: Jurisdiction)* [1991] 1 FLR 1 at page 6, courts should, as a general principle, act in comity to discourage the illicit transfer of children across international borders. And in addition to the driving imperatives of judicial comity, there is the wider comity between nations – comity with the judicial and other public authorities of a friendly State – to which a judge must have appropriate regard.[63]

---

60 [2009] CSOH 123, paras 44 and 45. See also *HS (Algeria) v. Secretary of State for the Home Department* [2009] CSOH 124; 2009 S.L.T. 1087, which arrives at the same conclusion on the relationship between the best interests principle and article 8 of the ECHR.
61 [2009] EWHC 498 (Fam); [2009] 2 F.L.R. 696.
62 See Chapter 2, section 2.5.2.2, for a brief account of the African Charter.
63 [2009] EWHC 498 (Fam), at para. 66.

On the facts, the judge held that the policy considerations pointed strongly in favour of the limited disclosure sought by the local authority.

3.5 The implementation of the convention on the rights of the child

The Committee's General Guidelines on how to prepare 'initial' and 'periodic' state reports (Committee on the Rights of the Child, 1991, 1995, respectively) group the provisions of the CRC into eight thematic clusters and request responses using this structure. This approach 'reflects the Convention's holistic perspective of children's rights: that they are indivisible and interrelated, and that equal importance should be attached to each and every right recognised therein'. There is a detailed account of the legal provenance of each article of the CRC given in Detrick (1999). In the following sections, however, an account of each of these eight 'clusters', as defined in the General Guidelines, is given with reference to the interactions between the states parties and the CtRC in the reporting process.

In this section, all the CtRC's 'concluding observations' for 2009 (concerning 17 state reports) and some earlier reports have been reviewed to prepare a summary and illustrative examples of the points discussed under each theme. It is hoped that this will enable the reader to obtain an understanding not only of the standard-setting achieved by the CRC, but also of the way in which it is actually being implemented in practice across a wide range of countries. The reader may also wish to consult the text of individual articles of the CRC that appear under each of the following eight headings.

3.5.1 General measures of implementation: articles 4, 42 and 44(6)

The CRC contains strongly worded provisions obliging states parties to implement and disseminate its provisions and principles. The CtRC has set out useful advice to states on how these obligations can be pursued: see General Comment No. 5 (2003). It commends the development of a comprehensive and rights-based strategy built on the framework of the CRC. The CtRC takes the view that economic, social and cultural rights, as well as civil and political rights, 'must be regarded as justiciable' (General Comment No. 5, 2003: para. 25). The 'general measures' theme in a 'concluding observation' usually opens with some commentary on the extent to which the CtRC's recommendations and concerns in the previous reporting round have been addressed. The CtRC frequently finds it necessary to encourage the further coordination of government implementation efforts. It has pointed out that the decentralization of government power does not in any way reduce states parties' direct responsibility to fulfil their responsibilities. Equally, such decentralization or devolution may require safeguards to protect groups from discrimination. The CtRC has encouraged states to adopt a continuous process of 'child impact assessment' and evaluation to be built into the policy-making process itself.

While approving governments' self-monitoring and evaluation, the CtRC also regards the independent monitoring of progress as essential. It encourages this, in particular, by recommending the establishment of independent human rights institutions. The CtRC 'considers the establishment of such bodies to fall within the commitment made by states parties upon ratification to ensure the implementation of the Convention and advance the universal realization of children's rights' (General Comment No. 2, 2002: para. 1). However, such independent institutions should be seen as complementary to government structures; governments ought not to merely delegate their monitoring functions to such bodies. The CtRC typically recommends the establishment of a Children's Commissioner or Ombudsman where there is none (CO Bolivia 2009). It may also approve of the establishment of such a body where this occurs (CO France 2009). The CtRC may also raise criticisms where it perceives that the body in question falls below the standard of independence as suggested by the 'Paris Principles'[64] (CO Malawi 2009).

The CtRC often points out the need for states to collect reliable statistical data, appropriately disaggregated, to enable the identification of discrimination and other disparities in realizing children's rights (General Comment No. 5, 2003: para. 12). It regularly requests data that identifies ethnic groups, age profiles, gender, street children, Roma children, refugee and asylum-seeker children, and encourages the development of nationally applicable and robust statistical indicators. The CtRC acknowledges that it is often difficult for states to be able to state definitively whether they have committed the 'maximum extent' of their available resources in pursuit of economic, cultural and social rights, under article 4, unless there is clear information about the extent of budgets impacting on children. The CtRC has noted that '[s]ome States have claimed it is not possible to analyse national budgets in this way. But others have done it and publish annual "children's budgets"' (General Comment No. 5, 2003: para. 51). The CtRC is likely to make criticisms where it perceives budgetary allocations are obviously inadequate, for example, in relation in particular to children living in rural areas (CO Moldova 2009). A benchmark for this type of critique in recent years has been the day of general discussion document on 'resources for the rights of the child' (Day of Discussion 2007). This document encourages states, inter alia, to consider legislating a specific proportion of public expenditure to be allocated to children, accompanied by a mechanism that allows for a systematic independent evaluation of such expenditure (Day of Discussion 2007: para. 23).

The CtRC has acknowledged that the obligations of the CRC, though placed on states, in practice stretch beyond state institutions and services and require the cooperation of civil society and the family. It urges governments to give NGOs non-directive support and develop sound links with them. The CtRC also stresses that article 4 requires international cooperation and urges states to meet internationally

---

64 'Principles Relating to the Status of Independent National Human Rights Institutions', adopted by General Assembly Resolution 48/134 of 20 December 1993.

agreed targets, for example, the UN target for international development assistance of 0.7 per cent of gross domestic product.

There were, at the time of writing, around 60 states parties who had current declarations and/or reservations on ratifying the CRC. We have already examined in some detail the declarations and reservations made by the United Kingdom (see section 3.4.1). The CtRC routinely urges states to withdraw reservations, and, as we have seen in the earlier discussion, all four of the UK's reservations made upon ratification have now been withdrawn. The facility to make reservations is often a useful diplomatic tool to persuade countries to ratify an international instrument. However, there are some limits to making them. Any reservation that is against the 'object and purpose' of the CRC would not be allowed,[65] and even if such reservations were not expressly prohibited in the CRC, they would be prohibited under the Vienna Convention on the Law of Treaties 1969.[66] The Netherlands has been criticised by the CtRC for its maintenance of reservations concerning children's rights to social security,[67] the application of adult penal law to children of 16 years and older in certain circumstances,[68] and exceptions to the right to legal assistance[69] (CO Netherlands 2009). The CtRC has been concerned that some reservations plainly breach article 51(2) (reservations incompatible with the CRC's 'object and purpose' are forbidden) 'by suggesting, for example, that respect for the Convention is limited by the State's existing Constitution or legislation, including in some cases religious law' (General Comment No. 5, 2003: para. 15).

Clearly, the assessment of the extent to which specifically 'legislative' measures[70] have contributed towards successful implementation of the CRC is a significant task that is performed in the reporting process. The CtRC is likely to welcome countries that proactively amend their national laws or even their Constitution to accommodate the legal standards set out in CRC. Bolivia, for example, has included a chapter on child rights in its recent constitution (CO Bolivia 2009: para. 3). The Committee can frequently be seen to encourage states parties to bring their domestic law into conformity with the CRC and to strengthen their efforts towards formal recognition of the CRC in domestic law (CO Sweden 2009: para. 10). However, the CtRC will go much further than a mere paper audit of child-friendly legislation. It will want to see that the legislation in question has a substantial impact in the real world. Regrettably, implementation is often measured by some states according to a rather narrow focus on the compatibility of its municipal legal system with CRC standards. Some countries have incorporated

---

65 CRC, article 51(2).
66 Article 19(c): see section 2.2.1.
67 CRC, article 26.
68 CRC, article 37.
69 CRC, article 40.
70 See CRC, article 4.

the whole of CRC into their domestic laws, but the relationship between municipal and international law is often a subtle one. France's *Cour de Cassation*, for example, has recognised the direct applicability of the CRC to domestic law, and the *Conseil d'État* followed suit, but the CtRC had to express concern that only a limited number of provisions of the CRC were recognised to have such direct effect (CO France 2009: 10).

The reporting process operated by the CtRC is deliberately aimed to encourage states to comprehensively review all their child-related legislation and policy. That process can engender new policy thinking and initiatives. It would appear, for example, that the influence of the CRC, alongside other national and international pressures, contributed to India's decision to universalise elementary education in 2001 as part of its general strategy to tackle poverty. In many societies, children have not been regarded as 'right holders'. Therefore, the duties to disseminate and publicise the CRC[71] are especially important. These duties often require relevant language translations for minority or indigenous groups, and programmes of rights awareness through mass media, professional training, school and other educational curricula. The involvement of NGOs and children themselves in such advocacy campaigns has become a hallmark of such activity. Indeed, the CtRC has concluded that: '[o]ne of the satisfying results of the adoption and almost universal ratification of the Convention has been the development at the national level of a wide variety of new child-focused and child-sensitive bodies, structures and activities' (General Comment No. 5, 2003: para. 9). However, the states parties' reports to the CtRC are still revealing low levels of awareness of the existence of the CRC (CO France 2009; CO Sweden 2009). A Northern Ireland study, for example, noted that 93.5 per cent of school pupils aged 14–16 surveyed had not heard of the CRC. The respondents had some understanding of human rights principles in relation to specific issues but 'no coherent, integrated understanding of human rights concepts' (United Kingdom 2002: para. 3.12.2). A nationwide survey in Germany, conducted by an opinion research institute in 1997, revealed that only 15 per cent of the German public were aware of the CRC (Germany 2003: para. 110). More optimistically, in the UK's combined 3rd/4th periodic report, it is stated that, in an online children's survey commissioned by the Department for Children, Schools and the Family (DCSF), about 70 per cent of respondents reported some awareness of the CRC (United Kingdom 2008: para. 61).

3.5.2 *Definition of the child: article 1*

The issue of the definition of a child was a crucial and contentious part of the negotiations in the original drafting of the CRC (Van Bueren 1994; Cantwell

---

71 CRC, articles 42 and 44(6).

1992: 26). Article 1 is essentially a compromise: it sets the international legal definition of a child as a person below 18 years, but subject to the proviso that a domestic law that sets legal majority at an earlier age will not be compromised. In some countries there is no uniform definition of the child in the laws and policies of the country and there may be, for example, conflicting legal minimum ages of children for marriage according to whether civil law or sharia law applies (CO Bangladesh 2009). There are often inconsistencies in the definition of a child at federal, provincial and territorial levels between secular and sharia law (CO Pakistan 2009). Where the general legal majority age is lower than 18 years, for example 17 years in Korea, the Committee encourages the states party to raise it to 18 years where possible. It characteristically comments unfavourably about the existence of low and/or discriminatory age rules in relation to marriage: for example, 16 years for boys and 14 years for girls in Bolivia (CO Bolivia 2009); 18 years for boys and 17 years for girls (CO Chad 2009); 18 years for boys and 15 years for girls (CO Niger 2009); 18 years for boys and 16 years for girls (CO Pakistan 2009). The prevention of early marriage according to the custom and practice of some countries is frequently targeted for action via awareness-raising campaigns to be led by traditional leaders in the country concerned (CO Malawi 2009).

In many countries the general age of majority is 18 years, for example, in Norway, Germany, Italy, China and the United Kingdom. However, such countries will also have specific legislation that offers legal capacity in particular areas. However, the setting of the upper age limit of 18 years for the definition of a child remains an important target for some countries, particularly those that, like India, still have problems with the prevalence of child marriages and child labour. The differential definitions of legal majority within a country can often deprive older children of essential services and care. For example, in Kyrgyzstan, assistance to families with children with HIV/AIDS has been provided only to children under the age of 16, and children aged 16 and over have been transferred to adult psychiatric care (CO Kyrgyzstan, 2004). Some countries still retain 21 years as an age of majority, at least for some purposes. In India, for example, the Child Marriage Restraint Act 1929 defined a child as a person who has not completed 21 years of age (if male) or 18 years of age (if female) (CO India 2003). A number of countries have attempted to synchronise the age at which 'light work' is permitted and the age at which compulsory education ends. However, there are still diverse rules relating to the age of criminal responsibility. As we have seen (section 3.4.2), the CtRC has expressed concern repeatedly about the United Kingdom's maintenance of an age of criminal responsibility of 8 years in Scotland and 10 years throughout the rest of the United Kingdom.

It is of greater difficulty to determine when childhood *begins*. Van Bueren discusses this issue at some length and notes that states 'hold such fundamentally conflicting views when childhood begins that they cannot be reconciled simply by the device of a treaty' (Van Bueren 1994: 33). She concludes that there is no universally agreed point of time when childhood begins, but it would appear that international law protects the beginning of childhood, at least from the moment of a live birth. States are not prevented from extending their definition of childhood to include periods in the womb, but such protection cannot be read into customary international law or into treaty provisions that protect the right to life. Some states have registered a number of reservations or declarations in order to clarify their country's position in relation to this question. As we have seen (section 3.4.1), the United Kingdom has made an interpretative declaration in respect of article 1, which applies the Convention only to a live birth.[72] However, other countries ratifying the CRC have specifically appealed to the ninth preambular paragraph of the CRC and the third preambular paragraph of the Declaration of the Rights of the Child of 1959 in support of the contention that the CRC confers rights on the human foetus, for example, in Argentina.[73]

3.5.3 General principles: articles 2, 3, 6 and 12

These are the foundational principles of the CRC. Article 2 (non-discrimination principle), article 3 (best interests principle), article 6 (right to life, survival and development) and article 12 (participation rights according to evolving capacities) are fundamental to an understanding of the CRC. States parties are expected to provide information not only in respect of these general principles but also, pervasively, in relation to how these general principles may impact on the implementation of other specific rights contained in the CRC.

3.5.3.1 The non-discrimination principle

One commentator has said:

> Art. 2 captures the child-specific dimension of child discrimination and has been used most effectively against the latter. The principle of non-discrimination of the child is guaranteed in a new protective way by art. 2

---

72 'As such it does not amount to a reservation representing less than complete compliance with the Convention, and it is likely to need to stand indefinitely.' (United Kingdom 2002: para 1.8.2).

73 Declaration made by Argentina upon signature and confirmed upon ratification: 'Concerning article 1 of the Convention, the Argentine Republic declares that the article must be interpreted to the effect that a child means every human being from the moment of conception up to the age of eighteen.' Declaration made by the Holy See: 'The Holy See recognizes that the Convention represents an enactment of principles previously adopted by the United Nations, and once effective as a ratified instrument, will safeguard the rights of the child before as well as after birth, as expressly affirmed in the 'Declaration of the Rights of the Child' [Res. 136 (XIV)] and restated in the ninth preambular paragraph of the Convention. The Holy See remains confident that the ninth preambular paragraph will serve as the perspective through which the rest of the Convention will be interpreted, in conformity with article 31 of the Vienna Convention on the Law of Treaties of 23 May 1969'.

and other special norms in the Convention, that contrast with earlier international anti-discrimination clauses from the 1950s and 1960s. It should also have become clear ... that, like other anti-discrimination clauses, art. 2 CRC is growing old. Special protection measures can have destructive discriminatory consequences on particularly vulnerable children whose integration should be our foremost goal. New inclusive approaches are yet to be sought therefore to avoid the 'ghettoization' of some cases of child discrimination.

(Besson 2005: 458)

   The principle applies in conjunction with all the substantive rights in the CRC, but does not provide an *independent* right to freedom from discrimination (Detrick 1999: 72). The words 'birth or other status' cover discrimination in relation to children born out of wedlock. The fundamental nature of the principle of non-discrimination is reflected by the fact that in some states the principle has been incorporated into their constitution (CO Chad 2009; CO Mauritania 2009). Of course, this does not necessarily provide sufficient protection. In Mauritania, for example, the constitutional protection has not been sufficient to prevent discrimination against children living in slavery or of slave descent, or children living in poverty (CO Mauritania 2009: para. 29). In many states, there have been moves to facilitate the assimilation of the legal status of legitimate and illegitimate children (CO Mozambique 2009; CO France 2009),[74] though in some countries discrimination against children born out of wedlock persists (CO Qatar 2009; CO Philippines 2009; CO Niger 2009). Roma children are frequently the recipients of discriminatory attitudes and practices (CO Moldova 2009; CO France 2009). Sometimes discrimination is directed against the girl child, reflecting more fundamental attitudes about females in the country in question (CO Philippines 2009; CO Niger 2009; CO Malawi 2009; CO Congo 2009). Such pervasive gender discrimination has drawn strong criticism from the CtRC, for example, in the case of Pakistan (CO Pakistan 2009: para. 28). The CtRC has also noted its concerns in relation to Sweden about discrimination and racist attitudes towards children of ethnic minorities, refugee and asylum-seeking children and children belonging to migrant families (CO Sweden 2009). The CtRC will respond to these various concerns with a range of possible recommendations. These often include urging the country in question to ensure that their domestic legislation is CRC-compliant, to adopt awareness-raising campaigns and to embark upon training programmes with the relevant professionals. The CtRC is further concerned that 'indigenous children enjoy all of their rights equally and without discrimination, including equal access to culturally appropriate services including health, education, social services, housing, potable water and sanitation' (Day of Discussion 2003: para. 9). As regards discrimination against children

---

74 See also the European Convention on the Legal Status of Children Born out of Wedlock 1975.

with disabilities, it is worth recalling that the CRC was the first human rights treaty to contain a specific reference to 'disability' (in article 2) and a separate article 23 which is exclusively dedicated to the rights and needs of children with disabilities.[75] One of the CtRC's General Comments notes that:

> [T]he Committee on the Rights of the Child ... has paid sustained and particular attention to disability based discrimination while other human rights treaty bodies have paid attention to disability based discrimination under "other status" in the context of articles on non-discrimination of their relevant Convention.
>
> (General Comment No. 9, 2006: para. 2)

The way in which the principle of non-discrimination applies in the context of education rights is given some explanation in the following extract.

> Discrimination on the basis of any of the grounds ... offends the human dignity of the child and is capable of undermining or even destroying the capacity of the child to benefit from educational opportunities. ... To take an extreme example, gender discrimination can be reinforced by practices such as a curriculum which is inconsistent with the principles of gender equality, by arrangements which limit the benefits girls can obtain from the educational opportunities offered, and by unsafe or unfriendly environments which discourage girls' participation. Discrimination against children with disabilities is also pervasive in many formal educational systems and in a great many informal educational settings, including in the home. Children with HIV/ AIDS are also heavily discriminated against in both settings. All such discriminatory practices are in direct contradiction with the requirements in article 29(1)(a) that education be directed to the development of the child's personality, talents and mental and physical abilities to their fullest potential.
>
> (General Comment No. 1, 2001: para.10)

The CtRC routinely draws states parties' attention to the principles of the Declaration and Programme of Action (Durban Declaration 2001), in addition to the outcome document[76] adopted at the 2009 Durban Review Conference. The CtRC typically welcomes warmly the establishment of a national body with responsibility to remedy problems of discrimination, particularly where it has the power to receive individual complaints, for example, the *Haute Autorité de Lutte contre Discriminations et pour l'Égalité* (CO France 2009).

---

75 Article 23 is usually dealt with under the 'basic health and welfare' theme: see section 3.5.6.1 below.

76 Available at: http://www.un.org/durbanreview2009/pdf/Durban_Review_outcome_document_En.pdf (accessed 22 December 2009).

3.5.3.2 The best interests principle

This principle first appeared, at the international level, in principles 2 and 7 of the Declaration on the Rights of the Child of 1959. The principle has appeared in various forms[77] in different countries and over a range of international legal instruments[78] for many years, in particular in relation to residence and contact decisions in the context of parental disputes about children's custody. Again, the fundamental nature of this principle has meant that some countries have integrated it with their constitution, though of course this is never a guarantee that the principle is actually fully integrated with the country's national laws or policies (CO Mozambique 2009). One persistent criticism of the best interests principle is that any one country's construction of its normative meaning will 'enable cultural considerations to be smuggled by States into their implementation of the rights recognised in the CRC' (Detrick 1999: 89). The CtRC typically urges states parties to make better efforts to integrate the principle into their domestic legislation and into projects, programmes and services that have an impact on children (CO Chad 2009), and it will chide countries that have a poor record in this respect (CO Congo 2009). Poor efforts at integrating the best interests principle are sometimes also tied with the allocation of insufficient resources for the respect and protection of children's rights (CO North Korea 2009: para. 21). The French *Cour de cassation* has recently aligned its jurisprudence with that of the *Conseil d'État* in acknowledging the direct applicability of article 3(1); however, the CtRC also noted 'the persisting differences in practice in understanding the application of this principle' (CO France 2009: para. 35). The CtRC has noted that, in respect of some states parties, customary law and practices can sometimes be an impediment to the implementation of the principle (CO Niger 2009). On occasion, a particular issue is singled out as lacking the application of the best interests principle; for example, in Romania the administration of juvenile justice was identified as an area where the principle was not operating as a primary consideration (CO Romania 2009). Also, particular groups of children have been identified with regard to practice in some states as lacking sufficient attention to the best interests principle; for example, in Sweden the best interests of asylum-seeker and migrant children were not taken sufficiently into account in asylum processes (CO Sweden 2009).

---

77 Principle 2 of the 1959 Declaration provides the stronger legal threshold, that is, 'the best interests of the child shall be the *paramount* consideration' in contrast to the '*primary* consideration' in the CRC. It has sometimes been argued that the 'paramountcy' standard should be the basic rule in international child law.

78 For example, The Hague Convention on Protection of Children and Co-Operation in respect of Intercountry Adoption 1993 provides, in article 1, that one object of that Convention is: ' a) to establish safeguards to ensure that intercountry adoptions take place in the best interests of the child and with respect for his or her fundamental rights as recognised in international law'. See also Sargent (2010).

3.5.3.3 The right to life, survival and development

The right to life, like its counterpart in the International Covenant on Civil and Political Rights[79] (ICCPR), is the only right in the CRC described as an 'inherent' right. Indeed, some commentators take the view that this is one of the 'peremptory norms of general international law', in other words, the *jus cogens* rule comes into play (see section 2.2.5). The right to life differs, however, from its counterpart in other major human rights treaties, as it additionally requires states to ensure 'to the maximum extent possible' the child's 'survival and development'. These were seen as complementary elements, implying, for example, the need for state measures to reduce infant mortality. Given the difficulties experienced in the drafting process to arrive at a satisfactory definition of the child (see section 3.5.2), it is not surprising that a few countries have made declarations or reservations to ensure that the interpretation of article 6 will not conflict with national abortion and family planning legislation. For example, China's reservation[80] aims to protect its 'one child' policy. Luxembourg, Tunisia and France have made declarations ensuring that article 6 does not interfere with their abortion legislation.[81]

The need to take measures to support survival and development has been underlined at a number of international conferences, for example, the *Special Session on Children* at the United Nations (UN 2002: para. 7(4)). The CtRC has expressed its concern with a number of article 6 issues in its examination of state reports, for example, high neonatal and infant mortality rates and child malnutrition (CO Bangladesh 2009; CO Chad 2009; CO North Korea 2009), which are made worse in states that have experienced armed conflict (CO Congo 2009). There is also concern in some states about high rates of suicide in places of detention (CO France 2009). The CtRC notes concern about the consequences of landmines from former conflicts and very high rates of road accidents (CO Mozambique 2009; CO Qatar 2009). The CtRC has also noted concern about the practice of euthanasia (conducted by a medical doctor under a strict code) in the Netherlands, which is applicable to children aged 12 years or older. It has recommended

---

79 Article 6.

80 '[T]he People's Republic of China shall fulfil its obligations provided by article 6 of the Convention under the prerequisite that the Convention accords with the provisions of article 25 concerning family planning of the Constitution of the People's Republic of China and in conformity with the provisions of article 2 of the Law of Minor Children of the People's Republic of China.'

81 'The Government of Luxembourg declares that article 6 of the present Convention presents no obstacle to implementation of the provisions of Luxembourg legislation concerning sex information, the prevention of back-street abortion and the regulation of pregnancy termination.'

'The Government of the Republic of Tunisia declares that the Preamble to and the provisions of the Convention, in particular article 6, shall not be interpreted in such a way as to impede the application of Tunisian legislation concerning voluntary termination of pregnancy.'

'The Government of the French Republic declares that this Convention, particularly article 6, cannot be interpreted as constituting any obstacle to the implementation of the provisions of French legislation relating to the voluntary interruption of pregnancy.'

the states party reviews its procedures on the termination of life of neonatal children (CO Netherlands 2009). It has also noted that one of the leading causes of death among older children in the Netherlands Antilles is homicide (CO Netherlands 2009). The CtRC has expressed concern about the 'still widespread and increasing problem of honour killings affecting children' (CO Pakistan 2009: para. 37). In the Philippines, serious concern was noted by the CtRC about extra-judicial executions, including those of children, committed by the armed forces, the national police and death squads (CO Philippines 2009: para. 32).

3.5.3.4 The right to express views and participate in decisions

One of the continuing concerns for children's rights advocacy has been the extent to which important decisions are made about children without children's own participation (see section 1.2.1.1). Article 12 obliges states parties to assure to the child who is capable of forming his or her own views a right to express views about matters affecting him or her. This article also confers on the child a right to be heard in any judicial or administrative proceedings affecting the child. This article is a key provision of the CRC. When read together with articles 5 and 13, it reflects a move away from merely identifying what decisions children are *not* competent to take, to the consideration of how children *can* participate. Van Bueren (1994: 137) comments that article 12(1) 'has great practical potential in improving the protection of the rights of the child, as it clearly places a duty on States parties to involve children when they wish in all matters which affect them'. Its importance has been underlined by the CtRC's production of recommendations following a day of general discussion (Day of Discussion 2006) and contained in a detailed and analytical General Comment which provides a comprehensive legal analysis of article 12, how this article relates to other important provisions of the CRC, and the implementation of the child's right to be heard in different settings and situations (General Comment No. 12, 2009). It concludes that states parties should avoid tokenistic approaches to the implementation of this article. Children's participation[82] should be understood as a process, not a one-off event. The General Comment recommends that all processes in which children are heard and participate must conform to a number of benchmarks (General Comment No. 12, 2009: para. 134(a) to (i)). They must be given accessible information about their right to express their views freely, how this participation will take place and its scope, purpose and potential impact. This should be

---

82 'A widespread practice has emerged in recent years, which has been broadly conceptualized as "participation", although this term itself does not appear in the text of article 12. This term has evolved and is now widely used to describe ongoing processes, which include information-sharing and dialogue between children and adults based on mutual respect, and in which children can learn how their views and those of adults are taken into account and shape the outcome of such processes'. (General Comment No. 12, 2009: para. 3). A number of typologies of children's participation are reviewed in Thomas (2007).

a voluntary process and children's views should be treated with respect. The issues on which children have a right to express their views must be of real relevance to their lives; children should be enabled to address issues they themselves identify as relevant. Environments and working methods should be adapted to accommodate children's evolving capacities. Participation should be inclusive, encouraging opportunities for marginalised children to be involved. Adults need support and training to facilitate children's participation. In certain situations, expression of views may expose children to risks and every precaution should be made to minimise any harmful risks. There is a need for accountability; any research or consultative process involving children should provide some evaluation and follow-up in order to inform children how their views have been interpreted and used and, where necessary, provide opportunities for children to challenge and influence the analysis of findings.

In their examination of state reports, the CtRC has noted some positive developments: for example, initiatives that set up children's interviews with policymakers and politicians and children's news agencies and news boards in schools (CO Bangladesh 2009); the establishment of democratic elections by children (CO Bolivia 2009), a 'Children's Parliament' in some countries (CO Chad 2009; CO France 2009; CO Mauritania 2009). The CtRC monitors closely the extent to which states parties' domestic legislation contains the child's right to be heard; in particular, it will note concern where a country's criminal laws and procedures contain no specific provisions for the hearing of child victims of crime, including sexual exploitation and abuse (CO Romania 2009). The CtRC has been at pains to build a culture of respect for children's views. Its concluding observations frequently alight upon traditional and societal attitudes that appear to limit children in freely expressing their views in schools, communities and within the family (CO Malawi 2009). It is interesting to note that the General Comment concedes that the comprehensive fulfilment of the obligations required by article 12 is likely to be a challenge for states parties:

> Achieving meaningful opportunities for the implementation of article 12 will necessitate dismantling the legal, political, economic, social and cultural barriers that currently impede children's opportunity to be heard and their access to participation in all matters affecting them. It requires a preparedness to challenge assumptions about children's capacities, and to encourage the development of environments in which children can build and demonstrate capacities. It also requires a commitment to resources and training.
>
> (General Comment No. 12. 2009: para. 135)

3.5.4 Civil rights and freedoms: articles 7, 8, 13–17 and 37(a)

During the drafting process of the CRC, the US delegation had proposed a single provision to include a child's right to civil and political freedoms, in particular a right to privacy (now article 16), a right to freedom of association (now article 15) and the right to freedom of expression (now article 13). The US delegation stated that children not only had the right to expect certain benefits from governments but they also had civil and political rights to protect them from abusive actions by governments. The consensus view during the drafting process had been that children should have broadly the same civil and political rights as applied to adults, other than the right to vote. However, the identity rights[83] contained in article 7 first appeared in the Declaration on the Rights of the Child of 1959[84] and were a novel addition in a major human rights treaty. The duty on states to ensure that systems are in place for the registration of every child at or immediately after birth is also a key provision.

3.5.4.1 Birth registration and identity rights (articles 7 and 8)

The existence of an enduring and robust birth registration system is a necessary precondition to the formulation of child policy and planning; a reliable and accurate demographic profile will be a valuable tool in such planning. Furthermore, where a child remains unregistered it is easier to abduct, sell or induce that child into prostitution, and a child may become stateless as a result of non-registration. The CtRC has recommended to states parties

> ... to undertake all necessary measures to ensure that all children are registered at birth, inter alia, by using mobile registration units and make birth registration free of charge. The Committee also reminds States parties of the importance of facilitating late registration of birth, and to ensure that children, despite being not yet registered, have equal access to health care, education and other social services.
>
> (Day of Discussion 2004: para. 2)

Consequently, the CtRC will often encourage states parties to enshrine their birth registration systems into legislation; for example, the plans for a National Registration Bill in Malawi that would make mandatory the registration of births, deaths and marriages (CO Malawi 2009). The CtRC will commonly express concern in relation to countries where there is a poor registration system. For example,

---

83 The rights to a name and a nationality are also dealt with by the Human Rights Committee in their General Comment on article 24 of the ICCPR, which states that the right to be registered immediately after birth and to have a name is of special importance in relation to children born out of wedlock; and that '[t]he main purpose of the obligation to register children after birth is to reduce the danger of abduction, sale of or traffic in children, or of other types of treatment.' Special attention was also needed in relation to the child's right to acquire a nationality in order to prevent a child becoming stateless (CCPR 1989: paras 7 and 8).

84 'The child shall be entitled from his birth to a name and a nationality.' Declaration of the Rights of the Child 1959, principle 3.

the CtRC noted with concern that more than 70 per cent of children in Pakistan were not registered at birth, especially girls and children belonging to a religious or minority group, refugee children and children living in rural areas (CO Pakistan 2009). The CtRC has also expressed concern about the extent of non-registration in Romania, in particular in relation to Roma children, street children, new-born babies abandoned in hospitals and home births (CO Romania 2009). The CtRC welcomes efforts to improve national systems of birth registration. For example, in Bangladesh progress has been made to increase birth registration to 50 per cent, though the absence of birth registration is still found to be a source of discrimination and exclusion from access to social services (CO Bangladesh 2009). The CtRC was concerned that, despite the adoption of a birth registration law providing for free registration, Chad had the lowest birth registration rate in West and Central Africa (CO Chad 2009: para. 39). Indeed, in some countries the progress in birth registration seems to have gone into reverse (CO Congo 2009; CO Niger 2009), or appears not to have progressed at all, for example, the low registration rate of 55 per cent in Mauritania. In such cases the CtRC may advise the state to seek technical assistance from UNICEF (CO Mauritania 2009). The CtRC is tireless in its encouragement of free birth registration. For example, Mozambique was praised for its efforts in increasing the free registration period from 30 days to 120 days, but expressed concern that the fees applicable for late registration might constitute an obstacle to achieving a higher birth registration rate (CO Mozambique 2009). In the Philippines the birth registration system is not free and fines have to be paid for late registration (CO Philippines 2009). The adoption of mobile registration units, particularly in rural areas, and the establishment of national electronic birth registration databases are encouraged where necessary (CO Bangladesh 2009). There are often particular concerns about birth registration of indigenous children as greater proportions of such children remain unregistered, and therefore are also at a high risk of becoming stateless (CO Philippines 2009; CO Bolivia 2009). The CtRC urges that states parties with indigenous populations should take special measures to ensure a robust, equitable and free-of-charge birth registration system (General Comment No. 11, 2009: paras 41–45). The text of article 7 also contains the child's right to know and be cared for by his or her parents. The CtRC interprets this to include the child's right to know their biological parents, so where national adoption systems include a mother's right to conceal her identity, this is likely to be criticised (CO France 2009: para. 43). Nevertheless, Luxembourg's reservation to article 7 seems to contradict this interpretation.[85]

The drafting of article 8 (preservation of identity) was originally proposed by Argentina and was prompted by the enforced disappearance of children and

---

85 'The Government of Luxembourg believes that article 7 of the Convention presents no obstacle to the legal process in respect of anonymous births, which is deemed to be in the interest of the child, as provided under article 3 of the Convention.'

adults in that country under the previous rule of a military junta. The CtRC commended the work done by Argentina's 'National Commission for the Right to an Identity' to recover children who had disappeared during the military regime (1976–83), and noted that out of an estimated 500 cases of disappearance of children, 73 had been found (CO Argentina 2002: para. 34). During the armed conflict in El Salvador (1980–92), more than 700 children had disappeared, of whom 250 had been traced by NGOs (CO El Salvador 2004). The right to acquire a nationality and a name has important implications for the right to obtain a passport and the right to vote. In general, under international law, nationality rules fall within the domain of municipal law, a point emphasised in the United Arab Emirates' reservation to article 7.[86] This has led to nations adopting different rules on nationality, and consequently there are persons who may fall between the various rules and become stateless. The CtRC urges states to ratify relevant international instruments, for example, the United Nations Convention Relating to the Status of Stateless Persons of 1954[87] (CO Niger 2009).

3.5.4.2 The rights to freedom of expression, thought, conscience, religion, association, no interference with privacy and access to information (articles 13–17)

The text of article 14 was one of the four principal areas of controversy in the drafting process of the CRC, according to Cantwell (1992: 26): see also Langlaude (2008). An earlier draft included 'the freedom to have or to adopt a religion … of his choice'. It was pointed out that a child's right to choose a religion did not exist under Islamic law; it could only apply to adults.

> This put the drafters in a delicate situation. What attitude was to be taken towards the elimination of a right of the child in the future Convention which was already conferred by a well established international human rights instrument [the International Covenant on Civil and Political Rights, article 18] without restriction as to the age of the beneficiary? Reluctantly, in the end, the proponents of retaining the full right agreed to drop all reference to choice, "in the spirit of compromise".
>
> (Cantwell 1992: 26)

The child's right to freedom of thought, conscience and religion (article 14) has been challenged in the context of France's constitutional arrangements that require a strict separation of Church and State: see generally, Eva (2006). New French laws which support a strictly secular public education system,

---

86 'The United Arab Emirates is of the view that the acquisition of nationality is an internal matter and one that is regulated and whose terms and conditions are established by national legislation.'
87 See Weis (1961) for an account of this Convention.

by prohibiting the wearing of religious signs or symbols in public schools, have been a cause for concern for the CtRC, though it has welcomed France's intention to review its legislation after 1 year (CO France 2004). The most recent concluding observation states the following:

> The Committee notes that the States party has undertaken measures to attenuate the consequences of the Law No. 2004-228 of 15 March 2004 banning the wearing of "signs or dress through which pupils ostensibly indicate which religion they profess in public, primary and secondary schools", including the establishment of a mediator in the national public education system. Nevertheless, the Committee endorses the concluding observations of CEDAW, that the ban should not lead to a denial of the right to education for any girl and their inclusion into all facets of the States party's society (CEDAW/C/FRA/CO/6, para. 20), as well as those adopted by the Human Rights Committee noting that respect for a public culture of laïcité[88] would not seem to require forbidding wearing such common religious symbols (CCPR/C/FRA/CO/4, para. 23).
>
> (CO France 2009: para. 45)

In Pakistan, while there are constitutional provisions giving a right of minorities to profess and practise their religions freely, the CtRC noted their concern that this was limited in practice and that citizens normally governed by secular law might sometimes be subject to sharia law. The CtRC was also concerned about reports that non-Muslim students had been forced to complete Islamic studies (CO Pakistan 2009: para. 43). As regards the child's right to freedom of association and peaceful assembly (article 15), the CtRC has expressed concern over the use in some countries of high-frequency ultrasound (aka 'mosquito devices'), flash ball devices and taser guns at public demonstrations and elsewhere (CO France 2009). Article 16 of the CRC, which protects children from arbitrary or unlawful interference with 'privacy, family, home or correspondence' and against unlawful attacks on the child's 'honour and reputation', is commented upon in some of the Committee's concluding observations. The CtRC has expressed its concern about the proliferation of databases in which personal data of children are gathered, stocked and used for a lengthy period, and that parents cannot oppose and/or are not informed of the registration of their children's data (CO France 2009). The CtRC will characteristically follow the recommendation of the Human Rights Committee[89] in this regard by calling upon states parties to ensure that such databases are lawfully regulated with clear aims, that the information cannot reach unauthorised recipients and that there are suitable rights

---

88 The nearest English translation is 'secularism', but this falls short of the pervading sense of Church/State separation that this phrase indicates to a French person.
89 Concluding observations of the Human Rights Committee, CCPR/C/FRA/CO/4, 31 July 2008, para. 22.

of access by children and their parents to such data. On occasion, the CtRC has been concerned where the media have disclosed information that might lead to the identification of child victims of crime (CO Mozambique 2009). It will urge states parties to respect the privacy of children in the media, particularly their participation in TV programmes and reality shows (CO Romania 2009).

3.5.4.3 Access to appropriate information (article 17)

The original draft of article 17 had been formulated in negative language, providing protection for children from the mass media, but was eventually reworked in more positive terms and acknowledged the educational role of mass media (Detrick 1999: 279). However, some of the CtRC's concluding observations register 'deep concern' that Internet providers, radio and satellite television channels operate with minimum regulations to protect children against harmful information and materials, including the exposure of children to digital pornography (CO Bangladesh 2009; CO Romania 2009). There may also be audiovisual media, including video games, with violent or pornographic content (CO France 2009). The CtRC will commonly identify the lack of sufficient mechanisms and guidance to monitor such media providers (CO Bolivia 2009; CO Mozambique 2009). Some states are at a more advanced stage in adopting protective measures in this field, for example, those where parental control software for Internet use is available (CO France 2009). The CtRC has noted with approval Sweden's adoption of a new law that criminalises any intent to approach children on the Internet under a fictitious identity (i.e. adults pretending to be a child) (CO Sweden 2009).

3.5.4.4 The right not to be subjected to torture or other cruel, inhuman or degrading treatment or punishment: in particular, corporal punishment (article 37(a))

The CtRC tries to ensure that the states parties have ratified other international instruments relevant to this right, in particular the UN Convention against Torture and Other Cruel, Inhuman or Degrading Treatment or Punishment of 1984 (CO Congo 2009). It will typically condemn legalised forms of corporal punishment, for example, whipping, amputation and stoning, and suggest suitable amendments to such penal codes (CO Mauritania 2009; CO Pakistan 2009). The CtRC has commented extensively about a wide range of conduct which breaches article 37(a). For example, it has noted concern about children in Koranic schools who are often chained up because of their difficult or rebellious behaviour. The CtRC also had concerns in relation to North Korea in respect of children subjected to severe ill-treatment while in detention (CO North Korea 2009). The CtRC has been concerned about reports of police officers illegally detaining children and subjecting them to torture and other ill-treatment (CO Mozambique 2009). The use of corporal punishment in the home, schools, institutions and workplaces is frequently a significant area of concern in the CtRC's concluding observations.[90] There is often a gap between the existence of laws preventing these practices and their implementation. A landmark study on 'Violence Against Children' was undertaken by the United Nations in 2005 (Pinheiro 2006), which included a number of regional consultations.[91] The study recommended, inter alia, the prohibition of all violence against children, ensuring accountability and ending impunity, the provision of recovery and social re-integration, the promotion of non-violent values and awareness-raising and the need to develop and implement systematic national data collection and research. The CtRC frequently refers countries to these recommendations in its concluding observations (e.g. CO Bangladesh 2009; CO Bolivia 2009).

The CtRC's General Comment No. 8 (2006) contains a useful analysis of the child's right not to be tortured or suffer cruel, inhuman or degrading treatment including corporal punishment:

> Article 37 of the Convention requires States to ensure that "no child shall be subjected to torture or other cruel, inhuman or degrading treatment or punishment". This is complemented and extended by article 19, which requires States to "take all appropriate legislative, administrative, social and educational measures to protect the child from all forms of physical or mental violence, injury or abuse, neglect or negligent treatment, maltreatment or exploitation, including sexual abuse, while in the care of parent(s), legal guardian(s) or any other person who has the care of the child". There is no ambiguity: "all forms of physical or mental violence" does not leave room for any level of legalised violence against children. Corporal punishment and other cruel or degrading forms of punishment are forms of violence and States must take all appropriate legislative, administrative, social and educational measures to eliminate them.
>
> (General Comment No. 8, 2006: para. 18)

The recommendations contained in this General Comment are frequently cited in the CtRC's concluding observations (e.g. CO Bolivia 2009). In some countries there has been progress in banning or limiting the use of corporal punishment in the context of disciplinary measures in schools and in the penal system, but such practices are often still prevalent in the family and alternative-care settings (CO Qatar 2009).

---

90 See also section 3.4.4.3 above for the CtRC's views about corporal punishment in the United Kingdom.
91 West Africa and Central Africa (Bamako, 23–25 May 2005); South Asia (Pakistan, 19–20 May 2005); Latin America (Buenos Aires, 30 May–1 June 2005); Europe and Central Asia (Ljubljana, 5–7 July 2005); East Asia and the Pacific (Bangkok, 14–16 June 2005); Eastern and Southern Africa (Johannesburg, 18–20 July 2005); Middle East and North Africa (Cairo, 27–29 June 2005).

3.5.5 Family environment and alternative care: articles 5, 18(1), (2), 9–11, 19–21, 25, 27(4) and 39

This cluster of rights relates to the integrity of the family unit and the way in which the state intervenes both to support families and to provide alternative care where the family environment has failed to function properly. The central theme underlying the CtRC's concluding observations reflects its perception of the appropriate balance between the state and the family (see section 1.1.4). In some countries there is evidence that the family unit has been fundamentally and structurally weakened, often as a result of civil strife, war and poverty. For example, one third of children in Rwanda have been orphaned (CO Rwanda 2004). In Equatorial Guinea, less than half of all children live with both parents as a result of large-scale poverty, HIV/AIDS, and the deterioration of traditional family solidarity (CO Equatorial Guinea 2004). Some of the relevant standards within this cluster of rights have been given further focus by the guidance given in Recommendation No. 7 (2004) and in a Day of Discussion (2005). The latter contains a statement of the core role of the state in preventing a child's separation from the family:

> The Committee emphasises that the family, as the fundamental group of society, is the natural environment for the survival, protection and development of the child and it acknowledges that there are several ethical and cultural values linked to the family. When considering the family environment, the Convention reflects different family structures arising from various cultural patterns and emerging familial relationships. In this regard, the Convention refers to various forms of families, such as the extended family, and is applicable in a variety of families such as the nuclear family, re-constructed family, joint family, single-parent family, common-law family and adoptive family. Socialization and acquisition of values are developed within the family and human relations within the family context are the most important links for the child's life in future.
>
> Acting on the basic premises that children do not develop properly outside of a nurturing "family" environment and that parents need a decent chance to raise their children, the Committee recommends that States parties develop, adopt and implement, in collaboration with the civil society, i.e. with non-governmental organizations, communities, families and children, a comprehensive national policy on families and children which supports and strengthens families. The national policy should not only focus on the State subsidies and material assistance to families in need but to provide families with support in the form of so-called service plans, including access to social and health services, child-sensitive family counselling services, education and adequate housing. The Committee recommends that the families and the family associations are integrated into the development of the national family policies and service plans.
>
> (Day of General Discussion 2005: paras 644–45)

The CtRC observed that there was a significant gap between states parties' obligations under the CRC and their practical implementation. It recommended that international standards for the protection of children without parental care be drafted and submitted to the General Assembly. The NGO Working Group on Children without Parental Care was established in 2005 and the United Nations Guidelines on the Appropriate Use and Conditions of Alternative Care for Children were drafted.[92] These guidelines, which elaborate on the principles and provisions of the CRC, have two principal aims: to ensure that children do not enter out-of-home care unnecessarily; and that, if they do have to enter care, the type and quality of out-of-home care is appropriate to children's rights and their specific needs.

3.5.5.1 Family environment

The CtRC welcomes states parties' efforts to strengthen family structures through investment in education, health and social services but will be concerned where a simple lack of financial resources is accepted as a reason to separate children from their families (CO Bolivia 2009; CO France 2009). It identifies the way in which family structures are threatened in circumstances where there are wider societal problems of armed conflict, an HIV/AIDS pandemic and extreme poverty (CO Chad 2009) and the neglect of orphans' inheritance rights (CO Malawi 2009). The CtRC urges states to provide more assistance to families in crisis situations due to poverty, absence of adequate housing or separation (CO France 2009). There are particular problems often caused in families where one or more parents migrate to another country, usually for economic reasons. In such circumstances, the CtRC will recommend that the state address the root causes for economic migration[93] and implement measures to mitigate the adverse effects on children left behind (CO Moldova 2009; CO Philippines 2009; CO Romania 2009): see also UNICEF (2006). There are also likely to be problems where children migrate and/or become unaccompanied by their parent(s). The CtRC's guidance on the treatment of unaccompanied and separated children draws attention to their particularly vulnerable situation and outlines the multifaceted challenges faced by states parties and others to enable such children to access and enjoy their rights. The issuing of a General Comment on the subject was motivated by the CtRC's 'observation of an increasing number of children in such situations' (General Comment No. 6, 2005: para. 2). Further problems are also noted with concern by the CtRC in relation to the increasing number of

---

92 The Human Rights Council on 17 June 2009 adopted by consensus resolution A/HRC/11/L.13 submitting the 'Guidelines for the Alternative Care of Children' to the General Assembly and these guidelines were adopted on the 20th anniversary of the CRC on 20 November 2009.

93 This issue is also commented upon by the Committee on Migrant Workers. See CMW/C/PHL/CO/1, 22 May 2009.

child-headed households, often a result of the HIV/AIDs pandemic and/or armed conflict (CO Mozambique 2009).

The particular ways in which parental responsibility is exercised (articles 5, 18(1), (2)) is a persistent subject of commentary by the CtRC. It has expressed concern, for example, that the practices of polygamy and repudiation have an adverse effect on children's rights (CO Mauritania 2009; CO Niger 2009). The CtRC has also been concerned about the persistence of a custom that is practised following divorce cases, where a child under 7 years old is automatically entrusted to the mother and thereafter to the father, without taking into account the child's views or considering the child's best interests (CO Niger 2009).

The limited degree to which fathers take parental responsibility is sometimes a cause for concern: see CO Qatar (2009). The CtRC has also identified legislative and *de facto* gender discrimination in sharing parental responsibility. It has recommended that 'States parties take all necessary measures to ensure that parents, both mothers and fathers equally, are able to meet their parental responsibilities' (Day of Discussion 2005: para. 647). On occasion, the Committee's ideological commitment to supporting the family as the preferred source of nurture for children, and its distaste for too much state intervention in family life, is plain to observe. The CtRC was:

> ... concerned at the excessive degree of [North Korea's] involvement in childcare, diminishing the active involvement of parents in the upbringing and hindering psycho-social and cognitive development of their children, in particular the widespread practice of leaving children in nurseries from Mondays to Saturdays, and the care of twins and triplets being relinquished to the State.

> (CO North Korea 2004)

The CtRC characteristically urges states parties to build their capacity of alternative care within a family-type environment and expresses concern where such arrangements are practically non-existent (CO Bangladesh 2009), or where family-type care is being institutionalised (CO Bolivia 2009). The automatic institutionalization of triplets in North Korea has again been criticised by the CtRC (CO North Korea 2009). The Committee is likely to criticise the omission of the 'best interest' principle in legislative standards, for example, in relation to parental custody disputes. In some countries, age limits are used as the underlying criterion in parental custody disputes: see CO Pakistan (2003) and CO Indonesia (2004).

3.5.5.2 Children without parental care

A state's efforts to provide alternative care are frequently tested when children are, for a number of possible reasons, deprived of their family environment. Sometimes children are abandoned simply because of harsh economic and other conditions, and there has evolved a predominant use of institutional care. Where the preference is for family forms of alternative care, for example, fostering, this may be accompanied by inadequate institutional care (CO Pakistan 2009). The CtRC will characteristically disapprove of high numbers of children being accommodated in institutional rather than family-friendly forms of alternative care (CO Philippines 2009), and some states need to be reminded that such care should only be a last resort (CO Chad 2009; CO North Korea 2009). Institutional care often suffers from poor living conditions; children with very different needs are provided inappropriately with the same service; and there may be a lack of any systematic review (see article 25) of the conditions children are living in. There are obvious dangers to children where institutional and other alternative-care settings lack sufficient monitoring mechanisms (CO Congo 2009), and indeed where some operate without being registered and regulated by the government at all (CO Malawi 2009).

In some states, the CtRC has noted the application of *kafalah* of Islamic law,[94] which is provided for in article 20(3) as a form of alternative care (CO Mauritania 2009; CO Pakistan 2009). The high profile internationally of the Romanian orphanages scandal in the 1990s has prompted some progress in that country (Lataianu 2003; Sargent 2004). The CtRC observed that decisions had been made in Romania to close down institutions and replace them with family-type homes, and between 2000 and 2007 the number of children in child protection institutions had more than halved, foster carers had been recruited and trained and the number of children in foster care had almost tripled. However, one unfortunate impact of these changes was that the abandonment of newborns often resulted in their spending many months in hospital wards. Also, a Romanian law forbidding the placement of any child under 2 years old into residential care, except children with severe disabilities, opened the way for discriminatory practice (CO Romania 2009). The principles of non-separation from parents (article 9) and family reunification (article 10) have generated adverse comments from the CtRC, for example, where there is a lack of opportunities to implement a child's right to maintain contact with his or her parents (CO France 2009).

3.5.5.3 Adoption

Article 21 of the CRC specifies that '[s]tates parties that recognise and/or permit the system of adoption shall ensure that the best interests of the child shall be the

---

94 'Traditional Muslim law does not appear to allow formal adoption because it refuses to accept the legal fiction which an adoption creates, namely that an adopted child can become equal to a blood relative of the adopting father' (Pearl and Menski 1998: 408). Placing children in *Kafalah* is similar to adoption, but not necessarily with the severing of family ties, the transference of inheritance rights, or the change of the child's family name. See also the reference to the *kafalah* in CRC, article 20(3).

paramount consideration', followed by five paragraphs setting out further details of states parties' obligations. It should be remembered that this area was one of the four principal issues of controversy identified by Cantwell (1992: 26). Since the Western notion of adoption – the full severing of the legal relationship between parent and child – is not recognised under Islamic law, the aim was to ensure that the text did not compel the Islamic states to recognise or establish systems of adoption. However, new thinking on adoption had already emerged in the form of a Declaration[95] approved by the General Assembly in 1986.

> This Declaration contained a number of fundamental principles that deserved inclusion in the Convention, and indeed translated the new thinking on inter-country adoption in particular, whereby emphasis was to be placed on guaranteeing the protection of the children concerned rather than on facilitating the process. The revised text of Article 21 took due account of all these questions.
>
> (Cantwell 1992: 26)

The Romanian orphanages scandal has led, inter alia, to that country now permitting intercountry adoption only in cases where a family relationship exists between the child and the prospective adoptive parents. The CtRC has recommended that Romania, in conformity with the Hague Convention on Intercountry Adoption and article 21 of the CRC, withdraw the existing moratorium on intercountry adoptions (CO Romania 2009: para. 55). The examination of the duties of states parties to combat the illicit transfer and non-return of children abroad (article 11) and to conduct an appropriate domestic and intercountry system of adoption (article 21) has prompted the CtRC to remind states parties to ratify the Hague Conventions on international child abduction and intercountry adoption. As regards the latter, France has been criticised as a receiving country of intercountry adoptions in that the main sending countries of origin have not ratified the Hague Convention on Intercountry Adoption and a high percentage of intercountry adoptions are carried out through individual channels and not through accredited bodies (CO France 2009). There are indeed a number of sending countries where intercountry adoption remains almost entirely unregulated (CO Niger 2009). In some countries, the system of domestic adoptions has remained informal and unregulated and often occurs within extended family structures, and intercountry adoptions are not always conducted consistently with article 21. There may be a marked preference given to intercountry over domestic adoption. The CtRC has recommended that all possibilities of domestic adoption

---

95 Declaration on Social and Legal Principles relating to the Protection and Welfare of Children, with special reference to Foster Placement and Adoption, Nationally and Internationally. General Assembly, 95th plenary meeting, A/RES/41/85, 3 December 1986. Available at: http://www.un.org/documents/ga/res/41/a41r085.htm (accessed 23 December 2009).

be considered under the 'subsidiarity principle'[96] before resorting to intercountry adoption. It has observed that, for example in Mozambique, the municipal legislation makes no distinction between intercountry and domestic adoption and is therefore violating the subsidiarity principle (CO Mozambique 2009). The legal protection for children involved in the traditional customary practice of 'intra-family' adoptions may also be weak (CO Chad 2009). The CtRC noted with concern the practice in the Philippines whereby, due to the high costs of the adoption process there, many non-biological parents resorted to a 'simulation of birth' or the fraudulent registration of birth to avoid the formal adoption process (CO Philippines 2009). There are also concerns in European states about cases of illegal adoptions, often the consequences of so-called 'weak' adoptions following internet sale and surrogacy arrangements (CO Netherlands 2009).

3.5.5.4 Abuse and neglect

The obligation to prevent the abuse and neglect of children (article 19), including their physical and psychological recovery and social reintegration (article 39), produces many criticisms of state practice, or rather a lack of adequate mechanisms to tackle these problems. Abuse and neglect can of course occur in a number of settings: the home, school, foster care, residential care and within other settings, including cases of sexual abuse in religious institutions (CO Philippines 2009). The CtRC reported starkly that one states party 'lacks a child protection system to monitor and report child abuse and neglect, leaving child victims unprotected' (CO Niger 2009: para. 51). The CtRC will characteristically recommend public awareness campaigns, the provision of information and parental guidance and the better training of professionals working with children, in addition to measures to strengthen support for both victims of abuse and neglect and the offenders (CO Bolivia 2009). However, the abuse and neglect that often occurs in the home, in schools, in children's homes, in detention centres and in the street regrettably 'is often legitimised by custom' (CO Chad 2009: para. 53).

3.5.6 Basic health and welfare: articles 6, 18(3), 23, 24, 26, 27(1), (2) and (3)

3.5.6.1 Children with disabilities

The CtRC has noted the historical exclusion of disabled children from participation in 'normal' childhood activities and the fact that 'their plight rarely figured

---

96 'An adoption within the scope of the Convention shall take place only if the competent authorities of the State of origin –
... b) have determined, after possibilities for placement of the child within the State of origin have been given due consideration, that an intercountry adoption is in the child's best interests;' (Hague Convention on Intercountry Adoption 1993, article 4(b)).

high on the national or international agenda, and they tended to remain invisible' (Day of Discussion 1997: para. 312). The CtRC has provided more recent guidance (General Comment No. 9, 2006) on children with disabilities and the United Nations has also produced a Convention on the Rights of Persons with Disabilities 2006,[97] along with an Optional Protocol that will allow the Committee on the Rights of Persons with Disabilities (CRPD) 'to receive and consider communications from or on behalf of individuals or groups of individuals subject to its jurisdiction who claim to be victims of a violation by that States party of the provisions of the Convention'.[98] One of the eight general principles of the Convention on the Rights of Persons with Disabilities 2006 is '[r]espect for the evolving capacities of children with disabilities and respect for the right of children with disabilities to preserve their identities'.[99] There is also a discrete provision in this Convention relating to children with disabilities which complements article 23 of the CRC:

Children with disabilities

1. States Parties shall take all necessary measures to ensure the full enjoyment by children with disabilities of all human rights and fundamental freedoms on an equal basis with other children.
2. In all actions concerning children with disabilities, the best interests of the child shall be a primary consideration.
3. States Parties shall ensure that children with disabilities have the right to express their views freely on all matters affecting them, their views being given due weight in accordance with their age and maturity, on an equal basis with other children, and to be provided with disability and age-appropriate assistance to realise that right.

(UN Convention on the Rights of Persons with Disabilities 2006, article 7)

The CtRC is not likely to miss an opportunity to recommend that states parties ratify these related international instruments. Its concluding observations frequently refer to the need for the states party to take into account the General Comment No. 9 (2006) and the Standard Rules on the Equalization of Opportunities

97 Adopted by General Assembly resolution on 13 December 2006. Opened for signature on 30 March 2007. This Convention came into force on 3 May 2008. As at 13 May 2010, it had 144 signatories and 86 states parties. The United Kingdom ratified this Convention on 8 June 2009. An Optional Protocol to this Convention was also adopted at the same time as the main Convention and opened for signature and came into force on the same dates. The Optional Protocol had 88 signatories and 53 states parties. The United Kingdom ratified this Optional Protocol on 7 August 2009.
98 Optional Protocol to the Convention on the Rights of Persons with Disabilities, article 1.
99 UN Convention on the Rights of Persons with Disabilities, article 3(h).

for Persons with Disabilities.[100] The CtRC frequently expresses concern that disabled children continue to suffer discrimination and that there is often a lack of training for teachers and other professionals working with such children and a lack of collection and analysis of data concerning children with disabilities (CO Bolivia 2009; CO Congo 2009). In some countries, the CtRC has observed an absence of modern approaches to special education, often with the consequence that many children are institutionalised or leave school altogether (CO Moldova 2009). In some states there is a lack of a robust infrastructure to manage the needs of children with disabilities. In Pakistan, for example, the CtRC has observed that 'the traditional charity-based welfare approach to addressing the needs of children with disabilities prevails' (CO Pakistan 2009: para. 58). In countries where there are more sophisticated infrastructures there are still opportunities for improvement. For example, the CtRC has urged the Netherlands to improve its access to public buildings and public transport by children with disabilities and to develop and strengthen early identification and intervention programmes (CO Netherlands 2009). It has also noted, in relation to Sweden, its concern about the limited participation of children with disabilities in cultural and recreational activities (CO Sweden 2009).

In some countries, views that children with disabilities are an 'embarrassment' to their parents and should not be integrated into mainstream society persist: see CO Botswana (2004) and CO Niger (2009). In others, the CtRC has observed a high prevalence of disability among children due to, for example, malnutrition and insanitary living conditions resulting from extreme poverty, and that 'children continue to face de facto discrimination and that they have an invisible role in society' (CO Philippines 2009: para. 53). There is also some evidence from the country reports that the social stigmatization of children with disabilities has led to some children being kept 'hidden' in the home by their parents (CO Romania 2009: para. 60).

3.5.6.2 Health and access to health services

The right to health and access to health services (article 24) is discussed at some length in the reporting process. Child mortality rates have been a cause for deep concern by the CtRC, and indeed the reduction of child mortality is one of the UN's 'millennium development goals' (MDGs).[101] Although deaths of children under 5 years of age worldwide declined from 93 to 72 deaths per 1,000 live births between 1990 and 2006, a child is 13 times more likely to die within the first 5 years of life in a developing country than in an industrialised country; and Sub-Saharan Africa accounts for around half the deaths of children in the developing world. About 27 countries, mostly in Sub-Saharan Africa, made no progress in reducing childhood deaths (UNDPI 2008). Mozambique had one of the highest

---

100 General Assembly resolution 48/96, A/RES/48/96, 85th plenary meeting, 20 December 1993.
101 'Target 1: Reduce by two thirds, between 1990 and 2015, the under-five mortality rate' (MDG 4).

infant mortality rates (CO Mozambique 2009). In Pakistan, the CtRC noted that there were an estimated 500,000 under-5-years infant deaths each year due to preventable causes (CO Pakistan 2009: para. 60). The CtRC observed that some countries have high rates of early childhood diseases, such as acute respiratory infections and diarrhoea, and recommended states to improve overall health strategies (e.g. CO North Korea 2009). High maternal deaths are also a subject of concern to the CtRC (CO Bolivia 2009; CO Chad 2009; CO Congo 2009) and also comprise an area targeted in the MDGs.[102] Indeed, the CtRC has observed the need for some states parties (e.g. CO Philippines 2009) to review their maternity legislation in order to support women by providing the recommended 14 weeks of paid maternity leave in accordance with the Maternal Protection Convention of 2000.[103]

The CtRC urges states parties to encourage the exclusive breastfeeding of infants up to the age of 6 months, and states that fall below this standard are urged to adopt legislation based on the 1981 World Health Organization's (WHO) International Code of Marketing of Breast-milk Substitutes (CO Congo 2009; CO Netherlands 2009). It will criticise states where the implementation of this standard remains inadequate and where the aggressive promotion of breastmilk substitutes remains common (CO France 2009). Only 30 per cent of children less than 6 months of age were exclusively breastfed in Mozambique (CO Mozambique 2009). Equally, some states parties are praised for maintaining an overall high rate of breastfeeding (CO Mauritania 2009).

The critical shortage of health care workers also figures in many of the CtRC's observations (e.g. CO Malawi 2009). One persistent concern of the international community has been to establish the structures necessary to tackle vaccine-preventable diseases with low-cost immunization programmes. Medical facilities are all too often concentrated in urban areas and, consequently, poor health standards are often disproportionately worse in rural areas (CO Mauritania 2009). Discriminatory practices may also be present in access to health care in some countries. For example, the CtRC noted their concern about migrant children's access to health services in the Netherlands (CO Netherlands 2009). Interestingly, the CtRC has observed that complementary and alternative medicine is a recognised field of medicine, in Europe and globally, and has criticised Sweden for prohibiting its use for the examination, treatment and care of children below 8 years of age (CO Sweden 2009).

3.5.6.3 Adolescent health

In some countries, the nature and extent of adolescent health problems are not well understood, and the CtRC will characteristically advise that a comprehensive study is made as a basis for the formulation of adolescent health policies and

---

102 'Target 1: Reduce by three quarters the maternal mortality ratio. Target 2: Achieve universal access to reproductive health'. (MDG 5).
103 ILO Convention No. 183 . This Convention came into force on 7 February 2002, but only had 18 ratifications, as at May 2010.

practices (CO Bangladesh 2009; CO Niger 2009). The CtRC has observed, for example, that in Pakistan 'the notion of adolescent health and in particular adolescent reproductive health has still gained little acceptance' (CO Pakistan 2009: para. 64). Adolescent health issues have also prompted special mention from the CtRC via a detailed General Comment No. 4 (2003). The CtRC has noted its concern about mental health issues, including eating disorders and suicide or attempted suicide rates in some countries (CO France 2009). The CtRC has also had concerns over long waiting lists for mental health services (CO Netherlands 2009). There have also been concerns about emerging trends of obesity, psychological and mental health problems (CO Qatar 2009; CO Sweden 2009). The CtRC has noted a high teenage pregnancy rate, sexually transmitted infections and high incidences of drug, tobacco and alcohol abuse in some countries (CO Bolivia 2009; CO Congo 2009) and unsafe abortions in others (CO Chad 2009; CO North Korea 2009). It has observed the difficulties that teenagers may have in gaining access to reproductive health services and information. It also shares the view expressed by the Committee on the Elimination of Discrimination Against Women (CEDAW) on the importance of including adequate sex education in school curricula (CO Mozambique 2009). The CtRC has expressed serious concern about inadequate reproductive health services and low rates of contraceptive use; for example, in the Philippines, only 36 per cent of women relied on modern family planning methods in 2006 (CO Philippines 2009: para. 61).

3.5.6.4 Harmful traditional practices

The way in which customary and traditional practices have had an impact on the maintenance of health standards has been a persistent theme in the CtRC's examination of state reports: for example, female genital mutilation (FGM), a practice said to be very prevalent (45 per cent) in Chad, with a majority of girls being excised between the ages of 5 and 15 (CO Chad 2009: para. 61). There is relatively less FGM occurring in the Congo, but this country lacks any legislation prohibiting the practice and domestic law sets the age for marriage at 15, and in practice early and forced marriages are not uncommon (CO Congo 2009). FGM occurs within certain ethnic groups in Malawi (CO Malawi 2009). Even where FGM has been forbidden by municipal law, the evidence is often that this practice remains and the prohibition is not adequately enforced, with the practice affecting some 70 per cent of girls in Mauritania (CO Mauritania 2009). In some states there have been significant efforts to eradicate FGM through legislation combined with awareness-raising campaigns organised through partnership with traditional chiefs (CO Niger 2009). Early marriage remains a common practice in Mauritania and girls continue to be subjected to forced feeding ('gavage'[104]).

---

104 Force-feeding had been a practice in some Middle Eastern and North African countries where fatness was considered a marriage asset in women and voluptuous figures were perceived as

The CtRC has also been deeply concerned about forced sexual intercourse with children during initiation ceremonies on reaching puberty (CO Malawi 2009; CO Mozambique 2009). The CtRC has expressed concern about exchange marriages (*vani* and *swara*)[105], marriages with the Holy Koran and sentences of *sina* (CO Pakistan 2009).

3.5.6.5 The prevalence of HIV/AIDS

The prevalence of HIV/AIDS is obviously a source of profound concern in many nations. A General Comment provides a detailed commentary about this issue and its relevance in the context of the CRC. It is noted, for example, that:

> Initially children were considered to be only marginally affected by the epidemic. However, the international community has discovered that, unfortunately, children are at the heart of the problem. According to the Joint United Nations Programme on HIV/AIDS (UNAIDS), the most recent trends are alarming: in most parts of the world the majority of new infections are among young people between the ages of 15 and 24, sometimes younger. Women, including young girls, are also increasingly becoming infected. In most regions of the world, the vast majority of infected women do not know that they are infected and may unknowingly infect their children. Consequently, many States have recently registered an increase in their infant and child mortality rates. Adolescents are also vulnerable to HIV/AIDS because their first sexual experience may take place in an environment in which they have no access to proper information and guidance. Children who use drugs are at high risk.
>
> (General Comment No. 3, 2003: para. 2)

In some countries the incidence of HIV/AIDS is high and overall awareness of the disease may be low (CO Chad 2009). In addition to recommending that states parties attend to the guidance in General Comment No. 3 (2003), the CtRC recommends they take into account the International Guidelines on HIV/AIDS and Human Rights (UNAIDS 2006). The formulation of these guidelines represented a culmination of a number of international, regional and national declarations and activities. Many of these confirmed that discrimination on the basis of actual or presumed HIV/AIDS status was prohibited by existing international human rights standards, and clarified that the term 'or other status' used in

---

indicators of wealth. Girls are forced, usually by their female relatives, to overeat, often accompanied by physical punishment.

105 This refers to a custom that is widespread across Pakistan and used as a method of resolving disputes and settling debts between families and tribes. Female members from the offending male's family are married or given to the victim's family as a reparation or penance.

the non-discrimination clauses of such texts 'should be interpreted to include health status, such as HIV/AIDS'.[106] This, and other, human rights aspects of the HIV/AIDS epidemic have proved to be key elements in preventing a stigmatization and marginalization process that might otherwise prevent open access to health care services. In some countries HIV/AIDS continues to be a culturally and religiously sensitive topic which poses challenges in terms of transmission channels, treatment and preventive measures (CO Pakistan 2009: 72). The Guidelines are designed as a practical tool for states in managing their HIV/AIDS policies and strategies. High incidences of HIV and children orphaned by HIV have been reported, for example, in the Democratic Republic of Congo (CO Congo 2009). In some countries there is a very low coverage of antiretroviral treatment for the prevention of mother-to-child transmission, and the human capacity constraints of trained health care workers with regard to children have been reported (CO Malawi 2009). The CtRC has been deeply concerned about increasing rates of sexually transmitted infections, including HIV/AIDS in Moldova, and has noted a lack of respect for confidentiality in relation to the HIV status of patients. The Committee recommended in particular the use of peer education within the adolescent population as an integral part of the state's strategy (CO Moldova 2009).

3.5.6.6 Standard of living

The CRC obliges states to recognise every child's right to a standard of living 'adequate for the child's physical, mental, spiritual, moral and social development'. Parents have the primary responsibility to secure living conditions necessary for a child's development. States parties are in turn obliged to take appropriate measures to assist parents and others responsible for the child to implement this right, and 'in case of need provide material assistance and support programmes, particularly with regard to nutrition, clothing and housing' (article 27(1)–(3)). Child poverty is therefore a key concern. These provisions of the CRC resonate with MDG 1, to halve the proportion of people whose income is less than $1 a day between 1990 and 2012.[107] In particular, child poverty impacts frequently on marginalised and minority groups of children. For example, the CtRC observed that while poverty among the Roma population in Romania had dropped between 2003 and 2006, the poverty risk among the Roma population was still four times that for the majority population (CO Romania 2009: para. 74). In Sweden there

---

106 Commission on Human Rights resolutions: 1990/65, 1992/56, 1993/53, 1994/49, 1995/44 and 1996/43.
107 Millennium Development Goal 1. Target 1: Halve, between 1990 and 2015, the proportion of people whose income is less than $1 a day. Target 2: Achieve full and productive employment and decent work for all, including women and young people. Target 3: Halve, between 1990 and 2015, the proportion of people who suffer from hunger.

was concern about the much higher rates of poverty amongst immigrant children, along with concern that the recession that commenced in 2007 might have a severe impact on the situation of such vulnerable groups of children (CO Sweden 2009).

Some states, like the United Kingdom (see section 3.4.4.5), are attempting to eliminate child poverty entirely by 2020; the CtRC encourages the adoption of legislation to achieve that target, including the adoption of measurable indicators (CO France 2009). In other countries, child poverty is pervasive and persistent. The CtRC noted with deep concern, for example, the widespread poverty and lack of access to, and availability of, food, safe drinking water and sanitation in the Democratic People's Republic of Korea (North Korea 2009). The CtRC found that in Bolivia 70 per cent of children live in poverty, of which 45 per cent live in extreme poverty (CO Bolivia 2009: para. 61). It found that children constitute 28 per cent of the population living in poverty in Moldova (CO Moldova 2009). Access to clean, potable drinking water and safe sanitation systems is also a concern in this context (CO Chad 2009; CO Congo 2009).

The residual obligation of states to provide state social assistance[108] is often the subject of commentary in the CtRC's concluding observations. It found, for example, that in Bangladesh such assistance was 'limited in view of the magnitude of the problems' and such programmes were not adequately evaluated for their short- and long-term impact (CO Bangladesh 2009: para. 71). Although the CtRC noted with approval the provision of social cash transfer schemes in Malawi in seven out of 28 districts that targeted child poverty and encouraged school attendance, it regretted the persistent widespread poverty and lack of basic services available, particularly in rural areas (CO Malawi 2009).

3.5.7 Education, leisure and cultural activities: articles 28, 29 and 31

3.5.7.1 The right to education

Article 28 of the CRC obliges states parties to recognise the right of the child to education, and 'with a view to achieving this right progressively and on the basis of equal opportunity' states are obliged in particular to work towards five goals. These goals are: to make primary education compulsory and free to all, an objective also reflected by MDG 2[109]; to encourage different forms of secondary education;

---

108 CRC, article 27(3).
109 Millennium Development Goal 2. Achieve universal primary education. Target 1: Ensure that, by 2015, children everywhere, boys and girls alike, will be able to complete a full course of primary schooling.
    Millennium Development Goal 3. Promote gender equality and empower women. Target 1: Eliminate gender disparity in primary and secondary education, preferably by 2005, and in all levels of education no later than 2015.

to make higher education accessible to all on the basis of capacity by every appropriate means; to make educational and vocational information and guidance available and accessible; and to take measures to encourage regular school attendance. The CRC has also provided standards about the content and aims of education (article 29) in a General Comment:

> Article 29(1) not only adds to the right to education recognised in article 28 a qualitative dimension which reflects the rights and inherent dignity of the child; it also insists upon the need for education to be child-centred, child-friendly and empowering, and it highlights the need for educational processes to be based upon the very principles it enunciates. The education to which every child has a right is one designed to provide the child with life skills, to strengthen the child's capacity to enjoy the full range of human rights and to promote a culture which is infused by appropriate human rights values. The goal is to empower the child by developing his or her skills, learning and other capacities, human dignity, self-esteem and self-confidence. 'Education' in this context goes far beyond formal schooling to embrace the broad range of life experiences and learning processes which enable children, individually and collectively, to develop their personalities, talents and abilities and to live a full and satisfying life within society.
>
> (General Comment No. 1, 2001: para. 2)

The CtRC urges states parties to consider and understand the importance of education and implementing children's rights in early childhood (General Comment No. 7, 2005; CO Mozambique 2009). The CtRC encourages states parties to increase primary and secondary school enrolment where possible and to conduct awareness-raising campaigns to improve the overall quality of the school experience, in particular to combat the mistreatment of children and prevent bullying of children (CO Bangladesh 2009). The establishment of schools that can maintain a safe environment for children is an obvious priority. In some countries there have been high levels of sexual abuse and harassment which have deterred, in particular, girls from attending school (CO Mozambique 2009). Constitutional or legislative guarantees of free and compulsory primary and secondary education do not necessarily result in their complete realization; indigenous children, for example, may not achieve the same access to free education, school fees may continue to be charged, and a continued gender disparity persists to the detriment of the girl child (CO Bolivia 2009; CO Chad 2009). The CtRC will also be concerned where it identifies a gap between the maximum age limit for education and the minimum age of employment under ILO Convention No. 138 (CO Chad 2009; CO Pakistan 2003, 2009).

In some countries the educational infrastructure is simply very poor: low enrolment rates, particularly for girls and children living in rural areas and from vulnerable groups; schools are poorly equipped; there are small numbers of qualified teachers (CO Congo 2009; CO Moldova 2009). In other, more developed nations there are persistent problems of educational disadvantage amongst particular groups; for example, Roma and traveller children, asylum-seeking children and teenage mothers (CO France 2009). In the Netherlands there is a persistent problem of de facto ethnic segregation in the city schools (CO Netherlands 2009). In Sweden, there is a problem of undocumented children without a residence permit and 'children in hiding' who in effect do not enjoy a right to education (CO Sweden 2009). The CtRC has also been concerned at reports that the *madrases*[110] have been used to recruit children to participate in armed conflicts despite renewed efforts to monitor these schools more carefully (CO Pakistan 2003, 2009).

3.5.7.2 The right to rest, leisure, play, recreational and cultural activities

Article 31 of the CRC obliges states parties to recognise, respect and promote the child's right to rest and leisure, to engage in play and recreational activities and to participate freely in cultural life and the arts. Furthermore, states must encourage the provision of appropriate and equal opportunities for cultural, artistic, recreational and leisure activity. During the drafting process the German and Japanese delegates doubted whether it was advisable to proclaim a universal right of the child to rest and leisure. The German representative 'indicated his preference for dealing with the issue in the context of the provision against economic and social exploitation' (Detrick 1992: 416). Nevertheless, the text of the article was agreed and no country has entered a reservation in relation to this article. The CtRC's concluding observations record that facilities for such activities are somewhat limited (CO Bangladesh 2009) and sometimes not really integrated in community and urban development planning (CO Bolivia 2009). In other countries, the CtRC has observed a decrease in, for example, playground space for children (CO France 2009) and a need in some countries to increase their existing playground spaces (CO Romania 2009). Some of the CtRC's observations simply do not make any mention of article 31 issues at all (CO Congo 2009; CO Malawi 2009; CO Mauritania 2009; CO Moldova 2009; CO Mozambique 2009; CO Niger 2009).

3.5.8 Special protection measures: articles 22, 32–36, 37(b), (c), (d), 38, 39 and 40

This section is divided into eight categories which follow the sub-headings used in the CtRC's concluding observations.

---

110 Religious schools in Islamic countries.

3.5.8.1 Refugee children

The CtRC has observed in relation to Bangladesh 'that no durable solution has yet been found to comprehensively address the rights of refugee children' (CO Bangladesh 2009: para. 78). The CtRC will typically recommend that states parties, which have not yet done so, should consider ratifying the Convention relating to the Status of Refugees of 1951, the Convention Relating to the Status of Stateless Persons of 1954 and the Convention on the Reduction of Statelessness of 1961. The CtRC characteristically recommends that states parties take measures to ensure that asylum claims by children are analysed under a refugee status determination procedure that takes into account the specific needs and rights of child asylum seekers in accordance with international refugee and human rights law (CO Bolivia 2009). The CtCR also draws attention to General Comment No. 6 (2005) on the treatment of unaccompanied and separated children outside their country of origin. In some countries the creation of refugee camps, though potentially beneficial in that these may contain living, educational, medical and other services, also may produce a range of problems. For example, the CtRC was concerned at the high level of ethnic tension and violence amongst children in camps where corporal punishment is inflicted by teachers. There had also been sexual violence against girls in the camp and economic exploitation of refugee children placed in foster families (CO Mozambique 2009). The CtCR's concluding observations also extend the Committee's concern to 'internally displaced persons' (IDPs) within a states party in addition to refugees from another country (CO Congo 2009).[111] The CtRC expressed concern in relation to Niger about the lack of information on IDPs, including children who had been forcibly displaced from their homes due to ongoing armed conflict in the northern part of the country (CO Niger 2009). The CtRC expressed its deep concern about the situation of unaccompanied children in the waiting zones of French airports, where placement decisions cannot be legally challenged and the legal requirement of the appointment of an ad hoc administrator is not systematically applied. The use of a bone test to determine age rather than more recent methods was also criticised (CO France 2009). The CtRC was also concerned that the institution of the *Kafalah*[112] is not applied within the context of family reunification.[113] The Democratic People's Republic of Korea's position is that it has no refugee children. Nevertheless, the CtRC expressed concern about 'returnee' children,

---

111 The CtRC recommended the actioning of the findings of the Representative of the Secretary-General on the human rights of IDPs, following his mission to the Democratic Republic of Congo in January 2009 (CO Congo 2009: para. 75).

112 See also the reference to the *Kafalah* in CRC, article 20(3).

113 See also the decision of the *Conseil d'État*, of 24 March 2004, which held that the decision made by the French local authorities to prevent a child from entering France to join her *Kafalah* parents infringed the right to respect private and family life. However, the concluding observation noted that this decision had yet to be implemented (CO France 2009: para. 90).

that is, persons who had crossed the border into neighbouring countries who may face harsh treatment upon return or repatriation (CO North Korea 2009). The CtRC observed with approval the efforts made in Mauritania to resolve the position of those who were exiled two decades ago, though there appeared to be no comprehensive returns strategy (CO Mauritania 2009). The Netherlands has made a restrictive declaration concerning article 22.[114] While the CtRC noted with approval that the Netherlands admits a high number of asylum seekers it also expressed concern about the practice of detention of unaccompanied children and families with children and that children continue to disappear from reception centres (CO Netherlands 2009). The CtRC has also welcomed Pakistan's generosity 'in hosting the world's largest and longest-lasting refugee population over the past three decades'. However, it also noted the harsh living conditions in the refugee camps, where a large number of children live without access to basic health and other services (CO Pakistan 2009: para. 82).

3.5.8.2 Children in armed conflict

The issue of children in armed conflict (article 38) and the physical and psychological recovery and social integration of such children (article 39) has been of great significance in both the drafting of the CRC and its subsequent development. The age at which children should be permitted to take part in armed conflict was one of four principal areas of controversy identified by Cantwell (1992: 26): see further, Chapter 8 (Children and Armed Conflict). In part because of the unsatisfactory compromises reached in relation to the drafting of article 38, there is now an Optional Protocol to the Convention on the Rights of the Child on the involvement of children in armed conflict (OPAC) that entered into force in 2002, which has built upon the text of article 38: see generally, Chapter 8.

The CtRC's concluding observations under this head are usually somewhat brief summaries of their (separate) concluding observations of states parties' initial reports made under OPAC. As the second reports under OPAC arrive, the CtRC's consideration of them will be reintegrated into their consideration of state reports under the main Convention. As we have seen (section 3.5.4.1 above), defects in a country's birth registration system have a number of unfortunate

---

114 'With regard to article 22 of the Convention, the Government of the Kingdom of the Netherlands declares:

    a) that it understands the term "refugee" in paragraph 1 of this article as having the same meaning as in article 1 of the Convention relating to the Status of Refugees of 28 July 1951; and

    b) that it is of the opinion that the obligation imposed under the terms of this article does not prevent
        – the submission of a request for admission from being made subject to certain conditions, failure to meet such conditions resulting in inadmissibility;
        – the referral of a request for admission to a third State, in the event that such a State is considered to be primarily responsible for dealing with the request for asylum.'

consequences, one of which arises in this context; the difficulty to determine the age of a person recruited or used in hostilities and thereby to identify how the obligations of article 38 and OPAC are being implemented (CO Bangladesh 2009). In some countries, the minimum age for voluntary or compulsory recruitment is not specified in law, and children as young as 13 years old can enrol in military schools and be taught basic handling of firearms (CO Niger 2009). The CtRC has expressed grave concerns about the recruitment and use of children by the Sudanese rebel movement and by Chadian forces and the small number of children demobilised since 2007 (CO Chad 2009). The CtCR took note of the recommendations of a Security Council working group that examined the situation in Chad (Security Council 2008). It also expressed 'grave concern' about the situation in the Democratic Republic of Congo, that the states party, through its armed forces, 'bears direct responsibility for violations' and has failed to protect children from non-state militias. It was particularly concerned about 'the very high number of children who have been abducted by armed groups for use in hostilities and are victims of violence, rape, sexual and commercial exploitation' (CO Congo 2009: para. 67): see also Security Council (2008a). The CtRC noted that while North Korea is still in a state of armistice[115] the perception remains that it is under constant threat and pressure from outside forces. The consequent political climate has been damaging for children; in particular, the aims of education (article 29) have been skewed by military aspects of the education system (CO North Korea 2009). The Committee noted with approval that the minimum age for recruitment was 18 years in Mauritania but that the Ministry of Defence had a discretion to lower this age limit to 16 years. The CtRC has urged Mauritania to raise the age to 18 in all circumstances, in accordance with the African Charter on the Rights and Welfare of the Child (see section 2.5.2.2) (CO Mauritania 2009). Almost inevitably, there is often a lack of data produced by countries plagued by armed conflicts, making the task of reintegration and recovery (article 39) more difficult. The CtRC expressed concern 'that former girl soldiers as well as girls and young women who were exploited as slave labour or abducted into sexual slavery in armed forces have often been excluded from programmes for reintegration of former soldiers' (CO Mozambique 2009: para. 77). The CtRC also received reports of forced underage recruitment and training of children by non-state groups in Pakistan for armed actions and terrorist attacks, including suicide attacks (CO Pakistan 2009). Despite some positive efforts in the Philippines, the CtRC noted concerns about the continuance of recruitment of

---

115 An armistice of 1953 ended the Korean War between North and South Korea that had begun in 1950. However, a peace treaty was never signed and there have been tensions between the two states ever since. The United States and North Korea (a socialist republic) do not have diplomatic relations and remain officially at war. The United Kingdom established diplomatic relations with North Korea on 12 December 2000. Both North Korea (the Democratic People's Republic of Korea) and South Korea (the Republic of Korea) were accepted into the United Nations in 1991.

children by armed groups 'to serve as combatants, spies, guards, cooks or medics and at the lack of prosecution of perpetrators of such crimes' (CO Philippines 2009: para. 69).

3.5.8.3 Economic exploitation including child labour

Exploitative child labour is not only regulated by the CRC, but is also controlled by the 1973 Minimum Age for Admission to Employment Convention (ILO Convention No. 138) and the Elimination of the Worst Forms of Child Labour Convention of 199 (ILO Convention No. 182): see generally, Chapter 4. Indeed, in the CtRC's concluding observations there are often references to these instruments and to the need for some countries to seek technical assistance from the International Labour Organization (ILO) and from its International Programme to Eliminate Child Labour (IPEC) and from UNICEF. Under article 32 of the CRC states parties are obliged to recognise the right of the child to be protected from economic exploitation and from performing any work that is likely to be hazardous or interferes with the child's education or is harmful to a child's development. Within a general duty on states to take all legislative and other measures to ensure the implementation of these obligations, states must in particular: provide for a minimum age for admission to employment, provide for the regulation of hours and conditions of employment, and provide appropriate penalties or other sanctions to ensure effective enforcement. The CtRC has noted the important efforts in Bangladesh to eliminate child labour from the ready-made garment sector, though it also notes the high incidence of child workers in five selected worst forms of child labour, that is, welding, auto workshops, road transport, battery recharging and recycling, and work in tobacco factories (CO Bangladesh 2009). One characteristic feature of exploitative child labour is its prevalence in the informal sector, in small family businesses, for example. Some of the CtRC's concluding observations note the lack of hard data on activities within the informal sector (CO Qatar 2009). Concerns have also been expressed in relation to hazardous work in mining (CO Bolivia 2009; CO Congo 2009), the position of *mouhadjirin* children[116] (CO Chad 2009), the engagement of school children in work that far exceeds vocational educational goals and is physically highly demanding (CO North Korea 2009), the widespread use of child labour in the agricultural sector and the need to harmonise the minimum age of admission to employment with the minimum age for the end of compulsory education (CO Mauritania 2009), the employment of children in commercial cotton, tobacco and tea plantations (CO Mozambique 2009) and the high incidence of child begging (CO Romania 2009). In some countries the use of child labour is widespread and awareness of the consequent damage is low. In Niger, for example, the CtRC

116 Children entrusted to *marabouts* (religious teachers) to study the Koran.

noted its concern that 74 per cent of children under 15 years of age work, many of them in hazardous conditions in mines and quarries which may expose them to mercury, and in crushing and hoisting ore (CO Niger 2009: para. 74). The use of bonded and forced labour and an absence of appropriate labour inspectorate machinery continue in some countries (e.g. CO Pakistan 2009).

3.5.8.4 Street children

Children living and working on the street are obviously in a vulnerable situation and may be prime targets for organised child- and drug-trafficking operations, susceptible to abuse, and may be charged with the crime of vagrancy (CO Bangladesh 2009; CO Bolivia 2009). There are reports of large numbers of street children in some countries, though the data is often incomplete (CO North Korea 2000; CO Mauritania 2009; CO Moldova 2009; CO Pakistan 2009). There are many poverty-related causes that contribute towards the appearance of street children. In some countries, the occurrence of HIV/AIDS orphans provides a supply of children living on the street and at heightened risk of sexual and economic exploitation (CO Chad 2009). In Romania, the forced eviction of Roma families has resulted in a number of street children and a high number of children go missing from child protection institutions (CO Romania 2009). The CtRC frequently urges states parties to undertake a systematic assessment of the situation of street children in order to obtain a better understanding of root causes (CO Mozambique 2009). In Mauritania and Niger there is a growing problem with *talibés* children,[117] forced by *marabouts* to beg (CO Mauritania 2009; CO Niger 2009).

3.5.8.5 Sexual exploitation and sexual abuse

Chapter 7 deals generally with the subject of sexual exploitation. Article 34 of the CRC obliges states parties 'to undertake to protect the child from all forms of sexual exploitation and sexual abuse'. The text of the article mandates states to take all appropriate national, bilateral and multilateral measures to prevent: the inducement or coercion of a child to engage in unlawful sexual activity; the exploitative use of children in prostitution or other unlawful sexual practices; and the exploitative use of children in pornographic performances and materials. The CtRC has noted with approval the establishment of a regional strategy for seven countries of the South Asian Association for Regional Cooperation to

---

117 *'Talibés'* are followers of a *'marabout'*, to whom they were entrusted by their families to learn the Koran. The *marabouts* frequently do not have the means to support them. See generally, Perry (2004) for an account of the conflicts between children's rights advocacy and the maintenance of *talibés* as traditional institutions. See also Anti-Slavery International (2009) for an account of *talibes in Senegal:* available at: *http://www.antislavery.org/includes/documents/ cm_docs/2009/f/forced_child_begging_in_senegal_july_2009.pdf.*

combat sexual abuse and exploitation of children (CO Bangladesh 2009). The CtRC characteristically advises states parties to implement appropriate policies and programmes in accordance with the Declaration and Agenda for Action and the Global Commitment adopted at the 1996, 2001 and 2008 World Congresses against Commercial Sexual Exploitation of Children (see Chapter 7). The CtRC examines carefully states parties' criminal/penal codes to ensure compliance with the CRC in this area. For example, in Mauritania the crime of rape had not been clearly defined in domestic legislation and girl victims of sexual abuse are criminalised according to sharia law, including charges of *zina* (i.e. extramarital and premarital sexual intercourse) (CO Mauritania 2009). The CtRC observed in another state that its domestic legislation did not cover certain sexual offences against children, including forced sexual relations and sexual exploitation (CO Mozambique 2009). It also urges that child victims of sexual exploitation are not themselves subject to criminalization or marginalization (CO Chad 2009) and that appropriate measures be taken to end impunity for perpetrators of sexual offences (CO Congo 2009). This is again an area where some states are not collecting sufficient information to guide policy and legislative initiatives. An extreme example of this shortfall in objective information was the statement in the report from North Korea that there had been no cases of sexual exploitation and abuse of children reported (CO North Korea 2009: para. 66). Undoubtedly, vulnerable groups such as street children are particularly exposed to sexual exploitation (CO Philippines 2009).

3.5.8.6 Sale of children and trafficking

The problem of trafficking and the sale of children has become a global one, and has attracted increasing international attention. A Special Rapporteur was established by the UNCHR in 1990 and an Optional Protocol to the Convention on the Rights of the Child on the Sale of Children, Child Prostitution and Child Pornography (OPSC) entered into force in 2002 (see Chapter 7). Article 35 of the CRC obliges states parties to take all appropriate national, bilateral and multilateral measures to prevent the abduction, sale or traffic in children for any purpose or in any form. An earlier draft of this article had initially been combined with the text of article 34 (sexual exploitation and abuse), but delegates agreed there should be two separate articles:

> [t]he problem of the sale or traffic of children was wider in scope than that of sexual exploitation and children were subjected to sale or traffic for many reasons: economic exploitation, sexual exploitation and sexual abuse, as well as for reasons of adoption or labour.
>
> (Detrick 1992: 430)

One example of a multilateral measure has been the 2005 Multilateral Cooperation Agreement to Combat Trafficking in Persons, and the Joint Plan of Action against Trafficking in Persons, Especially Women and Children, in the West and Central African region (CO Niger 2009). The obvious elements of criminality associated with this activity make it a difficult subject on which to gather reliable data or analysis. The CtRC characteristically recommends the establishment of strong monitoring mechanisms and supporting programmes and information campaigns to prevent trafficking (CO Philippines 2009). The CtRC noted that some countries continue to be both a source and a destination country for victims of trafficking (CO Bolivia 2009; CO Pakistan 2009). 'Reports of trafficking' are noted by the CtRC in relation to several countries, but the information given is sometimes little better than anecdotal. There are reports – for example from Mauritania – of children sold for use as camel jockeys and young girls as brides to the Middle East (CO Mauritania 2009). The CtRC has observed in relation to Mozambique that there is 'continuous' trafficking of children from rural to urban areas for forced labour and that girls are trafficked to and from the state for sexual exploitation and domestic servitude. Such activity is rarely followed by prosecution and conviction (CO Mozambique 2009).

3.5.8.7 Administration of juvenile justice

Article 37(b) provides that no child shall be deprived of his or her liberty unlawfully or arbitrarily and any arrest, detention or imprisonment shall be in conformity with the law and only used as 'a measure of last resort and for the shortest appropriate period of time'. Article 37(d) provides that every child deprived of liberty shall be treated with 'humanity and respect for the inherent dignity of the human person'. In particular, children deprived of liberty must be separated from adults 'unless it is considered in the child's best interests not to do so' and such children have the right to maintain contact with their family 'through correspondence and visits, save in exceptional circumstances'. Finally, article 37(d) provides that children deprived of their liberty shall have the right to 'prompt access to legal and other appropriate assistance'; the right to challenge the legality of the deprivation of liberty before a court or other 'competent, independent and impartial authority'; and to a prompt decision on any such action. Article 40(1) obliges states parties to recognise the right of every child in conflict with the penal law to be treated in a manner consistent with the promotion of the child's sense of dignity. Paragraph 2 of this article additionally specifies particular guarantees to the child alleged as or accused of having infringed the penal law: see the full text of article 40(2). Paragraph 3 obliges states to promote the establishment of laws, procedures, authorities and institutions 'specifically applicable to children' in conflict with penal law, and in particular to establish a minimum age of criminal responsibility. States are also obliged to seek measures other than judicial proceedings for such children. Paragraph 4 of article 40 stipulates that there should be a variety of dispositions (some are listed in the text) as alternatives to 'institutional care'.

The CtRC has devoted a Day of Discussion (1995a), a Recommendation No. 2 (1999) and General Comment No. 10 (2007) to the administration of juvenile justice. The Recommendation recalls 'that since the beginning of its work, the administration of juvenile justice has received consistent and systematic attention from the Committee' and notes that the CtRC's juvenile justice standards 'are in many instances not reflected in national legislation or practice, giving cause for serious concern'. The CtRC characteristically calls states parties to bring their juvenile justice systems into conformity with a number of international guidelines and agreements: the United Nations Standard Minimum Rules for the Administration of Juvenile Justice ('the Beijing Rules'),[118] the United Nations Guidelines for the Prevention of Juvenile Delinquency (the 'Riyadh Guidelines'),[119] the United Nations Rules for the Protection of Juveniles Deprived of their Liberty ('the Havana Rules')[120] and the Vienna Guidelines for Action on Children in the Criminal Justice System.[121] The CtRC also notes that child victims and witnesses of crime should be treated in a manner consistent with the United Nations Guidelines on Justice in Matters Involving Child Victims and Witnesses of Crime.[122] It will often call upon states to take into account specifically the relevant parts of General Comment No. 10 (2007). On occasion it will recommend that the states party considers seeking technical assistance from UNICEF and the United Nations Interagency Panel on Juvenile Justice[123] (CO North Korea 2009).

The CtRC has noted concern, in relation to some countries, that children less than 18 years old had been subjected to the death penalty (CO Bangladesh 2009; CO Pakistan 2009). It has also noted its concern over the imposition of life imprisonment sentences (CO Bangladesh 2009). Children are also held in pre-trial detention in some countries for long periods, and in Malawi such detention appeared to lie with an executive discretion unsupervised by any judicial means (CO Malawi 2009). The CtRC's advice is that such measures must be ones of last resort and for the shortest periods of time (CO Congo 2009). The use of isolation of children as a punishment in youth detention centres in Sweden has been criticised by the CtRC, which has taken the view that solitary confinement should not be used unless judged to be absolutely necessary and that the period of isolation should not exceed 24 hours (CO Sweden 2009).

Where possible, the CtRC – consistently with the international standards in this area – advises the development of alternatives to prison. However, it has expressed concern in relation to some countries about the limited use of diversion to such alternatives (CO Philippines 2009). The CtRC has frequently criticised

---

118 Adopted by General Assembly resolution 40/33 of 29 November 1985.
119 General Assembly, A/RES/45/112, 68th plenary meeting, 14 December 1990.
120 Adopted by General Assembly resolution 45/113 of 14 December 1990.
121 Recommended by Economic and Social Council resolution 1997/30 of 21 July 1997. In resolution 1997/30, paragraph 1, ECOSOC welcomed the Guidelines and invited all parties concerned to make use of them in the implementation of the CRC with regard to juvenile justice.
122 Economic and Social Council resolution 2005/20 of 22 July 2005.
123 The Interagency Panel on Juvenile Justice was established by the United Nations Economic and Social Council (ECOSOC) resolution 1997/30, to act as a 'coordination panel on technical advice and assistance in juvenile justice'.

the low age of criminal responsibility existing in some states; for example, in one country (CO Bangladesh 2009) the CtRC noted concern that the age of criminal responsibility had only been raised to 9 years old whereas it recommends it is raised to at least 12 years old with a view to raising it further, as recommended in the General Comment No. 10 (2007). In several countries the age of criminal responsibility was set at 7 years old, too low in the CtRC's opinion (CO Malawi 2009; CO Mauritania 2009; CO Pakistan 2009; CO Qatar 2009). In France, no age of criminal responsibility has been established (CO France 2009). In North Korea children aged 14 to 17 years who had committed crimes were subjected to 'public education measures', though the CtRC noted with concern that the states party had produced little information to explain what these consisted of and whether they were CRC-compliant (CO North Korea 2009).

As in the case of the United Kingdom (see section 3.4.1), there has also been concern over the frequency of children accommodated in adult jails (CO Bangladesh 2009; CO France 2009), sometimes in precarious conditions (CO Bolivia 2009). In some countries there may be hardly any, or only a rudimentary, development of a distinct juvenile court system (CO Congo 2009), or otherwise the situation may fall short of a fully-fledged juvenile justice system compliant with the CRC and other international agreements (CO North Korea 2009).

3.5.8.8 Children belonging to a minority or an indigenous group: article 30

As can be seen from the discussion in the previous sections, the position of minority and indigenous groups of children is frequently a more vulnerable one, consequent upon discriminatory attitudes which have often become institutionalised. The rights of indigenous children have been the subject of one of the CtRC's Days of Discussion (2003). The resultant recommendations called generally for a more comprehensive review of the situation of indigenous children (General Comment No. 11, 2009). A more comprehensive international instrument addressing the rights of indigenous persons appeared in the form of the United Nations Declaration on the Rights of Indigenous Peoples in 2007:[124] see Chapter 9. The CtRC's concluding observations also make reference to the findings of a Special Rapporteur on the situation of human rights of indigenous peoples;[125] for example, the illegal appropriation of indigenous lands by farm operators, the pollution of waters and soils traditionally used by indigenous communities, situations of servitude or forced labour, the failure to adapt the national education system to traditional cultures, the limited access to health services, and persistent

---

124   Adopted by resolution of the General Assembly, A/RES/61/295, 2 October 2007.
125   In 2001, the Commission on Human Rights appointed a Special Rapporteur on the situation of human rights and fundamental freedoms of indigenous people, as part of the system of thematic 'Special Procedures'. The Special Rapporteur's mandate was renewed by the Commission on Human Rights in 2004, and by the Human Rights Council in 2007.

manifestations of racism against indigenous peoples (CO Bolivia 2009).[126] Article 30 of the CRC asserts that children, in states that contain ethnic, religious or linguistic minorities or persons of indigenous origins, should 'not be denied' rights to enjoy their own culture, profess and practise their own religion, or use their own language. Despite some suggestions during the drafting process that this wording should be changed to a more positive obligation, 'a child...shall have the right...', the final text of article 30 retains the negative language. In part this was because the CRC Working Group did not want to pre-empt other international discussions of indigenous rights and how these could be framed in international law (Detrick 1999: 408–414). Reflecting some of these debates, for example, that selecting such minority groups of children was itself discriminatory, France has made a reservation in respect of article 30 disapplying this provision in the light of article 2 of the Constitution of the French Republic. The French Constitutional provision provides a guarantee of 'equality before the law to all citizens without distinction on the basis of origin, race or religion'.[127] However, the CtRC takes the view that 'equality before the law' may be insufficient to ensure equal enjoyment of rights by minority and indigenous groups in France's overseas departments and territories (CO France 2009). Venezuela takes the position, in its interpretative declaration, that article 30 'must be interpreted as a case in which article 2 of the Convention [the principle of non-discrimination] applies'.

3.6 Failure of the United States and Somalia to ratify the CRC

As we have seen, a distinctive feature of the CRC has been its near universal ratification. The United States and Somalia remain the only countries that have not ratified it. It should, however, be noted that both countries are signatories to the CRC.[128] The act of signature is not without some legal effect.

> Where signature is subject to ratification, acceptance, or approval ..., signature does not establish consent to be bound. However, signature qualifies the signatory state to proceed to ratification, acceptance, or approval and creates an obligation of good faith to refrain from acts calculated to frustrate the objects of the treaty.

> (Brownlie 2008: 610)

---

126 See also 'Report of the Special Rapporteur on the situation of human rights and fundamental freedoms of indigenous people, Mr. James Anaya – Mission to Bolivia', A/HRC/11/11, 18 February 2009.

127 'La France est une République indivisible, laïque, démocratique et social. Elle assure l'égalité devant la loi de tous les citoyens sans distinction d'origine, de race ou de religion. Elle respecte toutes les croyances'. (Constitution of the Fifth French Republic, 15 October 1958, article 2).

128 The USA on 16 February 1995 and Somalia on 9 May 2002.

Article 18 of the Vienna Convention on the Law of Treaties provides that states are bound not to do anything that would defeat the object and purpose of the relevant treaty until the state has made its intention not to ratify clear. In the case of Somalia, there has been no ratification to date as the combined effects of civil war since 1991 and successive waves of further inter-clan tensions have in effect produced a failed state that has lacked the governmental infrastructure of public institutions and sufficient stability to maintain diplomatic activity and contribute to international relations in the normal way.

The United States' failure to ratify the CRC remains a significant weakness of this international instrument, given its global power and influence. President Clinton decided that the United States would sign the CRC but that, in sending it to the Senate for their 'advice and consent' to ratification, he would 'ask for a number of reservations and understandings ... [to] protect the rights of the various states under the nation's federal system of government and maintain the country's ability to use existing tools of the criminal justice system in appropriate cases'.[129] Madeleine Albright, acting as the US delegate to the United Nations, signed the CRC on behalf of the United States on 16 February 1995.

Rutkow and Lozman (2006) usefully explain the USA's failure to ratify the CRC in terms of four areas of concern: sovereignty, federalism, reproductive and family planning, and parental rights. In terms of sovereignty, the United States has often been very cautious about agreeing to international human rights treaties; for example, the United Nations Convention on the Elimination of All Forms of Racial Discrimination of 1965 was only ratified 28 years after being signed by President Lyndon B. Johnson.[130] There were several calls from both the US Congress and the US Senate for the United States to sign the CRC in the early 1990s (Rutkow and Lozman 2006: 170–71). In essence, there are some structural and constitutional difficulties that have posed obstacles to US ratification (Kilbourne 1998), though increasingly commentators argue that such obstacles are either misconceived or have been superseded by subsequent developments. The concern about federalism is based on the fact that family law matters generally fall within the competence of the State legislatures rather than the Federal government,[131] so there are fears that ratification would federalise an area of law traditionally within the States' competence. Under article VI of the US Constitution (the 'supremacy clause'),[132] an international treaty ratified by the

---

129 Press Release, The White House, 'White House Statement on U.S. Decision to Sign UN Convention on Rights of the Child' (10 Feb. 1995).

130 Signed on 28 September 1966, ratified on 21 October 1994.

131 The Tenth Amendment to the US Constitution ('The powers not delegated to the United States by the Constitution, nor prohibited by it to the States, are reserved to the States respectively, or to the people'.) restricts the Federal government's authority to legislate in this area.

132 'This Constitution, and the Laws of the United States which shall be made in Pursuance thereof; and all Treaties made, or which shall be made, under the Authority of the United States, shall be the supreme Law of the Land; and the Judges in every State shall be bound thereby, any Thing in

United States should be applied as part of the 'law of the land'; that is, it would be binding in State and Federal courts. In principle, therefore, such ratification would result in American courts being able to cite provisions of the CRC. However, in recent times, when the Senate has given its consent to the ratification of human rights treaties, it has often included a declaration that the rights-guarantee provisions are not 'self-executing' (Quigley 2002). The lower courts have relied on these declarations as depriving litigants of the right to rely on the guarantee provisions. However, it has been pointed out that:

> This Senate practice, and the deference given by courts, remain controversial. No court has yet explained in constitutional terms how a Senate declaration of non-self-execution acquires the force of law.
>
> (Quigley 2002)

One particular sticking point has been the conflict between the right to life in the CRC and the existence of the death penalty applicable to under-18-year-olds in some states in the United States. However, the Supreme Court in 2005 abolished juvenile executions in the United States.[133] There have also been concerns about reproductive and family planning matters, mainly on the basis of religious beliefs and that the CRC does not expressly offer protection of the foetus (Smolin 2006). However, as discussed in (sections 3.4.1 and 3.5.2), the identification of the beginning of childhood proved problematic in drafting the CRC, and the combination of the text of article 1 and the ninth preambular paragraph[134] in effect provides an opportunity for states parties to interpret the CRC as providing legal protection either from the moment of live birth or from conception, as the case may be.

The failure to ratify can also be explained by reference to certain objections in principle, in particular the issue of how far 'children's rights' might threaten 'parental rights'. In addition, it has been thought that the inclusion within the CRC of economic rights might be inconsistent with American concepts of the limits of government. Finally, there are political and social factors to consider, particularly the influence of 'moral rearmament' groups.

The CRC's provisions for the participatory rights of children are the ones that have often sparked resistance among U.S. interest groups. Arguments against these participatory rights have been expressed vehemently by conservative

---

the Constitution or Laws of any State to the Contrary notwithstanding'. (US Constitution 1787, article VI, clause 2).

133 *Roper v. Simmons*, 543 U.S. 551 (2005).

134 Bearing in mind that, as indicated in the Declaration of the Rights of the Child, 'the child, by reason of his physical and mental immaturity, needs special safeguards and care, including appropriate legal protection, before as well as after birth'.

> family rights activists and have contributed to the failure of the United States to ratify the CRC.
>
> (Rutkow and Lozman 2006: 165)

It is a matter of regret that the United States, though it signed the CRC in 1995, has still failed to transmit it to the US Senate for ratification, particularly in the light of its active interest and participation in the original drafting process and its support and ratification of both Optional Protocols to the CRC. It has also been an important strand to US foreign policy to encourage human rights observance in other states, a policy surely made more difficult by its own delays in ratifying such instruments and in particular its failure so far to ratify the CRC. The emergence of the Obama administration has given some hope to reformers that the United States may eventually ratify the CRC. Indeed, there is a vigorous campaign group[135] in the United States that, at the time of writing, is advocating strongly US ratification of the CRC.

3.7 The Optional Protocols

The CRC now has two Optional Protocols: on the involvement of children in armed conflict (OPAC) and on the sale of children, child prostitution and pornography (OPSC). Both came into force in 2002.[136] An 'Optional Protocol' is not an amendment to the text of a UN Convention. It is an addition to the main convention on any topic relevant in the original treaty. Such protocols are 'optional' as states may not wish to have the burden of additional duties to those in the main convention that they have already ratified. The ICCPR, for example, has two protocols: one enabling the Human Rights Committee to receive and consider communications from individuals claiming to be victims of violations of any of the rights set forth in the Covenant (1966), and another on the abolition of capital punishment (1989). The reporting regime and an account of the number of report processes applicable for both Optional Protocols has been dealt with in section 3.3.2. Both Optional Protocols to the CRC are discussed in further detail in Chapters 7 and 8, respectively. It is however of interest that the USA, which has conspicuously failed to ratify the CRC to date, has in fact ratified both Optional Protocols.

---

135 'The Campaign for US Ratification of the CRC': http://childrightscampaign.org/crcindex.php.

136 OPSC: adopted and opened for signature, ratification and accession by General Assembly resolution A/RES/54/263 of 25 May 2000, entered into force on 18 January 2002. OPSC had 117 signatories and 137 ratifications as at 14 May 2010.

OPAC: adopted and opened for signature, ratification and accession by General Assembly resolution A/RES/54/263 of 25 May 2000, entered into force 12 February 2002. OPAC had 125 signatories and 132 ratifications as at 14 May 2010.

Chapter 4

Child labour

4.1 The phenomenon of child labour

The complexity of the phenomenon of child labour is widely acknowledged. It can be viewed as an economic, structural, governmental, moral and ethical issue, including human rights concerns (Abernethie 1998: 83). The pervasive process of globalization has enabled a more intense international focus on the problem, but it has also added to the complexities in debates surrounding it (Muntarbhorn 1998: 255). Child labour involves not only concerns about children's welfare and development but also considerations of effects on macroeconomic and labour markets. Furthermore, the different grounds – economic, developmental, human-itarian and moral – that might justify the elimination of child labour sometimes conflict with each other. For example, the elimination of child labour from facto-ries might lead to an increase in adult employment and wage rates, but might also negatively affect children's welfare if there are no adequate schools available and the children's only remaining option is to undertake more hazardous work in the 'informal sector' of the economy (Anker 2000: 264). Furthermore, our image of child labour is too often that it is a phenomenon largely only relevant to the devel-oping countries, whereas there is evidence of child labour in industrialised Europe, the United States and other developed nations (Selby 2008; Kilkelly 2003). In the field of child labour, one needs particularly to be aware of the dif-ferent perceptions of childhood in Northern and Southern countries respectively. Some commentators argue that the ethnocentrism of industrialised countries inappropriately dominates the international discourse on children's rights (Boyden 1997). The following sections discuss the key elements of the phenom-enon of child labour.

4.1.1 Difficulties of definition and types of child labour

The concept of 'child labour' tends to conjure up several images which are not always helpful in properly identifying the nature of the problem. One such image is of children working in terrible conditions in sweatshops in India in the carpet or garment industries, or in the firecracker or matches industries in China.

Another such image focuses on exploitation in export-related jobs and sex tourism. However, the reality is that most child labourers in the world are employed in the agriculture sector.[1] It has been estimated that exploitation in export-related jobs accounts for a quite small proportion of the total number of child labourers, and that commercial sexual exploitation of children is dominated by local rather than foreign customers. There are also believed to be a large number of children working in the 'informal economy', that is, doing work that goes on outside of a country's formal employment sector. Such work may be exploitative, for example, where children are working long hours under bad conditions in family-run enterprises or even in illegal activities within an organised crime environment. But work in the informal sector may also be beneficial to an individual child, depending on the context – for example, work delivering newspapers, babysitting or gardening (Selby 2008: 170). Some studies have identified quite positive attitudes by children themselves towards 'light work' and helping out in the family and home environment (Ochaíta et al. 2000: 31).

It should be clear that, for the purposes of imposing a legal regime to reduce child labour or eliminate it entirely, we need to define more precisely what 'child labour' should mean for these purposes. The task of defining child labour has been much discussed and contested precisely because there are many different views about what type of work or work characteristics are consistent with a child's welfare and development and what types do not, or indeed may have deleterious consequences. It is now generally accepted and, as we shall see later in this chapter, also reflected in the international legal regime, that a distinction must be drawn between work that children do, either at home within the family or for an external employer, which may be beneficial and contribute to their development and wellbeing, and 'child labour' that is exploitative. However, this begs the question of what practices can be regarded as 'exploitative' for these purposes. Exploitation is a somewhat value-laden term that is difficult to define objectively (Anker 2000: 260–61). But of course not all forms of child labour are exploitative, and in some settings child work may be an 'integral part of the socialization process' (Alston 1989: 36). There is clearly a need to view the work that children do as lying on a continuum between dangerous and exploitative work on the one hand and beneficial work on the other. A reasonable attempt at defining these two locations on this continuum is given in the following:

> We can speak of dangerous and exploitative work when it has the following characteristics: it is carried out full-time at too early an age; the working day is excessively long; it is carried out in inadequate conditions; it is not sufficiently well-paid; it involves excessive responsibility; it undermines the child's dignity and self-esteem. On the other hand, beneficial work is defined

---

1 69 per cent, according to ILO (2006: 8).

as that which promotes or stimulates the child's integral development – physical, cognitive and social – without interfering in his/her scholastic or recreational activity or rest. This type of work contributes to children's socialisation, offering them the opportunity to carry out certain tasks that provide them with feelings of competence and independence that are fundamental to the proper development of their self-concept and self-esteem.

(Ochaíta *et al.* 2000:19–20)

It is now widely accepted that the dividing line between exploitative/dangerous and beneficial child work is identified by an examination of how such work impacts on a child's development. Indeed, as will be seen later, article 32 of the UN Convention on the Rights of the Child (CRC) obliges states to recognise the child's right to be protected from economic exploitation and from performing any work that is, inter alia, likely to be 'harmful to the child's health or physical, mental, spiritual, moral or social development'. However, economists and governments responsible for collecting national statistics may have a rather narrower definition of child labour if they define it initially as 'employment'. This might catch those with a 'contract of employment' and also those recognised as 'self-employed'. The definition of 'economic' used by the UN's System of National Accounts (SNA) is formulated in broader terms relating to the content and productive nature of the work; so gathering fuel for household use would come within the SNA definition, even though it often occurs outside a market context, and such children would be classed as child labourers. On the other hand, burning fuel in the process of cooking a meal would not be classified as economic and many would say this was a case of a child being engaged in household 'chores', a delineation that typically has gender consequences (Dorman 2008).

The International Labour Organization (ILO) (see section 2.4.1.4) currently uses three categories: 'economic activity', 'child labour' and 'hazardous work', for the purpose of constructing their global statistics. Their definitions are reproduced below:

"Economic activity" is a broad concept that encompasses most productive activities undertaken by children, whether for the market or not, paid or unpaid, for a few hours or full time, on a casual or regular basis, legal or illegal; it excludes chores undertaken in the child's own household and schooling. To be counted as economically active, a child must have worked for at least one hour on any day during a seven-day reference period. "Economically active children" is a statistical rather than a legal notion.

"Child labour" is a narrower concept than "economically active children", excluding all those children aged 12 years and older who are working only a few hours a week in permitted light work and those aged 15 years and above whose work is not classified as "hazardous". The concept of "child labour" is based on the ILO Minimum Age Convention, 1973 (No. 138), which represents the most comprehensive and authoritative international definition of minimum age for admission to employment or work, implying "economic activity".

"Hazardous work" by children is any activity or occupation that, by its nature or type, has or leads to adverse effects on the child's safety, health (physical or mental) and moral development.[2] Hazards could also derive from excessive workload, physical conditions of work, and/or work intensity in terms of the duration or hours of work even where the activity or occupation is known to be non-hazardous or "safe". The list of such types of work must be determined at the national level after tripartite consultation.

(ILO 2006: paras 20–22)

However, there is no universally accepted definition of 'child labour'. The phrase is used in public discourse to refer to 'child time in activities that are somehow harmful to the child' (Edmonds 2008: 1). Economists think in terms of 'opportunity costs' to determine what might be 'harmful', that is, what activities would the child participate in if s/he was not working, and on balance would these be more beneficial? In other words, 'harmful' could be understood as implying the child would be made better off by not participating in the activity. However, according to Edmonds, who reviewed a large number of academic papers and reports on this problem, this definition of child labour creates 'the problem of the counterfactual', that is, it is impossible to know what the children would be doing in the absence of work (Edmonds 2008: 1). He argues that this problem is implicitly recognised in the Convention concerning the Prohibition and Immediate Action for the Elimination of the Worst Forms of Child Labour of 1999 (hereafter 'ILO Convention No. 182'), where hazardous work and other 'worst forms' of child labour are identified on the basis of job characteristics. He concludes that the international definition of child labour needs to be based on the key ILO Conventions and defined on the basis of a list of job attributes and work characteristics that can be tracked; for example, total hours worked, numbers of children working in certain industries (manufacturing, mining & quarrying, hotels and restaurants, private residences other than child's family), and certain working conditions (streets, at night or predawn, low lighting, lack of ventilation, operating machinery or powered tools) (Edmonds 2008: 38).

A further problem with efforts to define child labour is that the pattern of child labour is frequently *intermittent*. Many children may move from school into work and back again several times; some children attend school and also work and these patterns may vary considerably over time. In one study, using longitudinal data from Brazil, where the authors tracked the employment patterns of thousands of children aged 10–16 during 4 months of their lives in the 1980s and

2 See ILO Convention No. 182, article 3(d).

1990s, it was concluded that 'intermittent employment is a crucial characteristic of child labour which must be recognised to capture levels of child employment adequately and identify child workers (Levison *et al.* 2007: 245). Such problems of definition also pose difficulties in attempting to construct credible measurements of the extent of child labour (see section 4.1.6).

4.1.2 Identifying the causes of child labour

The complexity of the phenomenon of child labour is particularly apparent in analyses of its causes. Some commentators have attempted to produce typologies of causation deploying categories which range from the dynamics of the family unit, through to the school system, the labour situation of adults and finally macrosystemic elements such as prevailing cultural attitudes towards childhood, economic and social policies and existing legislation (Ochaíta *et al.* 2000: 16–17). The income from child labour may reflect a family's strategy to simply subsist. A key feature of child labour is that it is not only *caused* by structural economic, educational and social disadvantage, but it also *contributes* to the maintenance of such inequalities. The research literature is replete with discussion of the linkage with poverty and the lack of education and health services.[3] In low-income countries, child labour tends to decline with increases in gross per capita domestic product (GDP) (Betcherman *et al.* 2004: 12–13). ILO states that in countries with a per capita income of US$500 or less the labour force participation rate of children is very high, at 30–40 per cent. That participation rate declines rapidly to 10–30 per cent for countries with per capita incomes between US$500 and US$1,000. However, this negative correlation becomes less marked for further increases in per capita income 'where cultural factors may come into play' (ILO 2006: para. 36).

The increasing recognition of child labour located within a poverty matrix indicates much about the remedial strategies to tackle the problem, that is, strategies which integrate anti-poverty and wider development goals (Cooper 1997: 429). The way in which the matrix of poverty, educational disadvantage and child labour are linked by both cause and effect prompted ILO to announce that '[w]e have surely reached a moment in history where the absolute number of child labourers, and the proportion of a country's children who are subject to child labour, particularly to its worst forms, should become key indicators of economic and social development' (ILO 2002, para. 63).

The role of education is a key component in any discussion about the causes of child labour. There is, perhaps unsurprisingly, a lot of evidence confirming the adverse impact of child labour on educational attainment (Betcherman *et al.* 2004: 13). In a study on Bangladesh it was observed that children from poorer

---

3 See also Dorman (2008), who reviews a rapidly expanding literature on the relationships between child labour, education and health.

households who had little access to secondary education became engaged in a range of economic activity some of which was hazardous (Masum 2002: 266). In developing countries, it is estimated that one in five children (aged 6–11) is not in school – more than 100 million children in total. Children drop out of school often because of poor teaching and learning conditions and they are predominantly poor, rural and disproportionately female (Betcherman *et al.* 2004: 17). If the states' obligations under the CRC[4] to make primary education compulsory and available free for all and the MDG goal to strengthen universal primary education[5] are to be achieved, then it follows that child labour will necessarily diminish. The persistence of child labour in any country is clearly a significant obstacle to achieving universal education (Betcherman *et al.* 2004: 2). It is also thought that school attendance will both prevent child labour from occurring and have the potential to rehabilitate rescued child labourers and ensure their social reintegration. It would seem that '[a]dvances in the right to education therefore cannot but go hand in hand with the elimination of child labour'(Noguchi 2002: 362). However, developing nations have often been reluctant to invest in universal education on the basis of the large costs involved, and that poor families rely upon their children's income. Such arguments, however, appear unsatisfactory when one considers the historical evidence which suggests a range of factors contributing to the introduction of universal education. Japan introduced compulsory education in 1872 and North and South Korea, Taiwan and China introduced compulsory education shortly after the Second World War; all at a time when per capita incomes in those countries were low and poverty widespread. Nevertheless, in one country after another the phased extension of the age of compulsory education accompanied further restrictions on the employment of children (Weiner 1994: 128).

However, it should not be thought that the causative factors underlying child labour follow the same pattern in every country. A reasonable assumption in the United Kingdom – the first industrialised nation – might be that child labour is intimately linked with the process of industrialisation. However, that assertion is belied when one examines the widespread incidence of child labour in India, where the majority of child labourers are employed in the small-scale enterprises and in agriculture (Weiner 1994: 122). The pervasiveness and durability of the causative mix of factors leading to child labour in any one country is explained better by detailed investigation of the national profile. This, at least, should enable the disposal of several myths that have grown up around the child labour issue, for example, that children's 'nimble fingers' enable them to handle more efficiently tasks such as producing knots in the weaving of carpets, picking tea

---

4 CRC, article 1(a).
5 Millennium Development Goal 2: Achieve universal primary education. Target 1: Ensure that, by 2015, children everywhere, boys and girls alike, will be able to complete a full course of primary schooling.

leaves and packing matches. A detailed study surveying the gem, brassware, glass, pottery and lock industries in India refutes a number of these claims (Burra 1995).

Given the causative significance of poverty to the existence and extent of child labour, it is tempting to conclude that any remedial strategy (see section 4.3) should prioritise the eradication of poverty. The problem is that such policies take many years, sometimes several generations, to make significant development gains. The UN's Commission on Human Rights (UNCHR)[6] stated long ago that '[p]overty is often the main cause of child labour, but generations of children should not be condemned, until poverty is overcome, to exploitation' (UNCHR 1993: para. 2). Human rights advocates are in agreement with this point:

> To argue that the enormous problem of poverty must be solved first and that the problem of child labor should be addressed gradually is antithetical to the inherent logic of human rights.
>
> (Silk and Makonnen 2003: 368)

But the reduction of educational disadvantage and poverty cannot be a complete answer to the problem of child labour. There have been significant efforts in India to reduce poverty and strengthen education. However, one study observes that '[n]otwithstanding these economic successes, the number of children working in India has not decreased significantly and may have even increased', and that it is important that Indian government stops thinking in terms of child labour being a problem simply associated with poverty (Agarwal 2004: 665, 713). Some empirical research shows that the relationship between poverty and child labour is weaker than is often believed (Betcherman et al. 2004: 3). Indeed, the causative strength of poverty and lack of education weakens when we consider the persistence of child labour within the developed nations. In Europe,[7] it seems likely that a significant number of children, rather than being motivated by family survival strategies typical in developing nations, are more motivated by the desire to obtain 'supplementary income necessary to meet their consumer desires and the demands of peer pressure' (Kilkelly 2003: 347).

4.1.3 The extent and location of exploitative child labour

ILO's global report on child labour announced optimistically in 2006 that 'a future without child labour is at last within reach' (ILO 2006: 1). The claim was

---

6 Replaced in 2006 by the United Nations Human Rights Council (UNHRC). See section 2.5.1.1.
7 Kilkelly argues that the problem of child labour in Europe is worthy of consideration on the basis that (i) the protection of fundamental rights and freedoms is one of the EU's essential objectives, and (ii) the EU has substantial weight as a political and economic player with global diplomatic reach to promote human rights and labour standards (Kilkelly 2003: 322).

principally based on the global trends in children's 'economic activity' across the various regions, as set out in Table 4.1, and the number of children in 'child labour' and 'hazardous work' (subsets of those in 'economic activity') as set out in Table 4.2.

Table 4.1 shows that the world population of children grew from 1.19 billion in 2000 to 1.2 billion in 2004, while the absolute number of 'economically active' children fell from 211 million to 190.7 million, reflecting a global fall in the economic activity rate of children from 17.6 per cent to 15.8 per cent in the same period. These figures are broken down by region. It can be seen that 'Asia and the Pacific' have much the greater share of all children and economically active children in absolute numbers. It can also be seen that in each region, other than 'Sub-Saharan Africa', there has been a lessening in the absolute number of economically active children. The reduction of this number in 'Latin America and the Caribbean' is particularly marked and yields an impressive fall in the activity rate from 16.1–5.1 per cent. Even the slight rise in absolute numbers of economically active children in 'Sub-Saharan Africa' is accounted for by the greater rise in total child population in that region and in fact a slight reduction in the activity rate from 28.8–26.4 per cent is recorded, though this remains the highest activity rate of all regions. 'Other regions' is described by ILO as a heterogeneous group consisting of developed countries, transition economies and the developing region of the Middle East and North Africa.

ILO also states that in 2004, of the 190.7 million 'economically active' children (aged 5–14) there were 166 million 'child labour', and a subset of 74 million child labourers were in 'hazardous work'. However, ILO also produces figures for the 5–17-year-old group in respect of which it estimates there were 317 million economically active children in 2004, of whom 218 million could be regarded as child labourers; of the latter, 126 million were engaged in hazardous work. These figures are set out in Table 4.2.

Table 4.1 Global trends in children's economic activity by region, 2000 and 2004 (5–14 age group)

Region	Child population (million)		Economically active children (million)		Activity rate (%)	
	2000	2004	2000	2004	2000	2004
Asia and the Pacific	655.1	650.0	127.3	122.3	19.4	18.8
Latin America and the Caribbean	108.1	111.0	17.4	5.7	16.1	5.1
Sub-Saharan Africa	166.8	186.8	48.0	49.3	28.8	26.4
Other regions	269.3	258.8	18.3	13.4	6.8	5.2
World	**1,199.3**	**1,206.6**	**211.0**	**190.7**	**17.6**	**15.8**

Source: ILO (2006: 8).

Table 4.2 Global trends in children's economic activity, child labour and hazardous work (5–17 age group)

Year	Economically active children (million)	Child labour (million)	Hazardous work (million)
2000	351.7	245.5	170.5
2004	317	218	126
% change (2000–2004)	−9.9%	−11.2%	−26.1%

Sources: Derived from ILO (2002: 18, Table 1); ILO (2006: 6).

It can be seen from Table 4.2 that in this period ILO claims there was: a significant overall fall (−9.9 per cent) in the number of economically active children; a slightly greater fall in the percentage of children in child labour (−11.2 per cent) and a dramatic fall (−26.1 per cent) in the number of children in hazardous work. ILO's estimates also identify a near 50/50 split of boys and girls in child labour and hazardous work for the 5–11-year-old group, though boys become proportionately more exposed than girls to child labour in the 12–14 year group (54.8 to 45.2 per cent) and the 15–17 year group (62.1 to 37.9 per cent). The ILO estimate of child labour by economic sector is: agriculture (69 per cent); services (22 per cent); and industry (9 per cent).[8]

Although the widely held assumption that exploitative child labour occurs mostly in the developing world, in countries like Africa, Asia and Latin America, is borne out by the ILO estimates (Table 4.1), it should not be thought that the occurrence of child labour in developed countries is insignificant (Dorman 2001). Indeed, even where the employment of children is lawful, such work may be injurious (O'Donnell and White 1999). Furthermore, relatively effective labour regulatory systems in the developed countries are unlikely to identify or exert much influence over children who are involved in informal or illegal work, outside the scope of health and safety legislation and hidden from national monitoring systems (Kilkelly 2003: 347).

ILO has observed that in Europe, there have always been a relatively large number of children working for pay, in seasonal activities, street trades, small workshops or in a home work setting. There is a similar pattern in the United States, where 'the growth of the service sector, the rapid increase in the supply of part-time jobs and the search for a more flexible workforce have contributed to the expansion of the child labour market' (ILO 1996: para. 13). Although ILO's headline estimates outlined earlier cannot be easily verified, the regional, gender

---

8 'The agricultural sector comprises activities in agriculture, hunting, forestry and fishing. The industry sector consists of mining and quarrying, manufacturing, construction and public utilities (electricity, gas and water). The services sector includes wholesale and retail trade, restaurants and hotels, transport, storage and communications, finance, insurance, real estate and business services, and community, social and personal services' (ILO 2006: 7).

and employment sector distributions they describe are broadly accepted as the best figures that are currently available. However, the profile of child labour for individual countries is often better demonstrated by reference to national studies which may or may not be consistent with such global trends. In a study of Bangladesh, for example, it was found that 63.5 per cent of child labourers worked unpaid in family enterprises and that wage employment accounted for only 8.5 per cent of total child employment (Masum 2002: 237). In a study in the United States, a high proportion of children, often from ethnic minorities and immigrant groups, were identified as working in agriculture (Davidson 2001: 206–07). Unfortunately, the variety of studies using different methodologies and statistical categories does not make the task of comparing one country's perform-ance with another any easier.

4.1.4 Cultural relativism and child labour

The general problem of 'cultural relativism' was discussed in Chapter 1 (section 1.3) and, as already noted at the beginning of this chapter, some commentators have argued that the ethnocentrism of industrialised countries inappropriately domi-nates the international discourse on children's rights (Boyden 1997). The issues touching upon cultural relativism in the child labour field are particularly poignant. Indeed, some regard for the differing perspectives of developing, non-industrialised countries has been built into the ILO Constitution.[9] Some of the earlier policy thinking about child labour was dominated by the idea that the ultimate goal should be to remove all children from work completely and that children's best interests would be served by freeing them to enjoy a childhood in caring family environments. This approach then became discredited on the basis that it depended on a Northern-country ideal of childhood and led to caution by Southern countries to open dialogue with Northern donors and development agencies on the issue of child labour (Crawford S 2000). In Southern countries, children's work is more likely to be considered an acceptable element of family survival strategy. In some studies, it is argued that the reality and need for children to work should be acknowledged, and therefore the design of education systems should try to accommodate the working child (Dachi and Garrett 2003: 11). The basic differences between underlining perceptions of childhood in Northern/developed/industrialised on the one hand, and Southern/developing/non-industrialised countries on the other, has provided ongoing obstacles to the reception of the international legal regime. As we shall see in the discussion of

---

9 'In framing any Convention or Recommendation of general application the Conference shall have due regard to those countries in which climatic conditions, the imperfect development of industrial organisation, or other special circumstances make the industrial conditions substantially different and shall suggest the modifications, if any, which it considers may be required to meet the case of such countries'. ILO Constitution, article 19(3).

the Minimum Age Convention of 1973 (ILO Convention No. 138) (see section 4.2.3), this arguably reflects ethnocentric ideas about children and work (Myers 2001: 47). However, although there may be credible arguments that minimum age rules are driven by the ethnocentric concerns of the developed nations, it is less easy to maintain such criticisms in relation to the desire to eliminate the *worst forms* of child labour. As one commentator notes, 'it is important not to confuse the argument that some types of employment may be acceptable with cultural relativist arguments that exploitative or harmful child labour may be tolerable because of cultural differences' (Selby 2008: 171).

4.1.5 Covert nature of child labour

It is widely accepted that a dominant and characteristic feature of child labour is that it frequently occurs covertly and in the co-called 'informal sector', for example, family-based enterprises outside of state regulatory regimes. In some countries the proportion of children in the informal economy is very high. In Bangladesh it has been reported that the informal segment within the private sector accounted for 94 per cent of total child employment (Masum 2002: 237). In one study on Africa it was noted that less than 10 per cent of the population were employed by the formal sector (Bonnet 1993: 381). In another study relating to Pakistan, it was observed that most child labourers work unpaid in the home and the government has no way to keep track of them; less than half of all children attend school, and there is no way to monitor these children (Johnson 1999: 170). The covert forms of child labour in the informal sector will often be outside the remit and/or practical reach of regulatory labour inspectorates. For example, in Lesotho's and Portugal's thriving shoe industries and in the Philippine garment industry 'entire families work at home, making inspection nearly impossible' (Davidson 2001: 220).

By definition, it is difficult to collect reliable data on child labour which is carried out covertly and/or in the informal sector of an economy. It does seem likely, however, that gender is an important element to help explain national child labour profiles. For example, in a study relating to Turkey it is reported that it is traditionally expected that a young woman remains chaste if she is unmarried, and consequently it is thought best to keep young females within the domestic setting to protect her and the honour of the family (Bakirci 2002: 56). These kinds of societal attitudes will often be responsible for a disproportionate number of girls being engaged in home-based, domestic settings for a range of child labour activities.

4.1.6 Measuring the extent of child labour

The definitional problems discussed in section 4.1.1 and the clandestine nature of much of the informal economy discussed in section 4.1.5 make the task of measuring its incidence much harder. However, despite the conceptual, technical and infrastructural obstacles to establishing reliable statistical profiles of child labour, the estimates do at least prompt attention to the considerable magnitude of the problem as a legitimate concern for the international community. The literature reviewing statistical work is often qualified by the view that such estimates that do exist will probably be *under*-estimations because of the covert nature of many of the forms of child labour. Nevertheless, international organizations, national governments and non-governmental organizations (NGOs) all have their own agendas and no doubt headline figures are often deployed for 'advocacy' purposes (Invernizzi and Milne 2002). In addition, national efforts to collect relevant data in the formal sector are variable and use different methodologies. Many of the national statistical surveys use different age ranges: some only cover children aged 10 years and above, others 5 years and above. The landscape of child labour is often fast-moving and 'intermittent' (Levison *et al.* 2007) and consequently difficult to capture. While human rights advocates may have an interest in overestimation to bring attention to the issue, national governments may have an interest in underestimating the extent of the problem; consequently it is unsurprising that official statistics may be underestimating the real size of the problem (Bakirci 2002: 55). In developing countries there may be the additional problem of a lack of governmental infrastructure to support accurate statistical survey activity. But it should not be assumed that there are no significant defects in the data relating to developed countries. It has been observed that many of the European states have insufficiently effective systems of data collection and there remains an overwhelming lack of such data in Europe (Kilkelly 2003: 326, 346).

ILO and other international bodies[10] have been aware for some time of the need for more reliable and appropriately calibrated statistical estimates in order better to inform the policy-making process at the global, regional, national and local levels. Indeed, there is a requirement in the Worst Forms of Child Labour Recommendation No. 190 of 1999[11] on ILO member states to compile and maintain detailed statistical data.[12] There have been attempts, since the 'International Year of the Child' in 1979, to collate reliable global statistics on the magnitude of child labour disaggregated by age, gender, region, formal/informal economy, economic sector, type of work and other criteria. There were quite different

---

10 The CtRC places a high premium on states parties producing detailed statistical data in the reporting process under the CRC: see Chapter 3, section 3.5.1.

11 ILO Recommendations are not binding in international law, 'but are frequently found by governments, by national parliaments, by employers' and workers' organisations and other interested groups to be a useful checklist of actions that may be taken to give effect to the obligations entered into by ratification of a Convention' (ILO 2002a: 35).

12 'Detailed information and statistical data on the nature and extent of child labour should be compiled and kept up-to-date to serve as a basis for determining priorities for national action for the abolition of child labour, in particular for the prohibition and elimination of its worst forms as a matter of urgency'. (R190 Worst Forms of Child Labour Recommendation of 1999, para. 5(1)).

estimates made by ILO, other international bodies and NGOs which prompted Alston to remark that '[t]hese divergences reflect the difficulty of obtaining any sort of precise figures in relation to a practice which is generally ignored by official statistics' (Alston 1989: 36).

In 1998, a unit within ILO's 'International Programme on the Elimination of Child Labour' (IPEC) (see section 4.2.5), the 'Statistical Information and Monitoring Programme on Child Labour', was established to provide more sophisticated estimates. It has been argued by one observer, who discusses the methodologies for measuring hazardous work, the worst forms of child labour and non-hazardous but unacceptable forms of child labour, that several estimates are needed to represent the different types of work and their location along the exploitative/beneficial continuum of child labour (Anker 2000: 265).

The first integrated study of the economic costs and benefits of eliminating child labour throughout the developing and transitional countries has been undertaken by ILO (2004). A general programme of action was developed and (hypothetically) applied in each country under examination, estimations being made of the costs and benefits from eliminating child labour. Estimates were made of the two principal benefits: first, the benefits of improved productivity and earning capacity resulting from greater education; and second, the benefits of reduced illness and injuries, due to the elimination of the worst forms of child labour. The study found that the total economic benefits, resulting from the elimination of child labour over the period 2000–2020, would be $5,106.3 billion, whereas the total economic costs would be $760.3 billion. In other words, there would be a total net economic benefit of $4,346.1 billion. The study concluded that the 'single most import result is that the elimination of child labour and its replacement by universal education is estimated to yield enormous economic benefits (IPEC 2004: 4).

4.2 International legal protection of child labour[13]

International concern with exploitative child labour first occurred as a result of the Industrial Revolution in Europe. Legislation regulating safety and other labour standards in factories and elsewhere arose as a result of these developments and were prompted by the pressures brought to bear by vigorous trade union movements. The ILO Conventions, discussed in the following paragraphs, first made their appearance in 1919. International concern was focused on child labour by a major international campaign run by the Anti-Slavery Society for the Protection of Human Rights in 1975, and in 1980 the United Nations appointed a Special Rapporteur, Mr Abdelwahab Bouhdiba, whose report provided further impetus for international action (Bouhdiba 1982).

---

13 For an excellent account of the challenges of child labour in international law, see generally, Humbert (2009).

There are three main international instruments to consider which in combination form the core of international legal standards in this area: (i) the Minimum Age Convention of 1973 (ILO Convention No. 138); (ii) various provisions of the CRC of 1989; and (iii) the Worst Forms of Child Labour Convention of 1999 (ILO Convention No. 182). It has been said that these three conventions reflect competing notions of childhood and the role of children's work. It is argued that ILO Convention No. 138 reflects rather traditional and Northern-country ethnocentric ideas about children and work, and that it treats children as helpless victims needing adults to intervene on their behalf and does not give children any participation rights. The CRC, on the other hand, reflects albeit a Euro-American view of more active children requiring adult partnership rather than imposed supervision. Finally, ILO Convention No. 182 reflects 'a more democratic model better structured to accommodate diversity while focusing on a realistic social objective against which progress can be monitored' (Myers 2001: 45–53).

One commentator identifies four stages in the development of the international legal protection of child labour (Smolin 2000: 943). First, there were five specific areas of work identified for minimum age regulation between 1919 and 1932 in ILO conventions.[14] The standards of these old conventions were low compared with contemporary ones. There were broad exemptions for work in a family business and domestic work within a family performed by family members. The abolition of child labour was not specifically identified as an ultimate goal, and the minimum age set for admission to employment was generally 14 years (but with younger ages permitted for India and Japan). However, these conventions began a process of recognition, in an increasingly competitive and industrialised world, that nations had to all move in the same direction in reducing child labour. This was seen as necessary because, putting aside any humanitarian or welfare argument, countries needed to maintain fair and economic positions in the context of an increasingly competitive and global economy. A second wave of ILO conventions raised the minimum age from 14–15 years.[15] There were also attempts to regulate certain hazardous forms of employment.[16] However, there was still an absence of any rhetoric naming the abolition of child labour as a core principle. A third stage saw a process of consolidation of the existing conventions in the form of ILO Convention No. 138, which would gradually replace the ten previous, more specific ILO conventions. Smolin's fourth stage of development

---

14 Minimum Age (Industry) Convention, 1919 (No. 5), Minimum Age (Sea) Convention, 1920 (No. 7), Minimum Age (Agriculture) Convention, 1921 (No.10), Minimum Age (Trimmers and Stokers) Convention, 1921 (No. 15), Minimum Age (Non-Industrial Employment) Convention, 1932 (No. 33).

15 Minimum Age (Sea) Convention (Revised), 1936 (No. 58), Minimum Age (Industry) Convention (Revised), 1937 (No. 59), Minimum Age (Non-Industrial Employment) Convention (Revised), 1937 (No. 60).

16 Minimum Age (Fishermen) Convention, 1959 (No. 112), Minimum Age (Underground Work) Convention, 1965 (No. 123).

begins in the 1990s and continues to the present (Smolin 2000: 945). This period is characterised by efforts to mainstream the issue of child labour within the core business of ILO and other international institutions.

The following sections deal with the three principal international instruments in addition to a further section on 'other international instruments'. The broader role of the CRC and the CtRC has been dealt with extensively in Chapter 3, but here we also look at the wider role of ILO as a key international actor in formulating, establishing and monitoring international labour standards.

4.2.1 The Minimum Age Convention of 1973 (ILO Convention No. 138)

The Minimum Age Convention was adopted by the International Labour Conference on 26 June 1973 and entered into force on 19 June 1976. The overall aim of the Minimum Age Convention was expressed in terms of the abolition of child labour and each ILO member state[17] was put under an obligation 'to pursue a national policy designed to ensure the effective abolition of child labour and to raise progressively the minimum age for admission to employment or work to a level with the fullest physical and mental development of young persons'.[18] Some commentators argue that ILO Convention No. 138 reflects ethnocentric, Northern-country ideas about children and work (Myers 2001: 47). The overall intention was that the Convention should apply throughout all spheres of economic activity, replacing the previous ILO conventions applicable to limited economic sectors. However the Convention did not supply much guidance as to the contents of such 'national policy'.[19] The phrase 'employment or work' is significant in that it encompasses child labour performed irrespective of whether there is a contract of employment; it will include the self-employed working under contracts for services in addition to those working in family arrangements without any formal legal status (Creighton 1997: 372).

The core obligation placed on each member state is to declare upon ratification a minimum age for admission to employment, and on means of transport registered in its territory.[20] Further declarations may raise the specified age. The general rule is that the minimum age must not be less than that for completion of compulsory education, and in any event not less than 15 years, though there is a concession for developing countries to specify a minimum age of 14 years.[21]

---

17 There are currently (January 2010) 183 member states of ILO.
18 Article 1.
19 There is some guidance on 'national policy' in ILO Recommendation No. 146, paras 1–5.
20 Article 2(1).
21 Article 2(3) and (4). Furthermore, '(1) Members should take as their objective the progressive raising to 16 years of the minimum age for admission to employment or work specified in pursuance of Article 2 of the Minimum Age Convention, 1973. (2) Where the minimum age for

Although it is necessary to achieve a nexus between compulsory education and the minimum permissible age for work, compliance with this provision, according to ILO's Committee of Experts on the Application of Conventions and Recommendations (CEACR), further requires appropriate restrictions on work undertaken *outside* school hours. In order to provide states with some flexibility according to their national profiles, the Convention contains a number of permissible departures from the declared minimum age contained in articles 4–7 of the Convention. One of the criticisms levelled against ILO Convention No. 138 has been its lack of flexibility. To an extent, this criticism has been strengthened by a lack of awareness and low take-up of these various departures from the prescribed obligations in the Convention.

First, article 4 allows the state's 'competent authority', after consultation with employers and workers, to exclude from the application of the Convention 'limited categories of employment or work in respect of which special and substantial problems of application arise'. There is no specification within the Convention as to which 'categories' might be excluded. The omission was deliberate, in order to allow national authorities a wide measure of discretion to apply the Convention appropriately to its own national profile; possible exclusions discussed during the Convention's preparatory stages included employment in family undertakings, domestic service in private households, homework, and other work outside the supervision and control of employers (Creighton 1997: 374). Each member state ratifying the Convention must list such excepted categories in its *first* report to ILO and give reasons for such exclusions.[22] Implicitly, the range of exclusions cannot be extended subsequently to the submission of the first report. There was some concern that this prescription might be too rigid and/or might lead countries to produce an expanded list of exclusions in the first report (Creighton 1997: 375). However, this does not appear to have occurred. Indeed, it would appear that member states' lack of awareness about this and other 'flexibility' clauses contributed to the slow pace of ratification of ILO Convention No. 138 (Creighton 1997: 375).

Second, under article 5, there is also a generic concession to member states 'whose economy and administrative facilities are insufficiently developed' (i.e. developing countries) which are 'initially' allowed to 'limit the scope of application' of the Convention. Where a member state does so limit the application of the Convention it must append a declaration to its ratification specifying 'the branches of economic activity or types of undertakings' to which it will apply the Convention.[23] However, as a minimum protective requirement the Convention

---

employment or work covered by Article 2 of the Minimum Age Convention, 1973, is still below 15 years, urgent steps should be taken to raise it to that level'. Recommendation No. 146, para. 7.

22 Article 4(2).
23 Article 5(2).

will *always* be applicable to the following activities, which cannot therefore be disapplied from the protection of the Convention:

> ... mining and quarrying; manufacturing; construction; electricity, gas and water; sanitary services; transport, storage and communication; and plantations and other agricultural undertakings mainly producing for commercial purposes, but excluding family and small-scale holdings producing for local consumption and not regularly employing hired workers.
>
> (Minimum Age Convention, article 5(3))

Third, article 6 provides that ILO Convention No. 138 does not apply to work done by children and young persons in schools or in other training institutions where this is done as an integral part of a course of education or training for which a school or training institution is responsible, or a training programme in an undertaking approved by the competent authority, or a programme of guidance to facilitate occupation choice or training. It is also inapplicable to work done in undertakings by persons of 14 years or more as part of an apprenticeship or similar arrangement. Care must also be taken that a 'training' relationship should not be used as a subterfuge to enable an employer to put children to work before the legal minimum age. The accompanying ILO Recommendation No. 146 therefore provides that measures should be taken 'to safeguard and supervise the conditions in which children and young persons undergo vocational orientation and training within undertakings, training institutions and schools for vocational or technical education and to formulate standards for their protection and development'.[24]

Fourth, article 7 provides that 'light work' may be authorised by national laws in relation to children aged 13–15 years on two conditions: first, it must be 'not likely to be harmful to their health or development'; and second, 'not such as to prejudice their attendance at school, their participation in vocational orientation or training programmes ... or their capacity to benefit from the instruction received'. National laws may also permit the employment of persons who are at least 15 years old but have not completed their compulsory schooling. Developing countries are given further concessions to the general rule on light work by allowing them to specify 12 instead of 13 years and 14 instead of 15 years.[25] Where national laws or regulations do permit light work, the competent authority must prescribe 'the number of hours during which and the conditions in which such employment or work may be undertaken'.[26]

In 2009, the CEACR issued a 'general observation' on the concept of 'light work' in ILO Convention No. 138 on the basis that 'the need to determine the

---

24 Recommendation No. 146, para. 12(2).
25 Article 7(4).
26 Article 7(3).

types of light work that are authorised and the related conditions are often poorly understood by States and therefore likely to give rise to abuse' (CEACR 2009: para. 121). The general observation (CEACR 2009a) notes that the Convention's 'preparatory work'[27] showed that differences of views had emerged during the drafting process,[28] but the drafting committee did adopt article 7 on the basis that it 'attempts to combine the measure of flexibility necessary to permit the wide application of the Convention (especially in view of its general scope) with the restrictions necessary to ensure adequate protection' (CEACR 2009a). It is noted that 'a large number of countries' have determined the age of admission to light work and, in particular, that in countries that have specified a minimum age for admission to employment or work of 15 or 16 years, the age from which employment on light work may be authorised has been set at 13 years, while in those countries which have determined a minimum age for admission to employment of 14 years, the age for admission to light work is 12 years. Furthermore, in respect of certain countries that had not determined an age of admission to light work, it was observed that 'in the great majority of these cases, this is because they have not regulated employment in these types of work'. As regards article 7(3), it was observed that only a few countries had determined the types of light work and established the hours of work and other conditions that could be undertaken (CEACR 2009a). The general observation notes that the types of light work most frequently determined by member states were as follows:

(1) agricultural work, such as the preparation of seeds and crops, the main-tenance of crops without the use of insecticides or herbicides, the harvesting of fruit, vegetables or flowers, picking and sorting in farms and herding;
(2) forestry work and landscaping, including the planting of bushes and the maintenance of public gardens, without the use of insecticides or herbicides;
(3) domestic work, such as kitchen help, household help or looking after children; and
(4) the distribution of mail, newspapers, periodicals or publicity.

(CEACR 2009a)

The Committee further noted that some countries had laid down the hours of work for light work, that is, between two and four-and-a-half hours a day and

---

27 International Labour Conference (ILC), 57th Session, 1972, Report IV(2), pp. 39–43; and ILC, 58th Session, 1973, Report IV(2), pp. 19–21.
28 '... the majority of governments were in favour of a provision on light work, one government advocated greater flexibility of application, and several governments opposed the inclusion of a provision in the Convention permitting exemptions authorizing light work on the grounds that such a provision would restrict the scope of the Convention and would not lead to the complete abolition of child labour'. (CEACR 2009a).

between 10 and 25 hours a week. Certain countries have established that the time spent in school and on light work shall not exceed 7 hours a day, while others prohibit light work during school term time. Furthermore, certain countries prohibit night work (between 8 p.m. and 6 a.m.) and work on Sundays and public holidays, while others provide for annual leave of up to 4 weeks a year (CEACR 2009a).

Finally, article 8 provides a general concession to the prohibition of work for children below the declared minimum age under article 2, which the competent authority can grant by permit 'in individual cases' and 'for such purposes as participation in artistic performances'. Such permits will limit 'the number of hours during which and prescribe the conditions in which employment or work is allowed'.[29]

The five 'flexibility' clauses (articles 4–8) discussed earlier all provide for concessions to the general rule[30] of a minimum age of not less than the age of completion of compulsory education, or in any event 15 years (or 14 years for developing countries). However, article 3 provides that the minimum age for admission to employment or work 'which by its nature or the circumstances in which it is carried out is likely to jeopardise health, safety or morals of young persons' must not be less than 18 years.[31] Although this appears to establish a prescriptive standard more demanding than the general obligation in article 2, the types of employment or work which are referred to in article 3 must be determined again 'by national laws or regulations or by the competent authority' after consultation.[32] In determining the types of employment or work to which article 3 applies, 'full account should be taken of relevant international labour standards, such as those concerning dangerous substances, agents or processes (including ionising radiations), the lifting of heavy weights and underground work' and the list of types of such employment or work 'should be re-examined periodically and revised as necessary'.[33] Furthermore, such national laws etc. may authorise employment from the age of 16 years, 'on condition that the health, safety and morals of the young persons concerned are fully protected'.[34]

As regards enforcement, article 9 provides that 'all necessary measures, including the provision of appropriate penalties' must be taken by the competent authority to ensure the 'effective enforcement' of the Convention. National laws or regulations or the competent authority shall define 'the persons responsible

---

29 Article 8(2).
30 Article 2(3) and (4).
31 Article 3(1). Furthermore, 'Where the minimum age for admission to types of employment or work which are likely to jeopardise the health, safety or morals of young persons is still below 18 years, immediate steps should be taken to raise it to that level'. (Recommendation No. 146, para. 9).
32 Article 3(2).
33 Recommendation No. 146, para. 10.
34 Article 3(3).

for compliance with the provisions giving effect to the Convention',[35] and they will also prescribe the 'registers or other documents' that must be kept and made available by employers of persons whom he employs and who are less than 18 years.[36] The guidance on enforcement given in Recommendation No. 146 emphasises the strengthening of labour inspection, and the inspectors' close coordination and cooperation with the services responsible for the education, training, welfare and guidance of children and young persons. It also states that special attention should be paid to the enforcement of provisions concerning employment in hazardous types of employment or work; and to the prevention of the employment or work of children and young persons during the hours when instruction is available. Measures to facilitate the verification of ages should include the maintenance of an effective system of birth registration, and a requirement that employers keep and make available registers or other documents not only of children and young persons employed by them but also of those receiving vocational orientation or training in their undertakings.[37] Finally, article 10 provides for the revision of the ten previous ILO conventions on minimum age-setting in various industries.

Despite the merits of ILO Convention No. 138, some commentators have concluded that it did not 'constitute an adequate response' to the problem of abusive child labour (Creighton 1997: 386). Creighton identified a number of problems, for example, a lack of flexibility:

> [A]rticle 7 proceeds on the assumption that employment or work for children under thirteen is to be impermissible in all circumstances. This means that it is not acceptable in terms of the Convention for a twelve-year-old to work on a morning or evening newspaper route, or for an eleven-year-old to wash cars or weed a neighbour's garden on a Saturday afternoon. Furthermore, since the Convention applies to employment or work, it would be necessary to regulate unpaid work by children or young people on a family farm or in a family restaurant.
>
> (Creighton 1997: 387)

Developing countries have had difficulties in complying with the Convention as it is premised on the assumption that child labour should be entirely eliminated, which is simply not a practical proposition for many countries. The Convention also fails to articulate clear national priorities. Much is left to the

---

35 Article 9(2).
36 Article 9(3).
37 Recommendation No. 146, paras 14–16. Furthermore, 'children and young persons working in the streets, in outside stalls, in public places, in itinerant occupations or in other circumstances which make the checking of employers' records impracticable should be issued licences or other documents indicating their eligibility for such work'. (Recommendation No. 146, para. 16(c)).

discretion of member states without sufficient guidance on setting priorities for national action. There has developed a growing awareness that the process of eliminating child labour must be an incremental one and strategies should be fully integrated with other measures to promote economic and educational development and protect employment standards (Creighton 1997: 396).

ILO Convention No. 138 was a significant advance over previous efforts, but it failed in its first two decades of existence to attract sufficient ratifications to truly deliver the intended reforms. Indeed, it is difficult to say that there was any real coherence in international standards on child labour prior to the late 1990s. By 1996, only 49 of the member states had ratified it. The Asian countries and other developing nations were conspicuously absent from the list of ratifying countries during this period. At the time of the adoption of the Worst Forms of Child Labour Convention (ILO Convention No. 182) on 17 June 1999, ILO Convention No. 138 had attracted only 76 ratifications. However, as will be seen in section 4.2.3, the success of ILO Convention No. 182 had the effect of speeding up the ratification rate of ILO Convention No. 138. Two years after the coming into force of ILO Convention No. 182 (in November 2002), the number of ratifications of ILO Convention No. 138 rose to 121, and currently stands at 155.[38]

An important contributory factor to an increasing international attention on child labour, following ILO Convention No. 132, has been the combination of ILO's focus on international labour standards with the recognition of their importance within the post-war human rights and children's rights movements. The arrival of the rights-based agenda of the CRC in 1989 has reinforced and helped to transform ILO's older approaches to labour standards, first commenced in 1919. ILO's formulation, a decade after the appearance of the CRC, of ILO Convention No. 182 reflected a convergence of some of these influences.

4.2.2 The UN Convention on the rights of the child and child labour

In the 1980s and 1990s there was further recognition of the rights of children at the international level, reflected in particular by the introduction of the CRC in 1989 (see generally, Chapter 3). There are a number of provisions of the CRC that, it can be claimed, provide a framework of rights relevant to child labour. The CRC has tended to produce standards of a broad general nature, as compared to those adopted by ILO which contain a more detailed and precise set of standards (Alston 1989: 37). In particular, article 32 (protection from economic exploitation and child labour) contains some core obligations in this area: see the text

---

38 As at 14 May 2010.

of article 32 contained in Appendix 1.[39] In the early days of its existence, the Committee on the Rights of the Child (CtRC) had held a 'day of general discussion'[40] on the issue of economic exploitation of children where '[s]ituations of child labour, including the question of domestic servants, child prostitution and pornography and sale of children, were considered by the participants' (Day of Discussion 1993: para. 193). The statement arising from that event recorded that '[m]ore than 100 million children are forced into jobs destroying their health or preventing them from going to school. In some cases their conditions amount to slavery'. The Committee stressed the need for countries to consider how children could be protected and child labour prevented in programmes of economic reform. It emphasised the need for a review of education policy and to ensure free and compulsory primary education. The Committee recommended that a system of inspection of workplaces was needed in each country and that the informal sector should be systematically regulated. It also recognised that in this field there was a compelling need for co-ordination of policy at the international and national levels, and that a mechanism, such as a National Committee or Commission on the Rights of the Child, would be in a position to ensure the required multi-disciplinary approach to address economic exploitation.

It can be seen that article 32(2) of the CRC in effect cross-refers to various duties under ILO Convention No. 138. The original proposal of article 32 during the drafting process of the CRC specifically placed duties on states parties to set a minimum age for admission to employment of 15 years, comparable to article 2 of ILO Convention No. 138. However, that proposal was not adopted and instead the phrase 'work' was used in the text of article 32 to cover both work within the employment relationship and work falling outside of that relationship (Detrick 1992: 418–19).

In its examination of state reports,[41] the CtRC continues to commend nations that have ratified the relevant ILO Conventions and has prompted recalcitrant states to do so, and indeed to take up membership of ILO: see CO North Korea (2004). The CtRC regularly cross-refers to the ILO Conventions (Nos. 138 and 182) in its 'concluding observations' on country reports. The CtRC has frequently identified the persistence of child labour in the informal and domestic sectors and on family farms. It has also noted the way in which the practice of child labour frequently makes children vulnerable to sexual and other forms of exploitation. The Committee has often recommended that states parties sharpen their methods of collecting relevant data and improve their systems of labour inspection:

39 See also other articles of the CRC relevant to child labour: CRC, articles 11 and 35 (combating trafficking in children), article 19 (protection against violence, abuse, neglect and exploitation), article 34 (the protection of children from sexual exploitation or abuse) and article 38 (setting international standards in relation to children and armed conflict).

40 See Chapter 3, section 3.3.1.

41 See Chapter 3, section 3.5.8.3.

see CO Brazil (2004) and CO Qatar (2009). On occasion, it has made quite specific recommendations in respect of particular sectors. For example, in Kyrgyzstan, the practice within state educational institutions of requiring children to work for the profit of those institutions was exposed. The Committee recommended immediate steps to eliminate such practices (CO Kyrgyzstan 2004). It has also recognised the efforts made in Bangladesh to eliminate child labour from the ready-made garment sector, though it also notes the high incidence of child workers in five selected worst forms of child labour, that is, welding, auto workshops, road transport, battery recharging and recycling and work in tobacco factories (CO Bangladesh 2009). The CtRC, perhaps prudently, has generally avoided expressing an opinion about the merits or otherwise of the linkage between international trade and labour standards: see section 4.3.3. The CtRC continues to refer to the ILO Conventions as the key framework in assessing national situations of child labour and systematically recommending that states parties ratify these conventions (Doek 2003: 243). But it is tempting also to draw comparisons between the effectiveness of the reporting processes undertaken by the CtRC and by ILO in the field of child labour. Some commentators take the view that in the field of child labour it is generally acknowledged that the UN supervisory regime is 'less rigorous and comprehensive than that of the ILO' (Creighton 1997: 369). Kilkelly (2003: 324) notes that many of the reports submitted to the CtRC 'fail to address the issue of economic exploitation of children under Article 32 in a complete manner, or at all'. Others view the CRC and ILO conventions and their respective monitoring procedures as increasingly operating in a more helpful complementary manner to each other (Noguchi 2002: 357, 368).

However, in the 1990s there was an increasing urgency within the international community about child labour issues. This was prompted to some extent by the recognition that the process of globalization was exposing more intense competitive behaviour which, it was feared, could generate *more* child labour rather than reduce it. Governments attending the ILO Conference in Geneva in June 1996 agreed that there was a pressing need to proceed immediately with the prohibition of the most intolerable features of child labour. The CtRC also lent its support to ILO's new project to establish a convention aimed at the 'worst forms of child labour', and indeed made observations on the drafts of the new ILO Convention (Noguchi 2002: 365).

4.2.3 Elimination of the worst forms of child labour convention of 1999 (ILO Convention No. 182)

The decision of ILO's Governing Body in March 1996 to place 'intolerable' forms of child labour on the Conference agenda for 1998 reflected the frustrations with the apparent failures of ILO Convention No. 138 (discussed in section 4.2.1). The disappointment with the slow ratification rate in relation to this convention encouraged the international community to design a new convention that was more narrowly focused in order that it could match the areas of concern where there was more obviously an emerging global consensus (Davidson 2001: 203). ILO also adopted in June 1998 a landmark 'soft law' instrument, the Declaration on Fundamental Principles and Rights at Work and its Follow-up, in which the International Labour Conference declared that all member states should respect principles concerning four 'fundamental rights', including the elimination of child labour. ILO Convention No. 182 was adopted on 12 June 1999 and came into force on 19 November 2000. Since 2002, the UN's 'World Day Against Child Labour' has been celebrated on 12 June of each year, marking the date of adoption of this landmark ILO Convention. The World Day highlights the continuing challenges, for example, with a focus on exploitation of girls in child labour in 2009.[42] ILO convention No. 182 is distinctive in that it was the only ILO Convention to have been unanimously adopted by the tripartite representation of member states, and it has had the best record in ILO history for rapid ratification. It had been ratified by 130 states within two and a half years from its adoption, and by 172 states at the time of writing.[43] It should be noted that ILO Convention No. 182 does not revise or replace ILO Convention No. 138. The latter remains the foundation for international action to abolish child labour, whereas ILO Convention No. 182 supplements and highlights this underlying aim by setting out standards to eliminate and prohibit the 'worst forms' of child labour. However, the policy aims of ILO Convention No. 182 were not to produce just another ILO convention to fill some gaps in the protective coverage missed in previous conventions. There was a more ambitious aim to adopt an instrument that would 'pack a real punch and be capable of encouraging real impact' (Crawford S 2000: 5). As already noted, the adoption of ILO Convention No. 182 also correlates with Smolin's fourth stage in the development of international legal protection of child labour – its mainstreaming within ILO (Smolin 2000: 945). Noguchi (2002: 362) also observes that child labour has been 'mainstreamed within the ILO's agenda during the last few years'.

A key innovative feature of ILO Convention No. 182 was to focus on areas where there clearly existed strong international agreement, that is, the elimination of the worst forms of child labour that had been generally recognised as intolerable. The identification of these areas also extended the policy areas of concern through the explicit inclusion of such (criminal) matters as prostitution, pornography and drug trafficking. These rather distinctive features of ILO Convention No. 182 have resulted in this Convention having an iconic presence in the international legal regime to eliminate child labour. Much of the commentary reflects

---

42 See the World Day Against Child Labour website at: http://www.ilo.org/ipec/Campaignandadvocacy/ WDACL/lang--en/index.htm (accessed 14 May 2010).

43 As at 14 May 2010.

the optimism that this Convention is both more analytically sound and has a better chance of making a real difference.[44]

The preambular paragraphs of ILO Convention No. 182 make it clear that the intention was to *complement* ILO Convention No. 138, not only by ensuring the elimination of the worst forms of child labour but also by providing for children's 'rehabilitation and social integration', a duty resonant with article 39 of the CRC.[45] It is also interesting to note the clear recognition of poverty as the root cause of child labour and that, according to the text, the solution indicated lies in 'sustained economic growth'. The preambular paragraphs also 'recall' the text of the CRC and the ILO's landmark 'Declaration on Fundamental Principles and Rights at Work and its Follow-up' (see section 4.2.5), adopted by the International Labour Conference in June 1998. ILO's Governing Body identified ILO Convention No. 182 as one of eight conventions[46] that it regards as being fundamental to people's rights at work, irrespective of the level of development of individual states.

The core duty contained in ILO Convention No. 182 is stark. Nothing less than 'immediate and effective measures' are required from member states to secure the results of both the 'prohibition' and 'elimination' of the worst forms of child labour 'as a matter of urgency'.[47] This does not mean that a state is violating the Convention if the worst forms of child labour are not immediately erased. The duty requires immediate 'measures', not necessarily 'results'. For example, this may mean the adoption of appropriate legislation and regulation that will, in the future, ensure the prohibition and elimination of child labour.

The definition of a child is taken as applying to all persons under the age of 18 years.[48] This does not imply, however, a comprehensive ban on work for all persons less than 18 years of age. The general minimum age for work is usually lower than 18 (see section 4.2.1) and such work is legitimate provided it does not fall foul of the criteria defining the worst forms of child labour. It should be noted that ILO Convention No. 182 does not make any exception to the 18 years limit. However, it should be remembered that not all countries have an adequate system of birth registration.[49]

---

44 For example, Betcherman *et al.* (2004: 29) state that ILO Convention No. 182 'reflects the lessons learned over the last three decades about the causes and effects of child labor'.

45 See Chapter 3, sections 3.5.5.4 and 3.5.8.2.

46 The other seven conventions are: Forced Labour Convention, 1930 (No. 29); Freedom of Association and Protection of the Right to Organise Convention, 1948 (No. 87); Right to Organise and Collective Bargaining Convention, 1949 (No. 98); Equal Remuneration Convention, 1951 (No. 100); Abolition of Forced Labour Convention, 1957 (No. 105); Discrimination (Employment and Occupation) Convention, 1958 (No. 111) and Minimum Age Convention, 1973 (No. 138).

47 ILO Convention No. 182, article 1.

48 Ibid., article 2.

49 See Chapter 3, section 3.5.4.1.

The international community found some difficulty in arriving at a definition of the 'worst forms of child labour'. There was the need to identify the common denominator of what a majority of countries would find to be intolerable. There was also a need for a formulation that would provide a reasonable fit with national law, in particular in relation to prostitution and the armed forces. Article 3 of ILO Convention No. 182 defines the meaning of 'worst forms of child labour' which comprises:

(a) all forms of slavery or practices similar to slavery, such as the sale and trafficking of children, debt bondage and serfdom and forced or compulsory labour, including forced or compulsory recruitment of children for use in armed conflict;

(b) the use, procuring or offering of a child for prostitution, for the production of pornography or for pornographic performances;

(c) the use, procuring or offering of a child for illicit activities, in particular for the production and trafficking of drugs as defined in the relevant international treaties;

(d) work which, by its nature or the circumstances in which it is carried out, is likely to harm the health, safety or morals of children.

(ILO Convention No. 182, article 3)

The first three categories (article 3(a)–(c)) provide unqualified protection, while the last (d) is necessarily more elusive and is left for further definition by the national authorities. The first three categories are often referred to as the 'intolerable forms of child labour' and the more elusive category (d) as 'hazardous work'.[50] It should be noted that category (a) conspicuously falls short of an outright ban on the use of children as soldiers in armed conflict; it only applies where recruitment is 'forced or compulsory'. It has been said that this was one of the most controversial aspects of the drafting negotiations and that the United States blocked a proposal that would have produced broader prohibition of child soldiers (Davidson 2001: 217). A further difficult issue in the drafting negotiations was the approach to be taken to category (d), 'hazardous work'. Worker representatives at ILO wanted a specific list of hazardous work conditions (e.g. work underground, at dangerous heights, or in confined spaces), thus removing discretion from governments to regulate such work. Most government representatives preferred a more flexible approach which permitted them to take into account circumstances in their countries that would make work more or less hazardous. A compromise was reached, allowing the discretion of member states to determine what constitutes hazardous work, and there was an understanding between employer and worker members that article 3(d) did not encompass situations

---

50 See ILO's working definition of 'hazardous work' in section 4.1.1.

where children work on their parents' family farms (Dennis 1999: 945).[51] The repeated use of the word 'work' (rather than 'employment') in articles 2 and 3 ensures that the definition of the worst forms of child labour does not have any link with the existence of a contractual employment relationship or production for commercial or trading purposes (Noguchi 2002: 360). ILO Convention No. 182 can therefore be applied to employment and work in both the formal and the informal sectors and in family settings where there is no commercial/trading product. The wording of article 3 above differs from that of article 3(1) of ILO Convention No. 138, which only deals with employment or work which 'is likely to jeopardise the health, safety or morals of young persons'. A state that has ratified ILO Convention No. 138 will still have to determine a list of hazardous work for the purposes of ILO Convention No. 182. In practice, the lists may be identical but they need not be so, given the different aims of these two conventions. In earlier ILO conventions, 'domestic' work had been expressly excluded from the protected areas. However, it is thought that domestic work is implicitly included in all categories contained in article 3. The literature on child labour consistently cites domestic work and the informal economy as areas where child labour is prevalent. Yet there are difficult distinctions between child labour that ought to be prohibited and that which ought to be regarded as legitimate precisely in this area.[52] Crawford observes that there are a number of 'hidden' forms of child labour that have not been fully drawn out in the text of article 3 (Crawford S 2000: 12–13).

The precise boundaries of meaning in the last category (d) are left to be determined at the national level after consultation, and in particular taking into account the guidance on hazardous work laid down in ILO Recommendation No. 190 of 1999.[53] The Recommendation[54] provides some detailed criteria for identifying the types of work referred to in category (d). It specifically provides that this category of work should be positively authorised by a state in respect of children aged 16 years or more, but only after due consultation with workers and employers and subject to the safeguards regarding children's health, safety, morals and sufficient training. The requirement on competent authorities to identify such work[55] was added in an amendment and was intended to ensure that countries positively investigated the existence of such practices rather than merely going

---

51 Michael J. Dennis was Attorney-Adviser, Office of the Legal Adviser, US Department of State, and served as a legal adviser to the US delegation to the 87th Session of the International Labour Conference and participated in the negotiation of Convention No. 182.
52 An IPEC report makes a useful distinction between children giving a 'helping hand' in their own home, an activity which can be seen as a positive experience, and 'child domestic labour', a reference to where children perform domestic tasks in the home of a third party or 'employer' under exploitative conditions. (IPEC 2004: 1).
53 The legal status of ILO Recommendations is noted at footnote 11.
54 Para. 4.
55 ILO Convention No. 182, article 4(2).

through a hypothetical exercise of definition. The duties to identify the various categories of child labour are also to be periodically reviewed and monitored by states.[56] This will enable countries to retain some flexibility in updating their lists of prohibited child labour in a changing industrial environment.

Each member state is under a duty to take all necessary measures to ensure the effective implementation of ILO Convention No. 182[57]. The Recommendation provides, in particular, that member states should compile '[d]etailed information and statistical data on the nature and extent of child labour' as 'a basis for determining priorities for national action'.[58] In addition, each member state must, after consultation with employers' and workers' organizations, 'establish or designate appropriate mechanisms to monitor the implementation' of the Convention.[59] This is again reinforced by the Recommendation, which urges member states to ensure coordination between the national competent authorities, to cooperate with any international efforts and to identify responsible persons in the event of non-compliance with national provisions.[60] Most importantly, member states 'shall design and implement programmes of action to eliminate as a priority the worst forms of child labour'.[61] Again, this is given some practical substance in the Recommendation, which states that such programmes should aim at the identification and prevention of the worst forms of child labour, giving due attention to vulnerable groups of children.[62]

Each member state has a mandatory duty to take all necessary measures to ensure the effective implementation of ILO Convention No. 182, including penal or other sanctions.[63] The guidance provided by the Recommendation indicates that member states should designate three categories as criminal offences (practices similar to slavery, child prostitution and other illicit activities).[64] This list is in fact identical to the wording of the first three categories of the Convention (articles 3(a) to (c)), with the addition of the regulation of 'firearms'. Additionally, the Recommendation advises that, where appropriate, member states should provide criminal penalties for violations of any national provisions prohibiting and eliminating the hazardous work referred to in article 3(d). It also suggests the 'special supervision of enterprises which have used the worst forms of child labour, and, in cases of persistent violation, consideration of temporary or permanent revoking of permits to operate'.[65] If a member state has also ratified the

---

56 Article 4(3).
57 ILO Convention No. 182, article 7(1).
58 ILO Recommendation No. 190, para. 5(1).
59 ILO Convention No. 182, article 5.
60 ILO Recommendation No. 190, paras 8–11.
61 ILO Convention No. 182, article 6(1).
62 ILO Recommendation No. 190, para. 2.
63 ILO Convention No. 182, article 7(1).
64 ILO Recommendation No. 190, para. 12.
65 ILO Recommendation No. 190, paras 13 and 14.

Forced Labour Convention of 1930, then the protection offered there against illegal compulsory labour would already be punishable as a criminal offence.[66] The Recommendation reinforces ILO Convention No. 182's provisions by urging cooperation with international efforts by exchanging information concerning such criminal offences.[67]

The centrality of education in efforts to eliminate child labour is confirmed in article 7(2) which obliges member states, in taking effective and time-bound measures, to take into account 'the importance of education in eliminating child labour'. IPEC has developed a number of 'time-bound' programmes[68] to reflect the commitment contained in article 7(2). One of the listed measures under this provision is to 'ensure access to free basic education, and, wherever possible and appropriate, vocational training, for all children removed from the worst forms of child labour'.[69] The relationship between exploitative labour and education was another key issue in the drafting negotiations.

> Some governments, including the United States, as well as all worker members, wanted the Convention to cover work that systematically prevents a child from taking advantage of available or compulsory education. Other delegations opposed this formulation, asserting that lack of access to education was fundamentally different from the other abuses targeted by the Convention and that its inclusion would harm the prospects for ratification.
>
> (Dennis 1999: 946)

There were also some discussions about the meaning of 'basic education'; some interpretations in other international instruments correlate this phrase with primary education. Dennis notes that the worker and employer members clarified the record with their understanding that a broader meaning should be given, that is, 'basic education means primary education plus 1 year (i.e., eight or nine years of schooling), such education being based on curriculum and not age' (Dennis 1999: 946). It should be noted that the aim of article 7(2)(c) is to provide rehabilitation and reintegration of children who have been 'removed' from the worst forms of child labour, a provision that resonates with the general duty in the CRC on states parties to achieve the recovery and social reintegration of a child victim of any form of neglect, exploitation or abuse.[70] The Recommendation further encourages 'adopting appropriate measures to improve the educational

---

66 'The illegal exaction of forced or compulsory labour shall be punishable as a penal offence, and it shall be an obligation on any Member ratifying this Convention to ensure that the penalties imposed by law are really adequate and are strictly enforced' (Forced Labour Convention of 1930, article 29).
67 ILO Recommendation No. 190, para. 11.
68 See section 4.2.5.
69 ILO Convention No. 182, article 7(2)(c).
70 CRC, article 39.

infrastructure and the training of teachers to meet the needs of boys and girls'.[71]

The growing acknowledgment that the problem of child labour was indeed a global one requiring action at the international level is reflected in the text of an article that obliges member states to 'take appropriate steps to assist one another' in giving effect to the Convention 'through enhanced international co-operation and/or assistance including support for social and economic development, poverty eradication programmes and universal education'.[72] The Recommendation indicates various measures on which states may cooperate, such as mutual legal assistance and technical assistance, including the exchange of information.[73] In the drafting negotiations, the worker and employer members, together with governments of most developing countries, had sought an amendment that would have committed governments to 'enhanced international cooperation and assistance, including support for social and economic development'. Some governments, however, felt this might create a legal obligation to increase financial contributions to other states or ILO child labour programmes. The ILO Deputy Legal Adviser confirmed that the final text did not create any legal obligations concerning the nature or amount of any cooperation or assistance (Dennis 1999: 947).

There seems little doubt that the arrival of ILO Convention No. 182 marked a new confidence in the growing coherence and influence of a worldwide movement to progress international labour standards.[74] The campaign work of ILO and NGOs that occurred before, during and after the adoption of ILO Convention No 182 has been very successful, certainly if success is measured by the fast rate of ratification. The optimistic environment that appears to have existed around the introduction of this Convention has also been significant in terms of providing international donors with some assurance about the strength of international support which has helped to increase funding for ILO campaigns against child labour. Noguchi (2002: 365) observes that this shows 'a recognition that, for an issue like child labour, changing people's perception and way of thinking is not an auxiliary action of public information but itself a substantive measure to tackle the phenomenon effectively and from its roots'.

---

71 ILO Recommendation No. 190, para. 15(j).
72 ILO Convention No. 182, article 8.
73 Recommendation No. 190, para. 16(b) and (c).
74 One commentator remarked: 'Before it had even arrived, the U.S. Senate had taken the unusual step of adopting, by a 98–1 roll-call vote, a sense-of-the-Senate amendment to the Foreign Relations Authorization Act that commended the ILO member states for negotiating this "historic convention" and "called for the U.S. to continue to work with all foreign nations and international organizations to put an end to abusive and exploitative child labour". Early ratification by the United States should encourage other states to follow suit'. (Dennis 1999: 948).

4.2.4 Other international instruments relating to child labour

There are a number of other UN international instruments relevant to eliminating child labour. The Supplementary Convention on the Abolition of Slavery, the Slave Trade and Institutions and Practices Similar to Slavery of 1956 provides that states parties to that convention 'shall take all practicable and necessary legislative and other measures to bring about progressively and as soon as possible the complete abolition or abandonment' of a number of listed institutions and practices, 'whether or not they are covered by the definition of slavery contained in article 1 of the Slavery Convention [of 1926]'. The four types of servile statuses are: (a) debt bondage, (b) serfdom, (c) forced marriage and (d) child exploitation.

> Any institution or practice whereby a child or young person under the age of 18 years, is delivered by either or both of his natural parents or by his guardian to another person, whether for reward or not, with a view to the exploitation of the child or young person or of his labour.
>
> (Supplementary Convention on the Abolition of Slavery,
> the Slave Trade and Institutions and Practices Similar
> to Slavery of 1956, article 1(d))

The kind of practice which the drafting committee had in mind underlying this provision is well illustrated by the following extract from the proceedings of an *ad hoc* committee on slavery in 1951:

> The Committee next turned to the practice, particularly prevalent in the Far East, which in some localities is known as '*mui tsai*'. This involves the sale of a child's working capacity and usually takes the form of the transfer of a small child, usually a girl, for employment as a domestic servant by means of an adoption procedure, sometimes fraudulent. The custom has been known to exist under other names in other regions of the world, including parts of Africa. The Committee recognised that in many cases an element of servitude may not be involved. Often the parents of the child affect such a transfer in what they believe to be the best interests of the child. The Committee therefore felt that a status or condition of servitude existed only when the conditions of the transfer were such as to permit the exploitation of the child regardless of its welfare.
>
> (Economic and Social Council, Report of the
> Ad Hoc Committee on Slavery (2nd.Session), UN Doc. E/1988,
> E/AC33/13, 4 May 1951, p. 20 – quoted in Allain (2008: 305))

A few years later, the following 'principle' was drafted in the (non-binding) Declaration of the Rights of the Child:

> The child shall be protected against all forms of neglect, cruelty and exploitation. He shall not be the subject of traffic, in any form.

The child shall not be admitted to employment before an appropriate minimum age; he shall in no case be caused or permitted to engage in any occupation or employment which would prejudice his health or education, or interfere with his physical, mental or moral development.

(Declaration of the Rights of the Child 1959, principle 9)

The International Covenant on Civil and Political Rights (ICCPR) of 1966[75] carries the following provision:

1. Every child shall have, without any discrimination as to race, colour, sex, language, religion, national or social origin, property or birth, the right to such measures of protection as are required by his status as a minor, on the part of his family, society and the State.

(ICCPR, article 24(1))

And the International Covenant on Economic, Social and Cultural Rights (ICESCR) of 1966[76] carries the following provision:

3. Special measures of protection and assistance should be taken on behalf of all children and young persons without any discrimination for reasons of parentage or other conditions. Children and young persons should be protected from economic and social exploitation. Their employment in work harmful to their morals or health or dangerous to life or likely to hamper their normal development should be punishable by law. States should also set age limits below which the paid employment of child labour should be prohibited and punishable by law.

(Article 10(3))

These various provisions, combined with the relevant provisions of the CRC and the two ILO Conventions discussed earlier, comprise a fairly comprehensive international legal regime addressing the economic exploitation of children in the employment/work context. However, ILO's role as a leader within the international community in this field requires further examination in order to appreciate how international policy has been formulated in the past and its likely direction for the future.

4.2.5 The wider role of ILO

The International Labour Organization (ILO) (see section 2.4.1.4) has been the most important and longstanding inter-governmental organization in the field of international labour standards generally and child labour in particular. The

---

75 The ICCPR was opened for signature on 16 December 1966 and entered into force on 23 March 1976. It had 165 parties in May 2010.
76 The ICESCR was opened for signature on 16 December 1966 and entered into force on 3 January 1976. It had 160 parties in May 2010.

International Labour Conference adopted the Minimum Age (Industry) Convention 1919 (No. 5) at its very first session. Its membership now stands at 183 member states.[77] ILO's structure, and the way in which its standards are formulated[78] and monitored, are grounded in tripartism, that is, the involvement of governments and the worker and employer representation (the 'social partners'). This provides several advantages, in particular that ILO is uniquely positioned to monitor and report on child labour violations; the workers' groups give it access to data on current labour conditions and the employers' and government representatives 'lend it legitimacy with both private and public actors' (Ho 2006: 342). ILO has also forged partnerships with other international organizations better to facilitate its work of establishing international labour standards and meeting the challenges of child labour, for example, with the human rights treaty bodies, including the CtRC, with UNICEF, and with the World Bank (Betcherman *et al.* 2004: 30). Although other international organizations and NGOs have taken an interest in child labour issues, for example, the UNHRC,[79] UNICEF,[80] the International Organization of Employers, the Anti-Slavery Society and the International Confederation of Free Trade Unions, ILO 'has always considered itself to have a special mandate in this area' (Creighton 1997: 366). It has played a central role in producing international standards of protection. Although NGOs do not have a formal role in the preparation of new ILO standards, 'in practice NGOs do have opportunities to make a contribution' (Blagbrough 1997: 126).

In many ways the policy trends that have informed ILO's activities are punctuated by three 'soft law' instruments. First, there was the Declaration concerning the aims and purposes of the International Labour Organization, issued on 10 May 1944 (the 'Philadelphia Declaration'), which is now annexed to ILO's Constitution of 1944. The Declaration reaffirms the fundamental principles on which the organization is based, in particular, that:

(a) labour is not a commodity;
(b) freedom of expression and of association are essential to sustained progress;
(c) poverty anywhere constitutes a danger to prosperity everywhere;
(d) the war against want requires to be carried on with unrelenting vigor within each nation, and by continuous and concerted international effort in which the representatives of workers and employers, enjoying equal

---

77 As at 18 January 2010. ILO's relationship with the USA has been somewhat erratic (Davidson 2001: 208). The USA did not join ILO until 1934 and withdrew its membership in 1977, rejoining it in 1980.

78 For example, ILO Convention No. 182 specifically calls for tripartite consultation where states are taking measures to implement it, for example in determining the list of hazardous work and designing and implementing programmes of action and establishing monitoring mechanisms.

79 See, for example, UNHRC (1993).

80 See, for example, UNICEF (1997).

status with those of governments, join with them in free discussion and democratic decision with a view to the promotion of the common welfare.

(The 'Philadelphia Declaration' of 1944, § I)

The Declaration also observes that 'lasting peace can be established only if it is based on social justice' and affirms that 'all human beings, irrespective of race, creed or sex, have the right to pursue both their material well-being and their spiritual development in conditions of freedom and dignity, of economic security and equal opportunity'.[81] However, there is little in the way of specific provision relating to children, and it is certainly not couched in the language of children's rights discourse. Amongst the world programmes to which ILO declares its commitment is the 'provision for child welfare and maternity protection'.[82] ILO continued to produce a number of conventions in the post-war period through to the 1960s and 1970s. However, there was a shift away from 'standard-setting' in the international community in the early 1980s to public awareness campaigns (Cordova 1993) and, at the beginning of the 1990s, an emphasis on 'technical assistance' to member states (ILO 1996: para. 99). The appropriate balance between 'hard' and 'soft' law in international legal protection and their integration with practical programmes of assistance became an issue attracting greater attention.

Second, in June 1998, ILO adopted a soft law instrument, the 'Declaration on Fundamental Principles and Rights at Work and its Follow-up', in which the International Labour Conference declared that all member states should respect the principles of the (four) 'fundamental rights' that are the subject of ILO Conventions,[83] that is:

(a) freedom of association and the effective recognition of the right to collective bargaining;
(b) the elimination of all forms of forced or compulsory labour;
(c) the effective abolition of child labour; and
(d) the elimination of discrimination in respect of employment and occupation.

(Article 3)

In other words, these 'principles' should be binding on member states regardless of convention ratification. ILO's Director-General annually prepares a 'global report' on one of these fundamental rights in turn, providing a 4-year

---

81 The Philadelphia Declaration of 1944, § II(a).
82 The Philadelphia Declaration of 1944, § III(h).
83 See further: C87 and C98 on Freedom of Association; C29 and C104 on Forced Labour; C138 and C182 on child labour; and C100 and C111 on Employment Discrimination.

cycle of reporting on each of them.[84] There have been two global reports on child labour at the time of writing (ILO 2002; ILO 2006), and a third is expected to appear in 2010.[85]

The 1998 Declaration has been an important landmark in the history of ILO. Although it is a soft law instrument, its authority is enhanced by the fact that it was *unanimously* agreed by ILO member states. Some have argued that the Declaration provided the necessary flexibility required in an increasingly globalised world. Such core labour rights could be better universalised and reach further afield through the development of such principles. Alston (2004) provides a robust critique of this approach, noting that the Declaration marks a new normative hierarchy whereby the four core labour standards are privileged at the expense of ILO's careful construction of 'rights' in the various ILO Conventions over many years. Replying to these criticisms, Langille (2005) argues that these core labour standards are conceptually coherent and in fact support the existing international labour regime rather than undermining it.

ILO's global report on child labour in 2002 concluded with an action plan resting on three 'pillars':

- The first pillar is to reinforce the work of IPEC.
- The second pillar is to mainstream the abolition of child labour more actively across other ILO programmes and strengthen cross-sectoral collaboration and policy integration to this end.
- The third pillar is to forge closer partnerships with employers' and workers' organizations, as well as with other institutions and groups that share the goal of abolishing child labour.

(ILO 2002: 118–19)

ILO's global report of 2006 (ILO 2006) set out an action plan that is built upon the three-pillar approach, but in particular, given their analysis that real inroads into the problem of child labour had been made in the period from 2000–2004 (see section 4.1.3), it concluded that the elimination of the worst forms of child labour was within reach and set a goal to achieve this by 2016 (ILO 2006: 83–89).[86]

---

84 See Declaration on Fundamental Principles and Rights at Work, Annex, para. III.
85 The Dutch Ministry of Social Affairs, in collaboration with ILO, UNICEF and the World Bank, was, at the time of writing (January 2010), organizing an international conference for 10–11 May 2010 in The Hague: 'Towards a world without child labour – Mapping the road to 2016'. The event will feature the launching of the ILO Global Report on child labour for 2010. Conference website at: http://www.childlabourconference2010.com/ (accessed 19 January 2010). The third global report was published on 7 May 2010: see ILO (2010).
86 The report's summary concludes optimistically that '[t]his transformation in approach to global leadership will ensure that the ILO will contribute more effectively to consigning child labour to history'. (ILO 2006: 90).

Finally, ILO unanimously adopted a Declaration on Social Justice for a Fair Globalization on 10 June 2008. This Declaration builds on the Philadelphia Declaration of 1944 and the 1998 Declaration to express 'the contemporary vision of the ILO's mandate in the era of globalization' and, it is claimed, 'marks the most important renewal of the Organization since the Declaration of Philadelphia'.[87] The Declaration asserts that ILO's efforts 'to place full and productive employment and decent work at the centre of economic and social policies, should be based on the four equally important strategic objectives of the ILO' which can be summarised as: (i) promoting employment by creating a sustainable institutional and economic environment; (ii) developing and enhancing measures of social security and labour protection which are sustainable and adapted to national circumstances; (iii) promoting social dialogue and tripartism as the most appropriate method for implementing the strategic objectives; and (iv) respecting, promoting and realizing the fundamental principles and rights at work, which are of particular significance, as both rights and enabling conditions are necessary for the full realization of all the strategic objectives.[88] ILO also commits itself to 'review and adapt its institutional practices to enhance governance and capacity building'.[89]

The more integrated strategic approach that is signalled by both the ILO Declarations of 1998 and 2008 may go some way to address previous criticisms (e.g. Smolin 2000: 956) that ILO might lack experience and find difficulty in operating outside of the traditional concerns of the international labour movement. A key element in the development of this more integrated and holistic approach to the problem of child labour has been the very considerable achievements of the International Programme for the Elimination of Child Labour (IPEC) that ILO had introduced in 1991. By the time of the 1998 Declaration IPEC was running over 700 projects on child labour in over 40 countries (Detrick 1999: 562). The 'Time-Bound Programme' (TBP) approach[90] is an important method put in place by IPEC to assist countries in fulfilling their obligations under the Convention.

Time-bound programmes are designed as a comprehensive framework that governments can use to chart a course of action with well-defined targets. They comprise a set of integrated and coordinated policies and interventions with clear goals, specific targets and a defined time frame, aimed at preventing

---

87 Declaration on Social Justice for a Fair Globalization, preface, pp. 1 and 4.
88 Declaration on Social Justice for a Fair Globalization, § I, Part A (i)–(iv).
89 Declaration on Social Justice for a Fair Globalization, § II, Part A.
90 'This approach combines past experiences of sectoral, thematic and geographically based approaches – linking the action against child labour to the national development effort as a whole – and to economic and social policies of every kind, from macro-economic performance to education and labour market policies' (Noguchi 2002: 361).

and eliminating a country's worst forms of child labour. They emphasize the need to address the root causes of child labour, linking action for its elimination to national development policies, macro-economic trends and strategies, and demographic and labour market processes and outcomes, with particular emphasis on economic and social policies to combat poverty and to promote universal basic education and social mobilization. The TBPs' time horizon is set in accordance with the prevalence of the worst forms of child labour, the availability of resources, the level of local expertise and other conditions prevailing in the country. ...

IPEC sees the TBP as a key strategic approach for attaining large-scale impact on the worst forms of child labour.

(IPEC website: http://www.ilo.org/ipec/Action/
Time-BoundProgrammes/lang--en/index.htm
(accessed 18 January 2010)

El Salvador, Nepal and the United Republic of Tanzania were the first three countries to implement TBPs. Three other countries, the Dominican Republic, Costa Rica and the Philippines, started implementation during 2002–03. Several more countries have since begun the process, including: Bangladesh, Brazil, Cambodia, Ecuador, Ghana, Indonesia, Kenya, Lebanon, Madagascar, Mongolia, Pakistan, Senegal, South Africa, Turkey[91] and Yemen.[92]

4.2.6 ILO reporting, representation and complaints procedures

ILO has a unique supervisory mechanism that provides two types of international monitoring: regular supervision and *ad hoc* procedures (Noguchi 2002: 366). The system is based on the ILO Constitution, so separate conventions do not contain their own provisions on reporting and monitoring like the CRC. ILO relies (usually) on public shaming through documentation in ILO reports, together with technical expertise and financial assistance to promote compliance (Ho 2006: 341).

4.2.6.1 Regular supervision: reporting

Regular supervision is provided under article 22 of the ILO Constitution. Each member state ratifying an ILO convention agrees to make an annual report to the

---

91 It was concluded in one study that, despite Turkey's participation in 1992 as one of the original six countries in the IPEC programme, 'little has changed in relation to the extent of child labour and their working conditions' (Bakirci 2002: 71).

92 See IPEC's website for further details of the TBP approach: http://www.ilo.org/ipec/Action/ Time-BoundProgrammes/Implementation/lang--en/index.htm (accessed 18 January 2010).

International Labour Office on the measures it has taken to give effect to the conventions it has ratified. The Governing Body decides the form and content of such reports. They are then examined by the Committee of Experts on the Application of Conventions and Recommendations (CEACR). The Director-General must present summaries of the reports so received before the next conference.[93] The reports, when submitted to the conference, are then discussed by a tripartite committee. In practice, reports are submitted every 2 years for the so-called fundamental and priority conventions, and every 5 years for other conventions, unless the CEACR requests them sooner. Since 2003, reports have been submitted according to conventions grouped by subject matter. Governments are required to provide relevant legislation, statistics and documentation necessary for the full examination of their reports. Where a government has not satisfactorily provided such information, CEACR will write requesting it.

Although, in certain respects, there are distinct merits to the system of reporting under the CRC,[94] the ILO reporting procedures can be seen to have some advantages. There is, for example, an opportunity for a technical analysis by independent experts (the CEACR) in addition to an examination by the tripartite bodies of ILO (that is, governments, workers and employer representatives). Like the CRC system, there is regular monitoring on the basis of country reports and responses to reports, but there is also the opportunity under the ILO machinery for the use of *ad hoc* procedures in cases of severe violations. In the Follow-up to the Declaration of 1998, there is a system for gathering information from countries that have not yet ratified the relevant fundamental conventions through annual reports.[95]

The CEACR produces two types of commentary on the application of the conventions: 'observations' and 'direct requests'. 'Individual observations' contain comments on fundamental questions raised by the application of a particular convention by a particular government, and these are reproduced in the Committee's annual report (e.g. CEACR 2009). Occasionally, it also produces a 'general observation' on one of the conventions. For example, in 2009 the CEACR issued a 'general observation' on the concept of 'light work' in ILO Convention No. 138: see CEACR (2009a) and section 4.2.1. 'Direct requests' usually relate to more technical questions or questions of lesser importance and are not published in the report, but are communicated directly to the governments concerned.

---

93 ILO Constitution, articles 22 and 23.
94 See Chapter 3, section 3.3.2.
95 'The purpose is to provide an opportunity to review each year, by means of simplified procedures to replace the 4-year review introduced by the Governing Body in 1995, the efforts made in accordance with the Declaration by Members which have not yet ratified all the fundamental Conventions.
      'The follow-up will cover each year the four areas of fundamental principles and rights specified in the Declaration'. (Follow-up to the Declaration of 1998, § IIA(1) and (2)).

4.2.6.2 Ad hoc procedures

Where there are acute problems or persistent non-observance of a ratified convention, the ILO Constitution provides for *ad hoc* procedures.[96] As ILO depends greatly on a principle of voluntarism by member states, these procedures are not invoked routinely. There are two types of procedure to consider: 'representation' and 'complaints' procedures. There are two 'representation' procedures available. First, representations can be made, by either an industrial association of employers or workers, that any of the member states 'has failed to secure in any respect the effective observance within its jurisdiction of any Convention to which it is a party'. The Governing Body may then communicate this representation to the government concerned and invite it to make a statement. If either the government fails to make a statement in response, or the Governing Body does not deem its response satisfactory, then the latter may publish the representation and the statement, if any, made in reply to it.[97] Second, there is a 'reference' procedure[98] available for member states where another member has failed to respond to ILO standard-setting. A member state, when ratifying a convention or a recommendation, is under an obligation[99] to bring the measure 'before the authority or authorities within whose competence the matter lies, for the enactment of legislation or other action' within 1 year from the adoption of the measure or, in exceptional circumstances, 18 months. There is, additionally, a 'complaint' procedure[100] available. Member states have a right to file a complaint with the International Labour Office if they are not satisfied that any other member is securing the effective observance of any convention which both have ratified. The Governing Body has a discretion to request a statement from the government in question. If there is no satisfactory reply, or the Governing Body does not think it necessary to request one, it may appoint a Commission of Inquiry to consider the complaint and report. After full consideration of the complaint, the Commission must prepare a report setting out its findings of facts and such recommendations it may have as to the steps to be taken to meet the complaint and their timing. The Director-General must then communicate the report to the Governing Body and to each of the governments concerned in the complaint and arrange for its publication. Each of the governments must respond within 3 months, stating to the Director-General whether it accepts the recommendations contained in the Commission's report. If not, the governments may indicate that they propose to refer the complaint on to the International Court of Justice (ICJ).[101] The ICJ's decisions with regard to a complaint shall be final and

---

96 ILO Constitution, articles 24 and 26.
97 ILO Constitution, articles 24 and 25.
98 ILO Constitution, article 30.
99 ILO Constitution, article 19(5)(b) and (6)(b).
100 ILO Constitution, articles 26–28.
101 See Chapter 2, section 2.4.1.1.

'may affirm, vary or reverse any of the findings or recommendations of the Commission of Inquiry, if any'.[102]

ILO has reserved the use of Commissions of Inquiry for really grave and persistent violations of the international labour standards.[103] The Commission's report on Myanmar in 1998 (ILO 1998a) detailed the widespread and systematic use of forced labour in that country and a broad pattern of violation of fundamental human rights by the military government. The military in effect had used the civilian population (including women and children) as an unlimited pool of labourers to build and maintain a number of projects in construction, agriculture, and in hotels and other infrastructure projects.[104] A member state failing to carry out the recommendations of a Commission of Inquiry or a decision of the ICJ[105] will be vulnerable to the Governing Body recommending 'such action as it may deem wise and expedient to secure compliance therewith' to the Conference.

The involvement of ILO's 'social partners' in initiating *ad hoc* procedures and examining a case of representation is significant:

> They [the social partners] have a power to channel concerns of civil society into the mechanism of international standards. In the above-mentioned regular supervision, workers and employers organizations are very much encouraged to submit their comments and observations on the government's reports.
> (Noguchi 2002: 367)

4.3 Progressing the elimination of exploitative child labour

This section discusses how best the global movement to eliminate child labour can move forward. The rapid ratification of ILO Convention No. 182 and the substantial amounts of donor funding that have supported IPEC, discussed earlier, are encouraging developments, though there remain a few conspicuous omissions to the ratification list of ILO conventions Nos. 138 and 182.[106] It has been

---

102 ILO Constitution, articles 29, 31 and 32.
103 An example is the Commission of Inquiry set up in March 1997 following a complaint lodged by 25 worker delegates to the 83rd Session of the International Labour Conference in June 1996, to examine the application of the Forced Labour Convention of 1930 in Myanmar: see ILO (1998a). This situation also resulted in the unprecedented invocation of article 33 of the ILO Constitution which provides certain enforcement powers.
104 See generally, Sarkin and Pietschmann (2003) for an account of the Myanmar crisis.
105 ILO Constitution, articles 33 and 34.
106 India, for example, is thought to have a relatively large number of child workers, but had not ratified either ILO Convention No. 138 or 182 at the time of writing (May 2010). Bangladesh has not yet ratified ILO Convention No. 138, but it ratified ILO Convention No. 182 on 12 March 2001. The Indian Constitution provides that 'No child below the age of fourteen years shall be employed to work in any factory or mine or engaged in any other hazardous employment' (article 24). See Agarwal (2004), who discusses two public interest litigation actions in the

recognised that a holistic approach to the elimination of child labour is required to address the multi-faceted nature of this problem; its complexity is certainly no excuse for inaction. As one commentator remarked:

> The indivisibility and interdependence of all human rights, which is the lynchpin of the United Nations approach, is perhaps nowhere more evident tha[n] in the quest for solutions to the problem of the exploitation of child labour.
>
> (Alston 1989: 39)

Most commentators prefer an integrated strategy to tackle the elimination of child labour (e.g. Masum 2002). Earlier commentaries have remarked on the unwillingness of governments to acknowledge the existence or at least the extent of child labour within jurisdictions, and indeed official acknowledgment is a prerequisite in seeking international, technical or financial assistance (Alston 1989: 38). However, there are no uniform, pre-packaged solutions in this field. CEACR noted long ago that the uneven incidence of child labour within countries required detailed investigation followed by pilot programmes to determine the most effective measures (CEACR 1981: para. 407). It is clear that the elimination of child labour will involve legislative, judicial and administrative interventions, but these are only one element of measures taken at the national level; equally, the adoption of inappropriately tough legislation may make such practices go underground, Furthermore, a prerequisite for any credible programme to tackle child labour requires detailed and specific information; there is a continuing need for studies to provide robust analysis and policy prescriptions (Alston 1989: 40–46).

4.3.1 Child labour in international law: assessing the role of law and the enforceability problem

Much of public international law is vulnerable to the criticism that it lacks 'teeth', but that is often because inappropriate expectations are made of the extent to which it can deliver progress, particularly in relation to complex social, economic and cultural problems such as child labour. It should not be thought that the existence of law to eliminate child labour is necessarily the key type of intervention. The decline in child labour in the industrialised countries between 1880 and 1920 'is thought to be due to both economic and legal reasons, with the former predominating' (Betcherman *et al.* 2004: 25). It should also be remembered that international law has evolved alongside a deep history that supports the autonomy

Supreme Court of India in the 1990s to enforce India's domestic legislation in relation to events occurring in Sivakasi, the home of India's match and firecracker industries.

and equality of state sovereignty.[107] The principle of domestic jurisdiction is enshrined in the Charter of the United Nations.[108] It has been said that the lack of enforceability of conventions often reflects concern in the drafting process about the preservation of state sovereignty (Silk and Makonnen 2003: 363; Selby 2008: 175). Furthermore, international human rights instruments are the result of political consensus within the international community; they 'reflect what governments and interest groups could agree on, not necessarily what experts believe should be done' (Betcherman *et al.* 2004: 5). However, despite such limitations, these instruments do provide important standards from which national policy and benchmarks to assess policy interventions can be derived. In considering the 'enforceability' dimension to the three key international instruments discussed in this chapter, it should not be forgotten that these instruments ultimately rely heavily on national efforts. For example, it is particularly important that appropriate national systems of labour inspection are established given children's powerlessness in many work situations (Alston 1989: 44).

As we have seen (section 4.1.4), the dilemma between universal standard-setting and cultural relativity is a poignant one in relation to child labour. Northern countries tend to articulate children's rights against a background idea of childhood as a biologically driven natural phenomenon 'characterized by physical and mental growth stages that are everywhere roughly the same' (Myers 2001: 40). This dominant view of childhood tends to keep children separated off from adulthood and discourages participation in adult concerns, particularly the economic maintenance of the family. On the other hand, Southern societies stress collective family unity and solidarity and accept a much greater degree of participation and contribution to the economic maintenance of the family.

Discussion of the CRC and the reporting process – the main sanctioning mechanism – undertaken by the CtRC was considered earlier.[109] There are similar problems with the other human rights treaty bodies too (Lansdown 2000); indeed, some commentators have denoted these problems as a 'crisis' in the human rights treaty system (Alston and Crawford 2000). For example, although the Committee on Economic, Social and Cultural Rights (CESCR) has highlighted child labour in its concluding observations, 'the language of these conclusions is generally descriptive or hortatory, not mandatory, and is not coupled with any enforcement power' (Silk and Makonnen 2003: 364). The endemic problem of delay in the reporting processes has also affected the operation of CESCR and the Committee

---

107 'The sovereignty and equality of states represent the basic constitutional doctrine of the law of nations, which governs a community consisting primarily of states having a uniform legal personality.' (Brownlie 2008: 289).

108 Charter of the United Nations of 1945, article 2(1) and (7).

109 See Chapter 3, section 3.3.2.

on Human Rights (CCPR) in addition to CtRC.[110] Indeed, it has been observed that 'the system, established to oversee state compliance, depends for its continued functioning, on a high level of state default' (Crawford J 2000: 6).

The concerns about the delay and other problems with the CRC processes are comparable to defects in the enforcement available under the ILO machinery which, it is thought, have slowed the pace of reform in this area (Ho 2006: 340).

> The ILO enforcement system is both sophisticated and multifaceted. But it has few teeth. Its major drawback is its exclusive reliance on moral persuasion and such non-punitive techniques as publicity, shame, diplomacy, and dialogue to comply with the standards it establishes. Its option to use contentious proceedings is rarely utilized. Technical co-operation programmes, a favoured method of co-ordinating compliance with internationally agreed-to standards, seem so much more collegial and less adversarial.
>
> (Cooper 1997: 419)

It is to be hoped that ILO's recent commitment to reviewing its own institutional practices under the Declaration on Social Justice for a Fair Globalization of 2008 (see section 4.2.5) will enable further strengthening of the monitoring procedures.[111]

Some commentators have observed that the dilemma in this area is that there are (now) strong legal norms but weak enforcement mechanisms, a process which has in turn contributed to a rise in private action to prevent child labour (Silk and Makonnen 2003: 359). Silk and Makonnen offer a useful model of the evolution of human rights enforcement to consider. The identification of human rights abuses leads to the setting of strong international legal standards, but with weak institutions and processes of enforcement; this in turn leads to a range of NGO and IGO interventions of a non-law enforcement character aiming to achieve compliance with the established normative standards. Finally, aspects of these private initiatives may in turn be incorporated into effective, enforceable national and international law (Silk and Makonnen 2003: 369).

4.3.2 Partnership and coordination

It is widely accepted that the implementation of human rights standards generally will benefit greatly from well-planned partnerships between governments and NGOs. It has been said that NGOs may be able to be more robustly abolitionist

---

110   See Chapter 2, section 2.5.1.2 and Table 2.1 for the list of eight Human Rights Treaty bodies and the treaties/protocols monitored by them.

111   Selby (2008: 177) advocates building on the model of the monitoring role undertaken by the European Committee of Social Rights, which actively examines the affairs in member countries to ensure that practices meet their commitment to the European Social Charter.

in their stance towards child labour than official international institutions which are always dependent on political compromise and diplomacy (Silk and Makonnen 2003: 369). They have certainly undertaken some very successful anti-sweatshop campaigns in the 1990s, for example. NGOs are often able to strike clearer, principled aims and objectives. The increasing focus on the NGO contribution is derived, to an extent, from the growing recognition of the limitations of standard-setting. Most commentators agree that the complexity and multi-faceted nature of child labour in particular requires national governments to strike such constructive partnerships.[112] The development of NGO action around child labour issues has involved the emergence of, for example, voluntary codes of corporate conduct. Indeed, some of the independent monitoring schemes evolved in this way have been criticised by organised labour as a 'privatisation of law enforcement', undermining the traditional protections for workers – collective bargaining (Silk and Makonnen 2003: 365).

The increasing need for partnerships with NGOs and IGOs also assumes there will be successful coordination between all these bodies to achieve the required synergies. In the past there have certainly been criticisms that ILO has carried 'virtually singlehandedly' the burden of international efforts in relation to the elimination of child labour (Alston 1989: 48). There is greater coordination now, and other bodies such as UNICEF, the UN Development Program (UNDP) and the Food and Agriculture Organization (FAO) have more input in this field than they used to have. But it is not only coordination between the relevant international and other bodies concerned that is required. There is also a need to coordinate the policy approaches taken, particularly in relation to education at the national level. As we have seen (section 4.1.2), the role of education is central to debates about child labour, both causatively and consequentially. Finally, with regard to developing countries, where it seems likely that the worst forms of child labour will persist for longer, it is important to construct an approach that is integrated with the wider development policies[113] available to improve social conditions (Selby 2008: 178).

The research literature in this area has also raised interesting questions about the potential role of, and partnership with, the business community in assisting with efforts to eliminate child labour. Hassel (2008) argues that in the last decade, spurred on in particular by the ILO Declaration of 1998, there has been a fundamental change of approach by business and governments towards global labour

---

112 However, given the pervasiveness of child labour in some nations, a strategy of 'mobilization of shame' may also be counter-productive (Alston 1989: 38).

113 The Hague Global Child Labour conference planned for May 2010 (see footnote 85) will also feature a discussion of an interagency report on child labour and development. An expected outcome of the conference is a roadmap that will spell out how progress against child labour can be accelerated in the aftermath of the global economic crisis and prior to the target dates for the MDGs (2015) and the elimination of the worst forms of child labour (2016). See conference website at: http://www.childlabourconference2010.com/ (accessed 19 January 2010).

and social issues. International labour law has moved away from ILO conventions towards the principles of 'core labour standards'. This has in effect led to an indirect pattern of self-regulation. Indeed, it is argued that the proliferation of corporate codes and a variety of company-based independent monitoring schemes indicate 'an apparent shift from reliance on public international measures to private action' (Silk and Makonnen 2003: 363). Furthermore, the adoption by ILO of this 'soft law' approach fits better into the wider debate of linking trade with labour standards (Hassel 2008: 237).

4.3.3 Linking trade and labour standards

The frustrations with the defects in the international legal regime have opened up another front for action at the international level, the linkage of the issue of child labour with international trade regulation (Cooper 1997: 420). Supporters of the trade–labour linkage have relied on competition and human rights arguments. The competition-based argument is that countries with lower labour standards generally have lower production costs which offer them a competitive trade advantage. Consequently, there may be a 'race to the bottom', that is, lowering labour standards to remain competitive. The human rights argument is simply that by imposing the linkage the international community is protecting individuals against the violation of the core labour standards (including abolition of child labour) of the Declaration of 1998. The counter-argument relies on the theory of protectionism: in effect, that trade–labour linkage would allow developed countries to protect their interests by preventing less developed nations from exploiting their lower wage cost advantages and that would slow economic growth, further worsening the child labour problem (Ho 2006: 343). However, the protectionist argument is not as credible if applied to the *worst* forms of child labour. Nevertheless, there are those that do not see trade sanctions as a primary remedy for eliminating child labour. As one commentator observes, '[c]ountries with large, affluent populations of consumers will always have more leverage both in adopting sanctions against countries and deflecting them against themselves' (Cullen 1999: 25).

Trade–labour linkage supporters have argued either for a stronger enforcement mechanism within ILO, such as trade sanctions, or the addition of a labour clause in the World Trade Organization (WTO) agreements. Some argue the need to integrate child labour elimination into national economic regulation.[114] Various organizations have advocated the need to link trade and labour standards. For example, the International Confederation of Free Trade Unions has advocated the prohibition of imports of any goods produced with exploitative child labour.

---

114 For example, by using a 'preferences' model like the general system of preferences (GSP) scheme used in the European Union (Selby 2008: 178).

In essence, the proposition to have a 'social clause'[115] inserted into WTO and other trade agreements will involve an obligation by parties to the agreement to respect labour standards, including the elimination of child labour, and recognition that the obligation can be enforced with trade sanctions.

However, the advocacy to establish trade–labour linkages has met with fierce resistance, mainly on the basis that such a linkage could be seen as a disguised form of protectionism and an attempt to undermine the competitive advantage of developing countries (Cooper 1997: 421). National trade boycotts have had a mixed reception. When a bill that would ban entry of any goods into the United States manufactured with the use of child labour was introduced into Congress by Senator Harkin in 1993, employers in Bangladesh laid off tens of thousands of children. Subsequent UNICEF studies showed that none of these children returned to school (Cooper 1997: 423), though in the aftermath of international pressure there were a number of improvements achieved (English 1997: 439). The Child Labor Deterrence Act in India, which prescribed fines for employers, made the employment of children more costly, but this caused the wages of children to drop, 'causing either more children in the household to work or those already working to work more hours' (Betcherman *et al.* 2004: 27). Simplistic measures such as dismissal of child labourers without any effort to rehabilitate and reintegrate them into the community should be avoided (Muntarbhorn 1998: 305). Consumer boycotts can be effective, but there is a need for such campaigns to be a part of a comprehensive strategy to avoid such negative consequences. Labelling campaigns can also be useful to assure consumers that products have been manufactured without child labour.[116] There has also been some imaginative collaboration between multinational corporations and their local suppliers, in combination with international organizations, to eliminate child labour in a specific industrial sector. For example, international concerns over the widespread use of children to hand-stitch footballs persuaded the Sialkot region in Pakistan to sign a memorandum of understanding with ILO, UNICEF and Save the Children–UK in Atlanta in 1997.[117] This started a unique programme in Pakistan, coordinated by IPEC.

115 There are, of course, a number of different models of 'social clause' that have been proposed (Muntarbhorn 1998: 271).

116 For example, the *Rugmark* system established in 1994. *Rugmark International* is an international NGO working to end illegal child labour in the handmade rug industry and to offer educational opportunities to children in India and Nepal. *Rugmark* is currently being phased out and replaced by *Good Weave*. See their website at: http://www.rugmark.net/ (accessed 8 January 2010). See also the Child Labor Free Consumer Information Bill of 1999, S. 1549, 106th Cong. (1999), introduced by Senator Harkin, that would have established guidelines for attaching labels indicating 'child labor free' to imported products made without child labour.

117 See Cooper (1997: 427), Muntarbhorn (1998: 292) and Johnson (1999) for accounts of this collaboration in the football stitching industry.

However, it would seem, for the present at least, that the option of persuading WTO to embrace a social clause is not available. WTO rejected in principle the formulation of a trade–labour link at the Singapore Ministerial Conference in 1997.[118] WTO has in effect moved the discussion back to ILO and has since refused to consider any sort of trade–labour linkage (Ho 2006: 344). Equally, ILO has been averse to pursuing the link as it 'is concerned to protect its institutional legitimacy which is founded on tripartism and voluntarism' (Cullen 1999: 29). As the options that might have been possible via WTO and ILO action appear to be closing, Ho argues that a nationalised trade–labour linkage would better provide enforcement against child labour violations than trying to create a strong international system (Ho 2006: 349). The argument is that, analogously to the idea that the International Criminal Court should move towards becoming a 'hybrid court', that is, it should be reliant on national authorities to enforce international criminal law, the system of child labour regulation could be best accommodated by focusing on ILO facilitating a nationalization of the international movement to abolish child labour (Ho 2006: 338). The basic idea is that developed countries, such as the United States, could create unilateral or bilateral trade agreements through which trade benefits or sanctions are not determined by individual countries but by ILO findings. Arguably, such a nationalised trade–labour linkage would better provide enforcement against child labour violations than efforts to create a strong international system (Ho 2006: 349).

---

118 Ministerial Conference of the World Trade Organization, Singapore Ministerial Declaration, adopted 13 December 1996, 36 I.L.M. 218 (1997). Available at http://www.wto.org/english/ thewto_e/minist_e/min96_e/wtodec_e.htm (accessed 14 May 2010).

Chapter 5

International parental child abduction

5.1 International parental child abduction[1]

The act of removing children from their usual abode to another country and in the context of a parental dispute will almost inevitably be damaging to the welfare of the child(ren). A child is likely to feel uprooted from a familiar environment, especially in circumstances where the child loses contact with friends and relatives. The move may disrupt not only the child's relationships but also his or her education and general sense of security, particularly if such a move is conducted in the context of a parental dispute. In a US review of the research literature on parental child abduction, it was concluded:

> The research on parental abduction indicates that these incidents can be highly traumatic for both children and left-behind parents and that the longer the period of separation, the more damaging the impact is for the child and the left-behind parent. Parental abduction is a crime in all 50 States and the District of Columbia. However, for a variety of reasons, the criminal justice system's response to these cases has historically been inadequate and sporadic. Improved education—for law enforcement personnel, prosecutors, and the public-at-large—is needed to ensure a quicker and more effective response to the children and families affected by these crimes.
>
> (Chiancone 2001)

In a study undertaken in the United Kingdom, involving interviews with 30 adults[2] and 10 children, it was concluded that 'abduction and its effects linger for many years after the ending of the abduction' and 'the lack of contact between

---

1 I am grateful to an anonymous reviewer of the first edition for the title of the chapter and a number of other points, most of which I have addressed in this chapter. See generally, Lowe *et al.* (2004) for a detailed, comprehensive and authoritative account of both lawful movement and abduction of children into and out of the United Kingdom, including full coverage of the criminal law.
2 The adults interviewed were 25 abducting or left-behind parents, three adults abducted as children, one grandparent and one non-abducted sibling.

parents and children during the period of the abduction is a source of immense continuing anxiety for those concerned, many years after the abduction' (Freeman 2006: 46). Furthermore, it did not appear that the age of the child when abducted, or the gender of either the parent or the child, made 'any significant difference' to the quality of the effects suffered. Interestingly, Dr Freeman also indicated that 'children abducted by their primary carers usually do not perceive the experience as one of abduction but, when abducted by their non-primary carers, they do' (2006: 63). She also stressed the importance of post-abduction contact with both parents:

> Where continued contact is not facilitated and encouraged between separated siblings and other separated family members it appears to result in complete misery for those involved. It also appears to lead to an undesirable ability to detach, as some of the data has revealed.
>
> (Freeman 2006: 64)

In many national jurisdictions child abduction is regarded as a sufficiently serious matter to require the protection of the criminal law. For example, the English common law developed a criminal law offence of 'kidnapping', defined by the House of Lords as the taking or carrying away of one person by another, by force or by fraud, without the consent of the person taken or carried away and without lawful excuse.[3] Furthermore, section 1(1) of the Child Abduction Act 1984 provides that 'a person connected with a child under the age of 16 commits an offence if he takes or sends the child out of the United Kingdom without the appropriate consent'. The maximum penalty for a conviction is 7 years imprisonment. Of course child abduction also occurs where the abductors are not the parents or other carers of the child concerned, but are intent on the sexual and/or economic exploitation of the child. Such abductions by strangers will usually be covered by the national criminal code relevant to the country in which the abduction took place.[4] There are also various provisions in the UN Convention on the Rights of the Child (CRC) and its Optional Protocol on the Rights of the Child on the sale of children, child prostitution and child pornography of 2000 (OPSC)[5] relevant to those scenarios. OPSC, for example, is intended to both strengthen the international criminalisation of such practices and provide welfare protection for child victims (Buck 2008). Some national jurisdictions also provide civil regulation of child abduction carried out within their own borders. In the United Kingdom, for example, the Family Law Act 1986 provides for common jurisdictional rules to apply and a set of rules for the mutual recognition and enforcement

---

3 *R v. D* [1984] AC 778, at 800.
4 See Newiss and Fairbrother (2004) for figures relating to mainly criminal aspects of child abduction in the United Kingdom.
5 See generally, Chapters 3 and 7, respectively.

of custody orders in each territory of the United Kingdom. However, 'once a child has been removed from the United Kingdom, parental abduction is usually treated as a civil matter'.[6]

The focus of this chapter is on the private international law[7] aspects of the parental/carer abduction of the child and, in particular, the operation of the Hague Convention on the Civil Aspects of International Child Abduction of 1980 (hereafter, the 'Hague Convention'). However, before analysing this set of rules, it is worth considering for a moment the social phenomenon of international parental child abduction. What are the underlying causes? Are there any distinctive characteristics of those parents who abduct children? What kind of dysfunctional family scenario is likely to result in abduction? Are men more likely to abduct children than women? Are babies and infants more likely to be abducted than older children? There is some empirical evidence available to address these questions.

When the Hague Convention was being prepared in the 1970s the paradigm case was that of the father taking the child abroad and possibly attempting to conceal his own and the child's whereabouts from the left-behind mother. He may have been motivated by bitter feelings generated by a deteriorating relationship with the mother, and he may have been frustrated by restrictions on his access. He may have lost legal custody of the child(ren). However, even the few surveys that were available in the 1990s challenged this stereotype (Beaumont and McEleavy 1999: 9–10). The statistical evidence on international parental abduction has not yet been fully developed, although the work of Lowe *et al.* (1999, 2006) has influenced the Hague Conference to develop its own statistical database.[8] Although it would seem that a higher proportion of fathers abduct in the United States *within* the US jurisdiction, there is some evidence that examines specifically international abductions that suggests the proportion of female and male abductors is about equal (Chiancone *et al.* 2001: 4). Greif and Hegar's study of 371 abductions found that 45 per cent of abductors were female, while others found in their examination of 630 cases that 52.5 per cent were female (Johnston *et al.* 1985; Greif and Hegar 1991, 1993). The stereotype of a non-custodial father removing or retaining his children has no resemblance to reality in the context of the Hague Convention of 1980. Lowe *et al.* (2006: 21–23) calculated from their examination of 1259 incoming return applications received by 45 contracting states that 68 per cent of abductors[9] were mothers and 29 per cent fathers while the remaining 3 per cent were grandparents and other relatives and bodies, and that in 68 per cent of these cases the 'taking person' was the primary carer or joint

---

6 See the International Child Abduction and Contact (ICACU) website at: http://www.officialsolicitor.gov.uk/os/icacu_law.htm (accessed 20 January 2010).

7 See Chapter 2, section 2.1.

8 On 28 September 2007 an electronic statistical database, INCASTAT, was launched, which generates the annual statistical forms covering return and access applications relating to the Hague Convention of 1980; it also produces statistical charts. INCASTAT is available only to the central authorities designated under the 1980 Child Abduction Convention.

9 Lowe *et al.* (2006) deploy the less pejorative phrase of 'taking person'.

primary carer of the child. Sixty seven per cent of the children involved were single children and 33 per cent were part of a sibling group.

The emerging picture of international parental abduction is that although the absolute number of abductions remains modest – for example, the US Department of State reports[10] that at any given time there are 1,000 open cases of American children either abducted from the United States or wrongfully retained in a foreign country, and there are about 500 children abducted from the United Kingdom each year[11] – it would appear that the number is rising as the process of globalization provides more opportunities for international marriages or partnerships to take place.

Motivations to abduct vary from parents wanting to force reconciliation with the left-behind parent, to having a desire to blame or punish the left-behind parent, or to protect the child from a parent who is perceived to abuse or neglect the child (Chiancone 2001). It is difficult to find entirely reliable and disaggregated statistical profiles of the adults and children involved in international parental abduction, but it is becoming more widely accepted that there is an increasing number. One possible explanation lies in the impact of reformed custody laws. The international legal recognition of the child's right to contact with *both* parents has increasingly been observed.[12] Part of the explanation may also lie in the increasing number of persons who marry or cohabit with a person of a different nationality. When the relationship fails there may well be pressures on the couple to return to their respective countries of origin. It may appear to be the obvious course of action for the primary carer to return home with their children. It is also possible, all other things being equal, that children who are unlawfully abducted by the primary carer are less damaged by the experience than those abducted by the other partner, perhaps, as one highly informed commentator suggests, because such children 'do not perceive the experience as one of abduction' (Freeman 2006: 63).

5.2 Introduction to the international legal instruments

There are four international instruments that need to be considered in relation to international parental abduction: certain provisions of the CRC; the European

---

10 'International Abduction Resolution' passed by House, Washington, DC, House Concurrent Resolution 293, 23 May 2000.

11 '500 children a year abducted from UK', Helen Pidd, *The Guardian*, 9 August 2009.

12 'States Parties shall ensure that a child shall not be separated from his or her parents against their will, except when competent authorities subject to judicial review determine, in accordance with applicable law and procedures, that such separation is necessary for the best interests of the child. …

'States Parties shall respect the right of the child who is separated from one or both parents to maintain personal relations and direct contact with both parents on a regular basis, except if it is contrary to the child's best interests'. (CRC, article 9(1) and (3)).

Convention on Recognition and Enforcement of Decisions Concerning Custody of Children and on Restoration of Custody of Children of 1980; Council Regulation (EU) 2201/2003 (hereafter the 'Revised Brussels II Regulation'); and the Hague Convention of 1980. The first three are dealt with, in outline only, in the following three sections. This chapter is focused mainly on the Hague Convention of 1980, which is dealt with in more depth in subsequent sections.

5.2.1 UN Convention on the Rights of the Child of 1989

The principle of the non-separation of children from their parents is set out in article 9 of the CRC[13] in respect of domestic situations, and article 10[14] sets out the standards to be complied with in respect of separations between children and parents involving different countries. States parties must respect the right of the child who is separated from one or both parents 'to maintain personal relations and direct contact with both parents on a regular basis, except if it is contrary to the child's best interests'.[15] Children also have the right 'to maintain on a regular basis, save in exceptional circumstances, personal relations and direct contacts with both parents'.[16] This latter provision resonates with, and was in part based upon, the recognition given in the Hague Convention to the maintenance of relations between children and both parents, in particular where the parents are of different nationalities (Detrick 1999: 194). These provisions have generated adverse comments from the CtRC, for example, where there is a lack of opportunities to implement a child's right to maintain contact with his or her parents (CO France 2009). Furthermore, article 11[17] places a duty on states parties to

---

13 Ibid.
14 '1. In accordance with the obligation of States Parties under article 9, paragraph 1, applications by a child or his or her parents to enter or leave a State Party for the purpose of family reunification shall be dealt with by States Parties in a positive, humane and expeditious manner. States Parties shall further ensure that the submission of such a request shall entail no adverse consequences for the applicants and for the members of their family.
　　2. A child whose parents reside in different States shall have the right to maintain on a regular basis, save in exceptional circumstances, personal relations and direct contacts with both parents. Towards that end and in accordance with the obligation of States Parties under article 9, paragraph 1, States Parties shall respect the right of the child and his or her parents to leave any country, including their own, and to enter their own country. The right to leave any country shall be subject only to such restrictions as are prescribed by law and which are necessary to protect the national security, public order (ordre public), public health or morals or the rights and freedoms of others and are consistent with the other rights recognised in the present Convention'. (CRC, article 10).

15 CRC, article 9(3).
16 CRC, article 10(2).
17 '1. States Parties shall take measures to combat the illicit transfer and non-return of children abroad.
　　2. To this end, States Parties shall promote the conclusion of bilateral or multilateral agreements or accession to existing agreements.' (CRC, article 11).

take measures to combat the 'illicit transfer and non-return of children abroad'. This expression is a reference to international child abduction by a parent; '[i]t is to be distinguished from the specific form of exploitation of children which is referred to in article 35[18] as the "abduction of children"' (Detrick 1999: 201). In particular, states parties are obliged 'to promote the conclusion of bilateral or multilateral agreements or accession to existing agreements'.[19] During the drafting of this paragraph, specific mention was made of the Hague Convention of 1980. The CtRC will frequently criticise states that have not ratified the Hague Convention and encourage those that have done so.

5.2.2 European Convention on Recognition and Enforcement of Decisions Concerning Custody of Children and on Restoration of Custody of Children of 1980

The focus of this chapter is with the most important international legal instrument in this area, the Hague Convention of 1980, which aims to achieve universal application. However, there are also regional instruments relevant to the issue of international parental abduction. For example, there is a European Convention on Recognition and Enforcement of Decisions Concerning Custody of Children and on Restoration of Custody of Children of 1980 (hereafter, the 'European Convention of 1980').[20] In 2010, there were 82 contracting states to the Hague Convention of 1980 and 36 contracting states to the European Convention of 1980. All of the latter, except Liechtenstein, have also ratified or acceded to the Hague Convention of 1980. Some contracting states will have incorporated the relevant conventions into their domestic law. For example, the United Kingdom incorporated both conventions into English law in the Child Abduction and Custody Act 1985.[21] The European Convention of 1980 is concerned with the enforcement and recognition of custody orders and decisions relating to access. Consequently, and in contrast to the Hague Convention of 1980, it requires that there is a custody or access 'order' in existence as a necessary pre-condition for invoking its jurisdiction.

Under each convention, the contracting state must establish an administrative body (the 'central authority'[22]) which will collate and send information to the

---

18 'States Parties shall take all appropriate national, bilateral and multilateral measures to prevent the abduction of, the sale of or traffic in children for any purpose or in any form.' (CRC, article 35).
19 CRC, article 11(2).
20 ETS No. 105.
21 See Child Abduction and Custody Act 1985, section 1(2) and Schedule 1, and Part VI of the Family Proceedings Rules 1991, SI 1991/1247 (L.20).
22 The list of 'central authorities' for the purposes of the Hague Convention can be found at: http://www.hcch.net/index_en.php?act=conventions.authorities&cid=24 (accessed 25 January 2010).

appropriate agencies and, if necessary, initiate legal proceedings.[23] The underlying assumption behind each convention is that a peremptory return of the child to the *status quo ante* will ultimately be in the child's best interests. The European Convention of 1980 can be used to assist in finding the whereabouts of a child and/or securing the recognition or enforcement of a custody order. If an application is made within 6 months of abduction, it is likely that the restoration of custody will be immediate on establishing the facts of an unlawful removal. An application outside of this time limit, however, will have to satisfy further conditions. There are, however, some limited circumstances in which an application under the European Convention of 1980 may be the better remedy. First, if the application is made within 6 months, a return order will be virtually mandatory.[24] Second, there are some advantages where the main dispute concerns the enforcement of an *access* order. It would appear that, of the contracting states which have ratified *both* conventions, much more use is made of the Hague Convention of 1980 where applications for the return of children are founded on the concept of a breach of custody rights, rather than the registration and recognition of custody decisions in the receiving state.[25]

5.2.3 The Revised Brussels II Regulation of 2003

There is also Council Regulation (EU) 2201/2003 ('Revised Brussels II Regulation') to consider: see generally Lamont (2008). Since 1 March 2005, abductions and the enforcement of orders for contact or access within the European Union (other than Denmark[26]) will be governed by the Hague Convention of 1980 as modified by the Revised Brussels II Regulation. The regulation[27] has introduced a more streamlined process for dealing with parental abductions within Europe. The details of how this regulation interacts with the Hague Convention are quite complex.[28] In essence the position in the United Kingdom is that in order for a case to come under the Hague Convention: the child must be under 16 years, the child must

---

23 The Central Authority for England & Wales under the Hague and European Conventions on Child Abduction is the Lord Chancellor, who delegates the duties of the Central Authority to the International Child Abduction and Contact Unit (ICACU) which is based in the Office of the Official Solicitor and Public Trustee. The ICACU is also the designated Central Authority under the Revised Brussels II Regulation ICACU, having been appointed in accordance with article 67 of the regulation. For Scotland, the Minister for Justice in Scotland is the Central Authority under both the Hague and European Conventions of 1980.

24 European Convention of 1980, article 8.

25 For example, ICACU has estimated that, of the 500 children it considers annually, only 8 per cent of all applications received relate to the European Convention (Official Solicitor 1997, para. 11).

26 The Revised Brussels II Regulation does not apply to Denmark.

27 Also known as 'Brussels II bis' and 'Brussels II(a)'.

28 See generally, Lowe (2007) who reviews the difficulties of application, and Schulz (2008) where the first judgment of the European Court of Justice (ECJ) clarifying the relationship between the Hague Convention of 1980 and the Revised Brussels II Regulations is discussed.

have been 'habitually resident' in the United Kingdom prior to the abduction, the applicant must have and has been exercising 'rights of custody' in relation to the child, and the abduction must have taken place after the Hague Convention came into force between the United Kingdom and the country to which the child has been taken. The Revised Brussels II Regulation will apply to an abduction case where the same criteria as for the Hague Convention apply, but, in addition, the abduction must have been from or to a country within the European Union (other than Denmark) and the application for return must be made after 1 March 2005. The European Convention of 1980 will apply only where the applicant has a court order made in a country which is a party to that convention and which is not a member of the European Union (except Denmark). The overall impact of the Revised Brussels II Regulation is that in intra-European Union cases there is more focus on hearing the child's views, depending on the child's age and maturity, and the left-behind parent can express his or her views before a decision not to return is made. The regulation also restricts the scope for an article 13(b) defence in the Hague Convention (see section 5.3.4.3).[29]

5.3 The Hague Convention on the civil aspects of international child abduction (1980)

This Convention was made under the auspices of the Hague Conference on Private International Law, an inter-governmental organisation first convened in 1893: see generally, Chapter 2, section 2.4.2. The Hague Convention of 1980 puts contracting states under an obligation to take appropriate measures to implement the Convention's primary objectives: to secure the prompt return of children 'wrongfully removed to or retained in any contracting state' and to ensure that rights of custody and access are respected.[30] States must use 'the most expeditious procedures available'[31] to achieve these objectives. The assumption is that the main remedy in the Convention of a speedy return order will be appropriate to all the main participants involved in international child abduction. It will act as a deterrent to would-be abductors. It will reduce the harm done to the child(ren) and it will protect the rights of the left-behind parent. It should be noted that a Convention application can be activated only in relation to a child who has not attained the age of 16 years.[32]

---

29 It also 'allows for the left behind parent to litigate the issue of residence in their own country if a non return order is made. If an order is then made requesting the return of the child, the country which originally made the non return order has to enforce this subsequent return order and return the child'. See Scottish government website: http://www.scotland.gov.uk/Topics/Justice/law/17867/fm-children-root/18533/BrusselsIIa (accessed 20 January 2010).
30 Article 1.
31 Article 2.
32 Article 4.

Delay in a child abduction situation can, of course, have very serious and permanent consequences for the relationship between the child and the left-behind parent (Freeman 2003, 2006). Speed is therefore an important element to the structure of the Convention, and this is reinforced by a duty[33] on the relevant judicial or administrative authorities of each contracting state to reach a decision within 6 weeks of the date of commencement of proceedings. A failure to do so puts them under an obligation to provide written reasons for the delay.

It should also be noted that, in keeping with the practice of the Hague Conference on Private International Law, an *explanatory report* was produced on the Hague Convention of 1980 (Pérez-Vera 1980). Such explanatory reports have an especially persuasive status when the courts are trying to interpret the Convention's provisions (see section 2.2.1). Indeed, the essential aims of the explanatory report relating to the Hague Convention of 1980 are described as follows:

> On the one hand, it must throw into relief, as accurately as possible, the principles which form the basis of the Convention and, wherever necessary, the development of those ideas which led to such principles being chosen from amongst existing options. ... This final Report must also fulfil another purpose, viz to supply those who have to apply the Convention with a detailed commentary on its provision.
>
> (Pérez-Vera, 1980, paras 5–6)

The structure of the Convention (see Figure 5.1) can be summarised as follows. First, it defines what is meant by a 'wrongful' removal or retention. Second, if the facts fit this definition then an immediate duty arises for the court in the country to which the child has been abducted to make a return order. The child is returned to the country from which he or she has been removed to uphold the position as it was before the removal or retention. Further disputes about the child will then have to be addressed in domestic proceedings in the child's country of origin. The full force of the duty to order a peremptory return will last for 12 months from the date of removal or retention.[34]

Third, after the 12-month period has elapsed there is a proviso which permits the court to refuse to order a return if the court considers that the child is sufficiently 'settled in its (new) environment' to justify a departure from the underlying duty to return. Fourth, the duty to return may also be refused if one of the 'defences' applies. The abducting parent might, for example, show that the child's return would result in a grave risk of harm to the child. A child (adjudged as sufficiently mature) might object to the return, with adequate justification. It might be shown that a left-behind parent in fact consented to or acquiesced in

---

33 Article 11.
34 This is one of the reasons why the Hague Convention of 1980 is preferred over the European Convention of 1980 where the active time period is only 6 months.

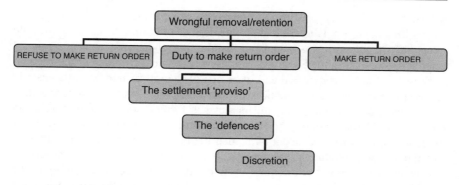

Figure 5.1 The structure of the Hague Convention of 1980.

the child's removal or retention. Alternatively, it could be that the left-behind parent had not actually exercised his or her rights of custody. Finally, even if one or more of these 'defences' are made out, the court will still have discretion to make the return order if it sees fit. It can choose to exercise its discretion in favour of the abducting parent and refuse to make a return order, or in favour of the left-behind parent by making the return order. The following sections examine these five steps in further detail.

5.3.1 *Wrongful removal or retention*

Article 3 defines what is a wrongful removal or retention.[35] The applicant who is seeking a return order under the Hague Convention has the evidential burden of showing that there has been a wrongful removal or retention. An application has to fail if the applicant cannot demonstrate this. It should be noted that the inclusion of the notion of a wrongful 'retention' ensures that a much wider number of situations are covered than would otherwise be the case. A typical retention might involve a child leaving his or her country of habitual residence with the agreement of person(s) having custody rights for a defined period of time (e.g. a holiday or visitation period). It was thought that a wrongful removal or wrongful retention were mutually exclusive concepts,[36] though this decision was distinguished

---

35 'The removal or the retention of a child is to be considered wrongful where –
 a) it is in breach of rights of custody attributed to a person, an institution or any other body, either jointly or alone, under the law of the State in which the child was habitually resident immediately before the removal or retention; and
 b) at the time of removal or retention those rights were actually exercised, either jointly or alone, or would have been so exercised but for the removal or retention.'
 'The rights of custody mentioned in sub-paragraph *a)* above, may arise in particular by operation of law or by reason of a judicial or administrative decision, or by reason of an agreement having legal effect under the law of that State.' (Article 3).
36 *Re H; Re S (Abduction: Custody Rights)* [1991] 2 AC 476, per Lord Brandon.

in *S. v. S. & S.*[37] In this case, the mother accepted that at the point of her departure from Lithuania to England she had no intention of returning the child on the date agreed by the father; it was concluded that the facts indicated a case of wrongful retention which subsumed a wrongful removal. Where a child is not returned on the expiry of an agreed period and in breach of the left-behind parent's custody rights, there is a wrongful retention, though a 'retention' may occur earlier than the agreed period if the abducting parent has formed such an intention at an earlier time.[38] Consequently, the Hague Convention is sufficiently broad to cover cases where the wrongful retention is identified as occurring some time after an initial (and lawful) 'removal' takes place. It can be seen from the text of article 3[39] that whether a removal or retention is 'wrongful' will depend largely upon the consideration of two key legal concepts: 'rights of custody' and 'habitual residence', which are discussed in the following sections. In some earlier cases there was some doubt whether the issue of 'consent' was relevant to the primary question of whether there had been a wrongful removal or retention, or to the 'defence' of consent contained in article 13(a). The Court of Appeal decided that the consent issue should be examined under article 13(a): see section 5.3.4.2.

5.3.1.1 Rights of custody

'Rights of custody' are defined non-exhaustively in article 5(a),[40] and the text of article 3(a)[41] confirms that the relevant law to determine whether rights of custody exist in any case will be the law of the country of the child's habitual residence immediately before the removal or retention.[42]

The Hague Convention indicates how rights of custody 'may' arise.[43] Rights of custody arise 'by operation of law' where the relevant domestic jurisdiction recognises that such rights would be *automatically* vested in a parent. In some jurisdictions a natural mother will always have parental rights (or 'parental responsibility', to use the UK terminology) vested in her. However, an unmarried father (in the United kingdom) must acquire parental responsibility by means of

---

37 [2009] EWHC 1494 (Fam).
38 There appears to be some doubt whether an uncommunicated decision not to return a child can amount to a wrongful retention: see *Re AZ (Abduction: Acquiescence)* [1993] 1 FLR 682; and *S v. S & S* [2009] EWHC 1494 (Fam).
39 See footnote 35.
40 'For the purposes of this Convention –
     a) "rights of custody" shall include rights relating to the care of the person of the child and, in particular, the right to determine the child's place of residence;
     b) "rights of access" shall include the right to take a child for a limited period of time to a place other than the child's habitual residence'. (Article 5).
41 See footnote 35.
42 Lowe *et al.* (2006: 39) calculate that this element accounts for 11 per cent of judicial refusals.
43 See the text of article 3 at footnote 35.

one of several prescribed methods, for example, by signing a parental responsibility agreement or by obtaining a parental responsibility order from the courts[44] or, following the Adoption and Children Act 2002, by virtue of being named on the birth certificate. Married partners will usually both have rights of custody by operation of law. This chapter focuses mainly on the position in the UK jurisdiction, but the reader should be aware that the laws on custody rights in various countries may differ greatly. Custody rights arising 'by reason of a judicial or administrative decision' will include court orders allocating parental responsibility and comparable administrative orders. It should be noted that the inclusion of 'administrative' decisions in this formula was agreed on the basis that in the Scandinavian countries an *administrative* authority generally makes custody decisions (Pérez-Vera 1980). Custody rights arising 'by reason of an agreement' is a broader category than merely narrow legal agreements such as the consensual 'parental responsibility agreement' available for parents to sign and lodge in the UK courts. In principle, this category will include all custody arrangements that are not specifically prohibited by law. A less formal parental agreement can therefore qualify under this heading. It will be a question of fact whether such an agreement will give rise to rights of custody.[45]

Some of the earlier cases took a formalistic view of whether custody rights existed. In *C v. S (Minor: Abduction: Illegitimate Child)*,[46] for example, the House of Lords considered a case where under the law of Western Australia the custody and guardianship of a child of unmarried parents was vested solely in the mother unless a court ordered otherwise. Since there was no order of the court giving the father custody rights at the time when the child was removed from Western Australia to England, the child's removal could not be wrongful within article 3 of the Convention. In later cases, however, the position of unmarried parents with *de facto* rather than strictly legal custody rights has been analysed with closer attention to the realities of the situation. Many would regard the breach of a married father's custody rights, the necessary trigger for a Hague Convention application, as socially and morally equivalent to the breach of an unmarried father's *de facto* custody rights. In *Re W and Re B (Child Abduction: Unmarried Father)*,[47] for example, the High Court held that a removal would be wrongful if an unmarried father had 'parental responsibility' either by agreement or court order, or there was a court order prohibiting it, or there were 'relevant proceedings' pending in a court, or the father was currently the primary carer of the child, at least if the mother had delegated such care to him. The House of Lords, in *Re D*

44 Children Act 1989, section 4.
45 See examples from the Icelandic and Israeli courts in *M v. K* (2000) HC/E/IS 363, and *Moore v. Moore* (2000) HC/E/IL 409, respectively.
46 [1990] 2 All ER 961.
47 [1998] 2 FLR 146.

(A Child) (Abduction: Rights of Custody),[48] has also recognised that 'rights of custody' may include a case where a person has a mere right of veto on the child's removal, even where there is no right to the actual care of the child; it did not matter whether the right of veto was the parent's or the court's, nor whether the right of veto arose by court order, by agreement or by operation of law.

The development of a more generous approach to enable the courts to identify 'rights of custody', a prerequisite for obtaining jurisdiction under the Convention, has been helped by the drafting of article 3. The words *'may* arise' allow the legal possibility of those rights coming into being by some other route than the three 'particular' elements mentioned in that article. Some of the cases have referred to the concept of 'inchoate rights' enjoyed by persons carrying out duties and enjoying privileges of a 'custodial or parental character'. For example, in *Re B (Minor) (Abduction),*[49] the Court of Appeal recognised such rights in respect of an unmarried father to whom the mother had entrusted the primary care of their child.[50]

Although this more liberal approach to the interpretation of 'rights of custody' opens the way to a potentially greater number of applications for return orders, there have to be some limits. In *A v. H (Registrar General for England and Wales and another intervening),*[51] for example, a child was born in London in August 2007 to Muslim parents. The British father and Dutch mother had gone through an Islamic wedding 3 days after the mother came to England in August 2006. This was not a legally valid marriage under English law. The birth of the child was registered by the father and he was named as the father on the birth certificate. On 31 March 2008 the mother, without notice to the father, took the child to the Netherlands. In June 2008 the father commenced Convention proceedings for the return of his son. The father raised several arguments to establish that he possessed rights of custody which were subsequently breached by the mother's unilateral removal of the child, but the court did not accept these. The argument that he had 'inchoate' rights of custody was specifically rejected on three grounds: there had been no abandonment of care to him; he did not have the right to determine where the child lived; and the mother had not recognised any rights of the father.

In a New Zealand case, *Fairfax v. Ireton,*[52] two unmarried partners had a child born in New Zealand in September 1996. The parents cohabited from 2 months after the boy's birth until they separated in late 1999/early 2000. In 2007 the parents agreed a parenting plan with the aid of a court-appointed counsellor which specified shared care of the child, although the plan was not put into a

---

48 [2007] 1 AC 619.
49 [1994] 2 FLR 249.
50 See *Re O (Child Abduction: Custody Rights)* [1997] 2 FLR 702 (Family Division), another case showing the courts protecting the primary carers, in this instance, the grandparents.
51 [2009] EWHC 636 (Fam).
52 [2009] 3 NZLR 289 (NZ CA).

formal court order. In February 2008 the mother took the child to Australia and the father then sought to secure the return of the child. The majority concluded that the father, even if not a guardian, had rights of custody under the parenting plan under New Zealand law, and even the dissenting judge agreed he had inchoate rights arising from the father's care of the child.

Although a finding of 'inchoate' rights of custody may found an application for a return order, mere 'rights of access', which are clearly distinguished from 'rights of custody' in the Convention, will not be sufficient to found an application. 'Rights of access' are separately protected under the Convention.[53] However, the practice relating to the enforcement of rights of access under the Hague Convention of 1980 varies considerably, and there have been significant weaknesses (HCCH 2001).

A further element of the definition of 'wrongful removal or retention' is that the custody rights must actually have been exercised (or would have been so exercised but for the removal or retention) at the time of the removal or retention. The purpose of this provision is to ensure that applications for return orders cannot be initiated by persons whose custody rights have in fact gone 'stale', for example, where a person has in effect abandoned all responsibility in relation to a child. This will generally occur through a failure to actively engage with the child(ren) over a significant period of time. Therefore, the mere existence of automatic parental rights, a formal court order or a parental agreement will not necessarily suffice as the basis of jurisdiction under the Hague Convention of 1980. There needs to be at least some evidence of the actual exercise of the custody rights in question to fulfil the legal requirements of a 'wrongful removal or retention'. In practice, however, it is unusual for this element of the definition to be a live issue. The desire on the part of the left-behind parent to make an application in the first place is generally prompted by having some form of active participation in the child's life prior to an abduction occurring.

The rights of custody in question must also be 'attributed to a person, an institution or any other body'.[54] Article 8 makes clear that it is '[a]ny person, institution

---

53 'An application to make arrangements for organising or securing the effective exercise of rights of access may be presented to the Central Authorities of the Contracting States in the same way as an application for the return of a child.'

'The Central Authorities are bound by the obligations of co-operation which are set forth in article 7 to promote the peaceful enjoyment of access rights and the fulfilment of any conditions to which the exercise of those rights may be subject. The Central Authorities shall take steps to remove, as far as possible, all obstacles to the exercise of such rights.'

'The Central Authorities, either directly or through intermediaries, may initiate or assist in the institution of proceedings with a view to organizing or protecting these rights and securing respect for the conditions to which the exercise of these rights may be subject.' (Article 21).

54 Article 3(a).

or other body' who may apply under the Convention for a return order.[55] Parents seek the majority of return petitions, but the drafting is wide enough to enable applications from public law bodies that have 'rights of custody'; for example, in *Re JS (Private International Adoption)*[56] the Family Division of the High Court considered that a licensed adoption agency in Texas could be properly regarded as having rights of custody. It is also clear that, in certain circumstances, a court might itself be properly regarded as having rights of custody. The House of Lords in *Re H (A Minor) (Abduction: Rights of Custody)*[57] considered, for example, the case of an unmarried father who had initiated proceedings in the Irish district court for guardianship and access, and later sought a return order when the mother had taken their daughter to England. It was held that the Irish court possessed custody rights in respect of the child by virtue of the father's pending guardianship application.

5.3.1.2 Article 15 declarations

Article 15[58] allows, as a matter of discretion, a request by the court or administrative authority that the applicant obtain a determination from the authorities of the state of the habitual residence of the child on the question whether the removal or retention was wrongful. In *Re D. (A Child) (Abduction: Rights of Custody)*,[59] it was held unanimously that where an article 15 declaration is sought the ruling of the foreign court as to the content of the rights held by the applicant must be treated as conclusive, save in exceptional cases where, for example, the ruling has been obtained by fraud or in breach of the rules of natural justice. This case is also authority for the proposition that the foreign court's determination would generally also be conclusive on how the content of domestic law should be viewed in Convention terms. It was also noted that recourse to article 15 would lead to delay and therefore the procedure should be used selectively; a balance had to be struck between acting on too little information and over-zealous examination.

---

55 'Any person, institution or other body claiming that a child has been removed or retained in breach of custody rights may apply either to the Central Authority of the child's habitual residence or to the Central Authority of any other Contracting State for assistance in securing the return of the child.' (Article 8).

56 [2000] 2 FLR 638.

57 [2002] 2 AC 291.

58 'The judicial or administrative authorities of a Contracting State may, prior to the making of an order for the return of the child, request that the applicant obtain from the authorities of the State of the habitual residence of the child a decision or other determination that the removal or retention was wrongful within the meaning of Article 3 of the Convention, where such a decision or determination may be obtained in that State. The Central Authorities of the Contracting States shall so far as practicable assist applicants to obtain such a decision or determination.' (Article 15).

59 [2006] UKHL 51; [2007] 1 A.C. 619.

5.3.1.3 Habitual residence[60]

'Habitual residence' is the second key concept within the definition of a wrongful removal or retention contained in article 3.[61] The identification of the country in which a child was habitually resident prior to a removal or retention is important in two respects. First, it locates the relevant jurisdiction to be examined in order to determine whether the left-behind parent has any 'rights of custody' (or can rely on the rights of custody vested in a court or other body) in the relevant domestic law. Second, the jurisdiction of the Hague Convention of 1980 will apply only to children who were habitually resident in a contracting state immediately before the breach of custody or access rights.[62] The idea behind the notion of habitual residence is that a child should be returned to the country where he or she has the most obvious connection prior to a wrongful removal or retention. This reflects the philosophy of the Convention to place the parties back into the position they were in prior to the alleged wrongful removal or retention. The country of the child's habitual residence is a logical and practical starting point. It is certainly a more appropriate connecting factor than the more abstract legal concepts of 'domicile' or 'nationality'. The notion of habitual residence is not defined in the Convention; it is left to be determined as a question of fact. This allows some flexibility for the courts and central authorities to come to practical solutions across the range of cases presented. The meaning of 'habitual residence' has been much litigated in the United Kingdom and in other contracting states. If an (abducting) parent can establish that the country to which he or she has removed the child has in fact become the child's 'habitual residence', then the left-behind parent will not be able to trigger the Convention's jurisdiction.[63]

There is a large body of case law concerning the notion of habitual residence (Beaumont and McEleavy 1999: 88–113). In the United Kingdom, habitual residence cannot be changed by the unilateral action of one parent. Earlier cases stressed the *factual* element; in other words, in which country did the child actually live prior to removal? Later cases, however, also identify the *mental* element of whether a person had a 'settled purpose' to establish habitual residence. It must also be remembered that it is ultimately the *child's* habitual residence at issue. Generally, it is difficult to make a factual distinction between a child's habitual residence and that of the child's parents. However, it is different when one considers the parties' settled purpose. If the test is based too much on the parties' settled purpose, it can result in the attribution of an artificial jurisdictional tie to the child. This is especially so in relation to very young children, who can hardly

---

60 See generally, Vivatvaraphol 2009.
61 Lowe *et al.* (2006: 39) calculate that this element accounts for 13 per cent of judicial refusals.
62 'The Convention shall apply to any child who was habitually resident in a Contracting State immediately before any breach of custody or access rights. The Convention shall cease to apply when the child attains the age of 16 years'. (Article 4).
63 See article 4.

be attributed with any meaningful intentionality with regard to their habitual residence.

There are a number of principles that emerge from the case law. In *C v. S (Minor: Abduction: Illegitimate Child)*[64] the House of Lords held that 'habitually resident' is not to be construed as a term of art with any special meaning, but rather it should be understood according to the natural meaning of the words. It is a question of fact to be determined by reference to all the circumstances of the case. The case also identified a significant difference between a person *ceasing* to be habitually resident and a person *commencing* habitual residence. Habitual residence could cease in a single day, whereas an 'appreciable period of time' and a 'settled intention' were necessary to establish habitual residence. However, this analysis meant, in effect, that during an 'appreciable period of time' when habitual residence is being established, a person is in a legal limbo, no longer habitually resident in the former country but not yet habitually resident in the prospective country. It is settled law in the United Kingdom that the child's habitual residence cannot be changed by the *unilateral* action of one parent.[65] Any other conclusion would undermine the usefulness of the Hague Convention of 1980. Transferring one habitual residence for another essentially requires cogent evidence that the child has spent some time in the country with the intention of adopting it as their regular abode. One problem with the concept of habitual residence arises where there is a fairly lengthy period spent abroad by a parent and the child(ren), often with initial parental consent. For example, in *Mozes v. Mozes*,[66] a US court conceded that, given enough time and positive experience, a child's life might become so firmly embedded in the new country as to make the child habitually resident there, notwithstanding lingering parental intentions to the contrary. Some of the English cases emphasise whether the individual has a settled purpose to take up a long-term residence; others focus more on whether a settled purpose for the time being, even if of short duration, would be sufficient to acquire a habitual residence.[67]

In *Re P.-J. (Children)*[68] the application related to five children, aged 4 to 13, who had lived with their Spanish father and Welsh mother in Spain until August 2007, when the children and mother moved to Wales for a 12-month period, to allow the children to spend an academic year abroad and to facilitate the renovation of the family home in Spain. In June 2008 the mother advised the father that she wished to end the marriage and to remain with the children in Wales.

---

64 [1990] 2 All ER 961.
65 See *N v. N (Child Abduction: Habitual Residence)* [2000] 3 FCR 84.
66 (2001) 239 F3d 1067 (9th Cir 2001).
67 While not giving a definitive view, the full Court of the Family Court of Australia indicated its preference for the latter position in *Kilah v. Director-General, Department of Community Services* (2008) Fam CAFC 81.
68 (2009) EWCA Civ 588.

Following their return to Spain for an attempted reconciliation, the mother unilaterally removed the children to the United Kingdom in October 2008. A return order was made in March 2009 and the mother appealed. Her central argument was that the children had acquired a habitual residence in England and Wales during their sabbatical year and that at the time of their removal in October 2008 they did not have a habitual residence in Spain. The Court of Appeal upheld the previous decision by the President of the Family Division that the children's habitual residence immediately before the removal was in Spain. Their ordered way of life was Spanish; their education had been undertaken there; their schooling in Wales was for a temporary period; their home was in Spain, not with their grandparents in Wales. The visit to Wales was a convenient respite to meet the dual objectives of increasing their language skills and refurbishing the Spanish home. Spain was where the family ordinarily lived. The mother's appeal against the return order was therefore rejected, and the return was ordered.

5.3.2 The duty to make a return order

Once the applicant has met the evidential burden of showing that there was a 'wrongful removal or retention' within the meaning of the Convention, then (in cases where less than 1 year has elapsed) the duty to return the child 'forthwith' arises.[69] Even where a period greater than 1 year has elapsed, a return order must still be made unless it can be demonstrated that the child is 'settled in its new environment' (for ease of reference, this provision[70] is referred to in this chapter as the 'proviso'). The policy of the Hague Convention is to support strongly the peremptory return of children to their countries of habitual residence; the merits of any particular parental dispute on residence and contact issues is left for the domestic courts to resolve.[71] Furthermore, the Convention also allows[72] two or more contracting states to agree amongst themselves that they will not utilise any of the available so-called 'defences' to a return order: see section 5.3.4.

---

69 'Where a child has been wrongfully removed or retained in terms of Article 3 and, at the date of the commencement of the proceedings before the judicial or administrative authority of the Contracting State where the child is, a period of less than 1 year has elapsed from the date of the wrongful removal or retention, the authority concerned shall order the return of the child forthwith.' (Article 12, para. 1).

70 'The judicial or administrative authority, even where the proceedings have been commenced after the expiration of the period of 1 year referred to in the preceding paragraph, shall also order the return of the child, unless it is demonstrated that the child is now settled in its new environment.' (Article 12, para. 2).

71 Indeed, it is expressly provided that '[a] decision under this Convention concerning the return of the child shall not be taken to be a determination on the merits of any custody issue'. (Article 19).

72 'Nothing in this Convention shall prevent two or more Contracting States, in order to limit the restrictions to which the return of the child may be subject, from agreeing among themselves to derogate from any provisions of this Convention which may imply such a restriction.' (Article 36).

5.3.3 'Settlement' cases

Once the period of 12 months from a wrongful removal or retention has expired, the underlying duty to return remains, but it is diluted by the possible application of the proviso. After the expiry of a period of 1 year, it will be open to an abducting parent to establish that the child has 'settled into its new environment'.[73] The date for assessing settlement is the date on which proceedings are commenced, not the date on which the application is determined.[74] The burden of proof to demonstrate settlement rests on the person (i.e. the abductor) opposing the return of the child. In earlier cases there had been some debate whether settlement prompted an obligation not to return, or simply provided a *discretion* not to order a return. This matter was resolved in favour of the latter position by the House of Lords in *Re M (Abduction: Zimbabwe)*.[75] It can be seen that where an abducting parent has deliberately concealed the whereabouts of the child, it would be inequitable if that provided an unjustified advantage in terms of the expiry of the period of time under the proviso.[76]

On the other hand, an *automatic* deduction of any period of time during which there was deliberate concealment might not provide the required flexibility for the court. The Court of Appeal approached the matter in *Cannon v. Cannon*[77] by examining more intensely the necessary elements of emotional and psychological settlement in concealment cases. Furthermore, settlement cases now involve almost invariably the separate representation of the child: see *Re D (A Child) (Abduction: Rights of Custody)*.[78]

5.3.4 The Article 13 'defences'

Notwithstanding the primary duty on authorities to order a return (discussed earlier) article 13 allows, exceptionally, the judicial or administrative authority of the state to which a child has been removed to refuse to make the usual return order in certain prescribed circumstances, but this is still subject to the overriding discretionary judgment of the court: see section 5.3.5.1. The text of article 13 of the Hague Convention of 1980 is set out in the following discussion.

> Notwithstanding the provisions of the preceding Article, the judicial or administrative authority of the requested State is not bound to order the

---

73 See the text of the 'proviso', i.e. article 12, para. 2, at footnote 70. Lowe *et al.* (2006: 39) calculate that this element accounts for 17 per cent of judicial refusals.
74 *Re N (Abduction)* [1991] 1 FLR 413.
75 [2007] UKHL 55, [2008] 1 FLR 251.
76 See *Re H (Abduction: Child of 16)* [2000] 2 FLR 51.
77 [2004] EWCA Civ 1330, [2005] 1 FLR 169, [2005] 1 W.L.R. 32.
78 [2006] UKHL 51, [2007] 1 AC 619, [2007] 1 FLR 961. See also Ranton (2009: 18).

return of the child if the person, institution or other body which opposes its return establishes that –

a) the person, institution or other body having the care of the person of the child was not actually exercising the custody rights at the time of removal or retention, or had consented to or subsequently acquiesced in the removal or retention; or

b) there is a grave risk that his or her return would expose the child to physical or psychological harm or otherwise place the child in an intolerable situation.

The judicial or administrative authority may also refuse to order the return of the child if it finds that the child objects to being returned and has attained an age and degree of maturity at which it is appropriate to take account of its views.

In considering the circumstances referred to in this Article, the judicial and administrative authorities shall take into account the information relating to the social background of the child provided by the Central Authority or other competent authority of the child's habitual residence.

(Hague Convention of 1980, article 13)

In essence, this article establishes a number of 'defences' to be raised by the person wishing to oppose a return. As with the 'settlement' cases[79] discussed earlier, the burden of proof to establish one or more of the defences rests with the person opposing the return, that is, the abductor. The drafters of the Convention envisaged that any routes to mitigate the inevitability of a return order should be narrowly construed (Pérez-Vera, 1980, para. 34). Generally, the courts therefore will interpret the defences quite restrictively; an over-generous approach to their interpretation would undermine the whole purpose of the Hague Convention to ensure that peremptory return orders are made where there has been a wrongful removal or retention. Each of these defences is examined in turn in the following sections.

5.3.4.1 Failure to exercise custody rights

The objective of the Convention is that a person should not be able to rely on a breach of rights of custody that have, in fact, been overtaken by subsequent events, or have gone 'stale'.[80] This defence, in effect, aims to preclude persons from making a claim who, while they might have technical 'custody rights', nevertheless have abandoned taking on any meaningful role in the child's life. It will be recalled that the failure to exercise custody rights is also an integral

---

79 Some commentators also categorise 'settlement' cases as a 'defence' to a return order.
80 Lowe *et al.* (2006: 39) calculate that this element accounts for 7 per cent of judicial refusals.

element to the way in which the Convention defines a wrongful removal or retention within the meaning of article 3: see section 5.3.1.1. This sub-provision of article 13 has not attracted much attention, at least in the UK courts. However, a useful distinction between the significance of the non-exercise of custody rights in articles 3 and 12 was identified in *Re W (Abduction: Procedure)*.[81] The court held that the former referred to rights of custody generally, whereas the latter was concerned specifically with rights of custody which were not being exercised by the person who has the care of the child, that is, a much narrower situation than the one envisaged by article 3.

What case law there is suggests that one must establish quite clear and unequivocal evidence of a failure to exercise rights of custody. One might suppose that a left-behind parent in prison could easily fall foul of this provision. However, in *H(MS) v. H(L)*,[82] the Supreme Court of Ireland held that the father's imprisonment did not divest him of his rights of custody. His rights were not nullified by a failure to play a significant part in the physical day-to-day care of the children. The court cited various other examples where a parent might have a low-level input to the routine physical care of a child: where a parent was disabled, incapacitated by sickness or accident, or in a job which necessitated long absences from home. On the facts, his children had visited him in prison and he had taken a sufficient interest to obtain a prohibited steps order. The court ruled that the mother had not discharged the burden required under article 13(1)(a). In the English jurisdiction several cases confirm that prisoners can still exercise rights of custody for the purposes of being consulted about a removal from the jurisdiction.[83]

5.3.4.2 Parental consent or acquiescence

Clearly, if a left-behind parent has consented to or acquiesced in a child's removal or retention in another country this can be regarded as merely a feature of normal family arrangements.[84] However, in keeping with a general need for the narrow construction of the defences, the evidence to establish consent in this context needs to be clear and compelling. The case law has stressed the need to find some *positive* element to consent. Normally, written evidence of consent will be required, but it is possible to infer consent from conduct,[85] so long as the evidence is definite and without ambiguity. Both the questions of consent and acquiescence are ultimately questions of fact. It would seem that the practical distinction

---

81 [1995] 1 FLR 878. I am grateful to Ranton (2009) for this point.
82 [2000] 3 IR 390.
83 See *Re A (Abduction: Rights of Custody: Imprisonment)* [2004] 1 FLR; *Re L (A Child)* [2006] 1 FLR 843.
84 Lowe *et al.* (2006: 39) calculate that the consent and acquiescence elements accounted for 9 and 5 per cent respectively of judicial refusals.
85 For example, *Re R (Abduction: Consent)* [1999] 1 FLR 828.

between consent and acquiescence is one of timing.[86] Consent will generally pre-date the removal or retention, whereas acquiescence occurs after such removal or retention.[87] Earlier case law identified different approaches for 'active' and 'passive' acquiescence, but the House of Lords in *Re H (Abduction: Acquiescence)*[88] stressed that the key question was whether the *subjective* state of mind of the left-behind parent constituted acquiescence. The only departure from this would be where any words or actions of the left-behind parent unequivocally showed, and led the abducting parent to believe, that the left-behind parent would not assert his or her right to summary return; then the court would be likely to hold that the left-behind parent had acquiesced.[89] The cases also illustrate that where the parties are merely undertaking negotiations with each other about where the child is to live, such negotiations will not amount to 'acquiescence'.[90] To take the opposite view would have undermined the support provided by the Hague Convention of 1980 to achieving *voluntary* settlement where possible.[91]

There remains some doubt whether delays consequent upon a lack of knowledge of the Convention can found a defence of acquiescence. One commentator has observed:

> Pending guidance from an appellate court, perhaps the clearest guidance that can be given about this concept is that the degree of knowledge of the remedies available on the part of the left-behind parent will be a relevant factor in each case. The weight to be attached to it will be case-specific. Once an applicant is aware of a Convention remedy, he *might* be considered to have acquiesced if it is not engaged promptly.
>
> (Ranton 2009: 22)

---

86 I am grateful to Ranton (2009) for this point.
87 *Re A (Minors) (Abductions: Acquiescence)* [1992] 1 FLR 14, 29.
88 [1998] AC 72. See also *Re S (A Child)* [2002] EWCA Civ 1941 which applies the approach in *Re H (Abduction: Acquiescence* [1998] AC 72.
89 See also *Re G (Abduction: Withdrawal of Proceedings, Acquiescence and Habitual Residence).* [2007] EWHC 2807 (Fam), [2008] 2 FLR 351, *D v. S* [2008] 2 FLR 393.
90 *Re I (Abduction: Acquiescence)* [1999] 1 FLR 778.
91 'Central Authorities shall co-operate with each other and promote co-operation amongst the competent authorities in their respective State to secure the prompt return of children and to achieve the other objects of this Convention. In particular, either directly or through any intermediary, they shall take all appropriate measures –
[*a*) –*b*) omitted]
c) to secure the voluntary return of the child or to bring about an amicable resolution of the issues'…
[*d*) – *i*) omitted]. (Article 7(c)).

5.3.4.3 Grave risk of harm or intolerable situation[92]

This defence is one of the most frequently pleaded.[93] Generally, it should be realised that some level of psychological harm is almost inevitable in a parental child abduction. However, something more than this (expected) threshold of harm is required in order to make out the defence.[94] The level of risk of harm must be 'grave', in other words, very serious. One factor that may take a case into this higher level of risk is where the court is satisfied that an established pattern of domestic violence may have induced the removal or retention in the first place.[95] However, it must be remembered that the provision requires harm to the child.[96] Domestic violence aimed at a parent is only relevant to the extent that such action can be shown to be damaging to the child(ren). Another factor which could heighten the risk of harm is where the court is not satisfied that there are sufficient institutional protective arrangements in the country of the child's habitual residence.[97] Normally, however, such protective arrangements will be assumed.[98] In *Re H (Children)(Abduction: Grave Risk)*[99], for example, a return order was made despite compelling evidence of significant violence suffered by the abductor on the basis that the Belgian court was in a position to protect the mother and children. As regards intra-EU cases, English courts will now assume other EU member states can provide sufficient protection in all but the exceptional case.[100] The defence can succeed, however, where the court identifies that there is a very specific risk of harm. For example, in *Re D (Article 13(b): Non-Return)*[101] the Court of Appeal refused to make a return order in circumstances where there had already been an attempt on the mother's life.

A difficult question, which arises in some of the cases, is where the (abducting) parent argues that he or she cannot return with the child to the country of habitual residence and that the consequent parent–child separation will constitute the harm contemplated in article 13(b). However, if this principle were to be

---

92 See the text of article 13(1)(b) at the beginning of section 5.3.4.

93 Lowe *et al.* (2006: 39) calculate that this element accounts for 19 per cent of judicial refusals globally.

94 A point stressed by the High Court of Australia in *DP v. Commonwealth Central Authority; JLM v. Director-General NSW Department of Community Services* [2001] HCA 39.

95 See *Sonderup v. Tondelli* 2001 (1) SA 1171 (CC) (Constitutional Court of South Africa); *Walsh v. Walsh* No. 99–1747 (1st Cir July 25, 2000) (US Court of Appeals for the First Circuit).

96 See also Weiner (2000: 704) where it is concluded that the Convention 'offers too little hope for the domestic violence victim who flees with her children to escape domestic violence and then faces her batterer's petition for the children's return'.

97 See *Q, A Petitioner* 2001 SLT 243 (Outer House of the Court of Session, Scotland); *TB v. JB (formerly JH) (Abduction: Grave Risk of Harm)* [2001] 2 FLR 515; *W v. W* [2004] 2 FLR 499.

98 For example, in *Re S (Abduction: Return into Care)* [1999] 1 FLR 843 (Family Division). See also *Re M (Abduction: Intolerable Situation)* [2000] 1 FLR 930.

99 [2003] 2 FLR 141.

100 See *F v. M (Abduction: Grave Risk of Harm)* [2008] 2 FLR 1263.

101 [2006] 2 FLR 305.

extended too generously it would allow abducting parents to over-control the outcome of proceedings by focusing on the damage caused by their own separation from the child.[102] The English courts have been reluctant to allow the circumstances flowing from an act of abduction to assist with formulating this defence.[103]

One category of case which has appeared in recent years concerns allegations of a grave risk of harm due to the security situation pertaining in the country of the child's habitual residence. It would seem that it does not matter whether it is actually a state of war or terrorist activity, or some other civil commotion. What is important is to assess the actual level of risk of harm to the child from the available evidence. The argument was not accepted in relation to an Israeli mother who had removed her child to England and argued that a return to Israel would expose her child to the difficult security situation there.[104]

Finally, it can be seen that a flexible and creative use of 'undertakings'[105] by the left-behind parent which address relevant article 13(b) concerns can be utilised to neutralise the court's acceptance of the defence. In such cases a return order is made, but often pending steps to be taken in the state of the child's habitual residence; for example, in *Re R (Abduction: Immigration Concerns)*[106] the return order was deferred pending the resolution of immigration matters that may have resulted in the separation of mother and child.

5.3.4.4 The child's objections

This defence is of particular interest in international child law as it touches upon the extent to which a child's 'autonomy rights' will be respected (see Chapter 1, section 1.2.1.2).[107] The requirement is not only that a child objects but also that the child 'has attained an age and degree of maturity at which it is appropriate to take account of its views'.[108] The question of a child's maturity is a matter of fact in which the court is required to exercise its judgment on the basis of the available evidence. For example, in *Re T (Abduction: Child's Objections to Return)*,[109]

---

102 See *Re C (Minors) (Abduction: Grave Risk of Psychological Harm)* [1999] 1 FLR 1145.

103 See *Re C (Abduction: Grave Risk of Psychological Harm)* [1999] 1 FLR 1145, and *Re C (Abduction: Grave Risk of Physical or Psychological Harm* [1999] 2 FLR 478.

104 See *Re S (A Child) (Abduction: Grave Risk of Harm)* [2002] EWCA Civ 908, [2002] 3 FCR 43.

105 There are now 'standard' undertakings relating to short-term financial provision and accommodation, and ones concerned with non-harassment and confirming the non-removal of the child pending a hearing on notice in the courts of the state of the child's habitual residence (Ranton 2009: 25).

106 [2005] 1 FLR 33.

107 Lowe *et al.* (2006: 39) calculate that this element accounts for 12 per cent of judicial refusals globally.

108 This resonates in the United Kingdom with the concept of the 'Gillick-mature child', though that was derived from a problem about consent and can be distinguished from the international law notion discussed here.

109 [2000] 2 FLR 192.

the Court of Appeal accepted that a child objected to being returned to her mother's care, and this was supported by a medical report indicating that she had suffered emotional abuse in her earlier life. Her consistent approach and the letter to her mother indicated that she was mature beyond her years and the article 13 defence was therefore accepted. The key question is about maturity rather than chronological age, though clearly the younger the child the less likely it is that s/he will have the appropriate maturity to make a credible decision.

The English courts have been reluctant to allow children to directly engage in Hague Convention litigation and there was a line of authority stating that a child could only be made a party to such proceedings in 'exceptional circumstances'.[110] However, the House of Lords in *Re D (A Child) (Abduction: Rights of Custody)*[111] considered this defence and noted that the procedural reforms introduced by the Revised Brussels II Regulation (see section 5.2.3) required that children should be heard unless this was inappropriate. Baroness Hale stated that this required more than the abductor presenting the child's views.[112] In addition to the usual Children and Family Court Advisory and Support Service (CAFCASS) officer report method, separate representation might be required, in particular where there were legal arguments which the adult parties were not putting forward, and there was no reason why the approach to be followed in EU cases should not be applied in all Hague cases. In a subsequent case in the House of Lords – *Re M (Abduction: Zimbabwe)*[113] – it was pointed out that 'settlement' cases (see section 5.3.3) were very likely to be combined with these 'child objections' cases and the court must consider at the outset how best to hear the child's views. Ordering separate representation would not be automatic, even in all child objections cases, but this might be more routinely ordered in settlement cases. The question for the directions judge would be 'whether separate representation of the child will add enough to the court's understanding of the issues that arise under the Hague Convention to justify the intrusion, the expense and the delay that may result'.[114]

Some of the cases have shown the difficulty of ordering a return in the face of a child who persistently objects to such a return.[115] The older the person, the more likely that greater weight will be given to that child. Pérez-Vera (1980: para. 30) concluded that 'it would be very difficult to accept that a child of, for example, 15 years of age, should be returned against its will'. However, the courts will be wary to exercise their discretion to refuse a return order where the evidence

---

110 See *Re H (Abduction)* [2007] 1 FLR 242.
111 [2006] UKHL 51, [2007] 1 AC 619, [2007] 1 FLR 961.
112 On the general role of the voice of the child in family proceedings, see Potter (2008).
113 [2007] UKHL 55; [2008] 1 FLR 251.
114 Per Baroness Hale, [2008] 1 FLR 251. This approach was adopted in *Re C (Abduction: Separate Representation of Children)* [2008] 2 FLR 6.
115 For example, in *Re HB (Abduction: Child's Objections) (No 2)* [1998] 1 FLR 564.

shows that a parent has heavily influenced and/or coached the child to adopt those objections.[116]

5.3.5 Exercising discretion

Even if, on the face of it, the abductor can meet the evidential burden of showing that one of the article 13 defences (or 'settlement' under article 12(2)) has been made out, the decision to make or refuse a return order will remain at the discretion of the court. There are two categories of 'discretion' considered in the following sections.

5.3.5.1 The court's discretion

Although earlier cases[117] based the discretion stage on the text of article 18,[118] this was expressly rejected in *Re M (Abduction: Zimbabwe)*[119] where it was pointed out that article 18 did not confer any new power to order the return of a child under the Convention, it merely contemplated powers conferred by domestic law. The court retains its discretion to make a return order. In *Re D (Abduction: Discretionary Return)*,[120] for example, the mother of two children applied for their return to France. After the couple's separation, a French court had made a residence order in favour of the mother, and the father was to have the children for holidays. The father retained the children in England at the end of a holiday. It was accepted on the facts that the mother had consented to this arrangement. The Family Division of the High Court exercised its discretion and ordered a return, mainly on the basis that if a return order had been refused it would conflict with the French residence order. The case demonstrates the more general point that this discretion is usually exercised consistently with the underlying philosophy of the Convention: to ensure that the examination of the case on its merits should occur in the country of the child's habitual residence.

In *Re M (Abduction: Zimbabwe)* the application related to two girls aged 13 and 10 at the time of the hearing. The parents were married but separated in early 2001, whereupon the mother moved abroad leaving the girls in the care of the father. In December 2004 the mother returned to Zimbabwe whereupon she had periodic contact with the children. In March 2005 the mother removed the children, taking them to England via Mozambique, Malawi and Kenya. The father learnt of his rights under the Convention in late 2006. Administrative delays led

---

116   See *AQ v. JQ* Outer House of the Court of Session (Scotland), 12 December 2001, HC/E/UK 415.
117   *Re S (A Minor) (Abduction)* [1991] 2 FLR 1; *Cannon v. Cannon* [2004] EWCA CIV 1330.
118   'The provisions of this Chapter do not limit the power of a judicial or administrative authority to order the return of the child at any time,' (Article 18).
119   [2007] UKHL 55, [2008] 1 AC, [2008] 1 FLR 251.
120   [2000] 1 FLR 24.

to his petition not being filed in the High Court until May 2007. On 19 June the High Court ordered the return of the children. The court accepted that the girls objected to going back and were of a sufficient age and maturity for their views to be considered, and that they were settled in their new environment, but the trial judge nevertheless exercised his discretion to make a return order. The mother unsuccessfully appealed to the Court of Appeal on 12 September. She was granted leave to appeal to the House of Lords on 24 October. The House of Lords allowed her appeal; the removal was wrongful, and it was accepted that the children had become settled in their new environment and objected to a return, but the court exercised its discretion not to make a return order. The House of Lords overturned a previous line of authority that suggested that the discretion could only be applied in 'exceptional' cases. It reasoned that making out any of the defences, in themselves, were 'exceptional' and therefore to impose a further layer of exceptionality at the discretion stage would be inappropriate. Baroness Hale held that 'the discretion is at large'.[121] The balance between the collective interests of supporting Convention policy to order returns and focusing on the individual child welfare considerations would vary from case to case. Furthermore, in *Re D (A Child) (Abduction: Rights of Custody)*[122] it was also held that the court's view of the morality of the abductor's actions ought not to affect the exercise of its discretion.

5.3.5.2 Discretion: article 20[123]

Article 20 provides the court with an additional, but little-used,[124] discretion to refuse a return order on the basis that otherwise the return of the child would breach fundamental principles of human rights. Article 20 was not expressly incorporated in the Child Abduction and Custody Act 1985. It was thought that the violation of primary human rights was likely to be a breach of article 13(1)(b) and therefore this article would have been otiose.[125] Baroness Hale observed in

---

121   [2008] 1 FLR 251, 266.
122   [2006] UKHL 51; [2007] 1 AC 619.
123   'The return of the child under the provisions of Article 12 may be refused if this would not be permitted by the fundamental principles of the requested State relating to the protection of human rights and fundamental freedoms,' (Article 20). Lowe *et al.* (2006: 39) calculate that this element accounts for 4 per cent of judicial refusals.
124   There were no article 20 cases cited in Lowe *et al.* (1999) and only eight cases (4 per cent of judicial refusals) in Lowe *et al.* (2006: 39), all relating to Chile.
125   The omission is similar to the non-incorporation of article 13 of the ECHR in the Human Rights Act 1998. Beaumont and McEleavy (1999: 172–76) discussed whether the United Kingdom and Finland might be in breach of their international obligations under the Hague Convention by not incorporating this article.

Re D (A Child) (Abduction: Rights of Custody)[126] that article 20 had in essence been given effect through the adoption of the Human Rights Act 1998.

The trend appears to be that this discretion will be used only where there is an obvious conflict with fundamental principles of human rights. For example, in *Director-General, Department of Families, Youth and Community Care v. Rhonda May Bennett*,[127] the Family Court of Australia noted that the regulation giving effect to article 20 was extremely narrow and should only be invoked exceptionally where the return of a child would utterly shock the conscience of the court or offend all notions of due process. It was held that the return of a child of Aboriginal or Torres Strait Islander heritage to a foreign country would not *per se* breach any fundamental principle in Australia relating to the protection of human rights and fundamental freedoms.

The few reported English cases that refer to article 20 suggest a reluctance to use this provision to refuse a return order. For example, the High Court did not accept any of the arguments that there had been a breach of the father's or the child's human rights in finding that the former was not considered to have rights of custody in *A v. H (Registrar General for England and Wales and another intervening)*.[128] In *N.J.C. v. N.P.C.*,[129] the Inner House of the Court of Session rejected a father's argument that the Convention proceedings had breached his right to a fair trial under article 6 of the ECHR; he may not have been able to focus his submissions as a professional lawyer would, but he had had every opportunity to address the relevant issues. In *Re M (Children) (Abduction: Rights of Custody)*[130] Baroness Hale declined to accept arguments based on article 20 and the ECHR. She held that returning the children against their will would be a graver interference with their rights than failing to do so would be with the rights of the father. Calculating the proportionality of interfering with his rights against the proportionality of interfering with the rights of the mother and the children would lead to the same result.

5.4 International parental abduction and non-convention countries

The Hague Convention of 1980 has been successful in many respects in securing the prompt return of children to the country of habitual residence prior to removal. An increasing number of states have ratified the Convention. The level of judicial and administrative co-operation has grown and become more sophisticated with the advent, for example, of international judicial seminars where the details of the Convention's mechanics can be fully aired: see HCCH (2000). However, there

---

126   [2006] UKHL 51; [2007] 1 A.C. 619.
127   [2000] Fam CA 253.
128   [2009] EWHC 636 (Fam).
129   [2008] CSIH 34, 2008 S.C. 571.
130   [2007] UKHL 55; [2008] 1 AC 1288.

remains the very significant problem of resolving international parental abductions where the abductor chooses to go to a country that has not ratified the Convention. The following two sections examine first, what the legal position is in relation to non-convention countries, and second, the recent adoption of a bilateral UK–Pakistan Protocol agreement.

5.4.1 Non-convention countries

Where an abductor has taken a child to a non-convention country then the left-behind parent must either arrive at an amicable solution with the abductor or commence proceedings in the domestic courts of that country; there are no international mechanisms available (except in Pakistan, see section 5.4.2). In some Islamic countries, non-Muslim mothers have very little chance of winning custody.[131] The Foreign & Commonwealth Office (FCO) and its network of embassies abroad will provide advice and support: for example, by providing lists of specialist overseas lawyers, liaising with overseas authorities, Interpol and other organizations for help in tracing the child(ren), or pressing the overseas courts to expedite the case.

For cases where an abductor had taken a child from a non-convention country to a convention country, the English courts had developed two lines of authority. One line of authority[132] favoured focusing on the welfare of the child as the court's paramount consideration.[133] A court would have to decline to order a return if that would be contrary to the child's welfare. Another line of authority[134] favoured applying the Convention machinery analogously to non-convention cases. However, in *Re J (Child Returned Abroad: Convention Rights),*[135] which concerned a Saudi father and a mother who had dual UK/Saudi nationality and their child, the mother and child had come to England with the father's consent, initially to study, and she later refused to return to Saudi Arabia. The case eventually arrived at the House of Lords, given the conflicting authorities. Baroness Hale rejected the approach of applying the Convention machinery analogously, though she conceded that the court could order an immediate return in appropriate cases. In all cases, the court must focus on the individual child.[136]

---

131 Scottish Government website, at: http://www.scotland.gov.uk/Topics/Justice/law/17867/fm-children-root/18533/13588 (accessed 25 January 2010).
132 *Re JA (Child Abduction: Non-Convention Country)* [1998] 1 FLR 231.
133 Children Act 1989, section 1. See also the decision of the Judicial Committee of the Privy Council in *McKee v. McKee* [1951] AC 352.
134 *Re E (Abduction: Non-Convention Country)* [1999] 2 FLR 642; *Re Z (Abduction: Non-Convention Country)* [1999] 1 FLR 1270.
135 [2005] 2 FLR 802.
136 See also *Re H (Abduction: Non-Convention Application)* [2006] 2 FLR 314 and *Re H (Abduction: Dominica: Corporal Punishment)* [2007] 1 FLR 72.

5.4.2 Non-convention countries: the UK–Pakistan Protocol[137] and the Cairo Declaration

The President of the Family Division and the Hon. Chief Justice of Pakistan, in consultation with senior members of the family judiciary of the United Kingdom and Pakistan, met on 15–17 January 2003 in the Royal Courts of Justice in London and agreed the (non-binding) bilateral 'UK–Pakistan Protocol'.[138] In essence, in a spirit of international judicial cooperation and assisted by a system of liaison judges, it is agreed in the protocol that '[i]n normal circumstances the welfare of a child is best determined by the courts of the country of the child's habitual/ordinary residence' and that '... the judge of the court of the country to which the child has been removed shall not ordinarily exercise jurisdiction over the child, save in so far as it is necessary for the court to order the return of the child to the country of the child's habitual/ordinary residence'.[139] Similarly, a (non-binding) arrangement with Egypt, known as the 'Cairo Declaration', was concluded on 17 January 2005,[140] comprising a number of agreed principles applying to cross-border cases.

5.5 Conclusions

A fundamental tension present in the Hague Convention of 1980 is that there is a persistent conflict between collective and individual rights. One can see that, in general, it will be in children's best interests to have a decision on their future made by courts located in their country of habitual residence. However, the children's rights agenda, considerably strengthened by the appearance of the CRC in 1989, also prompts a focus on the best interests of the child. To an extent, the availability of the 'settlement' proviso, the various defences in article 13 and the possibility of an article 20 argument, all provide possible routes whereby the centre of gravity of a Convention case can be pulled away from the underlying aim of peremptory return to the country of habitual residence and focus on the individual child's welfare interests. Nevertheless, the process of increasing international judicial co-operation and the holding of Special Commissions on the Convention has developed a recognisable way of dealing with these cases. The position of abductions to non-convention countries remains a worrying concern,

---

137 See generally, Freeman (2009, 2009a).
138 The text of the protocol can be found in Freeman (2009: Appendix 1), which also discusses the background and reviews the operation of the protocol. Available at: http://www.reunite.org/edit/files/Library%20-%20reunite%20Publications/Full%20Summary.pdf (accessed 15 May 2010).
139 UK–Pakistan Judicial Protocol on Children Matters of 2003, paras 1 and 2.
140 'Cairo Declaration Resulting from Anglo-Egyptian Meetings on Judicial Co-operation in International Child Abduction Matters between Egypt and the United Kingdom'. A copy of the declaration can be found at: http://www.reunite.org/edit/files/Library%20-%20International%20Regulations/Cairo%20Declaration.pdf (accessed 25 January 2010).

though the generation of bilateral agreements such as the UK–Pakistan Protocol appears to be a beneficial development.

Pressure groups such as Reunite and Parents and Abducted Children Together (PACT)[141] will no doubt continue to argue that the Convention is not doing the job it was intended to do. It was reported in 2009, for example, that more than one-third of children abducted from England and Wales had not returned home by the end of the year of being taken abroad without consent, according to figures released under the Freedom of Information Act.[142] Of 277 cases dealt with by the Ministry of Justice in 2008, only 103 led to children coming back to the United Kingdom. The founder of PACT, Catherine Meyer, stated:

> Despite the fact that parental child abduction is the subject of an international convention, the British government still tends to regard it as a private matter that does not require its vigorous intervention when the child of a British subject is illegally taken to another country.[143]

Some research has been conducted into whether mediation might be appropriate in the field of international parental abduction. In a study undertaken by Reunite it was concluded, after consideration of 28 cases which progressed to mediation, that 'there is a clear role for mediation in resolving these highly contentious and emotional disputes, and that parents are willing to embrace the use of mediation'. When mediation was undertaken fully in this study, three-quarters of parents (75 per cent) were able to agree a written 'memorandum of understanding' that focused on the best interests of their child (Reunite 2006: 53).

141 PACT's website is available at: http://www.pact-online.org/ (accessed 25 January 2010).
142 See 'Third of abducted children not returned home after a year', Helen Pidd, *The Guardian* (1 January 2010).
143 Ibid.

Chapter 6

Intercountry adoption

6.1 Introduction

Intercountry adoption is a subject that has seized much popular attention, with headlines in the news about celebrity adoptions.[1] These adoptions can be used to highlight many of the underlying legal issues and controversies which have remained unresolved within intercountry adoption. In one respect, intercountry adoption is seen as an act which provides a loving and secure home to a child who faces an otherwise bleak future. On the other hand, depictions of intercountry adoption include reports of child-trafficking, children being kidnapped, mothers relinquishing their children under dubious circumstances, and comments that intercountry adoption is an exploitation of poor countries and impoverished inhabitants of those states by wealthier and more powerful nations. Needless to say, then, intercountry adoption is not without controversy or widely divisive views on its utility and necessity.

Intercountry adoption is now regulated at the international level by the Hague Convention on Protection of Children and Co-operation in respect of Intercountry Adoption of 1993[2] (hereafter the 'Hague Convention of 1993'). However, this is by no means the only international instrument on intercountry adoption, nor is membership and ratification of this Convention required for states to carry out intercountry adoption.

6.2 Modern occurrence of intercountry adoption

Intercountry adoption is widely said to have started during and following the end of the Korean War in the 1950s (Hubinette 2006: 139). At the time there was no

---

1 For example, 'There's no mercy for Madonna as court blocks adoption', by Andy McSmith, *Independent* (4 April 2009); 'Madonna "ecstatic" over adoption', BBC News (12 June 2009).
2 The website of the Hague Conference on Private International Law (see Chapter 2, section 2.4.2) is available at: http://www.hcch.net/index_en.php (accessed 26 January 2010). This site carries the complete texts of all the Hague conventions. There is also a specialist area focusing on intercountry adoption, available at: http://www.hcch.net/index_en.php?act=text.display&tid=45 (accessed 27 January 2010).

international regulation of intercountry adoption. In the United States, for instance, private, and often religious-based, agencies promoted the adoption of Korean children. The rules on how intercountry adoption was to occur were only those that were made by the agencies, with very little oversight from either the South Korean or the American government. Agencies worked in tandem with the governments (Kim 2007a: 136). This is in keeping with the role that has been preserved for private agencies in the Hague Convention, although not without a great deal of controversy, as is further discussed in this chapter. One scholar comments on the occurrence of intercountry adoption in South Korea, the role of the agencies and government and the children who were sent to other countries:

> Of the many needy children, mixed-race children were most likely to be considered for homes abroad by the Korean government and private adoption agencies. Most mixed-race children were born to Korean women and U.S. soldiers stationed at U.S. bases in Korea during and after the war. The women who gave birth to mixed-race children were regarded as military prostitutes. Thus, those children bearing the stigma of their mothers' occupation are identified as a group of children who needed homes outside of Korea. In 1954, the South Korean government established the Child Placement Service ... to place biracial children in foreign adoption, particularly to their father's country, the United States.
>
> (Kim 2007a: 136)

While the occurrence of international law on intercountry adoption may seem like a common-sense approach in retrospect, the development of international law for intercountry adoption was a long time in coming. In part, this is because the idea of international human rights law was only starting to develop following the end of the Second World War.[3] It is only over time that the idea of a specific instrument of international human rights for children was created – the United Nations Convention on the Rights of the Child of 1989 (CRC), which, as we have seen, took several years to negotiate and draft.[4] The CRC, as discussed further in this chapter, contains some specific references to intercountry adoption. Finally, the Hague Convention of 1993 is an international instrument that is wholly focused on intercountry adoption, although there are also other relevant international instruments.

6.2.1 Early attempts to regulate intercountry adoption

When adoption from Korea to the United States began, there was little oversight of the activities by independent social services agencies under the leadership of one authority. There was in fact resistance to the idea that there should be strict

---

3 See further, Chapter 1, section 1.2.
4 See generally, Chapter 3, section 3.2.

regulation of the intercountry adoption process. One commentator observes that '[s]ocial service agencies ... firmly maintained that the welfare of adoptive children necessitated minimum standards of investigation placement, and supervision conducted only by social work professionals' (Choy 2007: 32). The oversight of intercountry adoption fell to individual states within the United States and to their governmental social services departments (Choy 2007: 32, 36–37).

International adoption without any unifying convention could prove complex (Jayme 1969: 290). In 1965 the Hague Convention on Jurisdiction, Applicable Law, and Recognition of Decrees Relating to Adoptions was concluded.[5] The purpose of this Convention was seen by one commentator as 'mainly concerned with recognition [of decrees relating to adoption] and its key provision is found in Article 8 under which every adoption governed by this Convention and granted by an authority competent under it shall be recognised without further formality in all contracting states' (Unger 1965: 463). That there should be a convention that dealt solely with international adoptions was found to need explanation:

> ... its scope is severely limited since, under Article 2(b), it will not apply in the ordinarily case where these parties are all nationals of the same state and are habitually resident in it. The machinery and conditions of recognition established by the Convention will therefore operate only in cases of what Article 6 describes as 'inter-country adoption'.
>
> (Unger 1965: 464)

It is apparent from this comment that two things seemed novel about this Convention: first, that its scope was limited to intercountry adoptions; and second, the use of the phrase 'inter-country adoption'. Nevertheless, the Convention received only limited success with just three states – Austria, Switzerland and the United Kingdom – ratifying it, and in accordance with article 23 it ceased to have any effect from 23 October 2008.[6]

6.2.2 Intercountry adoption and the UN Convention on the Rights of the Child

The CRC contains an article that deals specifically with intercountry adoption. The relevant part of this article states that:

> States Parties that recognize and/or permit the system of adoption shall ensure that the best interests of the child shall be the paramount consideration and they shall:

---

5 This Convention was concluded on 15 November 1965.
6 See the ratification status table on the Hague Conference website, at: http://www.hcch.net/index_en.php?act=conventions.statusprint&cid=75 (accessed 26 January 2010).

(a) [omitted]

(b) Recognise that intercountry adoption may be considered as an alternative means of child's care, if the child cannot be placed in a foster or adoptive family or cannot in any suitable manner be cared for in the child's country of origin;

(c) Ensure that the child concerned by intercountry adoption enjoys safeguards and standards equivalent to those existing in the case of national adoption;

(d) Take all appropriate measures to ensure that, in intercountry adoption, the placement does not result in improper financial gain for those involved in it.

(e) [omitted]

(CRC, article 21)

There are several noteworthy provisions in this article. First, there is the consideration of intercountry adoption as something that should be done if other arrangements cannot satisfactorily be arranged for the child in his or her country of origin. It should be noted that this is a debate that is also relevant to our following discussion of the Hague Convention of 1993. The United Nations Children's Fund[7] (UNICEF) released a statement in October 2007 to clarify its position on the priority that should be accorded to intercountry adoption. It states that:

> For children who cannot be raised by their own families, an appropriate alternative family environment should be sought in preference to institutional care which should be used only as a last resort and as a temporary measure. Inter-country adoption is one of a range of care options which may be open to children, and for individual children who cannot be placed in a permanent family setting in their countries of origin, it may indeed be the best solution. In each case, the best interests of the individual child must be the guiding principle in making a decision regarding adoption.
>
> (UNICEF website[8])

But this is not an unqualified endorsement on the value of intercountry adoption. The UNICEF statement goes on to state that:

> Over the past 30 years, the number of families from wealthy countries wanting to adopt children from other countries has grown substantially. At the same time, lack of regulation and oversight, particularly in the countries of origin, coupled with the potential for financial gain, has spurred the growth of an

---

7 See Chapter 2, section 2.4.1.2.

8 Statement available at: http://www.unicef.org/media/media_41118.html (accessed 26 January 2010).

industry around adoption, where profit, rather than the best interests of children, takes centre stage. Abuses include the sale and abduction of children, coercion of parents and bribery.

(UNICEF website)

The UNICEF statement was issued well after the entry into force of the Hague Convention on Intercountry Adoption. It notes the proliferation of many problems within intercountry adoption, including incidents of child-trafficking, and where, even if child-trafficking is not occurring, there is still an inappropriate focus on the profit to be made in the exchange of a child and not what is deemed to be in the best interests of the child.

But, as shown in the *Explanatory Report* to the Hague Convention of 1993 (Parra-Aranguren 1994), it was precisely these sorts of abuses and occurrences that spurred the need for a new Hague Convention dealing with intercountry adoption. Thus, even some years after the entry into force of the Convention,[9] the problems remained severe enough to be commented upon in the UNICEF statement.

Just what were the troubling occurrences in intercountry adoption that spurred the creation of the Hague Convention, and that persisted once it had entered into force? Given the lukewarm reception given to the 1965 Convention, what led to the formation and passage of a new convention on intercountry adoption? And with what success does intercountry adoption provide an alternative option to the placement of children in institutions, something that is seen by UNICEF and others as less preferable to adoption in another state? Two issues that frequently recur in discussions about intercountry adoption – the prevalence of inappropriate adoption of a child due to a profit motive, and the role of institutional placement of a child – are discussed in the following sections.

6.2.2.1 Adoption based on profit motives

How prevalent are situations where children are put up for intercountry adoption in a manner that implicates profit, rather than the best interests of the child, as the motivation? One commentator observes that 'thousands of children have been stolen, kidnapped, or purchased for purposes of intercountry adoption' and believes that his own research shows that 'estimating the number in the thousands is quite defensible' (Smolin 2007: 29, n.127). He goes on to say that these situations are often not recognised as 'more than a transient or insubstantial harm. Almost inevitably, one hears that such children are "better off", sometimes with a subtext that the acts of stealing, kidnapping and purchasing them were therefore either justified or only insubstantial wrongs' (Smolin 2007: 29).

---

9 The Hague Convention of 1993 was concluded on 29 May 1993 and came into force in international law in accordance with article 46 on 1 May 1995.

Smolin comments that the Hague Convention may in fact be insufficient to protect against child trafficking. He concludes that:

> ... in some ways a Hague-based intercountry adoption system could be even more vulnerable to child laundering schemes than the pre-Hague system. The Hague regime can appear to allocate the tasks of ensuring that children are truly orphans eligible for adoption to the sending country, despite the fact that many sending countries have significant problems with corruption, large-scale document fraud and inadequate legal, administrative, or governmental processes.
>
> (Smolin 2007: 54)

6.2.2.2 Institutional care and intercountry adoption

Proponents of intercountry adoption speak of the need to provide homes for children that are languishing in institutional care. They urge that intercountry adoption is one way to provide homes for these children, and that, until the UNICEF statement of 2007, the CRC was seen as stating that institutional care was to be preferred over intercountry adoption. There is sharp disagreement in the academic community about whether intercountry adoption is a successful method of reducing the number of children that are placed in institutions. One study undertaken set out to determine if, in fact, resort to intercountry adoption successfully reduces the number of children in institutional care (Chou and Browne 2008: 42). The results from this research demonstrated 'that countries with high proportions of outgoing international adoptions also had high numbers of young children in institutional care' (Chou and Browne 2008: 45). The final conclusion from the research was that 'evidence did not support the notion that international adoption reduces institutional care. On the contrary, survey data suggested that it may contribute to the continuation of institutional care and the resulting harm to children' (Chou and Browne 2008: 47). But the results of this study drew criticism on the selected research question and methodology employed. These critics argued that the results of the research were 'based on a badly formulated research question, that it draws on inaccurate data and that it proposes a misleading and unjustified set of conclusions' (Gay y Blasco *et al.* 2008: 63). Yet, in a rejoinder, Chou and Browne defend the results of their study, and stress that intercountry adoption becomes the option that is first sought for children:

> The fact that countries in transition use international adoption as a first resort rather than a last resort has been reported in a number of NGO reports. Therefore, it is naive to believe that sending countries make children available for intercountry adoption because children in institutions in their realms cannot be found homes locally.
>
> (Browne and Chou 2008: 73)

These are only a few of the current controversies that continue with intercountry adoption, even after the formulation and ratification of the Hague Convention of 1993. Further contemporary issues are discussed later in this chapter.

6.3 The Hague Convention on intercountry adoption

The need for the international regulation of intercountry adoption was summarised in the *Explanatory Report* on the Hague Convention (Parra-Aranguren 1994). Among the reasons highlighted were the need to identify when intercountry adoption was an 'appropriate' choice, and to work out how safeguards could be built to prevent profit motives driving intercountry adoption activity.

> The insufficiency of the international legal instruments to meet the present problems caused by intercountry adoptions was acknowledged in a 'Memorandum' prepared by the Permanent Bureau in November 1989, and the following requirements were mentioned:
> (a) a need for the establishment of legally binding standards which should be observed in connection with intercountry adoption (in what circumstances is such adoption appropriate; what law should govern the consents and consultations other than those with respect to the adopters?);
> (b) a need for a system of supervision in order to ensure that these standards are observed (what can be done to prevent intercountry adoptions from occurring which are not in the interest of the child; how can children be protected from being adopted through fraud, duress or for monetary reward; should measures of control be imposed upon agencies active in the field of intercountry adoption, both in the countries where the children are born and in those to which they will travel?);
> (c) a need for the establishment of channels of communications between authorities in countries of origin of children and those where they live after adoption (it would be conceivable, for example, to create by multilateral treaty a system of Central Authorities which could communicate with one another concerning the protection of children involved in intercountry adoption); and there is, finally,
> (d) a need for co-operation between the countries of origin and of destination (an effective working relationship, based on mutual respect and on the observance of high professional and ethical standards, would help to promote confidence between such countries, it being reminded that such forms of co-operation already exist between certain countries with results which are satisfactory to both sides).
>
> (Parra-Aranguren 1994: para. 7)

According to the *Explanatory Report*, the Convention drafters recognised that complex issues surround intercountry adoption and thus limited the purposes of the Convention. The drafters acknowledged that the Convention 'could not solve all problems related to children, no matter how important they may be'. The *Explanatory Report* explains that the Convention sought to address three main areas:

> ... the aims pursued are restricted to establish certain safeguards to ensure that intercountry adoptions take place in the best interests of the child, to provide a system of international co-operation amongst the States and to secure in Contracting States the recognition of adoptions made in accordance with the Convention.
>
> (Parra-Aranguren 1994: para. 59)

Article 1 of the Hague Convention of 1993 expressly states those three overall aims:

> The objects of the present Convention are—
> (a) to establish safeguards to ensure that intercountry adoption takes place in the best interests of the child and with respect for his or her fundamental rights as recognised in international law.
> (b) to establish a system of co-operation amongst Contracting States to ensure that those safeguards are respected and thereby prevent the abduction, the sale of, or traffic in children;
> (c) to secure recognition in Contracting States of adoptions made in accordance with the Convention.
>
> (Hague Convention of 1993, article 1)

The following sections examine the provisions of the Hague Convention of 1993 in the light of these three aims.

6.3.1 Intercountry adoption in the best interests of the child

The Hague Convention of 1993 addresses the principle of the 'best interests of the child' specifically in articles 4(b) and 16(d). The former provision requires that the sending state makes a finding that intercountry adoption is in the best interests of the child and specifies that the finding is to be made 'after possibilities for placement of the child within the State of origin have been given due consideration'.[10] The latter provision requires that the 'Central Authority' (see section 6.3.2) of the sending state makes a determination of whether a particular proposed placement is in the best interests of the child, following a determination that the child is 'adoptable'. This decision is to be made 'on the basis in particular

---

10 Hague Convention of 1993, article 4(b).

of the reports relating to the child and the prospective adoptive parents, whether the envisaged placement is in the best interest of the child'.[11] Thus, the sending state makes two key determinations regarding the best interests of the child in adoption. First, it determines whether intercountry adoption is in the best interests of the child; and second, whether a particular match of a child to a prospective intercountry adoptive parent is also in the best interests of the child.

6.3.2 System of international cooperation amongst states

Several provisions of the Hague Convention of 1993 are aimed at establishing a system of cooperation between states.[12] The central authority of each member state is key to the accomplishment of this aim of the Convention. A contracting state is obliged to designate a 'Central Authority' within its jurisdiction. The central authority is 'to discharge the duties which are imposed by the Convention upon such authorities'.[13]

The cooperative function of the central authority is stressed in a further provision. It states that 'Central Authorities shall co-operate with each other and promote co-operation amongst competent authorities in their States to protect children and to achieve the other objects of the Convention.'[14] Under the Convention, central authorities are granted the ability to delegate their duties. This can be a delegation to public authorities, accredited bodies or to other bodies or persons in the state. Accredited bodies are those that 'pursue only non-profit objectives'.[15] However, other 'bodies and persons' besides public authorities and accredited bodies can carry out some of the responsibilities of the central authority.[16]

The controversy over having central authority functions delegated to bodies and individuals that were neither public nor not-for-profit is seen in the provision of article 22, which allows states to declare that they will permit the sending of children for adoption only to states that restrict delegation of central authority tasks to public authorities or accredited bodies – that is, not-for-profit organisations:

> Any Contracting State may declare to the depositary of the Convention that adoptions of children habitually resident in its territory may only take place if the functions of the Central Authorities are performed in accordance with paragraph 1.
>
> (Hague Convention of 1993, article 22(4))

---

11 Hague Convention of 1993, article 16(d).
12 See generally, Hague Convention of 1993, Chapter III ('Central authorities and accredited bodies'), articles 6–13.
13 Hague Convention of 1993, article 6(1).
14 Hague Convention of 1993, article 7(1).
15 Hague Convention of 1993, article 11(1).
16 Hague Convention of 1993, article 22(2).

And paragraph one of that article provides that '[t]he functions of a Central Authority under this Chapter may be performed by public authorities or by bodies accredited under Chapter III, to the extent permitted by the law of its State.'[17] These articles are the answer to a larger controversy that was part of the Convention drafting negotiations, and that is: just who or what should be able to carry out the domestic functions of the central authority? It has been pointed out that the language used in the preliminary documents leading up to the Convention[18] in explaining the text of article 11 is a discrete reference to 'the fact that private or independent adoptions are very common in the United States, the country receiving the largest number of children' (Pierce 1995: 546). Pierce explains that the bodies that can be 'accredited' under article 11 exclude 'physical persons' (Pierce 1995: 546).

The disagreements over whether central authority functions could be handed over to individuals and organisations that did *not* have a non-profit objective is outlined in the *Explanatory Report*:

> The question as to whether the responsibilities assigned to Central Authorities by the Convention may be discharged by individuals or private organiza- tions, is a very sensitive issue because, according to experience, most of the abuses in intercountry adoptions arise because of the intervention of such "intermediaries" in the various stages of the adoption proceedings. For this very reason, some participants to the Special Commission did not want to accept that Central Authorities may delegate their responsibilities on accred- ited bodies, but others insisted on leaving to each Contracting State the determination of the manner in which to perform the Convention's duties.
>
> (Parra-Aranguren 1994: para. 242)

Thus, there were fears that adoptions done by 'individuals or private organiza- tions' might give rise to inappropriate adoption practices. The provisions in the Convention[19] that give room for the additional delegation to these 'individuals or private organizations' can be understood as a negotiated middle ground on the question of who should carry out adoption functions, according to the informa- tion in the *Explanatory Report*:

> The solution accepted by the draft (article 11) represented a compromise, permitting delegation only to public authorities and to private bodies duly accredited that comply, at least, with certain minimum requirements estab- lished by the Convention. However, as already remarked, this compromise became even more restricted when the matter was discussed in the Diplomatic Conference, because Article 8 of the Convention does not permit delegation

17 Hague Convention of 1993, article 22(1).
18 See, now, Parra-Aranguren (1994: para. 252).
19 Hague Convention of 1993, article 22(4).

to accredited bodies. Nevertheless, within the Convention's limits, each Contracting State is free to decide how the duties imposed upon the Central Authority are to be performed and to permit or not the possible delegation of its functions.

(Parra-Aranguren 1994: para. 243)

6.3.3 Securing recognition of adoptions in contracting states

Chapter V of the Convention[20] deals with those provisions that meet the third aim of the Convention; that of ensuring recognition of Convention-compliant adoptions amongst contracting states. Adoptions certified as compliant by one member state are to be recognised by other member states.[21] Furthermore, a state may refuse to recognise an adoption 'only if the adoption is manifestly contrary to its public policy taking into account the best interests of the child'.[22] Member states are enabled to *not* recognise adoptions that are made via agreements made by states who have an agreement as permitted in the following provision:

Any Contracting State may enter into agreements with one or more Contracting States, with a view to improving the application of the Convention in their mutual relations. These agreements may derogate only from the provisions of Articles 14 to 16 and 18 to 21. The States which have concluded such an agreement shall transmit a copy to the depositary of the Convention.

(Hague Convention of 1993, article 39(2))

The Convention explains what is included in the recognition of an adoption:
(a) the legal parent–child relationship between the child and his or her adoptive parents;
(b) parental responsibility of the adoptive parents for the child;
(c) the termination of a pre-existing legal relationship between the child and his or her mother and father, if the adoption has this effect in the Contracting State where it was made.

(Hague Convention of 1993, article 26(1))

6.3.4 Guide to good practice

Further explanation of the Hague Convention is provided in *The Implementation and Operation of the 1993 Intercountry Adoption Convention: Guide to Good*

---

20 Hague Convention of 1993, Chapter V ('Recognition and effects of the adoption'), articles 23–27.
21 Hague Convention of 1993, article 23.
22 Hague Convention of 1993, article 24.

Practice (HCCH 2008), which was the outcome of work done at a Special Commission of the Hague Conference held in 2005 (Special Commission 2006). The *Guide* addresses key issues that have been raised in intercountry adoption practice around the usage of the Hague Convention.

> [The *Guide*] is a project of post-Convention support initiated by the Permanent Bureau for the purpose of assisting States (whether or not already Contracting States) with the practical implementation of the Convention, in a manner which achieves the objects of the Convention, namely, the protection of children who are adopted internationally. It is the first such Guide for the 1993 Convention, and it identifies important matters related to planning, establishing and operating the legal and administrative framework to implement the Convention. It does not always claim to be a guide for best practices because some practices are necessarily different in different Contracting States.
>
> (HCCH 2008: para. 1)

Thus, the *Guide* emphasises its role in relation to the Convention, and not for necessarily setting out a prescribed method for how an intercountry adoption should be accomplished in all contracting states. Chapter 2 of the *Guide* (HCCH 2008: paras 37–110) addresses four 'general principles of the Convention', which reflect those contained in the Preamble[23] to the Hague Convention of 1993 and its objects as set out in article 1:[24]

- ensuring adoptions take place in the best interests of the child and with respect for his or her fundamental rights;
- establishing safeguards to prevent abduction, sale and trafficking in children for adoption;
- establishing co-operation between states; and
- ensuring authorisation of competent authorities.

These principles of course are closely related to the stated aims of the Convention, with the added specific mention of 'authorisation of competent authorities'. The issue of who can be an authority under the Convention to carry out delegated Central Authority tasks has been, as discussed, a contentious issue for intercountry adoptions carried out within the framework of the Convention. The *Guide* continues to address this issue, commenting that:

---

23 'Experts attending the Special Commission meetings insisted on the importance of the Preamble as guidance for interpretation when applying the Convention to particular situations' (HCCH 2008: para. 38).
24 See the text of article 1 in section 6.3.

In considering the place of intercountry adoption in a national child protection strategy, Contracting States need to consider the role of accredited bodies and whether to allow them to operate as part of the system. An additional question is whether to authorise approved (non-accredited) persons to operate in accordance with Article 22(2).

(HCCH 2008: para. 110)

The *Guide* has used the term 'approved (non-accredited) person' to refer to the same entities that were identified in the *Explanatory Report* as 'individuals or private organizations' (Parra-Aranguren 1994: para. 242). Both of these different sets of terminology address the provisions of article 22(2) of the Convention.[25] Further information is provided by the *Guide* on how such entities might function within the framework of the Hague Convention of 1993:

If Contracting States decide to allow approved (non-accredited) persons to perform the functions in Convention Chapter IV,[26] with the exception of Article 14, there must be a declaration made by the Contracting State to the Convention depositary in accordance with Article 22. Such persons do not have to meet all the eligibility requirements of accredited bodies. For example, they may undertake adoptions for profit. They are nevertheless required to meet certain standards of integrity, professional competence, experience and ethics. Furthermore, they may only perform their functions to the extent permitted by the law and subject to the supervision of the competent authorities of their State. Contracting States may therefore regulate or restrict the activities of approved (non-accredited) persons to any extent necessary, as they see fit.

Approved (non-accredited) persons have to be under the supervision of competent authorities. It is a matter for the Contracting State to authorise an appropriate competent authority to perform this task. If approved (non-accredited) persons, operating a business for profit, are contracted by accredited bodies to perform certain functions, accredited bodies may be legally and financially responsible for any duties performed for them by approved (non-accredited) persons.

(HCCH 2008, paras 217–18)

Thus, a person or group that does not fit the criteria for being an accredited body under the Hague Convention of 1993 can be delegated some of the Central Authority functions. But the functions have to be undertaken through the oversight of an accredited body in their state. The state must also make a declaration that a delegation of functions has been made to an approved person. Who can

---

25 See generally, section 4.4 of the *Guide* (HCCH 2008: paras 215–220).
26 Hague Convention of 1993, article 22(2).

perform intercountry adoptions has been a sensitive issue since the drafting stages of the Convention and continues to be so in its ongoing operation.

The *Guide* also addresses other key aims of the Convention, and the current interpretative or practical debates and barriers about their implementation. In its provisions on the best interests of the child, it addresses the debates over the order in which placement alternatives for a child should be pursued. This is called 'subsidiarity'. This debate was reflected in the UNICEF announcement (2007)[27] which stated that it was better for a child to be adopted via intercountry adoption than to be placed in their own country in a residential or institutional placement.

> 'Subsidiarity' means that states part[ies] to the Convention recognise that a child should be raised by his or her birth family or extended family whenever possible. If that is not possible or practicable, other forms of permanent family care in the country of origin should be considered. Only after due consideration has been given to national solutions should intercountry adoption be considered, and then only if it is in the child's best interests. Intercountry adoption serves the child's best interests if it provides a loving permanent family for the child in need of a home. Intercountry adoption is one of a range of care options which may be open to children in need of a family.
>
> The subsidiarity principle is central to the success of the Convention. It implies that efforts should be made to assist families in remaining intact or in being reunited, or to ensure that a child has the opportunity to be adopted or cared for nationally. It implies also that intercountry adoption procedures should be set within an integrated child protection and care system, which maintains these priorities. However, states should also ensure that efforts to achieve this goal do not unintentionally harm children by delaying unduly a permanent solution through intercountry adoption. States should guarantee permanency planning in the shortest possible time for each child deprived of his/her parents. Policies should work to promote family preservation and national solutions, rather than to hinder intercountry adoption.
>
> (HCCH 2008: paras 47 and 48)

These provisions point out important issues and interpretations regarding the use of intercountry adoption as a placement for children. Intercountry adoption is placed alongside other options that exist for child placement. The *Guide* stresses that intercountry adoption should not be seen as an isolated choice, but one that is within a 'range' of choices that can be made for child placement. The idea of 'permanency planning' for children is addressed, wherein plans are made for a child's placement. Above all, the *Guide* stresses the importance of subsidiarity both as a feature of the 'best interests' determination and of the function of the Convention itself:

---

27 See section 6.2.2.

The principle of subsidiarity should be interpreted in the light of the principle of the best interests of the child. For example:

- It is true that maintaining a child in his or her family of origin is important, but it is not more important than protecting a child from harm or abuse.
- Permanent care by an extended family member may be preferable, but not if the carers are wrongly motivated, unsuitable, or unable to meet the needs (including the medical needs) of the particular child.
- National adoption or other permanent family care is generally preferable, but if there is a lack of suitable national adoptive families or carers, it is, as a general rule, not preferable to keep children waiting in institutions when the possibility exists of a suitable permanent family placement abroad.[26]
- Finding a home for a child in the country of origin is a positive step, but a temporary home in the country of origin in most cases is not preferable to a permanent home elsewhere.
- Institutionalisation as an option for permanent care, while appropriate in special circumstances, is not as a general rule in the best interests of the child.

(HCCH 2008: para. 51)

This provision from the *Guide* as to the use of institutionalisation is similar to the later position announced by UNICEF in 2007.[28] The *Guide* also stresses the importance of a permanent home over a temporary home, and the need to not keep children waiting in institutional placements while an in-country home is sought, whilst at the same time there might be an intercountry adoptive home available.

Another issue explored in some detail in the *Guide* is the manner in which a child is matched with a prospective intercountry adoptive family. It stresses the importance of matching being done by professionals and not through a method in which interested adopters select a child from a photograph listed on the internet. Matching the needs of the child with the qualities of the adoptive parents and family is essential for the best interests of the child and should be done professionally. Prospective adoptive parents should be thoroughly and professionally assessed as suitable to adopt a child, particularly if the child has special needs (HCCH 2008: para. 64):

Matching should not be done by the prospective adoptive parents, either by selecting an appealing child in person or through a photo listing. Although photo listings can be a useful method of promoting adoption generally, as well as allowing prospective adoptive parents to express interest in adopting

28 See footnote 8.

a child, countries of origin should be careful that actual matching decisions are made by professionals and are based on the needs of the child with the qualities of the adoptive parents. Matching should not be done by computer.

(HCCH 2008: para. 65)

The *Guide* also stresses the importance of receiving appropriate consent from birthparents to place the child for intercountry adoption:

The requirement to obtain proper consents to the adoption is a key feature of the Convention in the fight against the abduction, sale and traffic in children. This means:

- obtaining consents from the legal custodian or guardian of the child [the person, institution or authority referred to in Article 4 *c)*(1)];
- ensuring that the person giving the consent understands the effect or consequences of their decision;
- ensuring the consents were given freely, and not induced or improperly obtained by financial or other reward;
- ensuring that a new birth mother does not give her consent until some time after the birth of her child;
- ensuring the consent of the child is obtained, when necessary.

(HCCH 2008: para. 77)

6.3.5 Intercountry adoption technical assistance programme

Compliance with the Hague Convention of 1993 poses a continuing concern for states. The Hague Conference has responded to this by creating 'The Hague Conference International Centre for Judicial Studies and Technical Assistance'. This has been the site for the 'Intercountry Adoption Technical Assistance Programme' (ICATAP), which 'was designed to provide assistance directly to the Governments of certain States which are planning ratification of, or accession to, the Convention, or which have ratified or acceded but are experiencing difficulties with implementation of the Convention' (ICATAP 2009: para. 13). The programme reports work being done within several states – 'Albania, Armenia, Belarus, Brazil, Cambodia, China, Colombia, Guatemala, Kenya, Paraguay, Romania, Ukraine, Viet Nam' – for the purpose of providing advice 'on adoption and related child protection matters' (ICATAP 2009: para. 13).

6.4 Contemporary issues in intercountry adoption

A survey of recent research is revealing of the persistent issues that are contemporary in intercountry adoption. One prominent issue, raised at the outset of this chapter, is that of 'high profile' intercountry adoption by celebrities. These adoptions are said to raise questions about the 'politics of intercountry adoption' where the perception is raised as to whether celebrities receive preferential treatment in adopting children from another country (Breuning and Ishiyama 2009: 89). The question is also raised as to what effect these adoptions have: see Gay y Blasco *et al.* (2008: 63), commenting on a press release on intercountry adoption research.

One commentator has considered the various ways in which intercountry adoption is depicted. King (2009) argues that intercountry adoption is perceived within legal research in a manner that perpetuates misconceptions about it, so that only part of the reality of intercountry adoption is presented. He identifies five common narratives found in relation to intercountry adoption in work by legal scholars. One narrative presents intercountry adoption as something that started from a 'humanitarian motive' (King 2009: 429). However, he suggests that this is an 'incomplete history' and that, instead, 'an alternative explanation is that Americans resorted to ICA [intercountry adoption], not solely for humanitarian reasons, but to atone for U.S. involvement in the wars and destruction of the native countries of these children' (King 2009: 430). The other narratives that King presents as providing only a partial picture, and therefore, not an accurate one, are: intercountry adoption as 'rescue' of a child; as a means to give the child an improved life; as a way to render the child's birth mother 'invisible' through the way in which adoption is carried out and depicted; and narratives about the need to 'rescue children from the developing world' as the focus of intercountry adoption rather than the adoption of 'war-orphans'.

Dubinsky discusses celebrity adoptions linked to the depiction of intercountry adoption as the rescue of children. She argues that adoptions by celebrities simply tell 'a classic rescue narrative, one with long roots in the history of adoption and child welfare' (Dubinsky 2008: 339). This is the same narrative that has been identified by King (2009). She argues that, instead, it would be more accurate to see intercountry adoption in another light; much as King argues that the common narratives do not present an entirely accurate picture on intercountry adoption. Dubinsky remarks that:

> Transnational adoption can easily be read (without squinting) as a metaphor for global inequalities of health care and bodily integrity, US foreign policy, and the increasing commodification of childhood.
>
> (Dubinsky 2008: 340)

Inequality is also featured as a theme of intercountry adoption in a recent book on intercountry adoption and global inequality. On the theme of inequality, the authors comment that:

> Transnational adoption emerged out of war. Only recently has it become, rather than an occasional practice, a significant way of forming a family for those who cannot have children. Even this new form of transnational adoption has been marked by the geographies of unequal power, as children move

from poorer countries and families to wealthier ones – and the forces that make a country rich and powerful are above all historical. In this sense, transnational adoption has been shaped by forces of colonialism, the Cold War and globalization.

(Briggs and Marre 2009: 1–2)

Dubinsky also points to the growing body of adult adoptees who are starting to comment upon intercountry adoption and their experiences as intercountry adoptees. This 'significant development' has its own impact in changing the way in which intercountry adoption is understood and presented (Dubinsky 2008: 342).

Other research examines the differences that sending countries in sub-Saharan Africa have in their laws. The researchers argue that 'there is much variation in these requirements and little research that might explain that variation. What determines whether a country has more or less restrictive policies regarding intercountry adoption?' (Breuning and Ishiyama 2009: 89). They conclude that the amount of 'economic interconnectedness' that a state has with other states 'appears to provide a better explanation as to why some African countries have lesser restrictions on intercountry adoption than does the Hague Convention' (Breuning and Ishiyama 2009: 89). They offer two possible explanations for this: first, that 'economic interconnectedness build sufficient trust to give sending governments the confidence that the child they send abroad will be raised by families in other countries will indeed find loving, stable families at their destination ...', or, alternatively, that 'the association between economic interconnectedness and lesser restrictions on intercountry adoption represents the commodification of children' (Breuning and Ishiyama 2009: 97).

6.5 Conclusion

Intercountry adoption is a complex phenomenon. Although the Hague Convention of 1993 is a relatively recent instrument, intercountry adoption was taking place well before the Convention was drafted. Problems that were being experienced in intercountry adoption were key motivators for developing the (second) Hague Convention on intercountry adoption. The present Convention has set up a framework to deal with broad aims that address concerns raised about intercountry adoption, but, as discussed in this chapter, concerns continue over those very issues. The *Guide* (HCCH 2008) provides valuable information about the Convention. Issues continue around who should be a provider of adoption services under the Convention, and whether using certain entities give rise to more adoption corruption, one of the very things that the Convention aims to protect against. It provides a contemporary explanation of the use of the Convention, and of the issues that arise in intercountry adoption. That there are persistent problems is apparent, as these receive mention from the impetus for drafting the Convention through to the appearance of the *Guide*. The ways in which intercountry adoption is seen are also changing, with challenges made to its representation as a humanitarian act that rescues children. Recent research brings into focus the question about the motivation for the adoption of children, and the reasons that some states have fewer restrictions on sending children than do others within their national laws.

As a matter of international law, there is more guidance than ever for the operation and use of the Convention with the advent of the *Guide*. To the extent that the *Guide* can be seen as a finger on the pulse of intercountry adoption, it is apparent that the difficult and complex issues that have been put to international law on intercountry adoption continue to be explored, and solutions located, within the framework of international law.

Chapter 7

Sexual exploitation

7.1 Introduction

It has been remarked that an outside observer would believe that the issue of child sexual abuse and exploitation is a modern concept (Phoenix and Oerton, 2005: 52), yet we know this is not true. The sexual abuse and exploitation of children has occurred for hundreds of years. However, it was not until the later years of the twentieth century that the issue of child sexual exploitation began to be taken seriously at a policy level in many countries, and certainly not until the 1990s that it began to feature notably at an international level. This chapter analyses how international law seeks to prevent the sexual exploitation and abuse of children.

7.1.1 What is sexual exploitation?

The first issue is to identify what sexual exploitation is. A variety of terms can be used in this area, but the two most often used are 'sexual abuse' and 'sexual exploitation'. There is disagreement as to what these terms mean and whether they are interchangeable. Some authors believe that each term is the equivalent of the other (Kempe 1978: 382) and it will be seen later that the UN Convention on the Rights of the Child (CRC) does not differentiate between the terms.[1] However some believe that a distinction can, and arguably should, be drawn. Van Bueren argues that abuse is the wider term and that 'all forms of exploitation are intrinsically abusive', although she then purports to draw a distinction between them by stating 'the distinguishing feature of sexual exploitation is that it generally involves notions of commercial gain'. Others would undoubtedly contest the argument that

---

1 'States Parties undertake to protect the child from all forms of sexual exploitation and sexual abuse. For these purposes, States Parties shall in particular take all appropriate national, bilateral and multilateral measures to prevent:

(a) The inducement or coercion of a child to engage in any unlawful sexual activity;
(b) The exploitative use of children in prostitution or other unlawful sexual practices;
(c) The exploitative use of children in pornographic performances and materials.' (CRC, article 34).

exploitation necessarily involves commercialisation, and Ost suggests that a more appropriate definition is 'a situation or context in which an individual takes unfair advantage of someone else for his own ends' (Ost 2009: 139). At the heart of this concept is Ost's belief, in the context of child pornography and child solicitation (and it is submitted that this applies equally to child prostitution and child trafficking), that exploitation involves an imbalance of power or abuse of a position of vulnerability (Ost 2009: 130). If Ost is correct, and it is submitted she is, then the commercial element sought by Van Bueren is unnecessary.

The natural meanings of the words 'exploitation' and 'abuse' would appear to confirm that there is a distinction between them and that exploitation is the wider term. A dictionary definition of 'exploit' is 'make use unfairly; benefit unjustly from the work or actions of' something.[2] This supports the definition adopted by Ost, and it is submitted that reference to unfairness and unjustness also implicitly support the notion of vulnerability, something particularly important in the context of the sexual exploitation of a child. Abuse is defined, inter alia, as 'treat with cruelty or violence; assault sexually; cruel and violent treatment'. Whilst there is undoubtedly some overlap, it would seem that sexual abuse could be considered to be the direct inappropriate sexual assault on a child whereas exploitation includes those who do not directly assault the child but use the child sexually for their own (material) benefit.

Child sexual abuse and exploitation remain inherently secretive phenomena and this causes significant difficulties in estimating their prevalence in society (Johnson 2004: 462). This is particularly true at the international level. As will be seen, international law commonly tackles the commercial sexual exploitation of children and indeed it has been noted that prior to the appearance of the CRC in 1989 sexual *abuse* rather than *exploitation* of a child never featured in international law: Van Bueren (1994: 46).

The focus on commercial sexual exploitation in international law is perhaps understandable as it has become a lucrative and global enterprise. A single child pornography website – 'Landslide Productions' – had receipts of $1.4 million per month (Taylor and Quayle 2003: 5) and this was by no means the only commercial child pornography website. Trafficking is similarly lucrative and has become a modern-day slave trade. Whilst it has been acknowledged that, given the nature of the behaviour, it is difficult to be precise as to the number of persons trafficked for the purposes of sexual exploitation (Riiskjær and Gallagher 2008: 5), estimates range from 800,000 to 1.7 million[3] people per year (Riiskjær and Gallagher 2008: 6). It has been suggested that the trafficking of persons is now more profitable than the smuggling of drugs and arms (Kelly 2002: 13).

2 Concise Oxford English Dictionary.
3 The higher figure comes from the International Labour Organisation (ILO) (see Chapter 2, section 2.4.1.4), which estimates 2.5 million people are trafficked each year but that one-third of these figures are for economic purposes rather than for sexual exploitation.

A child subject to sexual exploitation is not able to exercise free control over its activities. An adult can, in some situations, exercise a degree of choice over the activities that they participate in. Whilst the common perception of trafficking is based on coercion or abduction, it is clear that this is not necessarily always the case, with some women choosing to migrate to work in the sex industry (Melrose and Barrett 2006: 114). Similarly, it can be said that some adults make the choice to enter the sex industry as a sex worker[4] or choose to be involved in pornography. However, even though some argue that adult women have the ability to make this choice – although it should be noted that such an argument is fiercely resisted by others who argue that the sex industry is about the subjugation of women – a child does not have this choice, nor is he or she equipped to make the choice.

A child has the right not to be sexually exploited. At the first 'World Congress against Commercial Sexual Exploitation of Children' in Stockholm it was stated:

> The commercial sexual exploitation of children can result in serious, life-long, even life threatening consequences for the physical, psychological, spiritual, moral and social development of children ...
>
> (First World Congress 1996: 9)

The consequences for trafficking and prostitution include threats of violence (including threats to kill), pregnancy (including forcible terminations) and the acquisition of sexually transmitted diseases including AIDS. A premium can be charged for children and for not using condoms, the latter meaning that the risks are greater. The consequences of being involved in child pornography are similar. Where penetrative activity is being filmed the same risks above are present but, regardless of what type of pornography is filmed, it becomes a permanent record of the activity. Research suggests that once an image has been placed on the Internet it is almost impossible for it to be recovered as it is quickly downloaded, mirrored and disseminated (Taylor and Quayle 2003: 24). The impact on the child of this is that they fear, for the rest of their lives, that the photograph will be seen by someone known to them who may believe that they were willingly involved in the activity rather than being exploited (Palmer 2005), potentially leading to psychological difficulties. It has been cogently argued that child pornography can amount to the revictimisation of a child who has been sexually assaulted (Taylor and Quayle 2003: 31).

There is an inherent power imbalance between the adult photographer and the child (Taylor and Quayle 2003: 4), and the status of a child as a 'minor' makes this exploitative. The same logic can be found with the other forms of commercial

---

4 Collectives such as the International Union of Sex Workers (www.iusw.org) campaign for the right of adults to join a legalised sex work industry.

child sexual exploitation and it is this, together with the negative consequences of involvement, which requires action to be taken.

7.2 International action

Before turning to examine the principal international legislation that exists in this area it is worth pausing to note the bodies that have a mandate to combat child sexual exploitation.

7.2.1 Global bodies

The final decade of the twentieth century led to the issue of child sexual abuse and exploitation beginning to feature at the international level. In the broader policy context, the United Nations and its agencies began to take seriously the issue of child sexual exploitation and they began to assist non-governmental organisations (NGOs) who sought to work directly with victims and agencies trying to combat the sexual exploitation of children. Perhaps the most notable NGO to be set up was ECPAT ('Ending Child Prostitution And Trafficking'[5]), an international organisation which was established in 1990 by a series of researchers. Quickly ECPAT began to formalise and by 1996 it was acting in partnership with the United Nations. It remains an independent organisation (with its headquarters based in Bangkok, Thailand) but it has a close relationship with global, regional and local governments. At governmental level there are two bodies of particular note: the G8 and the United Nations.

7.2.1.1 G8

The G8 owes it origins to an economic summit in 1975 attended by the then five richest countries (France, Germany, Japan, the United Kingdom and the United States of America). By the end of the decade the group became the G-7 with the addition of Italy and Canada, but during the 1980s and 1990s the Soviet Union (and then Russia after the dissolution of the USSR) was invited to attend the meetings, which had begun to stray beyond mere economics and into more geopolitical issues. In 1998 the group formally changed its name from the G-7 to the G8. In 2001 the G8 established the Lyon/Roma group that was designed to tackle international crime. A sub-group of the Lyon/Roma group was specifically tasked to examine the issue of sexual exploitation, and by 2003 a strategy was created (G8 2003: paras 15–17). In 2009, following a global symposium on the issue of child pornography, the G8 issued a ministerial declaration on 30 May

---

5 Originally ECPAT meant 'Ending Child Prostitution in the Asian Territories'.

in Rome.[6] This declaration reaffirmed their commitment to tackling child pornography, and stated:

> Effective international cooperation would be achieved through a wider membership in multilateral task forces, sharing specialised software and closely coordinating on line undercover investigations and other international law enforcement operations.
>
> (G8 2009: 6)

This demonstrates how the G8 has evolved a policy role on tackling child pornography and, whilst it has not yet produced any treaties, its declaration arguably reaffirms the action that it has committed to in the various international instruments discussed in the following sections.

7.2.1.2 United Nations

The principal global player in this area is the United Nations. The final decades of the twentieth century led to the issue of child sexual abuse and exploitation beginning to feature on the United Nations global agenda, particularly through the United Nations Children's Fund (UNICEF) (see Chapter 2, section 2.4.1.2), the United Nations Human Rights Council (UNHRC) (section 2.5.1.1) and the UN Economic and Social Council (ECOSOC) (section 2.4.1). The United Nations also works closely with national governments, regional groupings and NGOs to fund and operate programmes that are designed to provide real assistance to victims of child sexual exploitation.

Arguably, the three most notable initiatives of the United Nations will all be discussed in this chapter. Two are legislative: the first is the CRC of 1989, which is discussed throughout this book but is considered later in the specific context of the sexual exploitation of children; the second instrument is the Optional Protocol to the Convention on the Rights of the Child on the sale of children, child prostitution and child pornography of 2000 (OPSC). This has quickly established itself as the leading instrument specifically designed to tackle forms of child sexual exploitation, and it will also be discussed later.

The third initiative is the establishment of the Special Rapporteur on the sale of children, child prostitution and child pornography.[7] Established in 1990,

---

6 'The Risk to Children Posed by Child Pornography Offenders', Ministers' Declaration, G8 Justice and Home Affairs Ministers, Rome, 30 May 2009. Available at: http://www.g8italia2009.it/static/G8_Allegato/declaration1giu2009,0.pdf (accessed 28 January 2009).

7 See the website of the Special Rapporteur at: http://www2.ohchr.org/english/issues/children/rapporteur/index.htm (accessed 30 January 2010). Previous mandate holders are Mr Vitit Muntarbhorn (1991–94), Ms Ofelia Calcetas-Santos (1994–2001) and Mr Juan Miguel Petit (2001–08). Ms Najat M'jid Maalla (Morocco) was appointed Special Rapporteur in May 2008.

following a resolution of the UN Commission on Human Rights,[8] the mandate has been continuously renewed. The current mandate[9] includes:

- To consider matters relating to the sale of children, child prostitution and child pornography;
- To continue, through continuous and constructive dialogue with Governments, intergovernmental organisations and civil society ... the analysis of the root causes of the sale of children, child prostitution and child pornography; addressing all the contributing factors, especially the demand factor;
- To identify and make concrete recommendations on preventing and combating new patterns of sale of children, child prostitution and child pornography;
- To continue ... to promote comprehensive strategies and measures on the prevention of sale of children, child prostitution and child pornography.[10]

In order to discharge her mandate, the Special Rapporteur will visit a number of countries (Buck 2008: 169) in order to have policy-level discussions and consider how the signatory states are discharging their obligations under OPSC. The Special Rapporteur produces an annual report to the Human Rights Council (e.g. Maalla 2009), which in turn reports to the UN General Assembly.

Buck, whilst observing the valuable work that the Special Rapporteur performs, notes that a difficulty is that the office is under-resourced (Buck 2008: 170). This is despite the fact that the mandate passed by the Human Rights Council requests the Secretary-General of the United Nations and the High Commissioner for Human Rights to 'provide all the human, technical and financial assistance' needed by the Special Rapporteur.[11] The under-resourcing of the office means that the Special Rapporteur is limited in the amount of research that can be commissioned and visits conducted. Ideally it would be beneficial for there to be an 'Office of the Special Rapporteur' that would employ a (small) number of staff to also conduct visits, commission and interpret research. Instead, a single mandate holder is in place and, whilst her role is invaluable, it does mean that its use is somewhat limited.

7.2.2 Regional bodies

It is not only global bodies that have a mandate to combat child sexual exploitation; some regional groupings also operate in this area. Regional mandates exist in part as a method of strengthening the work undertaken at global level but also to demonstrate a regional commitment to tackling this problem. The key difference

---

8 Resolution 1990/68 on the Rights of the Child.
9 Set out in resolution 7/13 at the 40th meeting of the Human Rights Council in March 2008.
10 See para. 2 of resolution 7/13.
11 See para. 4 of resolution 7/13.

between the global and regional mandates is that the regional ones, as their name suggests, ordinarily involve localised action. The mandate does demonstrate the political will to work towards combating child sexual exploitation. Examples of regional instruments include the Organisation of African Unity's (OAU) African Charter on the Rights and Welfare of the Child[12] and the South Asian Regional Association's Convention on Preventing and Combating Trafficking in Women and Children for Prostitution of 2002 which attempted to address one particular form of commercial sexual exploitation.

Perhaps the most active geopolitical area in seeking to combat child sexual exploitation is Europe. As is well known, there are two principal groupings within Europe; the Council of Europe (which consists of 47 member states) and the European Union (EU) (which has 27 member states). There are other groupings (e.g. the 'Council of Baltic States'), but these tend to work in conjunction with both of the other bodies.

The Council of Europe is best known for its work in human rights, particularly the European Convention on Human Rights (ECHR), but it has, in recent years, been active in seeking to combat exploitative actions against individuals, including the sexual exploitation of children. Most of its work has been on a legislative basis, although it does fund projects that seek to tackle these areas. Some of its legislation relates specifically to the exploitation of vulnerable persons (most notably the Convention on Action against Trafficking in Human Beings[13] and the Convention on the Protection of Children against Sexual Exploitation and Sexual Abuse),[14] but at other times the legislative action is found within more general provisions. Perhaps the most notable example of this is the Convention on Cybercrime,[15] which includes a provision that defines and mandates action against child pornography.[16]

The European Union has become involved in this area only comparatively recently (Akdeniz 1998), although this is perhaps unsurprising since prior to the Treaty of Maastricht of 1992 the European Community (as it was then known) was simply an economics vehicle. However, by the mid-1990s there was increased interest in child sexual exploitation (Akdeniz 2008: 167), eventually culminating in a number of legislative instruments of which a Council Decision on combating child pornography[17] and a Council Framework Decision[18] on combating the sexual exploitation of children and child pornography were the most notable. These instruments were designed to ensure that each member state had equivalent criminal offences that were punished rigorously, and required states to

---

12 The African Charter on the Rights and Welfare of the Child, article 16, requires signatories to protect children against abuse, including sexual abuse. See section 2.5.2.2 for an introduction to human rights protection in Africa.
13 CETS No. 197.
14 CETS No. 201.
15 CETS No. 1.
16 European Convention on Cybercrime, article 9.
17 2000/375/JHA.
18 2004/68/JHA.

act in an extraterritorial manner (explained in the following discussion) and provide programmes of assistance to victims of sexual exploitation.

The European Union's greatest impact, however, has probably been in its non-legislative action. The Treaty of Maastricht of 1992 established an European Law Enforcement Agency, 'Europol'[19], which is designed, inter alia, to facilitate cooperation between the law enforcement agencies of each member state. Europol came into existence in 1998 and as early as 2000 it had participated in international operations against child sexual exploitation (Europol 2009: 21), something it continues to this day. Its 'Internet Safety Programme and Internet Safety Plus' programme – Akdeniz (2008) provides a useful summary of these initiatives – has led to significant funding becoming available to ensure the safety of children from, for example, child pornography and grooming. Funding has also been used to establish *Inhope*[20] and *Insafe*,[21] both of which have been successful in safeguarding children from abuse.

7.3 International instruments

Having outlined the international action that is being undertaken to combat the sexual exploitation of children, it is now necessary to consider the international legal instruments that exist to tackle this phenomenon.

7.3.1 UN Convention on the Rights of the Child (CRC)

As has been noted already in other parts of this book,[22] the CRC is perhaps the most important international instrument relating to children's rights. It is a wide-ranging treaty that governs the social, civil and political rights of the child. Many of the provisions within the CRC are not directly relevant to the issue of sexual exploitation, but there are two articles that are specifically relevant to this issue. The first, and perhaps most significant, is article 34, although article 35 is also of relevance in this context.

Article 34 is the wider provision:

> States Parties undertake to protect the child from all forms of sexual exploitation and sexual abuse. For these purposes, States Parties shall in particular take all appropriate national, bilateral and multilateral measures to prevent:
> (a) The inducement or coercion of a child to engage in any unlawful sexual activity;

---

19 Europol's website is available at: http://www.europol.europa.eu/ (accessed 28 January 2010).
20 www.inhope.org. This is an international network of hotlines that allows members of the public to report websites they suspect of hosting child pornography or other exploitative material.
21 www.saferinternet.org. This is a network of contact centres that provide assistance and educational initiatives to the public and educators to safeguard children and young persons online.
22 See Chapter 3, section 3.1

   (b) The exploitative use of children in prostitution or other unlawful sexual
      practices;

   (c) The exploitative use of children in pornographic performances and
      materials.

At first sight this appears useful: it provides a clear statement that countries shall protect a child from both sexual abuse and sexual exploitation. Whilst this is a worthy statement, there is, however, difficulty in terms of how it is expressed. Article 34 does not make clear *how* a state should protect a child from sexual exploitation. Does it mean take civil steps? Criminal steps? Presumably both, but the article does not set this out clearly.

Article 34 seeks to define sexual exploitation in paragraphs (a) to (c), but again the specific terms used are not defined and this can lead to questions being raised as to what precisely article 34 seeks to protect. Some have argued that article 34 was a fudge and a compromise between the desire to protect children from exploitative practices and, at the same time, ensuring that adolescent experimentation was not the subject of mandatory intervention (Alexander *et al.* 2000: 482). The difficulty with compromised wording is that it allows debates to occur as to what its objectives are. For example, paragraph (a) refers to coercion or inducement but these can be said to be opposite ends of the same scale. What of situations where sexual activity takes place without coercion (which suggests pressure or force) or inducement (which suggests grooming or reward)? In paragraph (b) there is reference to 'child prostitution' but it is not clear what this covers. The term 'prostitute' covers a wide range of behaviour and indeed many argue the term is inappropriate (Pearce 2006). Without a clear understanding of what the term means, is article 34 seeking to protect only against, for example, the payment of money to a child for sex or does it cover other parts of the sex industry (e.g. online chatrooms, telephone sex lines etc.)? Does it cover situations where an adolescent has sex with someone in return for being given food or shelter?[23] Is this prostitution for the purposes of article 34?

It may seem pedantic to concentrate on the wording of the article when it could be argued that, like many of the other articles within the CRC, it was drafted deliberately wide to allow flexibility.[24] However the first Special Rapporteur noted that vague terminology can cause difficulties in assessing legal frameworks (Muntarbhorn 1991). This in turn makes the task of protecting children more difficult.

If article 34 suffers from a lack of precision, article 35 is perhaps even more problematic:

---

23 Research suggests that this is not uncommon: see, for example, Chase and Statham (2005) and
   Pearce *et al.* (2002).

24 See Chapter 3, section 3.2 for an account of the CRC's provenance.

States Parties shall take all appropriate national, bilateral and multilateral measures to prevent the abduction of, the sale or traffic in children for any purpose or in any form.

Article 35 does not even expressly mention the sexual exploitation of children. Sexual exploitation is undoubtedly covered since the provision refers to 'for any purpose or in any form', but it is not set out explicitly. Is this problematic? Arguably, it is, because the abduction of a child by a parent is considerably different to the trafficking of children for sex, and yet article 35 appears to cover both situations. A provision as wide as this raises the same issues as before. How can states be held to account for their legal systems if the benchmark they are being measured against – in this case, article 35 – is not sufficiently defined itself?

7.3.2 ILO Convention No. 182

In 1999 the International Labour Organisation (ILO), a specialist agency of the United Nations[25] charged with developing and enforcing labour standards, passed the Convention on the Worst Forms of Child Labour (ILO Convention No. 182).[26] At the time this Convention appeared, the ILO estimated that 250 million children were at work, with some 80 million involved in what it refers to as 'the worst forms of labour' (Geneva NGO Group, 2001: 5). ILO Convention No. 182[27] defines a child as a person under the age of 18. This can be contrasted immediately with the CRC which, whilst suggesting that the age of majority should be 18, allows that it can be lowered by domestic legislation.[28]

Article 3 defines the 'worst forms of child labour' and paragraph (b) includes 'the use of children for prostitution and pornography'. Paragraph (d) may also be of relevance as it refers to work that 'is likely to endanger the health, safety or morals of children'. The use of the term 'morals' may be of assistance in terms of dealing with some forms of commercial sexual exploitation that do not come within either prostitution or pornography.

Article 7 of the Convention commits signatory states, inter alia, to take measures to prevent a child's involvement in the worst forms of child labour and to provide assistance to those children who are working.

Accompanying the Convention is a recommendation (R190)[29] that provides guidance to signatory states on how to implement the Convention. The recommendation includes, for example, the suggestion that criminal offences should be

---

25 See Chapter 2, section 2.4.1.4.
26 See Chapter 4, section 4.2.3.
27 ILO Convention No. 182, article 2.
28 CRC, article 1.
29 See Chapter 4, footnote 11, for the legal status of ILO Recommendations.

invoked to tackle those who employ children in the worst forms of labour,[30] and also protocols on how information should be fed back to the ILO.

The ILO Convention does, at least, recognise that the commercial sexual exploitation of children is inappropriate and should be tackled. An advantage of ILO Convention No. 182 is that it brings together not just governments but also employers, NGOs and trade unions. Their diverse membership means that the issue of commercial sexual exploitation is raised at different levels.[31] That said, however, it is focused on very narrow areas, is restricted to commercial forms of child sexual exploitation (since otherwise they would not be 'labour') and does not provide appropriate definitions of the various terms. To an extent, therefore, it can be said to be additional recognition of the issue but it does not, by itself, take matters much further than the standards as formulated in the CRC.

7.3.3 Optional Protocol to the Convention on the Rights of the Child on the sale of children, child prostitution and child pornography of 2000 (OPSC)

As noted already, shortly after the drafting of the CRC the issue of child sexual exploitation, particularly sex tourism, became of great concern and the United Nations appointed its first Special Rapporteur on the sale of children, child prostitution and child pornography. The Special Rapporteur was concerned about whether the CRC was sufficient to tackle child sexual exploitation, and by 1994 the Commission on Human Rights[32] had created a working group to examine the possibility of an optional protocol to the CRC specifically related to the issue of (commercial) sexual exploitation.[33] Pressure to change increased with the holding of the first World Congress against the Commercial Sexual Exploitation of Children ('the Stockholm Conference').[34] An important outcome of this Congress was support for strengthening the international rules relating to commercial sexual exploitation, including the possibility of drafting a new legal instrument. Part of this pressure arose from the unsatisfactory wording of article 34, and it has been suggested that this was a major reason for the development of the Optional Protocol so soon after the CRC had come into force (Alexander *et al.* 2000: 482).

---

30 Recommendation No. 190, para. 12.
31 See further, Chapter 4, section 4.3, which discusses the strategic approach to progressing the elimination of child labour.
32 The UN Commission on Human Rights (UNCHR) was replaced by the UN Human Rights Council (UNHRC) in 2006: see Chapter 2, section 2.5.1.1.
33 See CHR resolution 1994/90.
34 See First World Congress (1996). There have subsequently been two more world congresses: in 2001, held in Yokohama, Japan; and in 2008, held in Rio de Janeiro.

Ultimately the demand for change led to the drafting of OPSC. The Protocol was open for signature on 25 May 2000 and, as of 2010,[35] some 137 countries have ratified it.[36] The Protocol came into force on 18 January 2002.

The Optional Protocol differs from the CRC in that it is more specific in terms of its definitions and its obligations on signatory states. The current Special Rapporteur has noted that the wording of OPSC is sufficient to allow her to 'implement her mandate within a clear legal framework and yet take into consideration endemic situations and emerging problems' (Maalla 2008: 6). That is not to say, however, that OPSC is perfect as, like any international instrument, it contains the negotiated wording resulting from the discussions and diplomatic compromises made by various states parties. Perhaps the most significant issue is that, unlike article 34 of the CRC, the Optional Protocol is arguably too narrow. OPSC does not refer to the sexual abuse or sexual exploitation of children (unlike, e.g., the Council of Europe's Convention on the Protection of Children against Sexual Exploitation and Sexual Abuse, which does seek to cover most forms), but rather it is focused specifically on commercial sexual exploitation. Indeed, it is clear from article 1 that it is restricted to three forms:

- child trafficking (the sale of children);
- child prostitution; and
- child pornography.

If the sexual behaviour is not within these three heads then it is outside the scope of OPSC. It is notable that OPSC is clearer than the CRC in terms of how it defines child prostitution. The wording of article 2 makes clear that it applies to sexual activity 'for remuneration or any other form of consideration' and, accordingly, the comments made earlier about youths providing sex in return for gifts or a place to stay overnight would come within this definition.

The technological revolution has, in recent years, arguably placed great strain on OPSC as there is evidence of exploitation which is not within these headings, most notably the issue of sexual solicitation or grooming:[37] see Petit (2004: 7). This will be discussed further later in respect of the criminalisation of the commercial sexual exploitation of the child.

---

35 OPSC was adopted and opened for signature, ratification and accession by General Assembly resolution A/RES/54/263 of 25 May 2000, and entered into force on 18 January 2002. OPSC had 117 signatories and 137 ratifications as at 17 May 2010.

36 It is notable that whilst the United Kingdom signed the Protocol on 7 September 2000 it did not ratify it until 20 February 2009.

37 For a discussion on the meaning of such terms see Gillespie (2002); Craven et al. (2006).

7.4 States' responsibilities

The international instruments discussed earlier place a number of responsibilities onto state signatories. For ease of analysis, these responsibilities will be considered in key themes. The themes are:

- criminalisation of child sexual exploitation;
- establishing jurisdiction over child sexual exploitation;
- international cooperation and support in tackling child sexual exploitation;
- measures to assist victims of child sexual exploitation.

7.4.1 Criminalization

Perhaps the most significant part of OPSC is the requirement in article 3 to ensure that 'as a minimum' a series of acts and activities are subject to the criminal law. The acts and activities are, inter alia:

(a) offering, delivering or accepting, by whatever means, a child for the purposes of its sexual exploitation,
(b) offering, obtaining, procuring or providing a child for child prostitution,
(c) producing, distributing, disseminating, importing, exporting, offering, selling or possessing for those purposes child pornography.

(OPSC, article 3(1))

Article 3(2) requires states to ensure that an attempt to commit an offence in article 3(1) is also an offence. The Protocol does not define what an attempt is but rather leaves this to each domestic legal system to identify.

Article 3(3) requires states to 'make these offences punishable by appropriate penalties that take into account their grave nature'. This is somewhat vague but could, in a positive sense, be read as meaning that there must be recognition that the crimes set out in article 3(1) are serious and should be reflected by strong punishments. However, in the more negative sense it is notable that the Convention has not, for example, suggested that they should ordinarily be punishable by imprisonment, or set minimum punishments. The reasoning behind this approach is that it is most unusual for treaties to set out minimum punishments,[38] in part because each jurisdiction will have its own system of punishments and agreeing a coherent approach could be difficult to negotiate. It was noted earlier that the CRC has been almost universally ratified and 137 countries have ratified OPSC to date. The drafters of the OPSC were no doubt careful to ensure that there was nothing in the Protocol that would restrict the likelihood of ratification.

---

38 The EU Framework Directive (2004/68/JHA) concerning, inter alia, certain forms of child sexual exploitation, does provide minimum standards but this is not a treaty per se but rather a legal instrument of the European Union.

7.4.1.1 Sale of children

Article 3(1) tackles the sale of children. The demarcation between this and child prostitution is open to debate but it is likely that this heading is designed to tackle those who treat children as a commodity, to be bought and sold. Whilst the term 'trafficking' is not used expressly, the language of the Protocol which refers to 'offering, delivering or accepting, by whatever means, a child' means it is likely that this is what was meant (UNICEF 2009: 9). That said, however, it has been noted that trafficking does not need to involve a child being physically sold (UNICEF 2009: 10), and this demonstrates a potential lacuna in the Protocol in that in the absence of a sale, or if it does not come within the definition of child prostitution, the trafficking of a child may not be included.

It is notable that the wording of article 3(1) includes 'offering', 'delivering' and 'accepting' and thus it tackles not only the person who sells the child but also an intermediary who 'receives' the child for another. 'Delivering' would seem to include those who are responsible for the actual movement of the child irrespective of whether they are necessarily involved in the sale itself. So, for example, X asks Y to smuggle V into country A. X is to be paid $5,000 for V. X is the one who has 'sold' V but Y is undoubtedly delivering her and accordingly would be covered in this Protocol. 'Offering' would seem to imply that the actual transaction need not take place, and advertising the sale of the child may be covered also. As will be seen, it is somewhat regrettable that the same is not true for either child prostitution or child pornography.

7.4.1.2 Child prostitution

It was noted in the first section of this chapter that 'child prostitution' is a controversial label and doubt exists over what precisely is covered. Article 3(1)(b) criminalises the 'offering, obtaining, procuring or providing' of a child for the purposes of child prostitution. The emphasis of the article would appear to be on those who control the child ('offering', 'procuring' and 'providing' must relate to the person who 'supplies' the child). What of the person who actually pays to have sexual contact with a child? It could be argued that the term 'obtains' covers this behaviour, although in the context of Article 3(1)(b) the term 'obtains' may be more apposite to describe a person who receives the child in order to control him or her. That said, the Special Rapporteur indicated his belief that OPSC did mandate the criminalization of the clients of child prostitutes (Petit 2006: 13) and, whilst it may have been preferable for the language of OPSC to be clearer, it is to be hoped states adopt that reasoning.

UNICEF (2009: 12) has noted that the issue of sex tourism is only mentioned in passing by OPSC but argues that sex tourism could come within this provision. The argument of UNICEF is that much sex tourism involves child prostitution. Presumably UNICEF means by this the fact that many sex tourists will seek to pay either a child or an agency for sexual activity with a child. Where this is the case, it should be possible to read article 3 in such a way that covers this activity.

This does, however, raise one issue in terms of the extent of the criminalization and the definition of child prostitution. The definition in article 2 appears to be focused quite specifically on the individual who supplies the child, but what of the person who controls the activities, or some of the activities, of a child prostitute? In the context of sex tourism this could involve the travel agent who knowingly sends a person to a particular country and, indeed, a particular villa or hotel. Can it really be said that this person has offered, procured or provided *a* child? The only possibility would be to suggest that he has procured child prostitution, but realistically it may still be one step away. Had OPSC referred to 'facilitates', then the issue would have been put beyond doubt.

7.4.1.3 Child pornography

Child pornography is something that continues to defy a precise definition (Gillespie 2010), but OPSC does, at least, define what it considers the term to mean. In article 2(c) it states child pornography is 'any representation, of whatever means, of a child engaged in real or simulated explicit sexual activities or any representation of the sexual parts of a child for primarily sexual purposes'. It is not the place of this chapter to critique this definition,[39] but it should be noted that the OPSC definition is arguably one of the widest and would include all forms of representation, including text, drawings and photographs.

Article 3(1)(c) requires a number of actions relating to child pornography to be criminalised. The first set of offences is concerned with the creation and dissemination of child pornography. The language of article 3 is deliberate and ensures that, for example, there is no doubt that the creation (production) of child pornography should be criminalised as should any form of the dissemination of child pornography. So, for example, the article is careful to ensure that dissemination includes not only distribution, but also the importing and exporting of material. The advent of communication technologies has meant that the clear majority of child pornography is hosted online (Taylor and Quayle 2003; Petit 2004), which does raise issues about whether information is 'imported' or 'exported' when it is merely accessed on the Internet as those terms are traditionally understood to mean the physical moving of an item into or out of the country.

An interesting issue in the wording of article 3(1) is whether the simple possession of child pornography is criminalised. The wording of article 3(1) suggests it is not, but that possession with the intention of disseminating the images is criminalised. This can be contrasted with, for example, the Convention on Cybercrime which states that simple possession of child pornography may[40] be a criminal activity (article 9), or the Convention on the Protection of Children

---

39 See Gillespie (2010) for further discussion.
40 Although Article 9(1)(e) is not equivocal, Article 9.4 provides that states may reserve, in whole or in part, the right not to apply that provision.

against Sexual Exploitation and Sexual Abuse (article 20). UNICEF has noted the potential lacuna in the wording of OPSC, although it suggests that the Committee on the Rights of the Child (CtRC) has attempted to fill this lacuna by making comments in national reports (Cedrangolo 2009: 9–10). In his first thematic report on child pornography, the then Special Rapporteur also noted this omission and recommended that simple possession be criminalised so as to tackle the 'participant chain' in the production and dissemination of child pornography (Petit 2004: 23). This has recently been reinforced by the current Special Rapporteur who, along with calling for simple possession to be criminalised, has argued that liability should additionally be extended to those who knowingly access or watch material online (Maalla 2009: 23).

7.4.1.4 Missing activities

It was noted previously that OPSC does not seek to criminalise all forms of child sexual abuse but is restricted to commercial forms of sexual abuse, as is ILO Convention No. 182. It will be remembered that the CRC itself does not provide expressly for the criminalization of any specific forms of behaviour, although article 34 does, at least, suggest that, inter alia, all forms of sexual abuse should be criminalized.

In response to technological advancements and the ways in which offenders have used information and communication technologies to seek children for abuse, the then Special Rapporteur recommended that states '... introduce legislation creating the offence of "internet grooming or luring"' (Petit 2004: 23). This was an interesting call since it would seem to fall outside the definitions put forward in OPSC (as grooming rarely involves any commercial aspect). The call could be taken as evidence of a desire to move OPSC beyond commercial sexual exploitation into a wider instrument to address the sexual abuse and exploitation of children. In the absence of a change to the text of the instrument, however, the Special Rapporteur can only make recommendations rather than ensuring that they form part of the obligations of a state. The effect of this is perhaps evident from the fact that in a recent report of the Special Rapporteur the same point about grooming is made (Maalla 2009: 23), and yet very few countries appear to have introduced legislation to tackle this form of behaviour in the 5 years between reports (Maalla 2009: 12).

7.4.1.5 Victims as criminals

It was noted in the preceding discussion that article 34 of the CRC was considered to be a compromise because of concerns that alternative wording may have led to adolescent sexual experimentation being criminalised. A more difficult problem is that in some countries it would appear that the victim of child sexual exploitation could be criminalised. It may be thought that this was only in less-developed countries, but it should be noted that, theoretically at least, under

English law a child involved in prostitution continues to be subject to the criminal law through, for example, soliciting (Gillespie 2007; Phoenix 2003). The Special Rapporteur has previously denounced the criminalization of victims of sexual exploitation (Petit 2006: 21) and the current Special Rapporteur has announced an advocacy programme with the intention of urging countries to decriminalise victims (Maalla 2008: 11).

A difficulty, however, is that international instruments are somewhat vague on this issue. The CRC merely states in general that non-judicial alternatives should be adopted where possible,[41] and OPSC requires only that 'the best interests of the child shall be a primary consideration'.[42] It is notable that OPSC says it should be *a* primary consideration and not *the* primary consideration. The absence of a definitive statement[43] is undoubtedly causing difficulties for some children – who may not report the fact that they are being exploited for fear of prosecution – and it is to be hoped that the Special Rapporteur is able to develop a presumption against the criminalization of victims.

7.4.2 Establishing jurisdiction

Article 4 of OPSC highlights the issue of jurisdiction. Article 4(1) requires states to ensure that their domestic laws establish jurisdiction of the criminal offences discussed earlier when committed in its territory, on board a ship or on an aircraft registered in that state. This can be said to be the traditional approach to jurisdiction (Hirst 2003) and it is relatively uncontroversial. However, OPSC goes further and suggests that jurisdiction should be extended in certain circumstances.

Article 4(2) requires states parties to ensure that jurisdiction over the offences referred to in article 3(1) (those discussed in section 7.4.1) should also be secured where the alleged perpetrator is a national or habitual resident of that state or where the victim is a national of that state.[44] Many countries have now adopted so-called 'sex tourism' legislation that seeks to tackle those who commit sexual offences abroad,[45] but few countries secure jurisdiction by reference to victims. Despite this provision in OPSC, it would seem that some countries continue to refuse to adopt the principle of extraterritoriality and many apply the principle of double jeopardy (Maalla 2009: 13). In this context, the rule of double jeopardy prevents somebody from being tried twice for the same offence. Accordingly, if D is prosecuted for crime X and is acquitted, then he cannot be prosecuted again.

---

41 CRC, article 40(3)(b).
42 OPSC, article 8(3).
43 It was originally intended that a definitive clause would be present, but several states objected to this (Cedrangolo 2009: 13).
44 See OPSC, article 4.2(a) and (b) respectively.
45 A useful history of this can be found in Hirst (2003: 268–69).

In the context of extraterritorial jurisdiction this would mean that if D is prosecuted in country X, where the crime took place, he could not then be prosecuted in country Y (the country of his residence). Some are concerned that the principle of double jeopardy can be misused in countries where sexual exploitation of a child will attract a very low penalty (Beaulieu 2008: 12). The Special Rapporteur has urged that double jeopardy should not apply to cases involving the sexual exploitation of children (Maalla 2009: 23) but, whilst some countries may agree to try individuals who have been prosecuted but not convicted, many countries would baulk at the notion that someone will be punished twice for the same conduct.

Even where countries adopt extraterritorial jurisdiction, some challenges remain. For example, in some jurisdictions there is the requirement of 'dual criminality'. Put at its most basic, this means that the crime must be illegal in *both* the country that is to try the offence (i.e. the state exercising extraterritorial jurisdiction) *and* the country where the act took place. In many instances this may well be appropriate, but in the context of commercial sexual exploitation, particularly in respect of sex tourism, this can be problematic. In some countries the age of consent remains extremely low and the principle of dual criminality would therefore permit a sex tourist the right to go to this country for the sole purpose of sexually exploiting a child. Abolishing the principle of dual criminality would mean that the same standard is expected of a country's citizens wherever they may go, but it does mean that a citizen of country X but resident in country Y may be prevented from doing something that is perfectly lawful in country Y. This can be particularly problematic where, for example, a citizen is a state of more than one country. Where dual criminality is no longer recognised, then it is presumably reliant on prosecutors to use their extraterritorial powers only where there is clear evidence of abuse or exploitation.

The far greater challenge for extraterritorial jurisdiction is the evidence. Whilst legislating for extraterritorial jurisdiction is relatively easy to do, securing its practical use is more challenging. In many countries the standard of evidence-gathering may be poorer than that which is expected by the courts of the country exercising jurisdiction. There is also the difficulty of securing witness testimony. That said, it can sometimes be a useful provision; an example could be:

> D is a citizen of country X. He went on holiday to country Y where he recorded himself having sexual activity with a child. Upon his return to country X he is arrested for an unconnected matter and his camera is analysed. The images show him sexually abusing the child in country Y. Applying extraterritorial jurisdiction, D could be tried in country X for the crimes committed in country Y, the photographs serving as the principal evidence.

Also, in the context of sex tourism, many would argue that it serves as a deterrent in that offenders know that they are not necessarily safe from prosecution when they return to their country of residence.

7.4.2.1 Refusal to extradite

Article 5 of OPSC, discussed in the following section, provides for rules relating to extradition. However some countries adopt an approach of not extraditing their citizens. Article 4(3) states that where an alleged offender is within state borders and the state refuses to extradite him, then domestic legislation should be sufficient to ensure that the person can be prosecuted in that state. It has been noted that although article 4(3) is silent as to nationality, it is likely that it means a citizen of that state (UNICEF 2009: 13). That said, there is no reason why it should be restricted to this and where, for example, domestic or international rules on extradition would prevent the extradition of non-citizens,[46] article 3(4) could ensure that they do not escape justice.

7.4.2.2 Extradition

Article 5 raises the issue of extradition. It is recognized that international travel makes it relatively easy for an offender to leave the state where a crime was committed or a state that seeks to prosecute him for the offence. The rules of extradition – that have existed for some time – allow for a country to remove a person from its state borders and deliver him to the requesting country. Extradition operates on a bilateral basis, with countries agreeing treaties amongst themselves as to how the extradition process operates. Article 5(1) requires the extradition treaties to be amended (and new treaties to be drafted) so as to include the offences contained within article 3.

Where an extradition treaty does not exist between parties, then article 5(2) requires the state to treat OPSC as a treaty authorizing extradition between signatory parties. Obviously this is limited to the offences contained within article 3(1) but, if state courts take this into account, it will allow for the extradition of an offender. Article 5(3) is related to this issue as it states that where a country is prepared to extradite in the absence of a treaty, it should recognise the offences within article 3(1) as extraditable offences. This is required because in the absence of such provision it is quite possible that only certain offences would be subject to extradition without a treaty.

Article 5(4) is an important provision in that it requires states to recognizse the extension of jurisdiction in article 4. Extradition ordinarily applies in respect of offences that are deemed to have been committed in the requesting country's territory. As noted in the previous discussion, article 4(2) asks countries to extend jurisdiction to include situations where a citizen of their country is alleged to have

---

46 For example, some instruments prevent extradition to countries where the perpetrator could be tortured or subject to capital punishment (see, most notably, the European Convention on Human Rights as set out in *Soering v. United Kingdom* (1989) 11 EHRR 439 and *Ahmed v. Turkey* (1997) 24 EHRR 278).

committed, or been the victim of, an offence. Article 5(4) requires countries to recognise this extended jurisdiction, meaning that country X could request country Y to extradite a citizen of country X where it is alleged that he committed an offence within Article 3(1) in country Z.

7.4.3 International cooperation and support

Article 6 of OPSC requires states to 'afford one another the greatest measure of assistance in connection with investigations or criminal or extradition proceedings ... including assistance in obtaining evidence at their disposal necessary for the proceedings'. It was noted earlier that a difficulty with extending jurisdiction is that the evidence may not be immediately available, and article 6 seeks to address this in part. Article 6 is reinforced by article 7 which requires, inter alia, states to take prompt measure to seize and confiscate goods, materials and proceeds of sexual exploitation,[47] including requests from other states.[48] The mischief of article 7 is obviously to ensure that those who are involved in commercial sexual exploitation do not profit from their activities. OPSC does not, however, say what should happen to the monies realised. It would have been useful if, at the very least, the Protocol had recommended that the monies were placed in a fund to assist victims.

International co-operation and support is not restricted to government agencies. Considerable co-operation exists at other levels, something hinted at by article 10(1) which, along with obliging states to co-operate internationally, requires states to work with international organisations and NGOs. The importance of broad cooperation is demonstrable from two initiatives highlighted by the Special Rapporteur. In his annual report of 2007, the then Special Rapporteur highlighted the creation of the 'Task Force to Protect Children from Sexual Exploitation in Tourism' (Petit 2008: 6). This body is constituted of government agencies, NGOs and those involved in the tourist industry, and is designed to produce a co-ordinated strategy against those who seek to sexually exploit children abroad.

In her annual report of 2009, the current Special Rapporteur highlights the work of the 'Virtual Global Taskforce' (VGT) (Maalla 2009: 21). The VGT was established in 2003 and is a group encompassing Interpol and agencies from Australia, Canada, Italy, the United Kingdom and the United States. The operation of the VGT allows for quick and efficient co-operation across national borders and its existence led, for example, to the arrest of Christopher Neil who had recorded himself sexually abusing children and placing these images on the Internet in such a way as to obscure his identity.[49]

---

47 OPSC, article 7(1).
48 OPSC, article 7(2).
49 ' "Swirly faced" paedophile sentenced for abusing Thai child', *The Times*, 15 August 2008, Times Online. Available at: http://www.timesonline.co.uk/tol/news/world/asia/article4537360.ece (accessed 30 January 2010).

Whilst welcoming the increased co-operation, the Special Rapporteur has suggested that additional partners be brought in. In the 2006 report the then Special Rapporteur suggested that financial institutions should also co-operate to tackle child sexual exploitation. During 2005 it was reported that some financial institutions had developed online payment processes that did not require a user to have a bank account. The Special Rapporteur noted that it was essential that there was a way of 'tracing' transactions where they have been used in the commercial sexual exploitation of children (Petit 2006: 5). Whilst most financial institutions have done this, it is notable that not every institution has and there are concerns that anonymous banking is possible (Gillespie 2008).

7.4.4 Assisting victims

A difficulty with the global nature of child sexual exploitation is that it makes the identification of victims somewhat difficult. A (local) police unit may receive, for example, a pornographic picture of a child or an advertisement for sex with a child but they may not know who that child is. If they recover children from trafficking or prostitution it may not necessarily be easy to identify where they came from. One commentator has noted that cooperation at the international level is necessary to safeguard children (Palmer 2005: 66), and this is reflected within the text of OPSC.

Article 10(2) requires states parties to cooperate 'to assist child victims in their physical and psychological recovery, social reintegration and repatriation'. OPSC goes further and notes that social and economic deprivation could be a causal link to sexual exploitation and that these matters must be addressed too (article 10.3), including by the provision of 'financial, technical or other assistance' at a multilateral, regional or bilateral level (article 10.4).

The principal provision that deals with assistance to victims is contained within Article 8 of OPSC. Article 8(1) requires a series of measures to be adopted 'at all levels of the criminal justice system'. The measures are:

(a) adapting the court proceedings to recognise the vulnerability of victims as witnesses,
(b) informing the child of their rights, their role and the timing and progress of the proceedings,
(c) allowing the views, needs and concerns of the child victim to be raised,
(d) providing appropriate support services to child victims throughout the process,
(e) protecting the privacy and identity of the child victim,
(f) providing, in appropriate cases, for the safety of the child victim and their family,
(g) avoiding unnecessary delay in the disposition of the case.

These are challenging measures for most judicial systems, including developed countries. It is an area that both the Special Rapporteur and the CtRC pay particular attention to, although the latest annual report of the Special Rapporteur suggests that the broad picture is that there is still inadequate provision of assistance to victims (Maalla 2009: 16).

Article 8(2) of OPSC states that where there is doubt as to the age of the child this should not prevent the initiation of criminal investigation. It should be noted that this provision does not state that criminal proceedings cannot be initiated – since in many jurisdictions identifying the age of the child would be critical to a prosecution – but it does require an investigation to occur as this may allow the age of the child to be ascertained.

Article 8(6) makes clear that the provisions of the article are not designed to prevent the accused from receiving a fair trial. This is an important point as other international instruments will uphold the right of a suspect to be treated fairly. The essence of article 8(6) is to ensure that the various states consider how to best balance the needs of the victim and the rights of the defendant.

7.5 Reporting mechanisms

The reporting mechanism of the CRC is discussed elsewhere and, obviously, signatory states are obliged to follow this in respect of article 34.[50] However, in the wider field of commercial sexual exploitation there are additional reporting mechanisms. There are two of primary relevance here; the Special Rapporteur and the mechanism provided in OPSC.

The office of the Special Rapporteur was outlined earlier, but part of her work is to visit countries to assess their approach to tackling the behaviour under her remit: see Maalla (2008: 9), who discusses the role of visits in the context of her mandate. These visits are summarized in each annual report and cross-references are also made to the reports submitted by countries under either the CRC or OPSC. The ability to visit and comment on countries should allow for an additional check to be made on the monitoring process, although it was noted earlier in this chapter (see section 7.2.1.2) that there are concerns about whether the office of the Special Rapporteur is adequately funded.

Article 13(1) of OPSC requires a state that has ratified the Protocol to provide a report to the CtRC giving comprehensive information about the measures taken to implement the Protocol in domestic law. After this initial report, states are required to report every 5 years.[51] Where a states party has also ratified the CRC, its report on OPSC should form a discrete part of its wider 5-yearly report on the CRC. Where a state has not ratified the CRC but has ratified OPSC (e.g. the United States), then its report will focus solely on the Optional Protocol.

---

50 See generally, Chapter 3, section 3.3.2, for an account of the reporting process under the CRC. See also Chapter 3, sections 3.5.8.5 (Sexual exploitation and sexual abuse) and 3.5.8.6 (Sale of children and trafficking).
51 OPSC, article 12(2).

It has already been observed that the reporting process of the CRC has suffered from delays, both in terms of the delay of the CtRC in processing reports and in the willingness of states to submit their country reports on time.[52] This has been a pervasive problem both in the CRC mechanisms and for other human rights treaty bodies, but there appears some evidence to suggest that this has improved in respect of the reports relating to the Optional Protocol. It is obviously crucial to the integrity of the process that the reports are considered promptly but also carefully. A 'rubber stamp' is of no assistance, but neither are delays of several years.

---

52 See Chapter 3, section 3.3.1 and Table 3.1.

Chapter 8

Children and armed conflict

Introduction

This chapter discusses the international framework relating to children's involvement and association with armed conflict. This takes a number of forms: the treatment of child civilians in armed conflicts; the general damaging impact of armed conflicts on children; the recruitment and use of children by state and non-state armed forces; the reintegration of child soldiers into society; and the international criminal justice available for those (including child soldiers themselves) who may have committed 'crimes against humanity' and 'war crimes'. This involves a consideration of both 'international humanitarian law' and 'international human rights law'.

There are some important contextual points to note before we examine the relevant international law. First, the international legal framework has had to respond to the changing patterns of armed conflicts over the past 50 years; inter-state wars are now significantly outnumbered by internal conflicts. In 2008, there were 16 major armed conflicts around the world and all of these conflicts were internal ones (SIPRI 2009). Second, the proportion of civilian casualties has greatly increased over the same period and the largest proportion of these has been women and children. Third, the ground-breaking Machel report (Machel 1996) on the impact of armed conflict on children (see section 8.2.2) galvanised a unique confluence of humanitarian concern and a growing presence of the children's rights agenda on the international stage. Finally, the United Nations has, following a series of Security Council resolutions (see section 8.2.1), mainstreamed issues around children and armed conflict within its primary mission of maintaining global peace and security.

8.1 Children and armed conflict: the international law framework

This section examines the influences of international humanitarian law, principally the Geneva Conventions of 1949 along with the Additional Protocols of 1977, followed by consideration of the main international human rights instruments relevant to this area, that is, the UN Convention on the Rights of the Child (CRC) along with the Optional Protocol to the Convention on the Rights of the Child on the involvement of children in Armed Conflict (OPAC), the African Charter on the Rights and Welfare of the Child and the Worst Forms of Child Labour Convention (ILO Convention No. 182).

8.1.1 International humanitarian law

This is the body of law that comprises 'all those rules of international law which are designed to regulate the treatment of the individual – civilian or military, wounded or active – in international armed conflicts' (Fleck 2008: 11). It famously includes the Geneva Conventions of 1949 and two Additional Protocols to these Conventions in 1977, though the term 'international humanitarian law' does not appear in any of these instruments.

8.1.1.1 The Geneva Conventions of 1949[1]

Most of the content of the Geneva Conventions is now considered to be declaratory of customary international law (Fleck 2008: 28).[2] The Geneva Conventions adopted prior to 1949 focused on combatants, not civilians. There was some protection for civilians in regulations annexed to the Hague Conventions of 1899 and 1907. Geneva Convention IV: Relative to the Protection of Civilian Persons in Time of War of 1949 was the first treaty to focus on the protection of civilians during armed conflict, though it is principally concerned with their treatment while 'in the hands of an opposing party or who are the victims of war, rather than with regulating the conduct of parties to a conflict in order to protect civilians' (Harvey 2003a: 7). The Geneva Conventions of 1949 very much reflected the experiences of the Second World War.[3] Geneva Convention IV contains a brief section (Part II[4]) concerning the general protection of the civilian population

---

1 The full text of the Geneva Conventions of 1949 and the Additional Protocols of 1977, along with commentaries, can be found on the International Committee of the Red Cross (ICRC) website. Available at: http://www.icrc.org/ihl.nsf/CONVPRES?OpenView (accessed 4 February 2010).

2 See Chapter 2, section 2.2.2, for an account of 'customary international law' as a discrete source of international law.

3 'Recent wars have emphasized in tragic fashion how necessary it is to have treaty rules for the protection of children. During the last World War, in particular, the mass migrations, bombing raids and deportations separated thousands of children from their parents. The absence of any means of identifying these children, some of whom were even too young to vouch for their own identity, had disastrous consequences. Thousands of them are irretrievably lost to their own families and thousands of fathers and mothers will always suffer the grief of their loss. It is therefore to be hoped that effective measures can be taken to avoid such harrowing experiences in the future.' ICRC commentary. Available at: http://www.icrc.org/ihl.nsf/COM/380-600028?OpenDocument (accessed 4 February 2010).

4 Geneva Convention IV, articles 13–26.

against certain consequences of war. Most of the Convention (Part III: Articles 27–141) addresses the status and treatment of protected persons, of which children form one category.

One provision of Geneva Convention IV allows that the parties to a conflict may establish 'hospital and safety zones' in order to protect from the effects of war, the 'wounded, sick and aged persons, children under fifteen, expectant mothers and mothers of children under seven'.[5] Another provision mandates parties to the conflict to 'endeavour to conclude local agreements for the removal from besieged or encircled areas' of a number of vulnerable groups including children.[6] Subject to certain conditions, there is also a provision that prescribes that contracting parties to the Convention must allow 'the free passage of all consignments of medical and hospital stores and objects necessary for religious worship', and this also requires the free passage of 'essential foodstuffs, clothing and tonics intended for children under fifteen, expectant mothers and maternity cases'.[7]

Geneva Convention IV also contains a general child welfare protective clause:

> The Parties to the conflict shall take the necessary measures to ensure that children under fifteen, who are orphaned or are separated from their families as a result of the war, are not left to their own resources, and that their maintenance, the exercise of their religion and their education are facilitated in all circumstances. Their education shall, as far as possible, be entrusted to persons of a similar cultural tradition.
>
> The Parties to the conflict shall facilitate the reception of such children in a neutral country for the duration of the conflict with the consent of the Protecting Power, if any, and under due safeguards for the observance of the principles stated in the first paragraph.
>
> They shall, furthermore, endeavour to arrange for all children under twelve to be identified by the wearing of identity discs, or by some other means.
>
> (Geneva Convention IV, article 24)

---

5 Article 14. 'Certain definite categories – children under fifteen and mothers of children under seven – were nevertheless chosen because the Conference considered that they were appropriate, reasonable and generally in accord with the requirements of the physical and mental development of children.' ICRC commentary. Available at: http://www.icrc.org/ihl.nsf/WebList?ReadForm&id=380&t=com (accessed 4 February 2010).

6 Article 17. 'Unlike Article 14 (Hospital and Safety Zones), the present Article does not fix an age limit up to which children are to be evacuated. The belligerents concerned are free to come to an agreement on the ... subject; the upper limit of 15 years of age, which applies to admission to a safety zone, seems reasonable and would appear to merit adoption in the present instance.' ICRC commentary. Available at: http://www.icrc.org/IHL.nsf/CONVPRES?OpenView (accessed 4 February 2010).

7 Article 23.

The International Committee of the Red Cross (ICRC) comments that the principles set out in this article 'apply to all the children in question who are living in the territory of a Party to the conflict, whether they are nationals of that country or aliens'.[8] The provision regarding accommodating children in a neutral country is based on the belief that '[h]owever well organised child welfare measures may be, they will never be able to protect the children completely from all the various privations suffered by the population of a belligerent country'.[9] Given the consistent use of the age of 15 years elsewhere in Convention IV, it is perhaps surprising to see the reference to an age limit of 12 years in relation to the third paragraph of article 24. This was chosen at an earlier international conference of the ICRC on the basis that 'it was considered that children over twelve were generally capable of stating their own identity'.[10] It would seem that there was some contention over this provision at the Diplomatic Conference in 1949.[11]

There are also provisions that mandate the 'occupying power', with the cooperation of the national or local authorities, to 'facilitate the proper working of all institutions devoted to the care and education of children'. The occupying power is also obliged to 'take all necessary steps to facilitate the identification of children and the registration of their parentage' and cannot change their personal status 'nor enlist them in formations or organizations subordinate to it'. For children whose identity is in doubt, there is provision for a special section of the 'official information Bureau'[12] to take responsibility for them. The occupying power is also obliged not to hinder any preferential measures regarding food, medical care and protection against the effects of war that were in place before an occupation 'in favour of children under 15 years, expectant mothers, and mothers of children under 7 years'.[13]

---

8 ICRC commentary. Available at: http://www.icrc.org/IHL.nsf/CONVPRES?OpenView (accessed 4 February 2010).

9 Ibid.

10 Ibid. The earlier XVIIth International Red Cross Conference, Stockholm.

11 'The idea of identity discs was treated with scepticism by many delegates, who pointed out for instance how mistakes could arise from children losing or exchanging their identity discs. That danger certainly exists and although experience of this method of identification in the armed forces has been generally satisfactory, that does not necessarily prove anything in regard to children'. ICRC commentary. Available at: http://www.icrc.org/IHL.nsf/CONVPRES?OpenView (accessed 4 January 2010).

12 This must be set up under the terms of Article 136 on the outbreak of hostilities or in case of occupation. 'The primary function of these Bureaux is ... to transmit to the State of origin all available information concerning measures taken in regard to its subjects by the Power in whose hands they are. The official Bureau which the Occupying Power is thus bound to open in occupied territory is a valuable source of information of all kinds. It is in a position to render useful service, particularly in the case of children whose identity has not been established by the local services concerned'. ICRC commentary. Available at: http://www.icrc.org/IHL.nsf/CONVPRES?OpenView (accessed 7 February 2010).

13 Article 50.

As regards to detainment, it is provided that members of the same family 'and in particular parents and children' must be accommodated in the same place of internment, subject to certain exceptions, and internees 'may request that their children who are left at liberty without parental care shall be interned with them'.[14] Furthermore, internees who are expectant and nursing mothers and children under 15 years 'shall be given additional food, in proportion to their physiological needs'.[15] There is also an obligation on the 'detaining power' to 'encourage intellectual, educational and recreational pursuits, sports and games amongst internees', and specifically the education of children and young people is protected; 'they shall be allowed to attend schools either within the place of internment or outside' and 'special playgrounds shall be reserved for children and young people'.[16] Finally, the rules regarding the release of interned persons by the detaining power privilege 'in particular children, pregnant women and mothers with infants and young children, wounded and sick, and internees who have been detained for a long time'.[17]

However, a significant weakness of the Geneva Conventions is that they apply only to international conflicts and not to the *internal* conflicts which, as already noted, have become the predominant mode of armed conflict in recent decades. The exception to this is found in an article which appears in all four Geneva Conventions[18] and places an obligation on parties to an 'armed conflict not of an international character' to provide a minimum floor of protection to non-combatants; an absolute prohibition on murder, mutilation, cruel treatment, torture, taking hostages, outrages upon personal dignity, and the passing of sentences and the carrying out of executions without due legal process.

8.1.1.2 UN Declaration on the protection of women and children in emergency and armed conflict of 1974

This (non-binding) Declaration was adopted by the General Assembly in 1974. It condemns and prohibits attacks and bombings on the civilian population, recognising that these inflict incalculable suffering, 'especially on women and

---

14 Article 82.
15 Article 89.
16 Article 94. 'This provision is one more proof of the interest shown by the Geneva Conventions in child welfare. It represents a most useful addition to the provisions contained in Article 50, which is one of the Articles (14, 17, 24, 26 etc.) laying down exceptions to the ordinary regulations in favour of children and contains special provisions dealing with their care and education.' ICRC commentary. Available at: http://www.icrc.org/IHL.nsf/CONVPRES?OpenView (accessed 5 February 2010).
17 Article 132.
18 Consequently, this is usually referred to as 'Common Article 3' of the Geneva Conventions of 1949.

children, who are the most vulnerable members of the population'.[19] It severely condemns the use of chemical and bacteriological weapons, recognising that this will inflict heavy civilian losses 'including defenceless women and children'.[20] States must make 'all efforts' in armed conflicts and military operations 'to spare women and children from the ravages of war' and '[a]ll the necessary steps shall be taken to ensure the prohibition of measures such as persecution, torture, punitive measures, degrading treatment and violence, particularly against that part of the civilian population that consists of women and children'.[21] It also indicates the *criminal* nature of violations of humanitarian law:

> All forms of repression and cruel and inhuman treatment of women and children, including imprisonment, torture, shooting, mass arrests, collective punishment, destruction of dwellings and forcible eviction, committed by belligerents in the course of military operations or in occupied territories shall be considered criminal.
>
> (UN Declaration on the Protection of Women and Children in Emergency and Armed Conflict, article 5)

Finally, the Declaration asserts that (civilian) women and children 'shall not be deprived of shelter, food, medical aid or other inalienable rights'.[22]

8.1.1.3 The Additional Protocols to the Geneva Conventions of 1977

Additional Protocol I[23] extended the protection of persons affected by international conflicts by, amongst other things, upgrading the standards relating to the conduct of hostilities. It also offered further protection for children in international conflicts, and contains a general child protection clause as follows:

> 1. Children shall be the object of special respect and shall be protected against any form of indecent assault. The Parties to the conflict shall provide them with the care and aid they require, whether because of their age or for any other reason.

---

19 UN Declaration on the Protection of Women and Children in Emergency and Armed Conflict, article 1.
20 Ibid., article 2.
21 Ibid., article 4.
22 Ibid., article 6.
23 Protocol Additional to the Geneva Conventions of 12 August 1949, and relating to the Protection of Victims of International Armed Conflicts (Protocol I), 8 June 1977.

2. The Parties to the conflict shall take all feasible measures in order that children who have not attained the age of fifteen years do not take a direct part in hostilities and, in particular, they shall refrain from recruiting them into their armed forces. In recruiting among those persons who have attained the age of fifteen years but who have not attained the age of eighteen years the Parties to the conflict shall endeavour to give priority to those who are oldest.

... [paras 3, 4 and 5 omitted]

(Additional Protocol I, article 77(1) and (2))

The remaining paragraphs of article 77: continue the protection offered by this article for children under 15 years who have taken a direct part in hostilities and have fallen into the hands of an adverse party[24]; prescribe that children who are arrested, detained or interned have separate quarters from adults[25]; and prohibit the death penalty for a child less than 18 years for offences related to the armed conflict.[26] A further provision of Additional Protocol I[27] provides some ground rules regulating the parties to a conflict in arranging the evacuation of children other than their own nationals to a foreign country.[28] This is only permitted for a temporary period 'where compelling reasons of the health or medical treatment of the children or, except in occupied territory, their safety, so require' and parental consent must be obtained. Article 78 attempts to ensure that 'each child's education, including his religious and moral education as his parents desire, shall be provided while he is away with the greatest possible continuity'. Finally, with a view to returning the children, the party arranging the evacuation and the authorities of the receiving country must establish a prescribed list of identity details for each child, which they shall send to the 'Central Tracing Agency' of the ICRC.

Additional Protocol II[29] was, significantly, the first binding international instrument to deal with the parties' conduct in non-international armed conflicts, that is, internal conflicts. It develops the basic guarantees of Common Article 3

24 Additional Protocol I, article 77(3).
25 Additional Protocol I, article 77(4).
26 Additional Protocol I, article 77(5). article 68 of Additional Protocol I also prohibits pronouncing the death penalty on persons under 18 years of age, a provision also adopted in the International Covenant of 1966 on Civil and Political Rights, article 6(5).
27 Additional Protocol I, article 78.
28 'This is to avoid the risk of removal for the purposes of ethnic cleansing and unnecessary removal of children, representing a major change in practice from World War II when mass evacuation of children took place.' (Harvey 2003a: 10).
29 Protocol Additional to the Geneva Conventions of 12 August 1949, and relating to the Protection of Victims of Non-International Armed Conflicts (Protocol II), 8 June 1977.

of the Geneva Conventions and contains an abbreviated version[30] of the child protection provisions contained in Additional Protocol I. Unfortunately, the restricted definition of the field of application of Additional Protocol II[31] means that it is applicable to a smaller range of internal conflicts than that covered by Common Article 3 of the Geneva Conventions.

8.1.2 International human rights influences

In addition to the international humanitarian law outlined above, this section considers the principal international human rights instruments impacting on children and armed conflict. It deals, in particular, with the CRC and the Optional Protocol (OPAC). It should be remembered that international concern for the plight of children in armed conflicts is not new. Indeed, it is clear that one of the main motivating factors underlying the adoption of the Declaration of the Rights of the Child in 1924 by the League of Nations had been the disastrous impact that the war in the Balkans had had on children (Marshall 1999: 106).[32]

8.1.2.1 UN Convention on the Rights of the Child of 1989 (CRC)

From the outset, the issue of children and armed conflict was of particular concern to the drafters of the CRC and to the Committee on the Rights of the Child (CtRC). Indeed, this topic formed the subject of the CtRC first 'day of general discussion': see Day of Discussion (1992). The CRC contains two significant articles relating to children and armed conflict. The first – article 38 – proved

---

30 'Children shall be provided with the care and aid they require, and in particular:

   (a) they shall receive an education, including religious and moral education, in keeping with the wishes of their parents, or in the absence of parents, of those responsible for their care;

   (b) all appropriate steps shall be taken to facilitate the reunion of families temporarily separated;

   (c) children who have not attained the age of 15 years shall neither be recruited in the armed forces or groups nor allowed to take part in hostilities;

   (d) the special protection provided by this article to children who have not attained the age of 15 years shall remain applicable to them if they take a direct part in hostilities despite the provisions of subparagraph (c) and are captured;

   (e) measures shall be taken, if necessary, and whenever possible with the consent of their parents or persons who by law or custom are primarily responsible for their care, to remove children temporarily from the area in which hostilities are taking place to a safer area within the country and ensure that they are accompanied by persons responsible for their safety and well-being.' (Additional Protocol II, article 4(3)).

31 'This Protocol shall not apply to situations of internal disturbances and tensions, such as riots, isolated and sporadic acts of violence and other acts of a similar nature, as not being armed conflicts.' Additional Protocol II, article 1(2).

32 See also Chapter 3, section 3.2.

to be one of the most controversial issues dealt with by the drafters of this Convention:[33]

1. States Parties undertake to respect and to ensure respect for rules of international humanitarian law applicable to them in armed conflicts which are relevant to the child.
2. States Parties shall take all feasible measures to ensure that persons who have not attained the age of fifteen years do not take a direct part in hostilities.
3. States Parties shall refrain from recruiting any person who has not attained the age of fifteen years into their armed forces. In recruiting among those persons who have attained the age of fifteen years but who have not attained the age of eighteen years, States Parties shall endeavour to give priority to those who are oldest.
4. In accordance with their obligations under international humanitarian law to protect the civilian population in armed conflicts, States Parties shall take all feasible measures to ensure protection and care of children who are affected by an armed conflict.

(CRC, article 38)

The first paragraph of this article ties in states parties' obligations to respect (and ensure respect for) the rules of international humanitarian law discussed in the previous section, though it does not appear to raise in any way the standards of humanitarian law. The second paragraph enjoins states parties to take 'all feasible measures', a formulation allowing states a certain amount of discretion, to ensure that persons under 15 years do not take a direct part in hostilities. As we have seen in the discussion above, the age of 15 years is frequently adverted to in the Geneva Conventions of 1949 and the Additional Protocols of 1977, and was therefore a natural age limit for the drafters of the CRC to alight upon and to do so consistently with the existing body of international humanitarian law and customary international law. However, there was substantial discomfort about the 15-year age limit. These are the only provisions of the CRC that do not apply to all children under 18 years. The third paragraph mandates states parties to refrain from recruiting under-15-year-old persons into the armed forces, and, in recruiting 15- to 17-year-olds, they must prioritise the recruitment of the oldest. By contrast, the comparable article appearing in the African Charter on the Rights and Welfare of the Child does not carry the 15-year limit and is more explicit in its application to internal armed conflicts.[34]

---

33 Cantwell (1992: 26) argues this provision and three others were the most controversial of all the articles in the CRC. See further, Chapter 3, section 3.2.
34 '1. States Parties to this Charter shall undertake to respect and ensure respect for rules of international humanitarian law applicable in armed conflicts which affect the child.

The fourth paragraph of article 38, for the avoidance of any doubt, makes it expressly clear that states parties must observe their obligations in international humanitarian law to protect children from the impact of armed conflict.

There was some general dissatisfaction by human rights groups and states parties about the 15-year threshold. Several states parties registered declarations or reservations in respect of article 38, disagreeing with the provisions in paragraphs 2 and 3 of this article concerning the participation and recruitment of children from the age of 15 years.[35] Others likewise rejected the 15-year threshold on the basis that this was, in any event, inconsistent with article 3(1) of the CRC which determines that the best interests of the child is a primary consideration.[36] Others expressly declared that 'it would have been preferable to fix that age at 18 years in accordance with the principles and norms prevailing in various regions and countries'.[37]

The second key provision of the CRC is article 39, which deals with the recovery and reintegration of the child following armed conflict:

> States Parties shall take all appropriate measures to promote physical and psychological recovery and social reintegration of a child victim of: any form of neglect, exploitation, or abuse; torture or any other form of cruel, inhuman or degrading treatment or punishment; or armed conflicts. Such recovery and reintegration shall take place in an environment which fosters the health, self-respect and dignity of the child.
>
> (CRC, article 39)

This provision recognises, inter alia, the serious and potentially long-lasting effects of armed conflict on children and reflects some aspects of international humanitarian standards as discussed above. The identification of the importance of achieving the recovery and reintegration into society of child soldiers and child victims of armed conflicts increasingly resonated with the sophisticated analyses given to the impact of armed conflict on children in the debates appearing in the UN institutions, as reflected in the ground-breaking Machel report (Machel 1996), discussed further in section 8.2.2.

---

2. States Parties to the present Charter shall take all necessary measures to ensure that no child shall take a direct part in hostilities and refrain in particular, from recruiting any child.

3. States Parties to the present Charter shall, in accordance with their obligations under international humanitarian law, protect the civilian population in armed conflicts and shall take all feasible measures to ensure the protection and care of children who are affected by armed conflicts. Such rules shall also apply to children in situations of internal armed conflicts, tension and strife'. (African Charter on the Rights and Welfare of the Child, article 22).

35 See declarations of Andorra, Argentina, The Netherlands and Spain. The declarations and reservations made by states parties to the CRC are available at: http://treaties.un.org/Pages/ViewDetails.aspx?src=TREATY&mtdsg_no=IV-11&chapter=4&lang=en (accessed 17 May 2010).

36 Ibid. See the declarations of Austria and Germany.

37 Ibid. See the declaration of Colombia and Uruguay.

As we have seen in Chapter 3, articles 38 and 39 of the CRC are considered in the CtRC's 'eighth cluster' in its reporting process. The CtRC's concluding observations on country reports reveal a number of ongoing concerns about the implementation of these provisions: see further, Chapter 3, section 3.5.8.2.

8.1.2.2 The Worst Forms of Child Labour Convention of 1999 (ILO Convention No. 182)

As we have seen from the discussion in Chapter 4, section 4.2.3, the definition of the 'worst forms of child labour' includes, inter alia, the 'forced or compulsory recruitment of children for use in armed conflict',[38] a definition that controversially fell short of a much broader prohibition on the use of children as soldiers in armed conflicts by some of the delegates to that negotiation.[39] The associated Recommendation to ILO Convention No. 190 also notes that states should provide that forced or compulsory recruitment of children for use in armed conflict is made a criminal offence.[40]

8.1.2.3 Optional Protocol to the Convention on the Rights of the Child on the involvement of children in armed conflict of 2000 (OPAC)

In part, precisely because of the unsatisfactory compromises reached in relation to the drafting of article 38 of the CRC, there was sufficient support to establish an Optional Protocol to the Convention on the Rights of the Child on the involvement of children in armed conflict in 2000 (OPAC). The appearance of a landmark report (Machel 1996) by the expert, Mme Graça Machel, appointed by the Secretary-General, which had followed two years of consultation, extensive research and field visits, was also a key influence in the production of OPAC. The UN Commission on Human Rights (UNCHR)[41] established a working group to draft OPAC in 1994. In 1996 the General Assembly recommended, in response to the Machel report, that the Secretary-General appoint for a period of three years a Special Representative on the impact of armed conflict on children: see section 8.2.2.

There were delays in the drafting process of OPAC, not least because of the need to deal with a number of difficult issues: the minimum age of persons participating in hostilities; the issue of direct or indirect involvement in hostilities; the age of recruitment (voluntary or compulsory) into the armed forces;

---

38   ILO Convention No. 182, article 3(a).
39   See Davidson (2001: 217) and Dennis (1999).
40   Recommendation No. 190, 'Worst Forms of Child Labour', para. 12(a).
41   The UNCHR was reconstituted as the UN Human Rights Council (UNHRC) in 2006: see Chapter 2, section 2.5.1.1.

and whether or not a clause should be included preventing child recruitment by non-governmental armed groups. The CtRC issued Recommendation No. 1 (1998) on the subject of children and armed conflict. The Recommendation expressed concerns about the delays in drafting the Optional Protocol. It also reaffirmed the belief that 'this new legal instrument is urgently needed in order to strengthen the levels of protection ensured by the Convention' and referred to its previous suggestion 'on the fundamental importance of raising the age of all forms of recruitment of children into the armed forces to 18 years and the prohibition of their involvement in hostilities'. In the meantime, another landmark international instrument was gaining attention, the Rome Statute of the International Criminal Court of 1998 (see section 8.3.1) which provided a mechanism of accountability for war crimes, crimes against humanity and other serious violations of humanitarian law.

OPAC was finally opened for signature on 25 May 2000 and came into force in international law on 12 February 2002.[42] It attempts to lay down a higher standard than the CRC to prevent the direct participation of under-18-year-olds in armed combat[43] or their compulsory recruitment.[44] However, OPAC falls short of achieving an absolute threshold of 18 years for participation and recruitment in armed conflict '... due to the reluctance of certain States, most notably the USA' (Harvey 2003a: 13). Article 3 of OPAC provides a mechanism whereby each state party must raise in years the minimum age for voluntary recruitment from that set out in article 38(3) of the CRC.[45] Furthermore, states parties must deposit a binding declaration upon ratification or accession that sets out the minimum age at which it will permit voluntary recruitment into its national armed forces and a description of safeguards it has adopted to ensure that such recruitment is not forced or coerced.[46] Those states parties that do permit voluntary recruitment under the age of 18 years must maintain a minimum floor of safeguards as follows:

(a) Such recruitment is genuinely voluntary;
(b) Such recruitment is carried out with the informed consent of the person's parents or legal guardians;
(c) Such persons are fully informed of the duties involved in such military service;

---

42 OPAC had 125 signatories and 132 ratifications as at 17 May 2010.
43 'States Parties shall take all feasible measures to ensure that members of their armed forces who have not attained the age of 18 years do not take a direct part in hostilities.' (OPAC, article 1).
44 'States Parties shall ensure that persons who have not attained the age of 18 years are not compulsorily recruited into their armed forces.' (OPAC, article 2).
45 OPAC, article 3(1). The requirement to raise the minimum age for voluntary recruitment does *not* apply, however, 'to schools operated by or under the control of the armed forces' that are in keeping with the education standards set out in the CRC: see OPAC, article 3(5).
46 OPAC, article 3(2).

(d) Such persons provide reliable proof of age prior to acceptance into national military service.

(OPAC, article 3(3)(a)–(d))

States parties may strengthen their declarations at any time by notification, which takes effect on receipt by the Secretary-General.[47]

A significant advance achieved in OPAC is the explicit recognition that armed groups, as distinct from the armed forces of a state,[48] have comparable impacts on children. Under article 4 of OPAC, such (non-state) armed militias or groups are *absolutely* prohibited from recruiting, or using in hostilities, under-18-year-olds.[49] One commentator observes that '[p]redictably, States have bound potential opponents with stronger obligations than they are prepared to accept for themselves, agreeing to stricter recruitment and deployment standards for rebel groups' (Harvey 2003a: 28). States parties are encouraged to prevent any recruitment and use of children in hostilities, including the adoption of 'legal measures necessary to prohibit and criminalise such practices'.[50] This article also carefully notes that its application 'shall not affect the legal status of any party to an armed conflict'.[51] Nothing in OPAC shall be construed as 'precluding provisions in the law of a State Party or in international instruments and international humanitarian law that are more conducive to the realization of the rights of the child'.[52]

States parties are under a duty, comparable to that contained in article 4 of the CRC,[53] to take all necessary measures to ensure OPAC's effective implementation and enforcement within their own jurisdictions and to disseminate its principles and provisions widely.[54] States parties are also under a duty to take 'all feasible measures' to ensure the demobilisation of children who are recruited or used in hostilities in contravention of the Protocol, and must 'when necessary' offer such persons appropriate assistance for their 'physical and psychological recovery and their social reintegration'.[55]

Article 7 of OPAC mandates states parties to co-operate in the implementation of the Protocol, including the prevention of activity violating the Protocol, and in the rehabilitation and social reintegration of victims. Technical cooperation

---

47 OPAC, article 3(4).
48 '*Condemning* with the gravest concern the recruitment, training and use within and across national borders of children in hostilities by armed groups distinct from the armed forces of a State, and recognizing the responsibility of those who recruit, train and use children in this regard' (OPAC, 11th preambular paragraph).
49 OPAC, article 4(1).
50 OPAC, article 4(2).
51 OPAC, article 4(3).
52 OPAC, article 5.
53 See Chapter 3, section 3.5.1.
54 OPAC, article 6(1) and (2).
55 OPAC, article 6(3).

and financial assistance is undertaken by the states parties and relevant international organisations.[56] States parties 'in a position to do so' must provide assistance through existing multilateral, bilateral or other programmes, 'or, *inter alia*, through a voluntary fund established in accordance with the rules of the General Assembly'.[57]

OPAC also contains its own reporting procedure: see chapter 3, section 3.3.2. States parties must submit to CtRC a report providing 'comprehensive information' on the measures it has taken to implement the Protocol within two years of the Protocol entering into force for that state party. That report will provide information and an account of the measures it has taken to implement the provisions on participation and recruitment.[58] Following the submission of this report, states parties that have ratified the CRC must also include in their reports in respect of the main Convention any further information with respect to the implementation of OPAC. Other states parties to the Protocol who have not ratified the CRC (the United States is the only country in this category) must submit a report every five years.[59] The CtRC may also request from states parties further information relevant to the implementation of the Protocol.[60] The remaining provisions of OPAC[61] deal, respectively, with: signature; entry into force; denouncement; amendment; and authentic text (Arabic, Chinese, English, French, Russian and Spanish).

By way of illustrating how OPAC works, the United Kingdom's[62] initial report under OPAC was considered by the CtRC in 2008 (CO United Kingdom OPAC 2008). The CtRC welcomed the fact that the United Kingdom is 'an active member of the United Nations Working Group on Children and Armed Conflict and provides strong support to the work of international criminal tribunals trying the most serious crimes of concern to the international community, including those against children' and had ratified several relevant international treaties.[63] However, the CtRC expressed a number of concerns about the UK's performance in implementing OPAC. First, it commented that there was insufficient dissemination of OPAC and it was 'not integrated in military school curricula or in training courses for the military'.[64] Second, CtRC had concerns about the wide scope of the UK's declaration in respect of article 1 of OPAC,[65] and recommended that

56 OPAC, article 7(1).
57 OPAC, article 7(2).
58 OPAC, article 8(1).
59 OPAC, article 8(2).
60 OPAC, article 8(3).
61 OPAC, articles 9–13.
62 The United Kingdom signed OPAC on 7 September 2000 and ratified it on 24 June 2003.
63 CO United Kingdom OPAC, 2008: para. 5.
64 Ibid, para. 7.
65 'The United Kingdom of Great Britain and Northern Ireland will take all feasible measures to ensure that members of its armed forces who have not attained the age of 18 years do not take a direct part in hostilities. The United Kingdom understands that article 1 of the Optional Protocol

the United Kingdom review this interpretative declaration and that children should not be exposed to the risk of taking direct part in the hostilities.[66] Third, the CtRC expressed regret that the UK's declaration under article 3, made upon ratification, set the minimum age for voluntary recruitment at 16 years and had no plans to raise this age threshold.[67] The CtRC noted that the United Kingdom's position that 'in order to compete in an increasingly competitive employment market, the British Armed Forces need to attract young people aged 16 and above into pursuing a career in the armed forces' (United Kingdom OPAC 2007: para. 18), but it was nevertheless concerned that the figures supplied by the United Kingdom showed that recruits under the age of 18 years represented approximately 32 per cent of the total intake of the United Kingdom's regular armed forces. The CtRC thought that such an active recruitment policy might lead to the targeting of children from, for example, ethnic minorities and children from low-income families, and that parents or guardians were only involved at the final stage of the recruitment process to give their consent.[68] Fourth, CtRC raised concerns that members of the armed forces under the age of 18 may be subject to the same military justice as adults and recommended that the United Kingdom ensure that such children are always dealt with under the juvenile justice system.[69] Finally, CtRC recommended that the United Kingdom expressly prohibit, within its legislation, the sale of arms to countries where children are known to be or may potentially be recruited or used in hostilities.[70]

8.2 The United Nations and children associated with armed forces or armed groups

8.2.1 Security Council resolutions and the 'Paris Principles'

In the late 1990s the UN Security Council[71] started to express its commitment to address the widespread impact of armed conflict on children in the context of its

---

would not exclude the deployment of members of its armed forces under the age of 18 to take a direct part in hostilities where:

a) there is a genuine military need to deploy their unit or ship to an area in which hostilities are taking place; and b) by reason of the nature and urgency of the situation:–

  i) it is not practicable to withdraw such persons before deployment; or
  ii) to do so would undermine the operational effectiveness of their ship or unit, and thereby put at risk the successful completion of the military mission and/or the safety of other personnel'.
(UK's declaration upon signature and ratification of OPAC).

66 CO United Kingdom OPAC, 2008: para. 10.
67 Ibid, para. 12.
68 Ibid, para. 14.
69 Ibid, paras 30–31.
70 Ibid, para. 33.
71 See Chapter 2, section 2.4.1.

primary responsibility for the maintenance of international peace and security. On an unprecedented occasion during the Security Council's new annual debate on children and armed conflict, a 14-year-old former child soldier from Sierra Leone addressed the Council.[72] A Security Council resolution in 1999,[73] reflecting the first Security Council debate on this issue, expressed 'grave concern at the harmful and widespread impact of armed conflict on children and the long-term consequences this has for durable peace, security and development' and strongly condemned the targeting of children in situations of armed conflict, 'including killing and maiming, sexual violence, abduction and forced displacement, recruitment and use of children in armed conflict in violation of international law', and called upon parties to comply strictly with their obligations under international law. A further resolution in 2000[74] welcomed the appearance of OPAC and reaffirmed its strong condemnation of the deliberate targeting of children in armed conflicts and the damaging impact such conflicts had on children and the long-term consequences for durable peace, security and development. It extended its list of concerns by, for example, also emphasizing 'the responsibility of all States to put an end to impunity and to prosecute those responsible for genocide, crimes against humanity and war crimes, and, in this regard, *stresses* the need to exclude these, where feasible, from amnesty provisions and relevant legislation'.[75] Another resolution in 2001[76] expressed readiness to include provisions for the protection of children when considering the mandates of peacekeeping operations and reaffirmed its readiness to include, where appropriate, child protection advisers in peacekeeping operations. It also committed itself to intensifying, monitoring and reporting activities on the situation of children in armed conflict. It built on previous resolutions with a list of concerns, for example, the need to pay attention to the rehabilitation of children affected by armed conflict in order to reintegrate them into society and to develop and expand regional initiatives. Furthermore, it requested the Special Representative (see section 8.2.2) to annex to her annual report a list of parties that recruit and use children. There are in fact two lists: one lists the parties that recruit or use children in situations of armed conflict which are on the Security Council's agenda;[77] and the second list includes parties that

---

72 'Child soldier asks United Nations for help', BBC News (21 November 2001). Available at: http:// news.bbc.co.uk/1/hi/world/africa/1667683.stm (accessed 5 February 2010).

73 S/RES/1261 (1999).

74 S/RES/1314 (2000).

75 Ibid, para. 2.

76 S/RES/1379 (2001).

77 The annual report of the Special Representative to UNHRC in 2009 lists parties in this category in: Afghanistan, Central African Republic, Chad, Democratic Republic of Congo, Iraq, Myanmar, Nepal, Somalia, Sudan and Darfur (SRSG 2009: annex I).

recruit or use children in situations of armed conflict which are not on the Security Council's agenda.[78]

A subsequent resolution in 2004[79] expressed deep concern 'over the lack of overall progress on the ground, where parties to conflict continue to violate with impunity the relevant provisions of applicable international law'. Significantly, it also requested the Secretary-General to devise urgently 'an action plan for a systematic and comprehensive monitoring and reporting mechanism', including timebound measures, that would utilise United Nations, national, regional and NGO expertise to provide reliable information on 'the recruitment and use of child soldiers in violation of applicable international law and on other violations and abuses committed against children affected by armed conflict'. It also expressed its intention to consider sanctions on parties failing to develop such action plans, for example, a ban on the export or supply of small arms and of other military equipment. In a further resolution in 2005,[80] the plans to devise monitoring and reporting mechanisms were strengthened. A working group of the Security Council[81] was established to review reports from the monitoring mechanisms and to review progress in the development of action plans. The Security Council also expressed grave concern about 'the documented links between the use of child soldiers in violation of applicable international law and the illicit trafficking of small arms and light weapons and stressing the need for all States to take measures to prevent and to put an end to such trafficking'. In the most recent Security Council resolution on children and armed conflict at the time of writing,[82] the success in bringing to justice some persons alleged to have committed crimes against children in situations of armed conflict was welcomed.[83] The resolution also expressed a conviction that 'the protection of children in armed conflict should be an important aspect of any comprehensive strategy to resolve conflict'. It reaffirmed the intention to take action against persistent perpetrators of crimes against children in armed conflict, and expressed deep concern:

> ... that children continue to account for a considerable number of casualties resulting from killing and maiming in armed conflicts including as a result of deliberate targeting, indiscriminate and excessive use of force, indiscriminate use of landmines, cluster munitions and other weapons and use of children as human shields and *equally deeply concerned* about the high

---

78 The following parties are listed in this category: Colombia, Philippines, Sri Lanka and Uganda (SRSG 2009: annex II).
79 S/RES/1539 (2004).
80 S/RES/1612 (2005).
81 The Security Council's Working Group's documents are available at: http://www.un.org/children/conflict/english/securitycouncilwgroupdoc.html (accessed 7 February 2010). See the group's latest annual report: SCWG (2009).
82 S/RES/1882 (2009).
83 See section 8.3.

incidence and appalling levels of brutality of rape and other forms of sexual violence committed against children, in the context of and associated with armed conflict including the use or commissioning of rape and other forms of sexual violence in some situations as a tactic of war ...

(UN Security Council resolution S/RES/1882 (2009))

The Secretary-General's now annual report on armed conflict includes information on compliance with the relevant international law relating to the recruitment and use of children in armed conflict and other grave violations committed against children affected by armed conflict. It also reports progress on the implementation of the monitoring and reporting mechanism and action plans mandated in the resolutions discussed above, and provides a brief summary of the conclusions of the Security Council's Working Group on Children and Armed Conflict. For example, the Secretary-General's 2009 report includes a proposal to strengthen the monitoring and reporting on rape and other grave sexual violence against children and also identifies a list of current concerns, including:

... internally displaced children and their particular risks for recruitment; terrorism and counter-terrorism measures and its impact on children; the accountability of child soldiers for acts committed during armed conflict, and special protections accorded to them; control on the transfer and use of arms and ammunitions, particularly to countries where children are known to be, or may potentially be, recruited or used in hostilities; and measures to achieve sustainable reintegration of children affected by conflict.

(UN Secretary-General 2009a: para. 2)

At a Paris Conference, 'Free Children from War', organised jointly by the French Ministry of Foreign Affairs and UNICEF on 5–6 February 2007, 59 states supported the adoption of the 'Paris Commitments to Protect Children Unlawfully Recruited or Used by Armed Forces or Armed Groups' and the 'Paris Principles and Guidelines on Children associated with Armed Forces or Armed Groups' (hereafter the 'Paris Commitments' and 'Paris Principles and Guidelines' respectively).[84] The 'Paris Commitments' are intended to strengthen political action to prevent association of children with armed conflict and to ensure their reintegration with society. States commit themselves to uphold and apply the 'Paris Principles', a set of operational guidelines. The language used in these

---

84 These documents are available from: http://www.un.org/children/conflict/english/parisprinciples. html (accessed 5 February 2010). The first ministerial follow-up forum on the Paris Commitments and the Paris Principles and Guidelines was held at UNHQ in New York on 26 September 2008. Nine additional countries endorsed the Paris Commitments, bringing the total number of country endorsements to 76.

documents had broadened out from referring to 'child soldiers' to a definition of 'a child associated with an armed force or armed group'.[85]

8.2.2 The special representative of the Secretary-General for children and armed conflict

A significant landmark in the international attention paid to children and armed conflict was the appearance of the UN commissioned report 'Impact of armed conflict on children' in 1996. The report was authored by Graça Machel, an expert designated by the Secretary-General to undertake the study, and has become known as the 'Machel report' (Machel 1996). It set out a comprehensive and detailed analysis of the problem:

> In 1995, 30 major armed conflicts raged in different locations around the world. All of them took place within States, between factions split along ethnic, religious or cultural lines. The conflicts destroyed crops, places of worship and schools. Nothing was spared, held sacred or protected – not children, families or communities. In the past decade, an estimated two million children have been killed in armed conflict. Three times as many have been seriously injured or permanently disabled, many of them maimed by landmines. Countless others have been forced to witness or even to take part in horrifying acts of violence.
>
> (Machel 1996: para. 2)

The report observed, for example, that 'the proportion of war victims who are civilians has leaped dramatically from 5 per cent to over 90 per cent' (Machel 1996: para. 24). Furthermore, it noted that children were rarely mentioned in reconstruction plans and advised that 'the seeds of reconstruction should be sown even during conflict' (Machel 1996: para. 243). The report was a powerful call to action and the General Assembly unanimously welcomed the report in a resolution[86] in which it also established the mandate of the Special Representative of the Secretary-General for Children and Armed Conflict.[87] The key elements of the mandate include: the assessment of progress and difficulties in strengthening the protection of children in situations of armed conflict; raising awareness and promoting the collection of data; and encouraging the development of networking and international cooperation to ensure the protection and rehabilitation of

---

85 '… any person below 18 years of age who is or who has been recruited or used by an armed force or armed group in any capacity, including but not limited to children, boys, and girls used as fighters, cooks, porters, messengers, spies or for sexual purposes. It does not only refer to a child who is taking or has taken a direct part in hostilities'. (Paris Principles, para. 2.1).

86 General Assembly, A/RES/51/77 (20 February 1997).

87 Ibid., paras 35–37.

children affected by conflict.[88] The Special Representative makes annual reports to the UN Human Rights Council (UNHRC).[89] Mr Olara A. Otunnu served as the first Special Representative of the Secretary-General for Children and Armed Conflict from 1998 to 2005.[90] The current Special Representative, Ms Radhika Coomaraswamy, was appointed by UN Secretary-General Kofi Annan as Under-Secretary-General, Special Representative for Children and Armed Conflict in April 2006 and was reappointed by the UN Secretary-General Ban Ki-moon in February 2007.

In September 2000, at the World Summit for Children, Canada hosted the International Conference on War-Affected Children in Winnipeg. In preparation for the conference, Canada commissioned the 'Machel Review 1996–2000', to review progress in protecting war-affected children and to serve as principal background document for the Conference. This review (Machel 2001) concluded that there had been some progress; for example, children were now more central to the UN's peace and security agenda and that war crimes against children had started to be prosecuted and violations against children were being documented more systematically, and that more is now known about how small arms and light weapons are damaging children's lives. However, the damaging impact on children by armed conflicts continues:

> In spite of this progress the assaults against children continue. An estimated 300,000 children are still participating in armed combat. Children in 87 countries live amid the contamination of more than 60 million landmines. At least 20 million children have been uprooted from their homes. Girls and women continue to be marginalised from mainstream humanitarian assistance and protection. Humanitarian personnel continue to be targeted and killed. Millions of children are abandoned to cope with the multiple and compounded effects of armed conflict and HIV/AIDS. Hundreds of thousands of children continue to die from disease and malnutrition in flight from conflict or in camps for displaced persons. Small arms and light weapons continue to proliferate excessively. Millions of children are scarred physically and psychologically.
>
> (Machel 2001: 61)

To mark the tenth anniversary of the landmark Graça Machel study (Machel 1996), UNICEF and the Special Representative of the Secretary-General (SRSG) have reviewed the current situation faced by children in armed conflict. The 'Machel Strategic Review' (SRSG 2007) identifies emerging challenges and priorities and the responses required for the next decade. It concludes with 15 recommendations: for example, urging the end of impunity for violations

---

88 Ibid.
89 See, for example, SRSG (2009).
90 Ms Sham Poo served as Interim Special Representative in Autumn 2005.

against children; strengthening the monitoring and reporting mechanisms; supporting inclusive reintegration strategies; operationalising the engagement of regional bodies; and integrating children's rights in peacemaking, peacebuilding and preventive actions (SRSG 2007: paras 103–117).

The main objectives of the current Special Representative's strategic plan are:

(1) to support global initiatives to end grave violations; (2) to promote rights-based protection for children affected by armed conflict; (3) to make children and armed conflict concerns an integral aspect of peacekeeping and peacebuilding; (4) to identify new trends and strategies for the protection of children through research; (5) to secure political and diplomatic engagement on CAAC [Children And Armed Conflict] initiatives and (6) to raise global awareness with regard to all issues relating to children and armed conflict.

(Special Representative for Children
and Armed Conflict website[91])

The Office of the Special Representative has also instituted a series of working papers 'to assist the community of practice working on the protection of children affected by armed conflict' (SRSG 2009a). The first of these working papers identifies the legal foundations of 'six grave violations' against children during armed conflict. The normative standards which are examined and clarified in the paper and which address these grave violations are headlined as follows:

- Parties to a conflict must protect children from being killed or seriously injured;
- Parties to a conflict must not recruit or deploy children as soldiers, and must prevent children from participating in hostilities;
- Parties to a conflict must not rape or otherwise abuse children;
- Parties to a conflict must not abduct children;
- Parties to a conflict must not attack schools or hospitals, other education or medical facilities ordinarily used by children; and
- Parties to a conflict must not deny humanitarian access for children even in a conflict zone.

(SRSG 2009a)

8.3 International courts and tribunals

Over the past two decades there have been important developments in international efforts to prosecute crimes against humanity, war crimes and other serious

---

91 Available at http://www.un.org/children/conflict/english/strategicplan.html (accessed 5 February 2010).

violations against international humanitarian law, including ending impunity for crimes against children. The arrest and trial of individuals in leadership positions alleged to have committed such crimes sends a powerful message that such behaviour may not be tolerated in the future. Combined with the various initiatives of the United Nations discussed earlier, these international justice mechanisms hold out some hope that relevant parties will be brought into compliance with international law standards in this field. The sections later focus on the International Criminal Court, the International Criminal Tribunal for the former Yugoslavia (ICTY), the International Criminal Tribunal for Rwanda (ICTR) and the Special Court of Sierra Leone. The international justice system, such as it is, remains challenged by the difficulties of dealing with child soldiers who have themselves been accused of war crimes, a problem that 'illustrates the complexity of balancing culpability, a community's sense of justice and the "best interests of the child"' (Machel 1996: para. 250). It would appear, however, that a consensus is emerging from the practice of the ICC and other international tribunals that children below the age of 18 years should not be prosecuted for such crimes by international courts and tribunals. There is also the political difficulty of whether the particular international court or tribunal is dispensing, or is seen as dispensing, 'victors' justice', a problem that undoubtedly impacts on the long-term legitimacy of such bodies.

8.3.1 International Criminal Court (ICC)

The Rome Statute of the International Criminal Court[92] of 1998 (ICC) provides a definition of 'war crimes' that includes, inter alia, '[c]onscripting or enlisting children under the age of 15 years into the national armed forces or using them to participate actively in hostilities'.[93] It also defines as a 'war crime' other serious violations of the laws and customs applicable in 'armed conflicts not of an international character', within the established framework of international law, including the conscription or enlisting of children under 15 years into 'armed forces or groups or using them to participate actively in hostilities'.[94]

As discussed in Chapter 2, the ICC's first trial of Congolese rebel militia leader Thomas Lubanga Dyilo, began on 26 January 2009, following an application for arrest made on 12 January 2006.[95] Lubanga is allegedly responsible for war crimes consisting of both of the offences referred to above. The number of children involved in fighting forces in the Democratic Republic of the Congo (DRC) conflict is estimated by the United Nations to be around 30,000. Lubanga was the President of the 'Union of Congolese Patriots' and is alleged to have

---

92 Adopted 17 July 1998 and entered into force on 1 July 2002.
93 Rome Statute of the International Criminal Court, article 8(2)(b)(xxvi).
94 Ibid., article 8(2)(e)(vii).
95 ICC-01/04-01/06, *The Prosecutor v. Thomas Lubanga Dyilo*.

served as commander-in-chief of the former military wing of the Union, namely the 'Patriotic Forces for the Liberation of Congo'. The Union of Congolese Patriots aimed to establish dominance of the Hema ethnic group through violence against mainly Lendu militias and civilians. Lubanga was arrested in 2005 and transferred from the DRC to the ICC a year later, in March 2006. After long delays, his trial started at the ICC on 26 January 2009. Lubanga is charged with responsibility for these crimes because of his alleged political and military leadership roles. If he is found guilty, the ICC can sentence him to prison and/or order his property to be taken so that reparations are paid to victims. The death penalty is prohibited under ICC rules. There is some disappointment that Lubanga has been charged only with the conscription/enlistment offences and not with further offences of murder and sexual violence. The person accused of committing crimes as Lubanga's deputy, Bosco Ntaganda, has similarly been charged only with enlisting, conscripting and using child soldiers in armed conflict. The trial was ongoing at the time of writing.[96]

The ICC has also issued arrest warrants for five senior members of the 'Lord's Resistance Army' in Uganda, including its leader, Joseph Kony, who is charged with 33 counts of war crimes and crimes against humanity, including the forcible enlistment and use of children under 15 years in hostilities.[97] Pre-trial proceedings at the ICC were ongoing at the time of writing.[98]

8.3.2 The International Criminal Tribunal for the former Yugoslavia (ICTY)

In May 1993, this Tribunal was established by the United Nations in response to mass atrocities taking place in Croatia and Bosnia and Herzegovina. This Tribunal is situated in The Hague, the Netherlands. The ICTY was the first war crimes court created by the United Nations and the first international war crimes tribunal since the Nuremberg and Tokyo tribunals. It was established as an *ad hoc* court by the Security Council in accordance with Chapter VII of the UN Charter. The Tribunal laid the foundations for what is now the accepted norm for conflict resolution and post-conflict development globally, namely, that leaders suspected of crimes against humanity, war crimes and other serious violations of international humanitarian law will be exposed to face justice. The work of the Tribunal showed that the mass murder at Srebrenica was indeed 'genocide'. Most of the key cases heard at the Tribunal have dealt with alleged crimes committed

---

96 See the Lubanga Trial website. Available at: http://www.lubangatrial.org/ (accessed 5 February 2010).

97 ICC-02/04-01/05 Case: *The Prosecutor v. Joseph Kony, Vincent Otti, Okot Odhiambo and Dominic Ongwen.*

98 See the ICC website. Available at: http://www.icc-cpi.int/Menus/ICC/Situations+and+Cases/ (accessed 5 February 2010).

by Serbs and Bosnian Serbs, but the Tribunal has also investigated and brought charges against persons from every ethnic background. It was estimated in 2009 that the trials should be completed by mid-2011, with the exception of that of Radovan Karadžić, which is expected to finish in late 2012. The ICTY has charged over 160 persons. Its indictments address crimes committed from 1991 to 2001 against members of various ethnic groups in Croatia, Bosnia and Herzegovina, Serbia, Kosovo and the Former Yugoslav Republic of Macedonia. More than 60 individuals have been convicted and currently more than 40 people are in different stages of proceedings before the Tribunal.

8.3.3 International Criminal Tribunal for Rwanda (ICTR)

The Security Council created the International Criminal Tribunal for Rwanda (ICTR)[99] in response to a recognition of the serious violations of humanitarian law committed in Rwanda between 1 January and 31 December 1994. The Tribunal is located in Arusha, United Republic of Tanzania. The purpose was to contribute to the process of national reconciliation in Rwanda and to the maintenance of peace in the region. ICTR was established for the prosecution of persons responsible for genocide and other serious violations of international humanitarian law committed in the territory of Rwanda. It also has jurisdiction to deal with the prosecution of Rwandan citizens responsible for genocide and other such violations of international law committed in the territory of neighbouring states during the same period. The ICTR has indicted around 90 individuals alleged to be responsible for the Rwandan genocide.

8.3.4 Special Court for Sierra Leone

The Special Court for Sierra Leone was established jointly by the Government of Sierra Leone and the United Nations.[100] It is now located at The Hague, the Netherlands. It is mandated to try those who bear the greatest responsibility for serious violations of international humanitarian law and Sierra Leonean law committed in the territory of Sierra Leone since 30 November 1996. Thirteen indictments were issued by the Prosecutor in 2003. Two of those indictments were subsequently withdrawn in December 2003 due to the deaths of the accused.

---

99   Security Council resolution S/RES/955 (8 November 1994).
100   'The Special Court shall, except as provided in subparagraph (2), have the power to prosecute persons who bear the greatest responsibility for serious violations of international humanitarian law and Sierra Leonean law committed in the territory of Sierra Leone since 30 November 1996, including those leaders who, in committing such crimes, have threatened the establishment of and implementation of the peace process in Sierra Leone'. [Statute of the Special Court of Sierra Leone, article 1(1)].

The trials of three former leaders of the Armed Forces Revolutionary Council in *The Prosecutor vs. Brima, Kamara and Kanu* (AFRC Case) have resulted in convictions and sentences. The Appeals Chamber, on 22 February 2008, upheld sentences of 50 years for Brima, 45 years for Kamara and 50 years for Kanu.[101]

In *The Prosecutor vs. Fofana and Kondewa (CDF Case)* in June 2003 the alleged leaders of the former Civil Defence Forces were indicted on various counts of war crimes, crimes against humanity, and other serious violations of international humanitarian law. In October 2007 Fofana was sentenced to a term of imprisonment of six years and Kondewa to eight years, minus time served. However, in May 2008 the Appeals Chamber, although overturning Kondewa's conviction for the enlistment of child soldiers, entered new convictions and increased sentences; Fofana was sentenced to a total of 15 years and Kondewa has been given a 20-year sentence.

In *The Prosecutor vs. Sesay, Kallon and Gbao (RUF Case)* five former leaders of the former Revolutionary United Front (RUF) were indicted on 18 counts of war crimes, crimes against humanity, and other serious violations of international humanitarian law. The RUF trial began on 5 July 2004, and on 25 February 2009 the Trial Chamber found Sesay and Kallon guilty on 16 counts and Gbao was found guilty on 14 counts. On 8 April 2009 Sesay was sentenced to 52 years, Kallon to 40 years and Gbao to 25 years. On 26 October 2009 the Appeals Chamber upheld these sentences.

In addition to these high-profile trials and convictions, the Special Court is also in the process of trying another high-profile case; that of the former Liberian President, in *The Prosecutor vs. Charles Ghankay Taylor*. The trial was in the 'defence phase' at The Hague at the time of writing. Charles Taylor has been prosecuted on 11 counts of war crimes and crimes against humanity, including conscripting or enlisting children into armed forces or groups and using them to participate actively in hostilities. The particulars of the latter count in the indictment read as follows:

> Between about 30 November 1996 and about 18 January 2002, throughout the Republic of Sierra Leone, members of RUF, AFRC, AFRC/RUF Junta or alliance, and/or Liberian fighters, assisted and encouraged by, acting in concert with, under the direction and/or control of, and/or subordinate to the ACCUSED, routinely conscripted, enlisted and/or used boys under the age of 15 to participate in active hostilities. Many of these children were first abducted, then trained in AFRC and/or RUF camps in various locations throughout the country, and thereafter used as fighters.
>
> (Special Court of Sierra Leone, Office of the Prosecutor, Indictment, 29 May 2007)

---

101 See the website of the Special Court of Sierra Leone. Available at: http://www.sc-sl.org/ (accessed 5 February 2010).

Chapter 9

Indigenous children

9.1 Introduction

This chapter discusses the rights of Indigenous children in international law. There is no single international instrument that is solely focused on the provision of the rights of Indigenous children. This is unlike other discussions of international law provision for children, such as parental child abduction (Chapter 5), intercountry adoption (Chapter 6), or even a general provision of rights such as the United Nations Convention on the Rights of the Child (CRC): see generally, Chapter 3. The discussion of Indigenous children's rights in this chapter requires an examination of where the international law relating to the rights of Indigenous *peoples* meets the rights of *children*.

The rights of Indigenous peoples have received an ever-increasing profile in international law, culminating most recently with the United Nations Declaration on the Rights of Indigenous People of 2007[1] (hereafter 'UNDRIP'). International estimates put the number of Indigenous people in the world at around 370 million in some 70 countries.[2] More recently, the United Nations issued a 'General Comment'[3] on the application of the CRC to the unique circumstances of Indigenous children (General Comment No. 11, 2009). The activity on an international level is summed up by a report issued by Professor S. James Anaya, who is currently the Special Rapporteur on the Situation of Human Rights and Fundamental Freedoms of Indigenous People[4]:

> During the last three decades, the demands for recognition of Indigenous peoples across the world have led to the gradual emergence of a common

---

1 United Nations Declaration on the Rights of Indigenous Peoples, United Nations General Assembly, 12 September 2007, A/61/L.67.
2 See, for example, the UN Permanent Forum of Indigenous Peoples (UNPFII) website, available at: http://www.un.org/esa/socdev/unpfii/en/history.html (accessed 1 February 2010).
3 See Chapter 3, section 3.3.1.
4 The website of this Special Rapporteur is available at: http://www2.ohchr.org/english/issues/Indigenous/rapporteur/index.htm (accessed 31 January 2010).

body of opinion regarding the content of the right of these peoples on the basis of long-standing principles of international human rights law and policy. This common normative understanding has been promoted by international and regional standard-setting processes; by the practice of human rights bodies, mechanisms and specialized agencies; and by a significant number of international conferences and expert meetings....The Declaration on the Rights of Indigenous Peoples is the most important of these developments globally, encapsulating as it does the widely shared understanding about the rights of Indigenous peoples that has been building over decades on a foundation of previously existing sources of international human rights law.

(Anaya 2008: para. 18)

Finally, it should be kept in mind that the international rights discussed in this chapter are dependent for the most part on *domestic* implementation, application and enforcement. That said, the international rights in the UNDRIP are not provided through the state, nor are they dependent upon recognition by the state, as is further discussed within this chapter. However, one of the largest dilemmas facing Indigenous rights is finding a way for them to be effectively transmitted to the state in a meaningful way, so that they do not simply become rights on paper without any practical effect (Anaya 2004).

9.2 Interpretative debates in international law

This section considers several international human rights concepts that are important in understanding Indigenous rights in an international law framework. Whilst these debates occur outside of an Indigenous law context, they take on a sharper focus when discussing Indigenous 'rights'. This section provides an overview of four of these: universal rights versus culturally relative rights; collective rights versus individual rights; issues of state sovereignty and the state as the focus for delivery of international rights; and lastly, the right to self-determination. These have been identified specifically by Anaya (2007) and Libesmann (2007) as important to understanding Indigenous law in relation to international legal frameworks.

9.2.1 Universal versus cultural relativity[5]

A long running and unresolved debate in international human rights law is what character international rights have. One school of thought is that international human rights have, by definition, a universal quality where rights are applied and interpreted uniformly, without regard for, or the need to consider, any local variation in cultures, communities or settings. Whilst this seems a praiseworthy

5 See also Chapter 1, section 1.3.

approach in instituting rights, it is not without its critics. A universal approach to human rights is said to be very Euro-centric in nature, with its stress upon Western dominant interpretations and the right of the individual stressed over the rights of groups or collective rights (Steiner and Alston 2000: 366–68). These debates become sharper when considering the rights of Indigenous peoples in international law, where Indigenous rights involve both issues of collective rights and culturally relative interpretations. These issues are both set out in further detail in further sections of this chapter. Steiner and Alston discuss the differences:

> The question of the 'universal' or 'relative' character of the rights declared in the major instruments of the human rights movement has been a source of debate and contention from the movement's start. These alternative understandings of the character of human rights have been cast in different but related ways—for example, 'absolute' rights (compare 'universal') as opposed to 'contingent' rights (compare 'relative') or imperialism in imposing rights (compare 'universal') as opposed to self-determination of peoples (compare 'relative').
>
> (Steiner and Alston 2000: 366)

Harris-Short (2001: 350) argues that a universalist interpretation can be highly limiting. Matters that do not lend themselves well to a universal interpretation of human rights are seen as troublesome. She considers that '[t]radition and culture are constantly presented as a "problem", rather than a potential strength' (Harris-Short 2001: 350).[6] She also argues that it is necessary to recognise rights as being culturally relative for improved functionality of the human rights legal regime:

> Achieving agreement on culturally legitimate universal norms is the first crucial step towards a more effective system of international human rights. The next step in seeking to ensure that human rights are meaningful to people across the world's social, cultural and economic divides is the process of interpretation and implementation.
>
> (Harris-Short 2001: 332)

Not all commentators find that there is a sharp divide between universal and culturally relative interpretations of rights. Donnelly argues that in fact appearances of differences are somewhat superficial (Donnelly 1984: 414). He presents the view that 'while human rights—alienable entitlements of individuals held in relation to state and society—have not been part of most cultural traditions,

---

6 See also the Committee on the Rights of the Child's (CtRC) treatment of 'harmful traditional practices': Chapter 3, section 3.5.6.4.

or even the west tradition until rather recently, there is striking similarity in many of the basic values that today we seek to protect through human rights'. In other words, whilst human rights regimes may introduce new normative ideas into cultures, they are not very different from the cultural traditions raised in debates about the cultural relativity of rights.

Yet another view is that of a deep suspicion over the claims of universality and neutrality of international human rights law documents. Mutua (2001) asserts that international human rights laws are established to perpetuate power imbalances between Western and European states and non-Western, non-European states. He describes the international human rights regime as being heavily imbued with European values that continue the unequal roles between states that existed in colonialism. Because of this, he concludes, there can be no candour in the claims made that international human rights can be interpreted as universal rights.

> The human rights corpus, though well-meaning, is fundamentally Eurocentric, and suffers from several basic and interdependent flaws.... First, the corpus falls within the historical continuum of the Eurocentric colonial project, in which actors are cast into superior and subordinate positions. Precisely because of this cultural and historical context, the human rights movement's basic claim to universality is undermined.
>
> (Mutua 2001: 204)

9.2.2 Collective versus individual rights

Another debate that occurs in international human rights regimes is over the provision for individual rights and the provision for collective rights. The development of Indigenous rights has had a profound impact on how rights are viewed within international law. Anaya argues that Indigenous peoples themselves have been instrumental in 'mov[ing] international law towards a recognition of collective rights' (Anaya 2007: 11–12). Buchanan comments that before Indigenous rights were raised as a matter of international law there was little conception of rights existing outside of the 'individual rights' paradigm (Buchanan 1993: 91). He explains that a 'focus on *collective* rights of Indigenous peoples constitutes a fundamental challenge to the core of normative assumption of post-Second World War international law: that a regime of individual human rights is sufficient for achieving an acceptable international legal order' (Buchanan 1993: 91).

The recognition of collective rights alongside individual rights is key to the delivery of Indigenous rights. Anaya identifies how the *collective* identification of Indigenous peoples is inherently important to the identification and provision of Indigenous rights. He comments that 'Indigenous groups are deemed to have collective rights in relation to their own lands, the maintenance and development of their culture, their own institutions of self-governance and their own laws and customs' (Anaya 2007: 6).

The tension between interpretations of rights is found in the General Comment's application of the CRC's best interest standard for Indigenous children:

> The application of the principle of the best interests of the child to Indigenous children requires particular attention. The Committee notes that the best interests of the child is conceived of as both a collective and individual right, and that the application of this right to Indigenous children as a group requires consideration of how the right relates to collective cultural rights. ... In the case of children, the best interests of the child cannot be neglected or violate in preference for the best interests of the group.
>
> (General Comment No. 11, 2009: para. 30)

This view, that the individual rights of a child should be lifted above those of a group, is shared by Eekelaar (2004: 191). However, he takes the position even further by arguing against the group having any rights whatsoever as a collective – that is, that there are no collective rights, and to the extent that individual members have cultural rights, the exercise of those rights is limited by the interests of the children in that group. But this view is strictly contradicted by the arguments put forth by Libesmann (2007), who considers that neither the child's individual rights nor the rights of the collectivity that are Indigenous Peoples can be recognised without the simultaneous recognition of both. Libesmann does not see the recognition of collective rights as in any way impairing the other rights that a child might hold; rather he sees the child's rights enhanced through the additional exercise of collective rights:

> Children are essential to the retention and development of Indigenous culture. Without Indigenous control over children how will Indigenous cultural, social and linguistic expression be developed? Likewise without the protection of Indigenous culture how are children to experience their rights under article 30 and more broadly their rights under the Convention?
>
> (Libesmann 2007: 307)

The tension over collective and individual rights for Indigenous children has been neatly summed up by Roby, who explains: '[t]he concept that the child belongs not only to himself but to the larger community is not a foreign idea, but one which is difficult for many to accept' (Roby 2004: 308) This tension takes on a particular significance when talking about the rights of Indigenous children. There are unresolved questions as to how provisions for both individual and collective rights should be weighed in human rights instruments relating to Indigenous children. Perhaps not unsurprisingly, there are calls for more traditional preferences of individual rather than collective rights provision. The appropriateness of this approach has been challenged, and it is questionable how well it fits into an Indigenous perspective of rights.

9.2.3 The state as the focus of international law and human rights law

Human rights and international law have traditionally focused on the state as being instrumental to the delivery of rights and law (Mutua 1996: 594; Anaya 2007: 4–5, 8). Anaya (2007) comments that Indigenous rights have been influential in bringing about a change in focus of international law from that of states to a recognition of collective rights within a state system. Mutua (1996) comments that international law has traditionally placed the state as 'the basic obligor' of human rights, with an overriding duty to 'protect the individual and property' (Mutua 1996: 594, n.14). In other words, according to Mutua, human rights cannot be delivered without the mechanism of the state to implement those rights. Anaya comments on how the focus of international law on the sovereignty of the state, as the basic principle for the formulation of international law, has been challenged by the development of Indigenous rights in an international law framework:

> A second, related way in which Indigenous peoples have helped forge change in the international legal order has to do with the doctrine of state sovereignty, a doctrine which is considered one of the bedrock doctrines within the international legal order. ... Indigenous peoples' demands, which include demands for recognition of Indigenous legal systems and related collective rights, are resulting in a more radical altering of the state sovereignty doctrine than that brought about by the internalization of individual rights. The assertion of Indigenous group rights, and the assertion of a space of Indigenous legal systems in particular, challenges the primacy and sphere of state governing authority in a much more fundamental sense than classic individual rights.
>
> (Anaya 2007: 8)

In other words, Indigenous rights alter the focus on states as the exclusive source of rights provision and protection. In the Indigenous context of rights delivery, the state is not the institution from which rights flow. The Indigenous collective, through its rights of self determination – discussed in the next section – have the ability to develop parallel systems to that found in the state for rights provision and protection.

9.2.4 Right to self-determination

The right to 'self-determination' has been one of the most contested in the establishment of Indigenous rights in international law.[7] Part of the debate has turned

---

7 See Sargent (2010a) for an account of the ramifications of the right to self-determination and the situation faced by Mayans in Guatemala.

on how the right to self-determination has been defined. Multiple definitions of the right at international law have been debated, with UNDRIP perhaps drawing a line under this debate by defining the right to be one of internal governance and not, as feared by state opponents of the right, the ability for Indigenous peoples to secede from the state.

The United Nations Charter of 1945 expressly set out the basic provision for the right of self-determination as one of the purposes of the United Nations:

> To develop friendly relations among nations based on respect for the principle of equal rights and self-determination of peoples, and to take other appropriate measures to strengthen universal peace.
>
> (United Nations Charter, article 1, para. 2)

The Indigenous claim to the right has been a cause of unease for states who viewed the assertion as tantamount to claims of a right to secede (Barsh 1994: 35). Instead, the Indigenous context for the right has been clarified in UNDRIP as one described as a right that includes internal self-governance, but not the right to secede (Barsh 1994: 35–36) and establish 'independent statehood' (Anaya 2004: 103; 1993: 143). UNDRIP clarifies the right as one that allows rights of self-governance within the structure of the Indigenous group:

> 3. Indigenous peoples have the right to self-determination. By virtue of that right they freely determine their political status and freely pursue their economic, social and cultural development.
> 4. Indigenous peoples, in exercising their right to self-determination, have the right to autonomy or self-government in matters relating to their internal and local affairs, as well as ways and means for financing their autonomous functions.
>
> (UNDRIP, articles 3 and 4)

Anaya, in his report as Special Rapporteur, clarifies that the right of self-determination in UNDRIP does not include a move to secession by Indigenous peoples, but rather it gives them a right both to be full citizens of the state in which they live and to have autonomy over Indigenous affairs:

> Together with affirming aspects of self-determination related to maintaining spheres of autonomy, the Declaration [UNDRIP] also reflects the common understanding that Indigenous peoples' self-determination at the same time involves participatory engagement and interaction with larger societal structures in which they live. In this connection, the Declaration affirms Indigenous peoples' right to 'participate fully, if they so choose, in the political, economic, social and cultural life of the State'; and to be consulted

in relation to decisions affecting them, with the objective of obtaining their prior, free and informed consent.[8]

(Anaya 2008: para. 39)

His comments re-emphasise that the articulation of self-determination found in UNDRIP is a right to internal self-governance rather than secession, while citizens retain their rights to full participation in the state in which they live. His further comments underscore this point:

> ... Reflecting the state of contemporary international law in relation to this principle [of self-determination] as well as the demands of Indigenous people themselves, the affirmation of self-determination in the Declaration is deemed compatible with the principle of territorial integr[ity] and political unity of States.

(Anaya 2008: para. 37)

9.2.4.1 Self-determination and Indigeneity Identification

The question of who it is that determines which persons are Indigenous (Corntassel 2003: 76) has been tied in with the right to self-determination (Barsh 1990: 215). Barsh argues that the ability of Indigenous peoples to self-identify their membership is critical, because 'state power to classify groups as nonindigeneous is power to extinguish their legal rights' (Barsh 1990: 215). The ability of Indigenous groups to set their own parameters for membership has been widely accepted, though not without controversy, as Corntassel explains:

> Despite the accepted practice of unlimited self-identification for Indigenous peoples within global forums, states 'hosting' Indigenous peoples within their borders have generally contested such an open policy. ... Debate over establishing definitional standards versus an unlimited right of Indigenous self-identification has exposed something of a dilemma over the construction of Indigenous identity.

(Corntassel 2003: 75–76)

In keeping with the position of Indigenous self-identification, UNDRIP does not define 'Indigenous'. This is also followed by CtRC which, in its General Comment, provides an unambiguous statement on the right of Indigenous peoples to self-define their group classifications:

> The presence of Indigenous peoples is established by self-identification as the fundamental criterion for determining their existence. There is no

---

8 See UNDRIP, articles 5 and 19.

requirement for States parties to officially recognise Indigenous peoples in order for them to exercise their rights.

(General Comment No. 11, 2009: para. 19)

For the time being, at least, the policy of Indigenous self-identification in international law has prevailed (Corntassel 2003: 75–76). The International Labour Organisation's (ILO) 'Indigenous and Tribal Peoples Convention of 1989' (ILO Convention No. 169), discussed in section 9.4.2, also gives the nod to self-identification of Indigenous peoples, whilst at the same time containing provisions that attempt to define the groups that might be covered under this Convention. This is a different approach from that of UNDRIP or CRC:

1. This Convention applies to:
   (a) tribal peoples in independent countries whose social, cultural and economic conditions distinguish them from other sections of the national community, and whose status is regulated wholly or partially by their own customs or traditions or by special laws or regulations;
   (b) peoples in independent countries who are regarded as Indigenous on account of their descent from the populations which inhabited the country, or a geographical region to which the country belongs, at the time of conquest or colonisation or the establishment of present state boundaries and who, irrespective of their legal status, retain some or all of their own social, economic, cultural and political institutions.
2. Self-identification as Indigenous or tribal shall be regarded as a funda-mental criterion for determining the groups to which the provisions of this Convention apply.

(ILO Convention No. 169, articles 1 and 2)

Corntassel (2003) raises cautions about the self-identification of Indigenous people within the international law framework. He cites the discomfort that states continue to have with self-identification as limiting in more than one way. The discomfort limits state willingness to ratify instruments on the one hand, and, on the other, the controversy over this means that other important issues are not addressed. He proposes that a new way to deal with Indigenous identification within international law must be found:

Dilemmas over self-identification polices versus established definitional approaches to documenting Indigenous peoples will continue, whether in global/regional forums, host state/Indigenous group interactions, or among Indigenous groups themselves. Can a self-identification policy work in tandem with a working definition of Indigenous peoples? Certainly this has been the case with key global instruments and policies relating to Indigenous peoples, such as ILO No. 169, the UN Working Group, the Organization of American States Declaration and the World Council on Indigenous People.

... Unfortunately, the discourse over defining Indigenous peoples has thus far been dominated by concerns of host states within international forums while de-emphasizing Indigenous goals of political, cultural, economic and social autonomy. ... Clearly the gap beyond praxis and theory must be closed if the global Indigenous rights discourse is to move beyond technical, definitional approaches and towards more substantive issues of self-determination, land rights and promoting cultural integrity.

(Corntassel 2003: 94)

How the issues of self-determination and self-identification are defined within international law frameworks is significant in setting the boundaries around a discernable law of rights for Indigenous children, as discussed further within this chapter.

9.3 Are Indigenous rights international customary law?

Questions have been raised as to whether Indigenous rights have reached the status of customary international law,[9] thus binding even upon those states that have not ratified specific treaties. Further, even non-binding documents such as UNDRIP would be considered binding if the rights contained therein were recognised to hold the status of international customary law. This 'core debate' (Oguamanam 2004: 397) remains an unsettled question, with the existence of 'a debate about whether the identified Indigenous claims have attained the status of *opinion juris*, that is whether there is a consensus among states that they are under obligation to recognise certain Indigenous claims as binding customary law' (Oguamanam 2004: 388). Even whilst this remains an unresolved question, Oguamanam argues that there is an acknowledgement that international law has set 'minimum standards' for Indigenous rights, with those reflected first in ILO Convention No. 169 (Oguamanam 2004: 393). Anaya says that the effect of international law efforts on Indigenous rights has been 'the gradual crystallization of a universal common understanding of the minimum content of the rights of these peoples as a matter of international law and policy' (Anaya 2008: para. 30).

The status of being a binding norm of international customary law is reached 'when a number of states or other international actors find a common understanding of the content of the norms and a willingness to conform to them' (Oguamanam 2004: 394). This status of customary binding international law then requires more than an agreement on the meaning of the norms; it requires additionally the voluntary willingness of states to conform to such norms. Arguably, it is that element which is most difficult to reach when it comes to Indigenous rights in international law.

---

9   See Chapter 2, section 2.2.2.

This issue remains unresolved with the status of the UNDRIP. Four states – Australia, New Zealand, the United States and Canada – have not voted in favour of it, arguing that 'they would not be bound by the Declaration, and that it is impossible for them to live up to it' (Kakungulu 2009: 2). However, subsequently, in April 2009 Australia has affirmed its support for the Declaration.[10]

Kakungulu argues that the four states that voted against the Declaration have something in common, and that is their use of the doctrine of *terra nullius* to justify their takeover of Indigenous lands and treatment of Indigenous peoples (Kakungulu 2009: 5–6). The doctrine of *terra nullius* refers to lands that are seen as 'empty ... uninhabited or occupied by people without settled laws or customs' (Kakungulu 2009: 9). This doctrine was 'elevated ... into a principle of international law' (Samson 2008: 5). Kakungulu concludes his argument by saying that even if there is no customary international law in force for Indigenous peoples, UNDRIP 'represents an authoritative common understanding, at the global level, of the minimum content of the rights of Indigenous peoples ...' (Kakungulu 2009: 13).

What place Indigenous rights have within international law is still unresolved. Whether or not such rights have risen to the level of international customary law has not been settled. If Indigenous rights are recognised as such, then they are binding upon all states, whether or not they have ratified the instruments that contain the rights. This would make the UNDRIP have the force of international law, even for those states that did not vote for it. Anaya has observed the following:

> Albeit clearly not binding in the same way that a treaty is, the Declaration relates to already existing human rights obligations of the States, as demonstrated by the work of the United Nations treaty bodies and other human rights mechanisms, and hence can be seen as embodying to some extent general principles of international law. In addition, insofar as they connect with a pattern of consistent international and State practice, some aspects of the provisions of the Declaration can also be considered as a reflection of norms of customary international law.
>
> (Anaya 2008: para. 41)

9.4 Indigenous rights in international law instruments

This section considers the key international instruments that deal with Indigenous rights. It focuses respectively on: the CRC and its provision for Indigenous children's rights; the Indigenous and Tribal Peoples Convention of 1989

---

10 See http://www.Indigenousportal.com/World/Australia-Government-endorses-UN-Declaration-on-the-Rights-of-Indigenous-Peoples.html (accessed 31 January 2010).

(ILO Convention No. 169); and the UN Declaration of the Rights of Indigenous Peoples of 2007 (UNDRIP).

9.4.1 The UN Convention on the Rights of the Child of 1989 (CRC)

One article of the CRC (see also, section 3.5.8.8) makes specific mention of Indigenous children:

> In those States in which ethnic, religious or linguistic minorities or persons of Indigenous origin exist, a child belonging to such a minority or who is Indigenous shall not be denied the right, in community with other members of his or her group, to enjoy his or her own culture, to profess and practise his or her own religion, or to use his or her own language.
>
> (CRC, article 30)

However, it should be noted that the CtRC has stressed that the whole range of rights contained in the CRC is applicable to *all* children, Indigenous or not (General Comment No. 11, 2009: paras 13–4, 21–2). This General Comment was issued for the purpose of identifying ways in which to ensure the application of the whole of the Convention to Indigenous children, in particular 'to explore the specific challenges which impede Indigenous children from being able to fully enjoy their rights and highlight special measures required to be undertaken by States in order to guarantee the effective exercise of Indigenous children's rights' (General Comment No. 11, 2009: para. 14). It recognises the special content in article 30 for Indigenous children as well as the links that this article has for the realisation of the rest of the rights in the CRC for Indigenous children:

> Article 30 of the Convention and the right to enjoyment of culture, religion and language are key elements of this general comment; however the aim is to explore the various provisions which require particular attention in their implementation in relation to Indigenous children. Particular emphasis is placed on the interrelationship between relevant provisions, notably with the general principles of the Convention as identified by the Committee, namely; non-discrimination, the best interests of the child, the right to life, survival and development and the right to be heard.
>
> (General Comment No. 11, para. 14)

The UNICEF Innocenti Research Centre likewise recognises the vulnerable position that Indigenous children occupy, as they are 'among the most marginalized groups in society and are frequently denied the enjoyment of their rights, including the highest attainable standard of health, education, protection and participation in decision-making processes that are relevant to their lives' (Innocenti Research Centre 2004: 2)

The marginalised status of Indigenous children highlights the importance of recognising and achieving the rights that have been granted to them under international law. Again, to repeat the point made at the outset of this chapter, the actual realisation of Indigenous rights is reliant upon sufficient domestic state action (see section 9.1) in this field.

As we have seen in the discussion of the CRC in Chapter 3, the duties placed on states to disseminate and publicise the CRC[11] are important and have often required relevant language translations for minority or Indigenous groups, and programmes of rights' awareness through mass media, professional training, school and other educational curricula.[12] The CRC also makes specific mention of the obligations on states to encourage the mass media to have regard to the linguistic needs of Indigenous children.[13] There is also another provision that specifically refers to persons of Indigenous origin in the context of state obligations to guide the direction of education.[14] Finally, as discussed in Chapter 3 (section 3.5.4.1), there are frequently concerns about the birth registration of Indigenous children as there tends to be a greater proportion of such children who remain unregistered and are therefore at a greater risk of becoming stateless (CO Philippines 2009; CO Bolivia 2009). The CtRC urges that states parties with Indigenous populations should take special measures to ensure a robust, equitable and free of charge birth registration system (General Comment No. 11, 2009: paras 41–45).

9.4.2 The Indigenous and Tribal Peoples Convention of 1989 (ILO Convention No. 169)

ILO Convention No. 169, which was issued in the same year as the CRC, is a binding international law instrument. It revises an earlier version of an ILO Convention on Indigenous rights,[15] which is now regarded as an outdated instrument (Barsh 1990: 209–10). At the time of writing, 20 states had ratified ILO

---

11 CRC, articles 42 and 44(6).

12 See Chapter 3, section 3.5.1.

13 'States Parties recognize the important function performed by the mass media and shall ensure that the child has access to information and material from a diversity of national and international sources, especially those aimed at the promotion of his or her social, spiritual and moral well-being and physical and mental health. To this end, States Parties shall:

   (d) Encourage the mass media to have particular regard to the linguistic needs of the child who belongs to a minority group or who is Indigenous; ...' (CRC, article 17(d)).

14 '1. States Parties agree that the education of the child shall be directed to:

   ... (d) The preparation of the child for responsible life in a free society, in the spirit of understanding, peace, tolerance, equality of sexes, and friendship among all peoples, ethnic, national and religious groups and persons of Indigenous origin; ...' (CRC, article 29(1)(d)).

15 ILO Convention No. 169, article 36. The Indigenous and Tribal Populations Convention of 1957 (ILO Convention No. 107) is the earlier instrument: it is currently (May 2010) ratified by 17 countries and denounced by 10 countries.

Convention No. 169.[16] It was adopted on 27 June 1989 by the International Labour Organisation, and came into force on 5 September 1991. ILO Convention No. 169 has some articles that refer *specifically* to the rights of Indigenous children. Article 28 addresses the importance of children being able to read and write in their Indigenous language(s).[17] Article 29 protects the right of children to become informed of, and participate in, the customary ways of their people.[18]

ILO Convention No. 169 is influential in many ways. One underlying purpose of its appearance in 1989 was to remove 'the assimilationist orientation of the earlier standards',[19] a point also noted by commentators in this field (e.g. Barsh 1994: 43; 1990: 209–10; Anaya 2004: 58). It establishes a new way of understanding Indigenous rights in a framework of self-determination. Formerly, state policies pressed for the assimilation of Indigenous peoples into the dominant society and were highly resistant to seeing Indigenous peoples as having any distinctive rights of their own, that is, a resistance to recognising collective rights that were distinct to Indigenous Peoples (Barsh 1994: 43–45; Anaya 2004: 58–59). ILO Convention No. 169 stopped short of vesting Indigenous Peoples with recognition of them as 'Peoples' within the broader international framework. Recognising a group as 'Peoples' was seen as granting them access to the right of self-determination. Access to this right was resisted by states, as discussed in the previous section. The contentiousness of the use of the word 'Peoples' in the text of ILO Convention No. 169 was mediated by the assurance within the body of the Convention that its use did not convey any wider access to international rights, including the right to self-determination.[20] Even with that limitation within the Convention, the usage of the term 'Peoples' is seen as a critical shift in international law from assimilationist views to self-determinative

16 The states that have ratified ILO Convention No. 169 are: Argentina, Bolivia, Brazil, Chile, Colombia, Costa Rica, Denmark, Dominica, Ecuador, Fiji, Guatemala, Honduras, Mexico, Nepal, Netherlands, Norway, Paraguay, Peru, Spain, Bolivarian Republic of Venezuela.
17 '1. Children belonging to the peoples concerned shall, wherever practicable, be taught to read and write in their own Indigenous language or in the language most commonly used by the group to which they belong. When this is not practicable, the competent authorities shall undertake consultations with these peoples with a view to the adoption of measures to achieve this objective.
    2. Adequate measures shall be taken to ensure that these peoples have the opportunity to attain fluency in the national language or in one of the official languages of the country.
    3. Measures shall be taken to preserve and promote the development and practice of the Indigenous languages of the peoples concerned.' (ILO Convention No. 169, article 28).
18 'The imparting of general knowledge and skills that will help children belonging to the peoples concerned to participate fully and on an equal footing in their own community and in the national community shall be an aim of education for these peoples.' (ILO Convention No. 169, article 29).
19 ILO Convention No. 169, 4th preambular paragraph.
20 'The use of the term peoples in this Convention shall not be construed as having any implications as regards the rights which may attach to the term under international law'. (ILO Convention No. 169, article 1(3)).

views on what rights should be accessible to Indigenous Peoples (Anaya 2004: 58–61; Barsh 1990: 210 and 215; Barsh 1994: 43–45).

Barsh remarks that the importance of the ILO Convention was to move Indigenous Peoples from 'objects to subjects' within international law – that rather than being the passive recipients of grants of particular rights within international law, they were now given 'legal personality' (Barsh 1994: 35).

The current Special Rapporteur on the situation of human rights and fundamental freedoms of Indigenous people, Professor Anaya (see section 9.1), identifies the significance of ILO Convention No. 169 in his first report to UNHRC as being 'historically the first international organisation to promote specific international norms and policies regarding Indigenous peoples' (Anaya 2008: para. 31). His report further underscores the importance of ILO Convention No. 169 in recognising the collective rights of Indigenous peoples within international law:

> Convention No. 169 provides significant recognition of Indigenous peoples' collective rights in key areas, including cultural integrity; consultation and participation; self-government and autonomy; land, territory and resource rights; and non discrimination in the social and economic spheres.
>
> (Anaya 2008: para. 32)

9.4.3 The United Nations Declaration on the Rights of Indigenous Peoples of 2007 (UNDRIP)

There has been a great deal of activity at the United Nations on the rights of Indigenous people in the past 30 years. The United Nations formed the Working Group on Indigenous Populations in 1982. In the 1980s, another group within the United Nations structure was formed, the United Nations Permanent Forum on Indigenous Issues (UNPFII).[21] The purpose of the Permanent Forum is to offer advice to the United Nations Economic and Social Council on Indigenous matters.[22] The United Nations has also declared two 'International Decades of the World's Indigenous People', the first from 1994 to 2004 and the second from 2005 to 2015.

In many ways UNDRIP reflects a culmination of more advanced thinking about the location and role of Indigenous people within international law. It builds upon the standards set out in ILO Convention No. 169 and was itself a product of several years' work (Anaya 2008: para. 34). As with the ILO Convention discussed in section 9.4.2 above, there are some articles in UNDRIP that also make specific references to children; for example, a specific right against the forced removal of Indigenous children, linking such a removal to an

---

21 This has since (significantly) been renamed the United Nations Permanent Forum on Indigenous *Peoples* (UNPFII), though it retains the old acronym.

22 See the website of UNPFII, available at: http://www.un.org/esa/socdev/unpfii/en/about_us.html (accessed 1 February 2010).

act of genocide.[23] Article 14 of UNDRIP (similarly to articles 28 and 29 in ILO Convention No. 169) protects the right to use Indigenous languages and to make the learning and use of such languages accessible, even and perhaps especially to Indigenous peoples who live away from their own community.[24] There is also a provision specifically protecting children from economic exploitation.[25]

It should however be noted that UNDRIP, in contrast to the ILO Convention No. 169 discussed above, is not a binding instrument in international law. On the other hand, UNDRIP explicitly makes use of the term 'peoples' with full consciousness that its use indicates rights of self-determination. However, the definition of self-determination in UNDRIP has been given a particular meaning; in essence, a right of Indigenous peoples to internal self-governance rather than a means by which a separate state could be declared (Anaya 2008: paras 30, 37–38).[26] Anaya also offers his review on the compatibility of the relationship between ILO Convention No. 169 and UNDRIP:

> The United Nations Declaration reflects the existing international consensus regarding the individual and collective rights of Indigenous peoples in a way that is coherent with, and expands upon, the provisions of ILO Convention No 169, as well as other developments, including the interpretations of other human rights instruments by international bodies and mechanisms.
>
> (Anaya 2008: para. 43)

Far from charting new ground, then, Anaya's comments stress that UNDRIP has simply gathered up a disparate set of rights and concepts and put them into a single international instrument. UNDRIP may add depth or clarity to existing

---

23 'Indigenous peoples have the collective right to live in freedom, peace and security as distinct peoples and shall not be subjected to any act of genocide or any other act of violence, including forcibly removing children of the group to another group'. (UNDRIP 2007, article 7(2)).

24 '1. Indigenous peoples have the right to establish and control their educational systems and institutions providing education in their own languages, in a manner appropriate to their cultural methods of teaching and learning.

2. Indigenous individuals, particularly children, have the right to all levels and forms of education of the State without discrimination.

3. States shall, in conjunction with Indigenous peoples, take effective measures, in order for Indigenous individuals, particularly children, including those living outside their communities, to have access, when possible, to an education in their own culture and provided in their own language.' (UNDRIP, article 14).

25 'States shall in consultation and cooperation with Indigenous peoples take specific measures to protect Indigenous children from economic exploitation and from performing any work that is likely to be hazardous or to interfere with the child's education, or to be harmful to the child's health or physical, mental, spiritual, moral or social development, taking into account their special vulnerability and the importance of education for their empowerment.' (UNDRIP, article 17(2)). See also Chapter 3, section 3.5.8.3, for an account of how article 32 (economic exploitation) of the CRC is implemented.

26 See also the discussion on this point in section 9.2.4.

international standards, but does not in itself add new rights. UNDRIP can be seen as a reiteration of international norms on Indigenous peoples. Anaya also points out that the the Declaration addresses past abuses of Indigenous Peoples, serving a sort of curative role:

> The Declaration's preamble thus stresses the essentially remedial purpose of the instrument. Far from affirming special rights per se, the Declaration aims at repairing ongoing consequences of the historical denial of the right to self-determination and other basic rights.
>
> (Anaya 2008: para. 36)

9.5 Indigenous children's rights

An examination of Indigenous children's rights brings together two disparate sources of international law – that of Indigenous peoples' rights and that of children's rights. Both have their own instruments and, unsettled debates on their interpretation and application as well. Within this framework of multiple instruments can there be said to be a discernible body of rights for Indigenous children? It is submitted that there is a discernible body of Indigenous children's rights. But the exact content and meaning of these rights are not well defined. The rights of Indigenous children in international law can be gleaned from a combination of international legal instruments. But the issue of what those rights are, and how they are to be applied consistently with Indigenous peoples' rights, is at this point very much an open question.

This section discusses the interpretative debates on the best interests of the child standard and the rights of Indigenous children. Within the space of this chapter, it is not possible to give a thorough discussion of the debates and conflicts that exist within the possible permutations of rights for Indigenous children. However, to outline the potential conflicts in rights interpretation, the example of the best interests of the child standard is used to demonstrate conflicts over rights provisions for Indigenous children.

9.5.1 The 'best interests' principle[27] and Indigenous children's rights

The CtRC's General Comment No. 11 (2009) speaks extensively on the best interests of the child standard, as located in article 3 of the CRC,[28] to be applied

---

27 'In all actions concerning children, whether undertaken by public or private social welfare institutions, courts of law, administrative authorities or legislative bodies, the best interests of the child shall be a primary consideration'. (CRC, article 3(1)). See also Chapter 3, section 3.5.3.2 for an account of how the 'best interests' principle is viewed within the CtRC's reporting process.

28 Ibid.

to Indigenous children. The CtRC highlights the tension between the competing interpretations of individual and collective rights. Its interpretation leaves little room for Indigenous interpretations that might well differ from those of the state:

> The application of the best interests of the child to Indigenous children requires particular attention. The Committee notes that the best interests of the child is conceived both as a collective and individual right, and that the application of this right to Indigenous children as a group requires consideration of how the right relates to collective cultural rights ... the best interests of the child cannot be neglected or violated in preference for the best interests of the group.
>
> (General Comment No. 11, 2009: para. 30)

The Comment also provides that a consideration of the best interests of Indigenous children by states cannot be done without taking into account the cultural rights of the child and that these rights are not exercised by the child in isolation:

> When State authorities including legislative bodies seek to assess the best interests of an Indigenous child, they should consider the cultural rights of the Indigenous child and his or her need to exercise such rights collectively with members of their group.
>
> (General Comment No. 11, 2009, para. 31)

In its General Comment No. 11 (2009) the CtRC observes the need for 'particular attention' to be paid to applying the best interests principle to Indigenous children, in particular that it is conceived both as a collective and an individual right. It asserts that the plight of Indigenous children has been obscured by wider concerns of Indigenous peoples, for example, in relation to land rights and political representation. Importantly, the CtRC states that the best interests of the child 'cannot be neglected or violated in preference for the best interests of the group' (General Comment No. 11, 2009: para. 30). It goes on to assert that the state's approach to the assessment of the best interests of the Indigenous child should encompass the child's need to exercise his/her cultural rights collectively with members of the group. Furthermore, the Indigenous community should be consulted about intended legislation, policies and programmes affecting Indigenous children, and such participation should include, where possible, 'meaningful participation of Indigenous children' (General Comment No. 11, 2009: para. 31). Although the CtRC makes a distinction between the best interests of the individual child and the best interests of children as a group, it clearly prefers an approach to the interpretation of states' obligations under the CRC whereby the former will override the latter in cases of conflict, though conceding that 'the collective cultural rights of the child is part of determining the child's best interests' (General Comment No. 11, 2009: para. 32). Finally, the need to encourage states' active implementation of the best interests standard should also involve, the CtRC notes, a range of training and awareness-raising among relevant professionals about the importance of considering collective cultural rights along with the determination of the best interests of the child (General Comment No. 11, 2009: para. 33).

It is of note that the CtRC identifies the Indigenous rights as cultural – thus not giving recognition to the many other types of rights that are held by Indigenous Peoples.Whilst acknowledging that group rights do exist for Indigenous children, the approach presented in General Comment No. 11 does two things. First, it discounts the collective rights of the Indigenous People and of the child as subordinate to the individual rights of the child. It utilises an approach that elevates the rights of the individual over the rights of the group. This fails to provide recognition that collective rights can stand alongside and in parity with individual rights. Preference for individual over group rights is only an interpretive approach and not a hard-and-fast rule of international law. Second, an approach that only looks to the state as a source of rights (a 'statist' approach) is taken to determine the rights and best interests of the Indigenous child. The General Comment addresses the rights and interpretations that a state should provide, with some nod to consultation with the child's Indigenous group. It does not address, however, that the Indigenous group itself, through the right of self-determination, may well have its own definitions, rules, laws, customs, and legal or other governance systems that deal with the issue in a legal system parallel to a state legal sytem. Nor does the CtRC acknowledge that, through the right of self-determination, the recognition of these systems may be incumbent upon the state as a matter of binding international customary law. The extent to which the source of Indigenous children's rights at international law may be found within Indigenous peoples' self-governance or internal governance mechanisms, and the extent to which states might give recognition to these elements, are not explored in the CtRC's General Comment.

Libesmann challenges the wisdom of the approach taken by the CtRC, arguing instead that more emphasis should be placed upon the viewpoint of Indigenous people with regard to determining the best interests of the child. He asserts that 'Indigenous peoples are in a good position to know and understand their own experiences. They are therefore in a good position to inform understandings about what is in the best interests of Indigenous children' (Libesmann 2007: 307). The disparity between statist approaches to defining the best interests of a child and the ways in which Indigenous peoples may do so themselves is highlighted in ethnographic research by Hand. She questions 'whose values should guide child welfare politics and practices' (Hand 2006 : 22). This challenges the unspoken assumptions made in General Comment No. 11 that the *state's* interpretations of the best interests of the child should predominate. Hand comments that 'it seems antithetical to impose one Euro-American child welfare paradigm on more than 500 culturally diverse First Nations communities' (Hand 2006: 22).

Hand's research shows that the Ojibwe culture can be seen to be more than simply a relic of the past. It is something that is seen as profoundly important to the survival of the Ojibwe people and is still very much a part of their present-day lives. Yet the vitality and importance of the practices of the Ojibwe people must exist alongside a state system which does not even see or recognise it and where state 'decision-makers sincerely believe there is no longer a culture' (Hand 2006: 40).

The recognition of 'collective cultural rights', called for in the interpretation of the best interests of the child standard in General Comment No. 11 (2009: paras 30–33), does not give sufficient credence to the place that a child's Indigenous culture plays in its life. Offering a statist view of culture may in fact overlie the belief that Hand's research revealed, namely the view that there is no culture. If Indigenous peoples were to give their view of the best interests of the child, Hand's research suggests that it would be based upon very different criteria than from a statist and Euro-influenced view.

Through the operation of the self-determination principle (see section 9.2.4) as is now located and defined within international law, Indigenous peoples may utilise this international law principle to gain recognition for their own body of rights for Indigenous children. That there is room for conflict between Indigenous interpretations of such rights and non-Indigenous interpretations is made clear in Hand's research. Ignoring Indigenous interpretations in favour of more individual, state-centred rights interpretations may do damage to Indigenous children's wellbeing; a point that is given little consideration in the CtRC's General Comment No.11. Future consideration of the rights of Indigenous children at international law must ensure that Indigenous interpretations are given due consideration.

9.6 Conclusion

As there continue to be developments in international law both on Indigenous people's rights and on children's rights, so will there be a growing focus on Indigenous children's rights. Further specific statements that clarify their rights are likely to appear in the future. The tension between collective and individual rights – an ongoing debate within international human rights law generally – takes on a poignant focus when we consider the rights specifically of Indigenous children. The changes that have been brought about in international law regarding Indigenous peoples are significant. Indigenous peoples' rights have an arguable claim as having attained the status of binding customary international law, a far different status than that of the doctrine of *terra nullius* used as the pretext for takeover and conquest of Indigenous lands and peoples in the past.

There remain areas of unresolved interpretation in Indigenous children's law. At one level, these are the challenges of realising the rights in the CRC for all children including Indigenous children. At another level, these reverberate in the ongoing tensions over the delivery of individual rights and the place of collective rights in international human rights law. Whilst there are statements that the rights of the individual child should be preferred over the rights of the Indigenous group as a collective, there are also sharp challenges to that view. Other unresolved debates on the interpretation of human rights also will likely sound in questions about the interpretation of Indigenous people's rights and the rights of Indigenous children. Are the rights of Indigenous people available to Indigenous children as children – is there a clash between the rights of children at international law and the rights of Indigenous children within an Indigenous rights framework? There are likely to be continued debates and developments and changes within international law on the subject of both international rights for Indigenous people and the rights of Indigenous children in international law.

Bibliography

Abernethie, L. (1998) 'Child labour in contemporary society: Why do we care?', 6(1) *International Journal of Children's Rights* 81–114.

Adjami, M.E. (2002) 'African Courts and Human Rights', abstracted from: Mirna E. Adjami, 'African Courts, International Law, and Comparative Case Law: Chimera or Emerging Human Rights Jurisprudence?', 24(1) *Michigan Journal of International Law* 103–67.

Agarwal, R.K. (2004) 'The Barefoot Lawyers: Prosecuting Child Labour in the Supreme Court of India', 21(2) *Arizona Journal of International & Comparative Law* 663–713.

Akdeniz, Y. (1998) 'The European Union and illegal and harmful content on the Internet', 3(1) *Journal of Civil Liberties* 31–36.

Akdeniz, Y. (2008) *Internet Child Pornography and the Law: National and International Responses*, Aldershot: Ashgate Publishing.

Akehurst, M. (1974) 'Custom as a source of international law', (1974–75) 47 *British Yearbook of International Law*, pp. i–xxx.

Alexander, S., Meuwese, S. and Wolthuis, A. (2000) 'Policies and Developments relating to the Sexual Exploitation of Children: The Legacy of the Stockholm Conference', 8(4) *European Journal on Criminal Policy and Research* 479–501.

Allain, J. (2008) *The Slavery Conventions: The Travaux Préparatoires of the 1926 League of Nations Convention and the 1956 United Nations Convention*, Leiden/Boston: Martinus Nijhoff.

Alston, P. (1989) 'Implementing Children's Rights: The Case of Child Labour', 58(1) *Nordic Journal of International Law* 35–53.

Alston, P. (2004) '"Core Labour Standards" and the Transformation of the International Labour Rights Regime', 15(3) *European Journal of International Law* 457–521.

Alston, P. and Crawford, J. (eds) (2000) *The Future of UN Human Rights Treaty Monitoring*, Cambridge: Cambridge University Press.

American Anthropological Association (1947) 'Statement on Human Rights', Executive Board, American Anthropological Association, 49(4) *American Anthropologist* 539–43.

Anaya, S.J. (1993) 'A Contemporary Definition of the International Norm of Self-Determination', 3(1) *Transnational Law and Contemporary Problems* 131–64.

Anaya, S.J. (2004) *Indigenous Peoples in International Law*, Second Edition, Oxford: Oxford University Press.

Anaya, S.J. (2007) 'Indigenous Law and its Contribution to Global Pluralism', 6(1) *Indigenous Law Journal* 3–12.

Anaya, S.J. (2008) *Report of the Special Rapporteur on the Situation of Human Rights and Fundamental Freedoms of Indigenous People*, Human Rights Council, Ninth session, A/HRC/9/9, 11 August 2008.

Anker, R. (2000) 'The economics of child labour: a framework for measurement', 139(3) *International Labour Review* 257–80.

Anti-Slavery International (2009) 'Forced child begging in Senegal', July 2009, Information on Senegal, Compliance with ILO Convention No.182 on the Worst Forms of Child Labour (ratified in 2000). London: Anti-Slavery International.

Archard, D. (1993) *Children: Rights and Childhood*, London: Routledge.

Ariès, P. (1962) *Centuries of Childhood*, London: Cape.

Arnstein, S.R. (1969) 'Eight rungs on the ladder of citizen participation', 35(4) *Journal of the American Institute of Planners* 216–24.

Bakirci, K. (2002) 'Child labour and legislation in Turkey', 10(1) *International Journal of Children's Rights* 55–72.

Barsh, R.L. (1990) 'An Advocate's Guide to the Convention on Indigenous and Tribal Peoples', 15(1) *Oklahoma City University Law Review* 209–36.

Barsh, R.L. (1994) 'Indigenous Peoples in the 1990s: From Object to Subject of International Law?', 7 *Harvard Human Rights Journal* 33–86.

Bauer, J.R. and Bell, D.L. (eds) (1999) *The East Asian Challenge for Human Rights,* Cambridge: Cambridge University Press.

Beaulieu, C. (2008) *Extraterritorial Laws: Why they are not working and how they canbe strengthened*, Bangkok: ECPAT International. Available at: http://www.ecpat.net/world congressIII/PDF/Journals/EXTRATERRITORIAL_LAWS.pdf (accessed 27 January 2010).

Beaumont, P. and McEleavy, P. (1999) *The Hague Convention on International Child Abduction*, Oxford: Oxford University Press.

Besson, S. (2005) 'The Principle of Non-Discrimination in the Convention on the Rights of the Child', 13(4) *International Journal of Children's Rights* 433–61.

Betcherman, G., Fares, J., Luinstra, A. and Prouty, R. (2004) 'Child labor, Education, and Children's Rights', Social Protection Discussion Paper Series, No. 0412, Washington, DC: The World Bank.

Bevan, H. (1989) *Child Law*, London: Butterworths.

Black, M. (1996) *Children First: The Story of UNICEF, Past and Present*, Oxford: Oxford University Press.

Blagbrough, J. (1997) 'Eliminating the worst forms of child labour – a new international standard', 5(1) *International Journal of Children's Rights* 123–27.

Bonnet, M. (1993) 'Child labour in Africa', 132(3) *International Labour Review* 371–89.

Bouhdiba, A, (1982) *Exploitation of Child Labour,* E/CN.4/Sub.2/479/Rev.l, U.N., Sales No. E.82.XIV.2, United Nations, New York: United Nations.

Boyden, J. (1997) 'Childhood and the Policy Makers: A Comparative Perspective on the Globalization of Childhood', in James, A. and Prout, A. (eds) pp. 187–226.

Breuning, M. and Ishiyama, J. (2009) 'The Politics of Intercountry Adoption: Explaining Variation in the Legal Requirements of Sub-Saharan African Countries', 7(1) *Perspective on Politics* 89–101.

Briggs, L. and Marre, D. (eds) (2009) *International Adoption: Global Inequities and the Circulation of Children*, New York: New York University Press.

Browne, K. and Chou, S. (2008) 'Child Rights and International Adoption: A Response to Critics', 32(2) *Adoption and Fostering* 69–74.

Brownlie, I. (2008) *Public International Law*, Seventh Edition, Oxford: Oxford University Press.

Buchanan, A. (1993) 'The Role of Collective Rights in the Theory of Indigenous Peoples' Rights', 3(1) *Transnational Law and Contemporary Legal Problems* 89–108.

Buck, T. (2008) 'International Criminalisation and Child Welfare Protection: the Optional Protocol to the Convention on the Rights of the Child', 22(3) *Children & Society* 167–78.

Burnett, J. (1983) 'The History of Childhood', 33(12) *History Today* 1–6.

Burra, N. (1995) *Born to Work: Child Labour in India*, India: OUP.

Campbell, T. (1992) 'The Rights of the Minor' in Alston, P., Parker, S. and Seymour, J. (eds) *Children, Rights and the Law*, Oxford: Clarendon Press.

Cantwell, N. (1992) 'The origins, development and significance of the United Nations Convention on the Rights of the Child', in Detrick, S. (ed.) (1992), pp. 19–30.

CCPR (1989) *General Comment No. 17: Rights of the child (Art. 24)*, in 'Report of the Human Rights Committee', General Assembly, Forty-fourth session, SUPPLEMENT No. 40 (A/44/40), New York: United Nations, Annex VI, pp. 173-75. Available at: http://daccess-dds-ny.un.org/doc/UNDOC/GEN/N89/229/15/IMG/N8922915. pdf?OpenElement (accessed 18 May 2010). 7 April 1989.

CEACR (1981) *General Survey by the Committee of Experts on the Application of Conventions and Recommendations: Minimum Age*, ILO, sixty-seventh session, Report III, pt 4B, Geneva: International Labour Office.

CEACR (2009) *General Report of the Committee of Experts on the Application of Conventions and Recommendations* 2009, International Labour Conference, ninety-eighth session, Geneva: International Labour Office. Available at: http://www.ilo.org/ilolex/gbe/ceacr2009.htm (accessed 7 January 2010).

CEACR (2009a) *General Observation concerning Convention No. 138*, International Labour Conference, ninety-eighth session, Geneva: International Labour Office. Available at: http://www.ilo.org/ilolex/gbe/ceacr2009.htm (accessed 7 January 2010).

Cedrangolo, U. (2009) 'The Optional Protocol to the Convention on the Rights of the Child on the sale of children, child prostitution and child pornography and the jurisprudence of the Committee on the Rights of the Child', Innocenti Working Paper No. 2009-03, Florence: UNICEF Innocenti Research Centre. Available at: http://www.unicef-irc.org/publications/pdf/iwp_2009_03.pdf (accessed 27 January 2010).

Champagne, D. (1993) 'Beyond Assimilation as a Strategy for National Integration: The Persistence of American Indian Political Identities', 3(1) *Transnational Law and Contemporary Problems* 109–129.

Chase, E. and Statham, J. (2005) 'Commercial and Sexual Exploitation of Children and Young People in the UK – A Review', 14(1) *Child Abuse Review* 4–25.

Chiancone, J. (2001) *Parental Abduction: A Review of the Literature*, UD Department of Justice, Office of Justice Programs/Office of Juvenile Justice and Delinquency Prevention. Available at: http://www.ncjrs.gov/html/ojjdp/190074/index.html (accessed 20 January 2010).

Chiancone, J., Girdner, L. and Hoff, P. (2001) 'Issues in Resolving Cases of International Child Abduction', *Juvenile Justice Bulletin*, December 2001, Washington DC: Office of Juvenile Justice and Delinquency Prevention. Available at: http://www.ncjrs.gov/pdffiles1/ojjdp/190105.pdf (accessed 15 May 2010).

Chief Secretary to the Treasury (2003) *Every Child Matters*, Cm 5860, London: The Stationery Office.

Chou, S. and Browne, K. (2008) 'The Relationship between Institutional Care and the International Adoption of Children in Europe' (2008) 32(1) *Adoption and Fostering* 40–48.

Choy, C.C. (2007) 'Institutionalizing International Adoption: The Historical Origins of Korean Adoption in the United States', in Bergquist, K.J.S., Vonk, M.E., Kim, D.S. and Feit, M.D. (eds) *International Korean Adoption: A Fifty-Year History of Policy and Practice*, Binghamton, NY: Haworth Press, pp. 25–42.

CO Argentina (2002) *Concluding Observation: Argentina's Second Periodic Report,* Committee on the Rights of the Child, UNCRC/C/15/Add.187, 9 October 2002.

CO Bangladesh (2009) *Concluding Observation: Bangladesh's Third/Fourth Periodic Report,* Committee on the Rights of the Child, UNCRC/C/BGD/CO/4, 26 June 2009.

CO Bolivia (2009) *Concluding Observation: Bolivia's Fourth Periodic Report*, Committee on the Rights of the Child, UNCRC/C/BOL/CO/4, 2 October 2009.

CO Botswana (2004) *Concluding Observation: Botswana's Initial Report*, Committee on the Rights of the Child, UNCRC/C/15/Add.242, 1 October 2004.

CO Chad (2009) *Concluding Observation: Chad's Second Periodic Report*, Committee on the Rights of the Child, UNCRC/C/TCD/CO/2, 12 February 2009.

CO Congo (2009) *Concluding Observation: Democratic Republic of Congo's Second Periodic Report*, Committee on the Rights of the Child, UNCRC/C/COD/CO/2, 10 February 2009.

CO El Salvador (2004) *Concluding Observation: El Salvador's Second Periodic Report*, Committee on the Rights of the Child, UNCRC/C/15/Add.232, 4 June 2004.

CO Equatorial Guinea (2004) *Concluding Observation: Equatorial Guinea's Initial Report*, Committee on the Rights of the Child, UNCRC/C/15/Add.245, 1 October 2004.

CO France (2004) *Concluding Observation: France's Second Periodic Report*, Committee on the Rights of the Child, UNCRC/C/15/Add.240, 4 June 2004.

CO France (2009) *Concluding Observation: France's Third/Fourth Periodic Report*, Committee on the Rights of the Child, UNCRC/C/FRA/CO/4, 11 June 2009.

CO India (2003) *Concluding Observation: India's Second Periodic Report*, Committee on the Rights of the Child, UNCRC/C/93/Add.5, 16 July 2003.

CO Indonesia (2004) *Concluding Observation: Indonesia's Second Periodic Report*, Committee on the Rights of the Child, UNCRC/C/15/Add.223, 30 January 2004.

CO Kyrgyzstan (2004) *Concluding Observation: Kyrgyzstan's Second Periodic Report*, Committee on the Rights of the Child, CRC/C/15/Add.244, 1 October 2004.

CO Malawi (2009) *Concluding Observation: Malawi's Second Periodic Report*, Committee on the Rights of the Child, UNCRC/C/MWI/CO/2, 27 March 2009.

CO Mauritania (2009) *Concluding Observation: Mauritania's Second Periodic Report*, Committee on the Rights of the Child, UNCRC/C/MRT/CO/2, 17 June 2009.

CO Moldova (2009) *Concluding Observation: Republic of Moldova's Second/Third Periodic Report*, Committee on the Rights of the Child, UNCRC/C/MDA/CO/3, 20 February 2009.

CO Mozambique (2009) *Concluding Observation: Mozambique's Second Periodic Report*, Committee on the Rights of the Child, UNCRC/C/MOZ/CO/2, October 2009.

CO Netherlands (2009) *Concluding Observation: Netherlands' Third Periodic Report*, Committee on the Rights of the Child, UNCRC/C/NLD/CO/3, 27 March 2009.

CO Niger (2009) *Concluding Observation: Niger's Second Periodic Report*, Committee on the Rights of the Child, UNCRC/C/NER/CO/2, 18 June 2009.

CO North Korea (2004) *Concluding Observation: Democratic People's Republic of Korea's Second Periodic Report*, Committee on the Rights of the Child, CRC/C/15/Add.239, 4 June 2004.

CO North Korea (2009) *Concluding Observation: Democratic People's Republic of Korea's Third/Fourth Periodic Report*, Committee on the Rights of the Child, UNCRC/ C/PRK/CO/4, 27 March 2009.

CO Pakistan (2003) *Concluding Observation: Pakistan's Second Periodic Report*, Committee on the Rights of the Child, UNCRC/C/15/Add.217, 27 October 2003.

CO Pakistan (2009) *Concluding Observation: Pakistan's Third/Fourth Periodic Report*, Committee on the Rights of the Child, UNCRC/C/PAK/CO/3-4, 15 October 2009.

CO Philippines (2009) *Concluding Observation: Philippines' Third/Fourth Periodic Report*, Committee on the Rights of the Child, UNCRC/C/PHL/CO/3-4, 2 October 2009.

CO Qatar (2009) *Concluding Observation: Qatar's Second Periodic Report*, Committee on the Rights of the Child, UNCRC/C/QAT/CO/2 14 October 2009.

CO Romania (2009) *Concluding Observation: Romania's Third/Fourth Periodic Report*, Committee on the Rights of the Child, UNCRC/C/ROM/CO/4, 12 June 2009.

CO Rwanda (2004) *Concluding Observation: Rwanda's Second Periodic Report*, Committee on the Rights of the Child, UNCRC/C/15/Add.234, 4 June 2004.

CO Sweden (2009) *Concluding Observation: Sweden's Fourth Periodic Report*, Committee on the Rights of the Child, UNCRC/C/SWE/CO/4, 12 June 2009.

CO United Kingdom (1995) *Concluding Observation: United Kingdom's Initial Report*, Committee on the Rights of the Child, UNCRC/C/15/Add.34, 15 February 1995.

CO United Kingdom (2002) *Concluding Observation: United Kingdom's Second Periodic Report*, Committee on the Rights of the Child, UNCRC/C/15/Add.188, 9 October 2002.

CO United Kingdom (2008) *Concluding Observation: United Kingdom's Third/Fourth Periodic Report*, Committee on the Rights of the Child, UNCRC/C/GBR/CO/4, 20 October 2008.

CO United Kingdom OPAC (2008) *Concluding observations of United Kingdom's initial report under article 8 of the Optional Protocol on the Involvement of Children in Armed Conflict*, Committee on the Rights of the Child, UNCRC/C/OPAC/GBR/CO/1, 17 October 2008.

Committee on the Rights of the Child (1991) *General guidelines regarding the form and content of initial reports to be submitted by States Parties under article 44, paragraph 1(a), of the Convention*, CRC/C/5, First Session, 30 October 1991. Available at: <http://www.unhchr.ch/tbs/doc.nsf/(Symbol)/CRC.C.5.En?Opendocument> (accessed 4 November 2009).

Committee on the Rights of the Child (1995) *General guidelines regarding the form and content of periodic reports to be submitted by states parties under article 44, paragraph 1(b), of the Convention*, CRC/C/58/Rev.1., Thirty-ninth session, 29 November 2005. Available at: <http://www.unhchr.ch/tbs/doc.nsf/(Symbol)/CRC.C.58. Rev.1.En?Opendocument> (accessed 4 November 2009).

Committee on the Rights of the Child (1995a) *Guidelines for the participation of partners (NGOs and individual experts) in the pre-sessional working group of the committee on the rights of the child* (in 'Annex VIII' of CRC's Report on the 22nd session, 7 December 1999, CRC/C/90, at p.111). Available at: <http://www.unhchr.ch/tbs/ doc.nsf/(Symbol)/da0ac735120e0703802568b20052b0c6?Opendocument> (accessed 4 November 2009).

Committee on the Rights of the Child (2005) *Provisional Rules of Procedure*, CRC/C/4/ Rev.1, 25 April 2005. Available at: <http://www.unhchr.ch/tbs/doc.nsf/(Symbol)/ CRC.C.4.Rev.1.En?OpenDocument> (accessed 4 November 2009).

Committee on the Rights of the Child (2009) 'Working Methods: Overview of the working methods of the Committee on the Rights of the Child', CtRC website document.

Available at: http://www2.ohchr.org/english/bodies/crc/workingmethods.htm (accessed 20 December 2009).

Cooper, J. (1997) 'Child Labour: legal regimes, market pressures, and the search for meaningful solutions', 52(3) *International Journal* 411–30.

Cordova, E. (1993) 'Some Reflections on the Overproduction of International Labour Standards', 14(2) *Comparative Labor Law Journal* 138–62.

Corntassel, J. (2003) 'Who is Indigenous? "Peoplehood" and Ethnonationalist Approaches to Rearticulating Indigenous Identity', 9(1) *Nationalism and Ethnic Politics* 75–100.

Corsaro, W. (2005) *The Sociology of Childhood*, Second Edition, London: Sage.

Council of the European Union (2007) *EU Guidelines for the Promotion and Protection of the Rights of the Child*, Brussels: Council of the European Union. Available at: <http://www.consilium.europa.eu/uedocs/cmsUpload/16031.07.pdf> (accessed 2 November 2009).

Council of the European Union (2008) *Annual Report on Human Rights for 2008*, Council of the European Union, 14146/2/08 REV 2, COHOM 105, Brussels, 27 November 2008. Available at: <http://www.consilium.europa.eu/uedocs/cmsUpload/st14146-re02.en08.pdf> (accessed 3 November 2009).

Craven, S., Brown, S. and Gilchrist, E. (2006) 'Sexual Grooming of Children: Review of the Literature and Theoretical Considerations', 12(3) *Journal of Sexual Aggression* 287–99.

Crawford, J. (2000) 'The UN Human Rights Treaty System: A System in Crisis?', in Alston, P. and Crawford, J. (eds), pp. 1–15.

Crawford, S. (2000) *The Worst Forms of Child Labour: A Guide to Understanding and Using the New Convention*, London: Department for International Development.

Creighton, B. (1997) 'Combating Child Labour: The Role of International Labour Standards', 18(3) *Comparative Labor Law Journal* 362–96.

Cullen, H. (1999) 'The limits of international trade mechanisms in enforcing human rights: the case of child labour', 7(1) *International Journal of Children's Rights* 1–29.

Cummins, S.J. (2008) *Digest of United States Practice in International Law 2007*, USA: Oxford University Press.

Cunningham, H. (2005) *Children and Childhood in Western Society since 1500*, Second Edition, Harlow: Pearson Education Ltd.

Cunningham, H. (2006) *The Invention of Childhood*, London: BBC Books.

Dachi, H. and Garrett, R. (2003) *Child Labour and its Impact on Children's Access to and Participation in Primary Education: A Case Study from Tanzania*, No. 48, Education Papers, London: Department for International Development.

Davidson, M.G. (2001) 'The International Labour Organization's Latest Campaign to End Child Labour: Will it Succeed Where Others Have Failed?', 11(1) *Transnational Law & Contemporary Problems* 203–24.

Day of Discussion (1992) *Children in Armed Conflicts*, CRC/C/10, 2nd Session, 19 October 1992.

Day of Discussion (1993) *Economic exploitation*, CRC/C/20, 8 October 1993.

Day of Discussion (1994) *The Role of the Family in the Promotion of the Rights of the Child*, CRC/C/34, 14 October 1994.

Day of Discussion (1995) *The Girl Child*, Committee on the Rights of the Child, UNCRC/C/38, 8th Session, 21 January 1995.

Day of Discussion (1995a) *Juvenile Justice*, Committee on the Rights of the Child, excerpted from UNCRC/C/43, Annex VIII, 10th Session, 13 November 1995.

Day of Discussion (1996) *The Child and the Media*, CRC/C/15/Add.65, 1996.

Day of Discussion (1997) *Children with Disabilities*, Committee on the Rights of the Child, UNCRC/C/66, Annex V, 16th Session, 6 October 1997.

Day of Discussion (1998) *Children living in a world with HIV/AIDS*, Committee on the Rights of the Child, CRC/C/80, 19th Session, 5 October 1998.

Day of Discussion (1999) *Tenth Anniversary: General Measures of Implementation*, Committee on the Rights of the Child, CRC/C/90, 22nd session, 30 September and 1 October 1999.

Day of Discussion (2000) *State Violence against Children*, Committee on the Rights of the Child, excerpted from CRC/C/97, 25th Session, 22 September 2000.

Day of Discussion (2001) *Violence against Children, Within the Family and in Schools*, Committee on the Rights of the Child, excerpted from CRC/C/111, 28th Session, 28 September 2001.

Day of Discussion (2002) *The Private Sector as Service Provider and its Role in Implementing Child Rights*, Committee on the Rights of the Child, excerpted from CRC/C/121, 31st Session, 20 September 2002.

Day of Discussion (2003) *The Rights of Indigenous Children*, Committee on the Rights of the Child, 34th Session, 15 September–3 October 2003.

Day of Discussion (2004) *Implementing Child Rights in Early Childhood*, 17 September 2004 (Summary record: CRC/C/SR.979, 22 September 2004).

Day of Discussion (2005) *Children without Parental Care*, 40th Session, CRC/C/153, 17 March 2006.

Day of Discussion (2006) *The Right of the Child to be Heard,* 43rd Session, 29 September 2006.

Day of Discussion (2007) *Resources for the Rights of the Child—Responsibility of States*, 46th Session, 5 October 2007.

Day of Discussion (2008) *The Right of the Child to Education in Emergency Situations*, Committee on the Rights of the Child, 49 Session, 15 September–3 October 2008.

DCSF (2009) *The protection of children in England: action plan—The Government's response to Lord Laming* (Cm 7589), Department for Children, Schools and Families, May 2009, London: The Stationery Office.

De Mause, L. (ed.) (1976) *The History of Childhood*, London: Souvenir Press.

Demetriou, A., Efklides, A. and Platsidou, M. (2000) *The Architecture and Dynamics of Developing Mind: Experiential Structuralism as a Frame for Unifying Cognitive Developmental Theories*, Monographs for the Society of Research in Child Development, Serial No. 234, Vol. 58, Nos 5–6, 1993, London: Wiley Blackwell.

Dennis, M.J. (1999) 'The ILO Convention on the Worst Forms of Child Labour', 93(4) *American Journal of International Law* 943–48.

Detrick, S. (ed.) (1992) *The United Nations Convention on the Rights of the Child: A Guide to the 'Travaux préparatoires'*, Dordrecht/Boston/Norwell: Martinus Nijhoff Publishers.

Detrick, S. (1999) *A Commentary on the United Nations Convention on the Rights of the Child*, The Hague/Boston/London: Martinus Nijhoff Publishers.

DHSS (1974) *Report of the Committee of Inquiry into the care and supervision provided in relation to Maria Colwell*, Department of Health and Social Security, London: The Stationery Office.

Doek, J.E. (2003) 'The Protection of Children's Rights and the United Nations Convention on the Rights of the Child: Achievements and Challenges', 22(2) *Saint Louis University Public Law Review* 235–52.

DoH (2000) *Adoption: A New Approach*, White Paper, Cm 5017, Secretary of State for Health, London: The Stationery Office.

Don Nanjira, D. (2003) 'The protection of human rights in Africa: The African Charter on Human Rights and People's Rights', in Symonides, J. (ed.) *Human Rights: International Protection, Monitoring, Enforcement*, Aldershot: Ashgate/UNESCO.

Donnelly, J. (1984) 'Cultural Relativism and Human Rights', 6(4) *Human Rights Quarterly* 400–19.

Dorman, P. (2001) *Child labour in the developed economies*, ILO/IPEC working paper, Geneva: ILO/IPEC.

Dorman, P. (2008) *Child labour, education and health: A review of the literature*, International Programme on the Elimination of Child Labour (IPEC), Geneva: International Labour Office.

Douglas, G. (1992) 'The Retreat from Gillick', 55(4) *Modern Law Review* 569.

Dow, U. (1998) 'Birth registration: the "first" right', in UNICEF, *The Progress of Nations*, pp. 5–11, New York: UNICEF.

Dubinsky, K. (2008) 'The Fantasy of the Global Cabbage Patch: Making Sense of Transnational Adoption', 9(3) *Feminist Theory* 339–45.

Durban Declaration and Programme of Action (2001) *Declaration and Programme of Action*, adopted at the World Conference against Racism, Racial Discrimination, Xenophobia and Related Intolerance 2001. Durban, South Africa, from 31 August to 8 September 2001. Available at: http://www.un.org/WCAR/durban.pdf (accessed 22 December 2009).

DWP (2003) *Measuring Child Poverty*, Department for Work and Pensions, London: The Stationery Office.

Edmonds, E.E. (2008) *Defining child labour: A review of the definitions of child labour in policy research*, Working paper, International Programme on the Elimination of Child Labour (IPEC), Geneva: International Labour Office.

Eekelaar, J. (1986) 'The emergence of children's rights', (1986) 6(2) *Oxford Journal of Legal Studies* 161–82.

Eekelaar, J. (2004) 'Children between Cultures', 18(2) *International Journal on Law, Policy and the Family* 178–94.

English, J. (1997) ' "Imitating the cries of little children": exploitative child labour and the growth of children's rights', 52(3) *International Journal* 431–44.

Ennew, J. (2008) Conference on Children's Rights, Presentation, Swansea University, 19 September 2008.

Europol (2009) *Ten Years of Europol: 1999–2009*, The Hague, Netherlands: Europol. Available at: http://www.europol.europa.eu/publications/Anniversary_Publication/Anniversary_publication.pdf (accessed 8 February 2010).

Eva, B. (2006) 'Above Children's Heads: The Headscarf Controversy in European Schools from the Perspective of Children's Rights', 14(2) *The International Journal of Children's Rights* 119–36.

Everall, M. and Nicholls, M. (2002) 'Brussels I and II—the impact on family law' [2002] *Family Law* 674–82.

Feinberg, J. (1980) *Rights, Justice and the Bounds of Liberty:* essays in social philosophy, Princeton, New Jersey: Princeton University Press.

First World Congress (1996) *Declaration and Agenda for Action*, 1st World Congress against Commercial Sexual Exploitation of Children, Stockholm, Sweden, 27–31

August 1996. Available at: http://csecworldcongress.org/en/stockholm/Outcome/index. htm (accessed 28 January 2010).

Fleck, D. (2008) *The Handbook of International Humanitarian Law*, Second Edition, Oxford: Oxford University Press.

Fortin, J. (2003) *Children's Rights and the Developing Law*, Second Edition, Cambridge: Cambridge University Press.

Fortin, J. (2006) 'Accommodating Children's Rights in a Post Human Rights Act Era' 69(3) *Modern Law Review* 299–326.

Fortin, J. (2009) *Children's Rights and the Developing Law*, Third Edition, Cambridge: Cambridge University Press.

Fox Harding, L. (1996) *Family, State and Social Policy*, Basingstoke: Macmillan.

Freeman, M. (2003) *The Outcomes for Children Returned Following an Abduction*, Reunite research unit, Leicester: International Child Abduction Centre.

Freeman, M. (2006) *International Child Abduction: The Effects*, Reunite research unit, Leicester: International Child Abduction Centre.

Freeman, M. (2009) *UK–Pakistan Protocol on Children Matters*, Reunite research unit, Leicester: International Child Abduction Centre.

Freeman, M. (2009a) 'When the 1980 Hague Child Abduction Convention does not Apply: The UK–Pakistan Protocol, *International Family Law* 181–85.

Freeman, M.D.A. (1983) *The Rights and Wrongs of Children*, London: Continuum International Publishing.

Freeman, M.D.A. (1992) 'The limits of children's rights', in Freeman, M. and Veerman, P. (eds) *The Ideologies of Children's Rights*, Dordrecht/Boston/London: Martinus Nijhoff Publishers.

Freeman, M.D.A. (2007) 'Why it Remains Important to Take Children's Rights Seriously', 15(1) *International Journal of Children's Rights* 5–23.

G8 (2003) *Justice and Home Affairs ministerial meeting—Paris, 5 May: President's Summary*. Available online at: http://www.g8.fr/evian/english/navigation/news/news_ update/justice_and_home_affairs_ministerial_meeting_-_paris__5_may_2003/final_ official_statement_-_presidents_summary.html (accessed 30 January 2010).

G8 (2009) *Final Declaration*, Ministers of Justice and Home Affairs, Rome, 30 May 2009. Available at: http://www.g8italia2009.it/static/G8_Allegato/declaration1giu2009,0.pdf (accessed 28 January 2010).

Gay y Blasco, P., Macrae, S., Selman, P. and Wardle, H. (2008) 'The Relationship between Institutional Care and the International Adoption of Children in Europe: A Rejoinder to Chou and Browne', 32(2) *Adoption and Fostering* 63–67.

GCO (2008) *Corporate Citizenship in the World Economy*, United Nations Global Compact Office, New York: UN Global Compact Office. Available at: http://www. unglobalcompact.org/docs/news_events/8.1/GC_brochure_FINAL.pdf (accessed 14 January 2010).

General Comment No. 1 (2001) *The Aims of Education*, Committee on the Rights of the Child, UNCRC/GC/2001/1, Twenty-sixth session, 17 April 2001.

General Comment No. 2 (2002) *The Role of Independent National Human Rights Institutions in the Promotion and Protection of the Rights of the Child*, UNCRC/ GC/2002/2, Thirty-first session, 15 November 2002.

General Comment No. 3 (2003) *HIV/AIDS and the Rights of the Child*, UNCRC/GC/2003/3, Thirty-second session, 17 March 2003.

General Comment No. 4 (2003) *Adolescent Health and Development in the Context of the Convention on the Rights of the Child*, Thirty-third session, UNCRC/GC/2003/4, 1 July 2003.

General Comment No. 5 (2003) *General Measures of Implementation of the Convention on the Rights of the Child (Arts 4, 42 and 44, para 6)*, UNCRC/GC/2003/5, Thirty-fourth session, 27 November 2003.

General Comment No. 6 (2005) *Treatment of unaccompanied and separated children outside their country of origin*, CRC/GC/2005/6, Thirty-ninth session, 1 September 2005.

General Comment No. 7 (2005) *Implementing child rights in early childhood*, CRC/C/GC/7/Rev.1, Fortieth session, 20 September 2006.

General Comment No. 8 (2006) *The right of the child to protection from corporal punishment and other cruel or degrading forms of punishment (arts 19; 28, para. 2; and 37, inter alia)*, CRC/C/GC/8, Forty-second session, 2 March 2007.

General Comment No. 9 (2006) *The rights of children with disabilities*, CRC/C/GC/9, Forty-third session, 27 February 2007.

General Comment No. 10 (2007) *Children's rights in juvenile justice*, CRC/C/GC/10, Forty-fourth session, 25 April 2007.

General Comment No. 11 (2009) *Indigenous children and their rights under the Convention*, CRC/C/GC/11, Fiftieth session, 12 February 2009. Available at: http://www2.ohchr.org/english/bodies/crc/docs/CRC.GC.C.11.pdf (accessed 31 January 2010).

General Comment No. 12 (2009) *The right of the child to be heard*, CRC/C/GC/12, Fifty-first session, 20 July 2009.

Germany (2003) *Second Report: Germany*, UNCRC/C/83/Add.7, 24 July 2003.

Gill, T. (2007) *No Fear: Growing up in a risk averse society*, London: Calouste Gulbenkian Foundation.

Gillespie, A.A. (2002) 'Child Protection on the Internet: Challenges for Criminal Law', 14(4) *Child and Family Law Quarterly*, 411–26.

Gillespie, A.A. (2007) 'Diverting Children Involved in Prostitution', [2007] 2 *Web Journal of Current Legal Issues*, published 27 April 2007. Available online at: http://webjcli.ncl.ac.uk/2007/issue2/gillespie2.html (accessed 27 January 2010).

Gillespie, A.A. (2008) *Child Exploitation and Communication Technologies*, Lyme Regis: Russell House Publishing.

Gillespie, A.A. (2010) 'Legal Definitions of Child Pornography', 16(1) *Journal of Sexual Aggression*, 19–31.

Goldstein, J., Freud, A. and Solnit, A. (1973) *Beyond the Best Interests of the Child*, London: Collier-Macmillan.

Goldstein, J., Freud, A. and Solnit, A. (1980) *Before the Best Interests of the Child*, London: Burnett Books Ltd.

Greif, G.L. and Hegar, R.L. (1991) 'Parents whose children are abducted by the other parent: Implications for treatment', 19 *American Journal of Family Therapy* 215–25.

Greif, G.L. and Hegar, R.L. (1993) *When Parents Kidnap: The Families behind the Headlines*, New York, NY: The Free Press.

Haanappel, P.P.C. (2003) *The Law and Policy of Air Space and Outer Space: a Comparative Approach*, The Hague: Kluwer Law International.

Hagemann, F., Diallo, Y., Etienne, A. and Mehran, F. (2006) *Global child labour trends 2000–2004*, Geneva: International Labour Office.

Hand, C. (2006) 'An Ojibwe Perspective on the Welfare of Children: Lessons of the Past and Visions for the Future', 28(1) *Children and Youth Services Review* 20–46.

Harris, S.R. (2000) 'Asian Human Rights: Forming a Regional Covenant', 1(2) *Asian-Pacific Law & Policy Journal* 1–22.

Harris-Short, S. (2001) 'Listening to "The Other"? The Convention on the Rights of the Child', 2(2) *Melbourne Journal of International Law* 304–50.

Hart, H.L.A. (1984) 'Are There Any Natural Rights?', in Waldron, J (ed.) *Theories of Rights*, Oxford: Oxford University Press.

Hart, R.A. (1992) *Children's Participation: From Tokenism to Citizenship*, Innocenti Essays No. 4, Florence: UNICEF.

Harvey, R. (2003) 'The UK before the UN Committee on the Rights of the Child' [2003] *International Family Law Journal* 33.

Harvey, R. (2003a) *Children and Armed Conflict—A guide to international humanitarian and human rights law*, University of Essex: Children and Armed Conflict Unit/ International Bureau for Children's Rights. Available at: http://www.essex.ac.uk/ armedcon/story_id/000044.pdf (accessed 4 February 2010).

Hassel, A. (2008) 'The Evolution of a Global Labor Governance Regime' 21(2) *Governance: An International Journal of Policy, Administration and Institutions*, 231–51.

HCCH (2000) *Best Practices: Common Law Judicial Conference on International Parental Child Abduction*, Washington, DC, 17–21 September 2000, The Hague: HCCH Publications.

HCCH (2001) *Conclusions and Recommendations of the Fourth Meeting of the Special Commission to Review the Operation of the Hague Convention of 5 October 1980 on the Civil Aspects of International Child Abduction*, 22–28 March 2001, The Hague: HCCH Publications.

HCCH (2001a) *Transfrontier Access/Contact and the Hague Convention of 25 October 1980 on the Civil Aspects of International Child Abduction. A Preliminary Report*, Preliminary Document No. 4 of February 2001, The Hague: HCCH Publications.

HCCH (2008) *The Implementation and Operation of the 1993 Hague Intercountry Adoption Convention: Guide to Good Practice – Guide No. 1*, Bristol: Family Law/Jordan Publishing Ltd.

Health Committee (2003) *The Victoria Climbié Inquiry Report* (HC 570), Sixth Report of Session 2002–03, 25 June 2003, London: The Stationery Office.

Hendrick, H. (1997) *Children, Childhood and English Society 1880–1990*, Cambridge: Cambridge University Press.

Heywood, C. (2001) *A History of Childhood: Children and Childhood in the West from Medieval to Modern Times*, Cambridge: Polity Press.

Hirst, M. (2003) *Jurisdiction and the Ambit of the Criminal Law*, Oxford: Oxford University Press.

Ho, J. (2006) 'The International Labour Organization's Role in Nationalizing the International Movement to Abolish Child Labor', 7(1) *Chicago Journal of International Law* 337–49.

Holt, J. (1974) *Escape from Childhood: The Needs and Rights of Childhood*, New York: EP Dutton and Co. Inc.

Home Secretary (1997) *Rights Brought Home: The Human Rights Bill* (Cmd 3782), White Paper, Secretary of State for the Home Department, London: The Stationery Office.

Hubinette, T. (2006) 'From Orphan Trains to Baby Lifts: Colonial Trafficking, Empire Building, and Social Engineering', in Trenka, J.J, Oparah, J.C. and Shin, S.Y. (eds) *Outsiders Within: Writing on Transracial Adoption*, New York: Southend Press, pp. 139–150.

Humbert, F. (2009) *The Challenge of Child Labour in International Law*, Cambridge Studies in International and Comparative Law, Cambridge: Cambridge University Press.

ICATAP (2009) *The Hague Conference International Centre for Judicial Studies and Technical Assistance: The Intercountry Adoption Technical Assistance Programme*, The Hague: HCCH Publications. Available at: http://www.hcch.net/upload/icatap_e.pdf (accessed 27 January 2010).

ILO (1983) *Report of the Director-General to the International Labour Conference*, 67th Session, Report III (part 4B), Geneva: International Labour Office.

ILO (1996) *Child Labour: What is to be done?* Geneva: International Labour Office.

ILO (1998) *Child Labour: Targeting the Intolerable*, International Labour Conference 86th Session, Report VI(1), Geneva: ILO.

ILO (1998a) *Forced Labour in Myanmar (Burma): Report of the Commission of Inquiry*, 2 July 1998, Geneva: International Labour Office.

ILO (2002) *A Future Without Child Labour*, Global report under the Follow-up to the ILO Declaration on Fundamental Principles and Rights at Work, Report of the Director-General, International Labour Conference 90th Session, Geneva: International Labour Office.

ILO (2002a) *Eliminating the Worst Forms of Child Labour: A Practical Guide to ILO Convention No. 182*, Geneva: ILO and Inter-Parliamentary Union.

ILO (2004) *Investing in Every Child: An Economic Study of the Costs and Benefits of Eliminating Child Labour*, International Programme on the Elimination of Child Labour, Geneva: ILO.

ILO (2006) *The End of Child labour: Within Reach*, Global report under the Follow-up to the ILO Declaration on Fundamental Principles and Rights at Work. Report of the Director-General, International Labour Conference 95th Session, Geneva: International Labour Office.

ILO (2010) *Accelerating action against child labour*, Global report under the follow-up to the ILO Declaration on Fundamental Principles and Rights at Work, Report of the Director-General, International Labour Conference 99th Session, Geneva: International Labour Office.

ILO Committee of Experts' Annual Report (2004) *Report of the Committee of Experts on the Application of Conventions and Recommendations*, Report III (Part 1A), General Report and observations concerning particular countries, ILC 92nd Session, Geneva: International Labour Office.

Innocenti Research Centre (2004) *Ensuring the Rights of Indigenous Children*, Innocenti Digest No. 11, Florence: UNICEF Innocenti Research Centre. Available at: http://www.unicef.at/fileadmin/medien/pdf/Digest11_FINALEnglish.pdf (accessed 31 January 2010).

Invernizzi, A. and Milne, B. (2002) 'Are children entitled to contribute to international policy making? A critical view of children's participation in the international campaign for the elimination of child labour', 10(4) *International Journal of Children's Rights* 403–31.

IPEC (2003) *Every Child Counts: New Global Estimates on Child Labour*, Geneva: IPEC.

IPEC (2004) *Helping Hands or Shackled Lives? Understanding Child Domestic Labour and Responses to it*, International Programme on the Elimination of Child Labour, Geneva: ILO.

James, A. and Prout, A. (eds) (1997) *Constructing and Reconstructing Childhood: contemporary issues in the sociological study of childhood*, Second Edition, London: Routledge/Falmer.

James, A., Jenks, C. and Prout, A. (1998) *Theorizing Childhood*, Oxford: Polity Press.

Jayme, E. (1969) 'Florida Spouses Adopt Italian Child in Germany: Multistate Adoption and Doctrine of "Hidden Renvoi" ', 21(3) *University of Florida Law Review* 290–94.

Jenks, C. (1996) *Childhood*. London: Routledge.

Johnson, C.F. (2004) 'Child Sexual Abuse', 364(9432) *The Lancet*, 462–70.

Johnson, S.M. (1999) 'Excuse me, but is that football "child-free"? Pakistan and Child Labour', 7(1) *Tulsa Journal of Comparative and International Law* 163–76.

Johnston, J.R., Campbell, L.E. and Mayes, S.S. (1985) 'Latency children in post-separation and divorce disputes', 24(5) *Journal of the American Academy of Child Psychiatry* 563–74.

Joint Committee on Human Rights (2003) *The UN Convention on the Rights of the Child*, Tenth Report of Session 2002–03 (HL Paper 117, HC 81), 24 June 2003, London: The Stationery Office.

Kaczorowska, A. (2008) *Public International Law*, Third Edition, Abingdon: Routledge-Cavendish.

Kakungulu, R. (2009) 'The United Nations Declaration on the Rights of Indigenous Peoples: A New Dawn for Indigenous Peoples Rights?', *Cornell Law School Inter-University Graduate Student Conference Papers*. Available at: http://scholarship.law.cornell.edu/lps_clacp/18/ (accessed 31 January 2010).

Kelly, F. (2005) 'Conceptualising the child through an "ethic of care": lessons for family law' 1(4) *International Journal of Law in Context* 375–96.

Kelly, L. (2002) *Journeys of Jeopardy: A Commentary on Current Research on Trafficking of Women and Children for Sexual Exploitation within Europe*, IOM Migration Research Series, MRS No. 11, International Organization for Migration, London: Stationery Office Books.

Kempe, C.H. (1978) 'Sexual abuse, Another hidden Pediatric Problem: The 1977 C. Anderson Aldrich Lecture', 62(3) *Pediatrics* 382–89.

Kilbourne, S. (1998) 'The wayward Americans – why the USA has not ratified the UN Convention on the Rights of the Child' [1998] *International Family Law* 104–12.

Kilkelly, U. (1996) 'The UN Committee on the Rights of the Child – an evaluation in the light of recent UK experience', 8(2) *Child and Family Law Quarterly* 105–20.

Kilkelly, U. (2003) 'Economic Exploitation of Children: A European Perspective', 22(2) *Saint Louis University Public Law Review* 321–58.

Kim, D.S. (2007) 'A Country Divided: Contextualizing Adoption from a Korean Perspective', in Bergquist, K.J.S., Vonk, M.E., Kim, D.S. and Feit, M.D. (eds) *International Korean Adoption: A Fifty-Year History of Policy and Practice*, Binghamton, NY: Haworth Press, pp. 3–24.

Kim, H. (2007a) 'Mothers without mothering: birth mothers from South Korea since the Korean War', in Bergquist, K.J.S., Vonk, M.E., Kim, D.S. and Feit, M.D. (eds) *International Korean Adoption: A Fifty-Year History of Policy and Practice*, Binghamton, NY: Haworth Press, pp. 131–54.

King, M. (2007) 'The Sociology of Childhood as Scientific Communication: Observations from a social systems perspective', 14(2) *Childhood* 193–213.

King, S. (2009) 'Challenging Monohumanism: An Argument for Changing the Way we Think about Intercountry Adoption', 30(2) *Michigan Journal of International Law* 413–70.

Kirkby, P. (2003) *Child Labour in Britain, 1750–1870*, Social History in Perspective, Basingstoke: Palgrave Macmillan.

Laming, H.W. (2009) *The Protection of Children in England: A Progress Report* (HC 330), The Lord Laming of Tewin, 12 March 2009. London: The Stationery Office.

Lamont, R. (2008) 'The EU: Protecting Children's Rights in Child Abduction', *International Family Law* 110–12.

Langille, B.A. (2005) 'Core Labour Rights—The True Study (Reply to Alston), 16(3) *European Journal of International Law* 409–37.

Langlaude, S. (2008) 'Children and Religion under Article 14 UNCRC: A Critical Analysis', 16(4) *International Journal of Children's Rights* 475–504.

Lansdown, G. (2000) 'The Reporting Process under the Convention on the Rights of the Child', in Alston, P. and Crawford, J. (eds), pp. 113–28.

Lansdown, G. (2010) 'The realization of children's participation rights: critical reflections', in Percy-Smith, B. and Thomas, N. (eds) *A Handbook of Children and Young People's Participation: Perspectives from Theory and Practice*, Abingdon: Routledge, pp. 11–23.

Lataianu, C.M. (2003) 'Social Protection of Children in Public Care in Romania from the Perspective of EU Integration', 17(1) *International Journal of Law, Policy and the Family*, 99–120.

Lee, N. (1998) 'Towards an Immature Sociology', 46(3) *The Sociological Review* 458–82.

Lee, Y. (2008) *Statement by Yanghee Lee: chairperson of the Committee on the Rights of the Child*, 63rd session of the General Assembly Third Committee, item 60, 15 October 2008, New York: UN General Assembly. Available at: <http://www2.ohchr.org/english/bodies/crc/statement.htm> (accessed 4 November 2009).

Levison, D., Hoek, J., Lam, D. and Duryea, S. (2007) 'Intermittent child employment and its implications for estimates of child labour', 146(3/4) *International Labour Review* 217–51.

Libesmann, T. (2007) 'Can International Law Imagine the World of Indigenous Children?', 15(2) *International Journal of Children's Rights* 283–309.

Lloyd, A. (2002) 'A theoretical analysis of the reality of children's rights in Africa: an introduction to the African Charter on the Rights and Welfare of the Child', 2(1) *African Human Rights Law Journal* 11–32.

Low Pay Unit (1997) *Fair Play for Working Children*, London: Low Pay Unit.

Lowe, N. (2007) 'The Current Experiences and Difficulties of Applying Brussels II Revised', 7(4) *International Family Law* 182–95.

Lowe, N., Armstrong, S. and Mathias, A. (1999) *A Statistical Analysis of Applications Made in 1999 under the Hague Convention of 25 October 1980 on the Civil Aspects of International Child Abduction*, The Hague: HCCH Publications.

Lowe, N., Atkinson, E. and Horosova, K. (2006) *A Statistical Analysis of Applications Made in 2003 under the 1980 Hague Convention on the Civil Aspects of International Child Abduction*, Vol. 1, Global Report (pp. 80); Vol. 2, National Reports (pp. 492); published as Preliminary Document No. 3 for the 5th Meeting of the Special Commission to Review the Operation of the Hague Convention of 25 October 1980 on the Civil Aspects of International Child Abduction. Available at: http://www.hcch.net/index_en.php?act=conventions.publications&dtid=2&cid=24 (accessed 25 January 2010).

Lowe, N., Everall, M. and Nicholls, M. (2004) *International Movement of Children: Law, Practice and Procedure*, London: Family Law/Jordan Publishing Ltd.

Lowe, V. and Crawford, J. (2009) *British Year Book of International Law 2008: Volume 79*, Oxford: Oxford University Press.

Maalla, N.M. (2008) Report submitted by the Special Rapporteur on the sale of children, child prostitution and child pornography. UN Human Rights Council, ninth session, A/HRC/9/21, 31 July 2008. Available at: http://daccess-dds-ny.un.org/doc/UNDOC/GEN/G08/148/41/PDF/G0814841.pdf?OpenElement (accessed 27 January 2010).

Maalla, N.M. (2009) *Report submitted by the Special Rapporteur on the sale of children, child prostitution and child pornography*. UN Human Rights Council, twelfth session, A/HRC/12/23, 13 July 2009. Available at: http://www2.ohchr.org/english/bodies/hrcouncil/docs/12session/A.HRC.12.23.pdf (accessed 27 January 2010).

MacCormick, N. (1982) *Legal Right and Social Democracy: Essays in Legal and Political Philosphy*, Oxford: Clarendon Press.

Machel, G. (1996) *Impact of Armed Conflict on Children*, General Assembly, A/51/306 and Add.1, 26 August 1996.

Machel, G. (2001) *The Machel Review 1996–2000: A Critical Analysis of Progress Made and Obstacles Encountered in Increasing Protection for War-Affected Children*, General Assembly, A/55/749 (26 January 2001).

Marshall, D. (1999) 'The construction of children as an object of international relations: The Declaration of Children's Rights and the Child Welfare Committee of League of Nations, 1900–1924', 7(2) *International Journal of Children's Rights* 103–47.

Masum, M. (2002) 'Eradication of hazardous child labour in Bangladesh: The need for an integrated strategy', 10(3) *International Journal of Children's Rights* 233–68.

Mayall, B. (2000) 'The sociology of childhood in relation to chidren's rights', 8(3) *International Journal of Children's Rights* 243–59.

Mayall, B. (2003) *Childhood in Generational Perspective*, Bedford Way Papers, London: Institute of Education.

Melrose, M. and Barrett, D. (2006) 'The Flesh Trade in Europe: Trafficking in Women and Children for the Purpose of Commercial Sexual Exploitation', 7(2) *Police Practice and Research* 111–23.

Moravcsik, A. (2000) 'The Origins of Human Rights Regimes: Democratic Delegation in Postwar Europe', 54(2) *International Organization* 217–52.

Muntarbhorn, V. (1991) *Report of the Special Rapporteur on the sale of children, child prostitution and child pornography*, UN Economic and Social Council, E/CN.4/ 1991/51.

Muntarbhorn, V. (1998) 'Child rights and social clauses: Child labour elimination as a social cause?' 6(3) *International Journal of Children's Rights* 255–311.

Mutua, M. (1996) 'The Ideology of Human Rights', 36(3) *Virginia Journal of International Law* 589–658.

Mutua, M. (2001) 'Savages, Victims, Saviors: The Metaphor of Human Rights', 42(1) *Harvard International Law Journal* 201–46.

Myers, W.E. (2001) 'The Right Rights? Child Labour in a Globalizing World', 575(1) *Annals of the American Academy of Political and Social Science* 38–54.

National Assembly for Wales (2000) *Children and Young People: A Framework for Partnership—consultation document*, Child and Families Division, November 2000, Cardiff: National Assembly for Wales.

Nesi, G., Luca Nogler, L. and Marco Pertile, M. (eds) (2008) *Child Labour in a Globalized World: A Legal Analysis of ILO Action*, Aldershot: Ashgate.

Newiss, G. and Fairbrother, L. (2004) 'Child abduction: understanding police recorded crime statistics', Findings 225, London: Home Office Research, Development and Statistics Directorate.

NGO Group (1998) *A Guide for Non-governmental Organizations Reporting to the Committee on the Rights of the Child*, revised 1998, NGO Group for the Convention on the Rights of the Child, Geneva: Defence for Children International. Available at: http://www.crin.org/docs/resources/publications/NGOCRC/NGOCRC-Guide-en.pdf (accessed 20 December 2009).

NGO Group (2001) *Do You Know About the ILO Worst Forms of Child Labour Convention?* Geneva: NGO Group for the Convention on the Rights of the Child.

NGO Group (2005) *Semantics or Substance? Towards a shared understanding of terminology referring to the sexual abuse and exploitation of children*, Subgroup against the Sexual Exploitation of Children, NGO Group for the Convention on the Rights of the Child, Bangkok: ECPAT International. Available at: http://www.crin.org/docs/resources/publications/Subgroup_Sexual_Exploitation_Semantics.pdf (accessed 30 January 2010).

Noguchi, Y. (2002) 'ILO Convention No. 182 on the worst forms of child labour and the Convention on the Rights of the Child' 10(4) *International Journal of Children's Rights* 355–69.

Ochaíta, E., Espinosa, A. and Calvo, E. (2000) 'Child Work and Labour in Spain: a First Approach,' 8(1) *International Journal of Children's Rights* 15–35.

O'Donnell, C. and White, L. (1999) *Hidden Danger: injuries to children at work in Britain*, London: Low Pay Unit.

Official Solicitor (1997) *The Hague and European Conventions Child Abduction Unit – Operation of Conventions*, Official Solicitor and Public Trustee website: www.offsol.demon.co.uk.

Oguamanam, C. (2004) 'Indigenous Peoples and International Law: The Making of a Regime', 30(1) *Queen's Law Journal* 348–99.

OHCHR (2005) *The United Nations Human Rights Treaty System: an introduction to the core human rights treaties and treaty bodies*, Fact Sheet No. 30, Office of the High Commissioner for Human Rights, June 2005, Geneva: OHCHR. Available at: <http://www.ohchr.org/Documents/Publications/FactSheet30en.pdf> (accessed 30 October 2009).

OHCHR (2010) *United Nations Special Procedures: facts and figures 2009*, Office of the High Commissioner for Human Rights, Geneva: OHCHR. Available at: http://www2.ohchr.org/english/bodies/chr/special/docs/Facts_Figures2009.pdf (accessed 19 May 2010).

Ost, S. (2009) *Child Pornography and Sexual Grooming: Legal and Societal Responses*, Cambridge: Cambridge University Press.

Palmer, T. (2005) 'Behind the Screen: Children who are the Subjects of Abusive Images', in Quayle, E. and Taylor, M. (eds) *Viewing Child Pornography on the Internet*, Lyme Regis: Russell House Publishing, pp. 61–74.

Parra-Aranguren, G. (1994) *Explanatory Report on the Convention on Protection of Children and Co-operation in Respect of Intercountry Adoption*, drawn up by Mr G. Parra-Aranguren, The Hague: HCCH Publications. Available at: <http://hcch.e-vision.nl/index_en.php?act=publications.details&pid=2279&dtid=3> (accessed 2 November 2009).

Parsons, T. and Bales, R. (1956) *Family: Socialisation and Interaction Processes*, London: Routledge and Kegan Paul.

Pearce, J. (2006) 'Finding the "I" in sexual exploitation: hearing the voices of sexually exploited young people in policy and practice', in Campbell, R. and O'Neill, M. (eds) *Sex Work Now*, Cullompton: Willan Publishing, pp. 190–211.

Pearce, J., Williams, M. and Galvin, C. (2002) *It's someone taking a part of you: a study of young women and sexual exploitation,* London: National Children's Bureau.

Pearl, D. and Menski, W. (1998) *Muslim Family Law,* Third Edition, London: Sweet & Maxwell.

Pérez-Vera, E. (1980) *Explanatory Report: Hague Convention on International Child Abduction,* The Hague: HCCH Publications. Available at: < http://hcch.e-vision.nl/index_en.php?act=%20publications.details&pid=2779> (accessed 3 November 2009).

Perry, D.L. (2004) 'Muslim Child Disciples, Global Civil Society, and Children's Rights in Senegal: The Discourses of Strategic Structuralism', 77(1) *Anthropological Quarterly* 7–45.

Petit, J.M. (2002) *Report of the Special Rapporteur on the sale of children, child prostitution and child pornography,* UN Economic and Social Council, E/CN.4/2002/88, Commission on Human Rights, Fifty-eighth session, 4 February 2002. Available at: http://www.unhchr.ch/Huridocda/Huridoca.nsf/0/bdd270749d8fdc9ec1256b990055c306/$FILE/G0210592.pdf (accessed 27 January 2010).

Petit, J.M. (2004) *Rights of the Child: Report submitted by the Special Rapporteur on the sale of children, child prostitution and child pornography.* UN Economic and Social Council, E/CN.4/2005/78, Commission on Human Rights, Sixty-first session, 23 December 2004. Available at: http://daccess-dds-ny.un.org/doc/UNDOC/GEN/G05/100/19/PDF/G0510019.pdf?OpenElement (accessed 27 January 2010).

Petit, J.M. (2006) *Rights of the Child: Report of the Special Rapporteur on the sale of children, child prostitution and child pornography,* UN Economic and Social Council, E/CN.4/2006/67, Commission on Human Rights, Sixty-second session, 12 January 2006. Available at: http://daccess-dds-ny.un.org/doc/UNDOC/GEN/G06/101/70/PDF/G0610170.pdf?OpenElement (accessed 27 January 2010).

Petit, J.M. (2008) *Report of the Special Rapporteur on the sale of children, child prostitution and child pornography.* UN Human Rights Council, seventh session, A/HRC/7/8, 9 January 2008. Available at: http://daccess-dds-ny.un.org/doc/UNDOC/GEN/G08/100/07/PDF/G0810007.pdf?OpenElement (accessed 27 January 2010).

Phoenix, J. (2003) 'Rethinking Youth Prostitution: National Provision at the Margins of Child Protection and Youth Justice', 3(3) *Youth Justice* 152–68.

Phoenix, J. and Oerton, S. (2005) *Illicit and Illegal: sex, regulation, and social control,* Cullompton: Willan Publishing.

Piaget, J. (1952) *The Origins of Intelligence in Children,* New York: The Norton Library, W.W. Norton and Co. Inc.

Piaget, J. (1960) *The Child's Conception of the World,* New Jersey: Littlefield, Adams and Co.

Pierce, W. (1995) 'Accreditation of Those who Arrange Adoptions under the Hague Convention on Intercountry Adoption as a Means of Protecting, through Private International Law, the Rights of Children', 12(2) *Journal of Contemporary Health Law and Policy* 535–61.

Pinheiro, P.S. (2006) *Report of the independent expert for the United Nations study on violence against children,* A/61/299, General Assembly, sixty-first session, 29 August 2006. Report of the independent expert for the United Nations, Paulo Sérgio Pinheiro, submitted pursuant to General Assembly resolution 60/231. Available at: http://www.unicef.org/violencestudy/reports/SG_violencestudy_en.pdf (accessed 6 January 2010).

Pollock, L. (1983) *Forgotten Children: Parent – Child Relations from 1500–1900,* Cambridge: Cambridge University Press.

Potter, M. (2008) 'The Voice of the Child: Children's "Rights" in Family Proceedings', *International Family Law* 140–48.

Quigley, J.B. (2002) 'US ratification of the Convention on the Rights of the Child', Justice for Children Project, Moritz College of Law: moritzlaw.osu.edu/jfc/staff/quigleyratification.pdf.

Qvortrup, J., Bardy, M., Sgritta, G. and Wintersberger, H. (1994) *Childhood Matters: Social Theory, Practice and Politics*, Aldershot: Avebury.

Ranton, D. (2009) 'Hague and Non-Hague Convention Abductions: notes for Reunite Website on Hague Convention Law as at 20th October 2009', Reunite website, at: http://www.reunite.org/edit/files/articles/Notes%20on%20Hague%20Convention%20Law.pdf (accessed 24 January 2010).

Raz, J. (1996) 'Liberty and trust', in George, R. (ed.) *Natural Law, Liberalism and Morality*, Oxford: Oxford University Press.

Recommendation No. 1 (1998) *Children in Armed Conflict*, UNCRC/C/80, 19th Session, September 1998.

Recommendation No. 2 (1999) *The Administration of Juvenile Justice*, UNCRC/C/90, 22nd Session, September 1999.

Recommendation No. 3 (2002) *The Methods of Work: Exceptional Submission of Combined Reports*, CRC/C/114, 29th Session, January 2002.

Recommendation No. 4 (2002) *The Organisation of Work: Content and Size of State Reports*, CRC/C/118, 30th Session, May 2002.

Recommendation No. 5 (2003) *Submission of Periodic Reports*, January 2003.

Recommendation No. 6 (2003) *Committee to Work in Two Chambers*, September 2003.

Recommendation No. 7 (2004) *Children Without Parental Care*, 37th Session, October 2004.

Recommendation No. 8 (2005) *Consideration of reports under the two Optional Protocols of the Convention on the Rights of the Child*, 37th Session, June 2005.

Reunite (2006) *Mediation in International Parental Child Abduction: the Reunite Mediation Pilot Scheme*, Leicester: Reunite International Child Abduction Centre.

Riiskjær, M. and Gallagher, A.M. (2008) *Review of the UNHCR's efforts to prevent and respond to human trafficking*, United Nations High Commissioner for Refugees, Policy Development and Evaluation Service, PDES/2008/07, Geneva: UNHCR. Available at: http://www.humansecuritygateway.com/documents/UNHCR-PDES_EffortsToPreventHumanTrafficking.pdf (accessed 27 January 2010).

Robertson, A. and Merrills, J. (1996) *Human Rights in the World: An Introduction to the Study of the International Protection of Human Rights*, Fourth Edition, Manchester: Manchester University Press.

Roby, J. (2004) 'Understanding Sending Country's Traditions and Policies in International Adoption: Avoiding Legal and Cultural Pitfalls', 6(2) *Journal of Law and Family Studies* 303–22.

Rutkow, L. and Lozman, J.T. (2006) 'Suffer the Children? A Call for United States Ratification of the United Nations Convention on the Rights of the Child', 19 *Harvard Human Rights Journal* 161–90.

Samson, C. (2008) 'The Rule of *Terra Nullius* and the Impotence of International Human Rights for Indigenous People', 5(1) *Essex Human Rights Review* 1–12. Available at: http://www.ehrr.org/ (accessed 31 January 2010).

Sargent, S. (2004) 'Suspended Animation: The Implementation of the Hague Convention on Intercountry Adoption in the United States and Romania', 10(2) *Texas Wesleyan Law Review* 351–80.

Sargent, S. (2010) *The Best Interests of the Child in Intercountry Adoption: A Constructivist and Comparative Account*, unpublished PhD thesis, Leicester De Montfort Law School, De Montfort University, Leicester, United Kingdom.

Sargent, S. (2010a) 'Indigenous Children's Rights—International Law, Self-Determination and Intercountry Adoption in Guatemala', 10(1) *Contemporary Issues in Law* 1–23.

Sarkin, J. and Pietschmann, M. (2003) 'Legitimate Humanitarian Intervention under International Law in the Context of the Current Human Rights and Humanitarian Crisis in Burma (Myanmar)', 33(2) *Hong Kong Law Journal* 371–416.

Sawyer, C. (2006) 'The Child is Not a Person: Family Law and Other Legal Cultures', 28(1) *Journal of Social Welfare and Family Law* 1–14.

Schulz, A. (2008) 'Guidance from Luxembourg: First ECJ Judgment Clarifying the Relationship between the 1980 Hague Convention and Brussels II Revised', (2008) *International Family Law* 221–25.

Schwebel, S. (1984) 'Authorising the Secretary-General of the United Nations to Request Advisory Opinions', 78(4) *American Journal of International Law* 869–78.

Schwebel, S. (1988) 'Preliminary Rulings by the International Court of Justice at the Instance of National Courts', 28(2) *Virginia Journal of International Law* 495–508.

SCWG (2009) *Annual report on the activities of the Security Council Working Group on Children and Armed Conflict (1 July 2008 to 30 June 2009)*, Security Council, S/2009/378 (22 July 2009). Available at: http://www.un.org/children/conflict/english/securitycouncilwgroupdoc.html (accessed 7 February 2010).

Secretary of State for Children, Schools and Families (2007) *The Children's Plan: Building brighter futures* (Cm 7280), Department for Children, Schools and Families, December 2007, London: The Stationery Office. Available at: http://www.dcsf.gov.uk/childrensplan/ (accessed 21 December 2009).

Security Council (2008) *Working Group on Children and Armed Conflict: Conclusions on children and armed conflict in Chad*, S/AC.51/2008/15, 5 December 2008. Available at: http://daccess-dds-ny.un.org/doc/UNDOC/GEN/N08/627/95/PDF/N0862795.pdf?OpenElement (accessed 23 December 2009).

Security Council (2008a) *The report of the Secretary-General on children and armed conflict in the Democratic Republic of Congo*, S/2008/693, 10 November 2008. Available at: http://daccess-dds-ny.un.org/doc/UNDOC/GEN/N08/595/42/PDF/N0859542.pdf?OpenElement (accessed 23 December 2009).

Selby, J. (2008) 'Ending Abusive and Exploitative Child Labour through International Law and Practical Action', 15 *Australian International Law Journal* 165–80.

Sen, A. (1997) 'Human Rights and Asian Values', Sixteenth Morgenthau Memorial Lecture on Ethics & Foreign Policy, New York: Carnegie Council on Ethics and International Affairs. Available at: <http://www.cceia.org/media/254_sen.pdf> (accessed 3 November 2009).

Shaw, M. (2008) *International Law*, Sixth Edition, Cambridge: Cambridge University Press.

Silk, J.J. and Makonnen, M. (2003) 'Ending Child Labor: A Role for International Human Rights Law?', 22(2) *Saint Louis University Public Law Review* 359–70.

SIPRI (2009) *SIPRI Yearbook 2009*, Solna, Sweden: Stockholm International Peace Research Institute (SIPRI). Summary of Yearbook available at: http://www.sipri.org/yearbook/2009/files/SIPRIYB09summary.pdf (accessed 7 February 2010).

Smolin, D.M. (2000) 'Strategic choices in the international campaign against child labour', 22(4) *Human Rights Quarterly* 942–87.

Smolin, D.M. (2006) 'Overcoming Religious Objections to the Convention on the Rights of the Child', 20(1) *Emory International Law Review*, 81–110.

Smolin, D.M. (2007) 'Child Laundering as Exploitation: Applying Anti-Trafficking Norms to Intercountry Adoption under the Coming Hague Regime', 32(1) *Vermont Law Review* 1–55.

Special Commission (1994) *Report of the Special Commission on the Implementation of the Hague Convention of 29 May 1993 on Protection of Children and Co-operation in respect of Intercountry Adoption,* 17–21 October 1994, The Hague: HCCH Publications. Available at: http://www.hcch.net/index_en.php?act=publications.details&pid=933 &dtid=2 (accessed 27 January 2010).

Special Commission (2001) *Report and Conclusions of the Special Commission on the practical operation of the Hague Convention of 29 May 1993 on Protection of Children and Co-operation in respect of Intercountry Adoption,* 28 November–1 December 2000, The Hague: HCCH Publications. Available at: http://www.hcch.net/index_en. php?act=publications.details&pid=2273&dtid=2 (accessed 26 January 2010).

Special Commission (2006) *Report and Conclusions of the second Special Commission on the practical operation of the Hague Convention of 29 May 1993 on Protection of Children and Co-operation in respect of Intercountry Adoption,* 17–23 September 2005, The Hague: HCCH Publications. Available at: http://www.hcch.net/index_en. php?act=publications.details&pid=3835&dtid=2 (accessed 26 January 2010).

Special Rapporteur (2004) *Rights of the Child*: Report submitted by Juan Miguel Petit, Special Rapporteur on the Sale of Children, Child Prostitution and Child Pornography to the Commission on Human Rights, E/CN.4/2004/9, 5 January 2004.

SRSG (2007) *Report of the Special Representative of the Secretary-General for Children and Armed Conflict*, General Assembly, A/62/228 (13 August 2007).

SRSG (2009) *Annual report of the Special Representative of the Secretary-General for Children and Armed Conflict*, Human Rights Council A/HRC/12/49 (30 July 2009).

SRSG (2009a) 'The Six Grave Violations against Children during Armed Conflict: The Legal Foundation', *Working Paper No. 1*, New York: Office of the Special Representative of the Secretary-General for Children and Armed Conflict. Available at: http:// www.un.org/children/conflict/_documents/SixGraveViolationspaper.pdf   (accessed 5 February 2010).

Stalford, H. and Drywood, E. (2009) 'Coming of Age?: Children's Rights in the European Union', 46(1) *Common Market Law Review* 143–72.

Steiner, H. and Alston, P. (2000) *International Human Rights in Context: Law, Politics, Morals*, Second Edition, Oxford: Oxford University Press.

Stone, L. (1990) *The Family, Sex and Marriage in England 1500–1800*, (abridged edition) London: Penguin.

Sutherland, P. (1992) *Cognitive Development Today: Piaget and his critics*, London: Paul Chapman Publishing.

Tardu, M. (2003) 'The European systems for the protection of human rights' in Symonides, J. (ed) *Human Rights: International Protection, Monitoring and Enforcement*, Aldershot: Ashgate/UNESCO.

Taylor, M. and Quayle, E. (2003) *Child Pornography: An Internet Crime*, London: Routledge.

Thomas, N. (2007) 'Towards a Theory of Children's Participation', 15(2) *International Journal of Children's Rights* 199–218.

UN (2002) *A World Fit for Children*, Twenty-seventh special session, Resolution adopted by the UN's General Assembly, A/RES/S-27/2, General Assembly, 11 October 2002.

Available at: <http://www.unicef.org/specialsession/docs_new/documents/A-RES-S27-2E.pdf> (accessed 19 May 2010).

UN (2008) *Report of the Committee on the Rights of the Child*. General Assembly, sixty-third session, supplement no. 41, A/63/41. Available at: http://daccess-dds-ny.un.org/doc/UNDOC/GEN/N08/426/47/PDF/N0842647.pdf?OpenElement) (accessed 30 January 2010).

UN Secretary-General (2009) *Composition of the Secretariat*, Sixty-fourth session, Secretary-General's report A/64/352, General Assembly, 15 September 2009. Available at: <http://daccessdds.un.org/doc/UNDOC/GEN/N09/515/01/PDF/N0951501.pdf? Open Element> (accessed 3 November 2009).

UN Secretary-General (2009a) *Children and Armed Conflict – Annual Report*, General Assembly/Security Council, A/63/785–S/2009/158 (26 March 2009).

UNAIDS (2006) *International Guidelines on HIV/AIDS and Human Rights*, Consolidated version 2006. Geneva: Office of the High Commissioner for Human Rights / Joint United Nations Programme on HIV/AIDS (UNAIDS). Available at: <http://data.unaids.org/Publications/IRC-pub07/jc1252-internguidelines_en.pdf> (accessed 1 December 2009).

UNCHR (1993) *Programme of Action for the Elimination of the Exploitation of Child Labour*, E/CN.4/RES/1993/79, Geneva: Office of the United Nations High Commissioner for Human Rights. Available at: http://ap.ohchr.org/documents/alldocs.aspx?doc_id=4160 (accessed 14 May 2010).

UNDPI (2008) *High-level Event on the Millennium Development Goals: Fact Sheet*, United Nations Headquarters, New York, 25 September 2008, New York: UN Department of Public Information—DPI/2517 J. Available at: http://www.un.org/millenniumgoals/2008highlevel/pdf/newsroom/Goal%204%20FINAL.pdf (accessed 30 November 2009).

UNGA (2009) *The girl child*, Sixty-fourth session, Third Committee, Agenda item 65(a), Promotion and protection of the rights of children (Namibia: draft resolution), A/C.3/64/L.20. General Assembly, 16 October 2009. Available at: <http://www.un.org/ga/third/64/propslist.shtml> (accessed 2 November 2009).

UNGA (2009a) *The Rights of the Child*, Sixty-fourth session, Third Committee, Agenda item 65(a), Promotion and protection of the rights of children, A/C.3/64/L.21, General Assembly, 19 October 2009. Available at: <http://www.un.org/ga/third/64/propslist.shtml> (accessed 2 November 2009).

Unger, J. (1965) 'Hague Conference on Private International Law: Draft Convention on Adoptions', 28(4) *Modern Law Review* 463–65.

UNICEF (1997) *State of the World's Children 1997*, New York/Oxford: OUP/United Nations Children's Fund.

UNICEF (2006) *The Situation of Children Left Behind by Migrating Parents*, January 2006, Chisinau, Moldova: UNICEF.

UNICEF (2007) Statement, 'UNICEF expresses strong support for the Hague Intercountry Adoption Convention', 5 October 2007. Available at: http://www.hcch.net/index_en.php?act=publications.details&pid=4135&dtid=28 (accessed 26 January 2010).

UNICEF (2009) *Handbook on the Optional Protocol on the Sale of Children, Child Prostitution and Child Pornography*, Innocenti Research Centre, Florence: UNICEF. Available at: http://www.unicef-irc.org/publications/pdf/optional_protocol_eng.pdf (accessed 27 January 2010).

United Kingdom (1994) *Initial Report: United Kingdom*, CRC/C/11/Add.1, 28 March 1994.

United Kingdom (2002) *Second Report: United Kingdom*, UNCRC/C/83/Add.3, 25 February 2002.

United Kingdom (2008) *Third and Fourth Periodic Reports: United Kingdom*, CRC/C/GBR/4, 25 February 2008.

United Kingdom OPAC (2007) *Initial Report of the United Kingdom under article 8 of the Optional Protocol on the Involvement of Children in Armed Conflict*, Committee on the Rights of the Child, CRC/C/OPAC/GBR/1, 3 September 2007.

Van Bueren, G. (1994) *The International Law on the Rights of the Child*, Dordrecht/Boston/London: Martinus Nijhoff Publishers.

Van Bueren, G. (1994a) 'Child sexual abuse and exploitation: A suggested human rights approach', 2(1) *International Journal of Children's Rights* 45–59.

Van Bueren, G. (1998) *The International Law on the Rights of the Child*, The Hague: Martinus Njjhoff / Kluwer Law International.

Vivatvaraphol, T. (2009) 'Back to Basics: Determining a Child's Habitual Residence in International Child Abduction Cases under the Hague Convention', 77(6) *Fordham Law Review* 3325–69.

Vygotsky, L. (1962) *Thought and Language*, edited and translated by Eugenia Hanfmann and Gertrude Vakar, Cambridge, MA: MIT Press; 1975 reprint (original Russian edition, 1934).

Wald, M. (1979) 'Children's Rights: A Framework for Analysis', 12(2) *University of California Davis Law Review* 255–82.

Ward, R. and Akhtar, A. (2008) *Walker and Walker's English Legal System*, Tenth Edition, Oxford: Oxford University Press.

Weiner, M. (1994) 'Child labour in developing countries: The Indian case. Articles 18a, 32 and 36 of the UN Convention on the Rights of the Child', 2(2) *International Journal of Child Rights* 121–28.

Weiner, M.H. (2000) 'International Child Abduction and the Escape from Domestic Violence', 69(2) *Fordham Law Review* 593–706.

Weis, P. (1961) 'The Convention Relating to the Status of Stateless Persons', 10(2) *International and Comparative Law Quarterly* 255–64.

Wellman, C. (1999) *The Proliferation of Rights: Moral Progress or Empty Rhetoric?* USA: Westview Press.

World Health Organization (1981) *International Code of Marketing of Breast-milk Substitutes*, Geneva: World Health Organization. Available at: <http://www.who.int/nutrition/publications/code_english.pdf> (accessed 8 November 2009).

Index

[NOTE: Page numbers followed by n denote footnotes.]